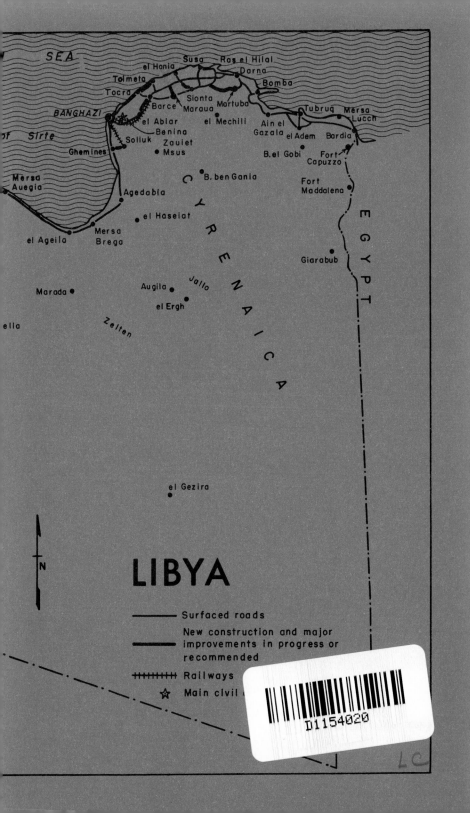

SEA

el Hania Susa Ras el Hilal
Darna
Tolmeta Bomba
Tocra
BANGHAZI Barce Sionta Martuba Tubruq Mersa Lucch
Maraua
el Ablar el Mechili Ain el Gazala
Benina el Adem Bardia
Solluk Zauiet B. el Gobi Fort Capuzzo
of Sirte Ghemines Msus
Fort Maddalena
B. ben Gania
Mersa Auegia Agedabia
el Haseiat EGYPT
Giarabub
el Ageila Mersa Brega

C Y R E N A I C A

Marada Augila Jallo
el Ergh
Zelten
ella

el Gezira

N

LIBYA

——— Surfaced roads

New construction and major
improvements in progress or
recommended

++++++++ Railways

☆ Main civil

LC

moδern liBya:

A Study in Political Development

By the Same Author

WAR AND PEACE IN THE LAW OF ISLAM
The Johns Hopkins Press

INDEPENDENT IRAQ
Oxford University Press

LAW IN THE MIDDLE EAST
*(Edited, in collaboration with H. J. Liebesny, for
The Middle East Institute)*

ISLAMIC JURISPRUDENCE: SHAFI'I'S RISALA
The Johns Hopkins Press

THE GOVERNMENT OF IRAQ
(Arabic and English)

AMERICAN WRITINGS ON THE MIDDLE EAST
(Edited in Arabic for the Franklin Publications)

THE ALEXANDRETTA QUESTION
(Arabic Publication)

King Idris I

Modern Libya

Libya

A Study in Political Development

by Majid Khadduri

THE JOHNS HOPKINS PRESS

BALTIMORE

1963

© *1963, The Johns Hopkins Press, Baltimore 18, Md*

Printed in the U. S. A. by J. H. Furst Co., Baltimore, Md.

Library of Congress Catalog Card No. 62–18509

This book has been brought to publication with the assistance of a grant from the Ford Foundation.

Preface

IN 1949, LIBYA WAS declared by the United Nations as
ready to be established as a united and independent
country. A decade earlier it had formed a "fourth shore"
for Italy and was subjected to demographic colonization. Its
people came very close to losing their identity when World
War II broke out, but the new circumstances gave them a
chance to recover their country. Following the war Libya
might have passed from Italian to other hands, but by a
combination of happy circumstances it attained an independent status without having to pass through even a semi-
sovereign stage.

Before Libya achieved independence, its name was merely
a geographical expression, for its people preferred to be called
Tripolitanians, Cyrenaicans, and Fazzanese rather than to be
identified by the geographical name of the country. Nor had
the term Libya ever been applied to a well-defined territory.
To the ancient Greeks, according to Herodotus, Libya meant
the entire North African area, while to Roman and Arab
geographers, it meant two different regions. Discarded from
antiquity in favor of names of local communities, the term
has been revived in the era of nationalism to be applied
specifically to the newly created Libyan state. This name is
used now with pride by a people who are anxious to have

their country identified with it and to occupy the well-deserved position given them in the community of nations.

Several studies on certain Libyan problems have been made, especially by United Nations experts; but no comprehensive study since Libya's liberation from Italian control has yet appeared, although extensive literature dealing with the period before Libya's rise to statehood exists. This work, designed to discuss Libya's political development since liberation, lays no claim to completeness, since the closely related economic problems are dealt with only insofar as they are related to domestic or foreign policy. The appearance in print of the report of the International Bank on the *Economic Development of Libya* (Baltimore, 1960), which discusses adequately Libya's economic problems, has rendered my task less difficult by enabling me to concentrate on Libya's fundamental political problems.

I have tried to verify material derived from published and unpublished sources by oral interviews with leading public men, who readily have given me their assistance. I am grateful in particular to His Majesty, King Idris, who graciously received me and candidly answered my questions. I should like also to mention the assistance given me by all of Libya's former Premiers, Governors, leading Ministers, and other political leaders. Furthermore, I am grateful to the opportunity given me by the Libyan Government when I was invited in 1957 to serve as Dean in the newly-created Libyan University. My work in Libya during that year inspired me with the idea of writing this book, since I had had the privilege of making the acquaintance, and sometimes winning the friendship, of a number of men who took a leading part in the public affairs of their country. Among those who were particularly helpful I should like to mention Mahmud al-Muntasir, Muhammad al-Saqizli, Mustafa Bin Halim, and 'Abd al-Majid Ku'bar, Libya's former Premiers; Husayn Maziq and Mahmud Abu Hidma, Governors of Cyrenaica; Fadil Bin Zikri and 'Abd al-Salam al-Busiri, Governors of Tripolitania; 'Ali al-Sahili and Busiri al-Shalhi, at the Royal Diwan; and 'Ali al-'Unayzi, 'Ali al-Jirbi, Sulayman al-Jirbi, 'Abd al-Rahman al-Qalhud, Khalil al-Qallal, Mansur Qadara, 'Ali Ju'uda, Mustafa al-Sarraj, former Ministers. Among those of opposition groups, I had the benefit of expert advice of 'Abd al-'Aziz al-Zaqalla'i, 'Abd al-Mawla Lanqi (now in the Cabinet), 'Ali al-Dib (Chief of the Executive Council of Tripolitania), Bashir al-Mughayribi (now member of Parliament), Mustafa Ba'aiu (now in the Foreign Office), Mahmud Makhluf, and Mahdi al-Mutardi. During my recent visit to Libya in 1961, the Prime Minister, Muhammad Bin 'Uthman, was particularly encouraging and his staff, especially Ahmad Fahmi al-Hammali, very helpful.

I have also frequently been assisted by valuable comments made on parts or the whole of the book. I should like to acknowledge in particular those comments made by Mustafa Bin Halim, former Prime Minister; W. G. C. Graham, former British Ambassador to Libya; Sir Duncan Cumming, former Chief Political Officer in Cyrenaica; and Professor J. N. D. Anderson, former liaison officer with the Sanusi force in Cairo. To Adrian Pelt, former United Nations Commissioner in Libya; Sir Alec Kirkbride, first British Ambassador to Libya; 'Abd al-Rahman 'Azzam, former Secretary-General of the Arab League; and E. A. V. de Candole, former Governor of Cyrenaica; I acknowledge their invaluable assistance. I should like to acknowledge the assistance of Harold Glidden who read the entire work and William Sands who read parts of it. Finally, I wish to acknowledge the grants extended by the Philosophical Society and the Rockefeller Foundation which enabled me to visit Libya in 1959 and 1961, while the book was in preparation.

None of these persons or institutions, however, is responsible for any errors which may be found in the volume or for the views expressed in it.

Majid Khadduri

January, 1962

Contents

moôern liByá:

A Study in Political Development

chapteR I

Introduction

THE NORTH AFRICAN SECTOR, though consisting virtually of an island between sea and desert, was overrun by
successive conquerors. Foreign ascendency, however, though re-
peatedly asserted, invariably proved to be transitory. Conquerors
who made their descent upon this island by the sea, pushing
natives to the desert, were confined to the coast. The perennial
struggle that ensued, which took the form of colonial war, was
essentially a struggle between desert and sown and almost always
the desert dwellers eventually won. When the desert dwellers
recovered the land, they were enriched by the wealth and culture
bequeathed by those who had departed.

The desert dwellers of the central sector, who played a remarkable role in recovering their lands from Greco-Roman ascendancy,
inherited the political division of the country and, perhaps, their
chronic local rivalry. There was no sense of unity in the ancient
polity, and the subsequent history of the native population was
largely a struggle either against further invasions or a relapse
into intertribal conflict.

But geography contributed no less a share in the internal
division of the country than history. The division of the central
coast, more than 800 miles as the crow flies, caused by the Gulf
of Sirte has created two principal entities: Tripolitania and
Cyrenaica. Beyond the narrow coastline lies the vast open desert,
extending south to Lake Chad and the Western Sudan, sparsely

3

populated by nomadic tribes who traverse the region from one oasis to another. The Fazzan province, consisting of this desert area, constitutes the third major division of the country.

Geography and history have left an indelible impress on Libya's polity. Her internal structure, which helped to preserve the national identity of the people, is no longer adequate for conditions of modern life. Libya's present struggle to become a modern state is in no small measure a struggle to rid herself of the legacy of the past and to overcome physical barriers.

The Ancient Heritage

From ancient times the two principal provinces have persisted as separate political units. Cyrenaica fell under Greek, and Tripolitania under Carthaginian and Roman influences. Each developed separate self-governing institutions. Cyrenaica comprised five Greek settlements, known as the Pentapolis; [1] and Tripolitania, as its name implies, consisted of three separate towns—the principal one of which survived to become the modern Tripoli. [2] Cyrenaica's towns were inhabited primarily by Greeks and Tripolitania's by Carthaginians and Romans. Beyond these settlements the vast open country was inhabited by Berbers, but doubtless the Berbers crowding round those settlements were gradually assimilated. Cyrenaica and Tripolitania enjoyed self-government and remained separate political units, until brought by Roman occupation under one imperial rule. Upon the break-up of the Empire, Tripolitania fell to the Vandals, while Cyrenaica suffered a decline that persisted after the two provinces were joined into a single unit by the Byzantines in the sixth century of the Christian era. Byzantine rule was limited by the growth of Berber power, and urban life scarcely extended outside the limits of the ever decreasing number of settlements held by garrisons. By the time the Arabs invaded the country, civilization had already been on the decline.

---

[1] It was later supplemented by other settlements and its principal towns included Cyrene (Shahhat), Apollonia (Susa), Barce (al-Marj), Ptolemais (Tolmeita), Berenice (Banghazi), and Teuchira (Tocra).

[2] The three seaports were Sabratha, Leptis Magna, and Oea. The last adopted the name of the three and became Tripoli.

The Arabization of Libya

The Arab invaders achieved what the Greeks and Romans strove for in vain. They made it clear to the Berbers at the point of the sword that their real interest lay with Islam and not against it. By an alliance with the Berbers, the Arabs turned first against the Byzantine and Roman settlers, bringing them under their control, and later the Berbers themselves fell under Arab domination. In the seventh century of the Christian era, the Arab invasion was confined to coastal control, leaving the desert to the Berbers. It was not until the eleventh century that the Arabs came to take up their residence and to spread tribewise and camp all over the vast desert region. Most of these tribes who came originally from Arabia had been unleashed in 1051 A.D. by the Fatimid rulers of Egypt. The Banu Hilal and Banu Sulaym, who left the Egyptian desert in quest of plunder, swept over eastern North Africa; but Libya, the first country penetrated by these tribes, attracted the Banu Sulaym who settled in Cyrenaica. A few of the Banu Hilal settled in Tripolitania, but Libya as a whole felt more deeply the crushing advance of these invaders. As Ibn Khaldun has observed:

> When the Banu Hilal and the Banu Sulaym broke their way in [from their homeland] to Ifriqiya and the Maghrib in the fifth [A.D. eleventh] century they struggled there for 350 years. They took the flat territory as their abode and it was completely devastated. Before this invasion, the whole region, extending from the Sudan to the Mediterranean, was [more densely] populated; the traces of an ancient civilization, such as monuments, architectural sculpture, and the visible ruins of towns and villages testify to the fact.[3]

While these invasions completed the destruction of ancient civilization, they speeded up the process of Arabization and the spread of Islam which had been going on since the Arab invasion of the seventh century. The commixture of Arabs and Berbers

[3] Ibn Khaldun, *al-Muqaddimah*, ed. Quatremère (Paris, 1858), Vol. 1, p. 273; English translation by F. Rosenthal (London, 1958), Vol. I, p. 305. See also al-Tahir Ahmad al-Zawi, *Ta'rikh al-Fath al-Arabi Fi Libya* (Cairo, 1954), pp. 197 ff.

became almost complete and the Arabic language became predominant. Even under Ottoman rule, when a new blood—the Turkish—was introduced, the Arabization process continued, and the Turkish language and Turkish elements were confined either to a small ruling class or to the Ottoman army (Quloghli).

The recent emphasis on the Arabic character of Libya may, therefore, be justified on the basis of the historical process that had been going on for centuries. However, it must be borne in mind that this commixture of cultures and races was not one in which only one culture or one racial element survived, but that the outcome was the product of the fusion of all into what constitutes the present population of Libya.[4] One thing is unquestionably Arabic—the Arab tongue, although Berber dialects may be found in certain small communities, and a number of old words and usages have been assimilated into the common parlance.

The Predominance of Islam

The Arab-Berber controversy, which played an important role in the shaping of North African society, stirred "national" feeling in both Arab and Berber communities to a high pitch until the fusion of Arabs and Berbers became almost complete. The disappearance of this stimulus, coupled with the triumph of the Islamic conception of universalism, facilitated the domination of North African countries by Muslim rulers regardless of their origin, especially their submission—except Morocco [5]—to Ottoman rule. Faced with Christian encroachments on their seaports during the age of European discoveries, North African rulers from Algeria to Libya invited the Ottoman sultan to extend his control to their countries. The easy occupation of North Africa by the Ottoman Porte in the sixteenth century demonstrated an attachment to Islamic rule—a loyalty to be contrasted with the

[4] See Louis Dupree, "The Arabs of Modern Libya," *The Muslim World*, Vol. XLVIII (1958), pp. 113–24; and "The Non-Arab Ethnic Groups of Libya," *The Middle East Journal*, Vol. XII (1958), pp. 33–44.

[5] Morocco, ruled by an 'Alid (Sharifi) dynasty, refused to submit to Ottoman rule.

Berber's opposition to early Arab invaders who had entered North Africa to spread the words of the Qur'an.

The Ottoman sultans governed Libya as they governed other Arab lands, not as Turkish rulers but as Muslim caliphs,[6] and their Islamic policy made their subjects, regardless of whether they were Turks or Arabs, feel at home under their rule. During the first Ottoman occupation (1522–1714), Libya's internal administration was left to local rulers and tribal chiefs, and the Ottoman Porte was satisfied with an annual tribute. This arrangement seems to have worked to the satisfaction of Libya's rulers and their Ottoman overlords, but the country fell into disrepute in Europe since her seaports, as well as the seaports of other North African countries, were infested with pirates who inspired fear among all who sailed the Mediterranean.

The power of the sultans, however, no longer remained even nominal and the taxes were often not paid. Early in the eighteenth century, the Qaramanli family, founded by one of the Sultan's janissaries, made Tripolitania virtually independent. Not unlike Muhammad 'Ali of Egypt, Ahmad al-Qaramanli (1711–1745) secured his position by force and paid tribute to the Ottoman Porte. He was an able ruler who extended his control to Fazzan and Cyrenaica. He and his successors preyed upon the commerce of the Mediterranean with great success, but this trade brought trouble with the Great Powers, especially with the United States.[7] It was not until France and England seized Algiers and Malta respectively and controlled the Mediterranean commerce that Qaramanli's power was curtailed. Internal weakness tempted the Ottoman Porte to send a fleet to Tripoli in 1835, which removed Qaramanli and appointed a new governor directly responsible to Istanbul. The return of Ottoman rule made little difference in improving the system of administration, although piracy came to an end and with it the prosperity of Tripoli.[8]

---

[6] The Ottoman sultans used the title of caliphs officially in the time of 'Abd al-Hamid I (1774–1789) vis-à-vis foreign powers and constitutionally in the time of 'Abd al-Hamid II (1876–1909).

[7] For American relations with North Africa, see Louis B. Wright and Julia H. Macleod, *The First Americans in North Africa* (Princeton, 1945).

[8] For the second Ottoman occupation, see Ahmad al Na'ib, *Kitab al-Manhal*

In Cyrenaica, unrest and the decline in population continued. But the rise of the Sanusi movement, a religious revival not unlike the Wahhabi movement, gave a sense of unity and supplied leadership which proved to be Cyrenaica's greatest asset. The founder of the movement, Muhammad Bin 'Ali al-Sanusi, like Ibn 'Abd- al-Wahhab of Arabia, was concerned with religious reform; but when Libya was captured by Italy, Sanusi followers rallied behind his authority to oppose Italian penetration into the country. The Sanusi order was founded on a network of Zawiyas (lodges), spread over the desert oases between the Sudan and Tripolitania, which supplied a kind of politico-religious organization under the head of the order and rescued the country from unrest and anarchy. The headquarters of the movement were established in the interior at Jaghbub, which constituted both a strategic center for consolidating Sanusi power and for spreading the creed among the tribes along the caravan routes. Sayyid al-Mahdi al-Sanusi, father of King Idris, brought pressure to bear upon the French after their occupation of Tunisia and expanded Sanusi preaching into the desert, although his activities were not entirely acceptable to the Ottoman Porte. It was, however, not until Italy declared war on the Ottoman Empire in 1911 and occupied Libya that the Sultan came to appreciate the value of Sanusi resistance and appointed Sayyid Ahmad al-Sharif, who succeeded Sayyid al-Mahdi as head of the order, as his deputy in central North Africa.

The Sanusi order was an Islamic revival movement which aimed at purifying Islam from accretions that crept into it during the past few centuries. It is a Sunni creed, following the Maliki school of law, and is adapted to desert life.[9] It supplied the Cyrenaican tribesmen with religious zeal and a sense of unity. The challenge which aroused the tribesmen to rally around Sayyid Ahmad and fight a religious war was Italy's attack on Libya; it was taken as an encroachment on Islam's territory,

---

al-'Adhib (Tripoli, n. d.), 2 vols.; L. Charles Féraud, Annales Tripolitaines (Paris, 1927); and A. J. Cachia, Libya Under the Second Ottoman Occupation, 1835–1911 (Tripoli, 1945).

[9] It is deemed outside the scope of this book to discuss the Sanusi creed; the reader, however, may be referred to the following studies: E. E. Evans-Pritchard, The Sanusi of Cyrenaica (Oxford, 1949); N. A. Ziadeh, Sanusiyah (Leiden, 1958).

and the war did not come to an end when the Sultan made peace with Italy. Thus before nationalism began to take the place of religion, under the impact of Europe, the Sanusis supplied the incentive for the Libyans to resist Italian occupation. But when nationalism became the new mode of loyalty, especially among the new generations, the Sanusi movement began to decline.

Rise of Nationalism

Ottoman rule in Libya was far from popular, and certain grievances against Ottoman misrule were often voiced, but Libyans managed to escape military service and they often were exempt from taxation. Under the impact of Islamic reform preached by Jamal al-Din al-Afghani and Muhammad Abduh on the one hand, and the nationalism advocated by Mustafa Kamil, leader of the Egyptian National Party, and the Egyptian press on the other, Libyans remained attached to Ottoman unity; but, like other loyal subjects of the Empire, they keenly felt the need for reform and the improvement of government administration. They therefore welcomed the Turkish Revolution of 1908 and the establishment of the parliamentary regime, in which Tripolitania and Cyrenaica were represented, and opposed those elements who sought to secede from Ottoman unity.[10]

As a result, nationalism in Libya and the other North African countries arose not as a reaction against Ottoman domination as in the Arab World east of Egypt, but in complete harmony and co-operation with Ottoman authority. North Africa had been the object of Christian invasions since the Crusades and the reconquest of Spain, and now that Algeria, Tunisia, and Egypt lay under Christian control, the Ottoman Porte was looked upon by Pan-Islamists and nationalists alike not as an enemy, but as a great supporter of North African national movements.

[10] Among those who represented Tripolitania and Cyrenaica during 1908–1911 were the following: Sulayman al-Baruni, Mukhtar Ku'bar, Mahmud Naji (Tripolitania), and 'Umar Mansur al-Kikhya, Yusif Shatwan, 'Abd al-Qadir (Cyrenaica).

Nationalism in Libya and the other North African countries was linked with religion. For, unlike the Arab nationalists in the Eastern Arab world, the primary object of their nationalism was not to attack the leading Muslim Power and Islam as a basis of the state, but to enlist Ottoman support and make use of Islam to enforce North Africa's resistance to Christian encroachments. While the nationalist in the Eastern Arab countries was clearly distinguished from, if not always opposed to, the Pan-Islamist, the two were hardly distinguishable in North Africa. Religion was indeed one of the most potent factors in the rise and development of nationalism in North Africa, and the sacred authority of the sultan-caliph was often invoked to bolster up the national cause.[11]

Italian Occupation

It is deemed outside the scope of our present study to discuss the origins and development of the Italian occupation of Libya, save insofar as it aroused the religious and national feeling of Libyans and inspired their leaders to work for the ultimate recovery of their country from Italian hands. It was the European diplomatic game which ultimately decided the fate of Libya,[12] although the Ottoman Sultan by no means had paid much attention to this African part of his dominion. For though the Sultan had known that Italy had cast covetous eyes on his African territory, his army was withdrawn from that territory to deal with a revolt in the Yaman. However, when Italy launched an attack on Libya, the Arab world showed its indignation and the Ottoman Porte was reproached for its failure to take adequate steps to resist the occupation. It was this indignation, aroused by the press, which induced the Turks and other Muslim nations to raise funds and dispatch continuous support

[11] Even though secular ideas, under the impact of the West, in recent years have begun to gain currency, the religious element in nationalism is still important, although religious orders are regarded by articulate nationalists as outdated.

[12] For the diplomatic background of Italy's occupation of Libya, see W. C. Askew, *Europe and Italy's Acquisition of Libya, 1911–1912* (Durham, 1942).

to Libyans even after the war between Italy and Turkey had
come to an end.

It was the religious tie between Libya and the Ottoman Empire
that prompted Libyans to fight with Ottoman forces, preferring
to remain the loyal subjects of a Muslim ruler than to become
Europeanized citizens under Christian rule. Thus, when Italy
was able to force the Sultan to surrender his sovereignty over
Libya by a peace treaty (1912), the legal transfer of sovereignty
from Ottoman to Italian control in accordance with international
practice seemed meaningless to Muslims, who fought the war
not in the name of Ottoman sovereignty over Libya but in the
name of Islam.

The Italian expeditionary force, superior to the Ottoman
garrison stationed in Libya, did not expect a long war and was
encouraged by certain initial successes; [13] but when the natives,
both in Tripolitania and in Cyrenaica, rallied to the support
of Ottoman forces, the Italians began to appreciate the resistance
that lay ahead of them. First, tribal shaykhs and Sanusi followers
gave the Italians no respite and often inflicted heavy losses. The
Ottoman Porte, encouraged by local resistance, sent a few able
men, such as Enver Pasha (one of the triumvirate who ruled
Turkey), Mustafa Kemal (later the well-known Ataturk), and a
few Arab army officers. Without native support the Ottoman
Porte could not have possibly continued to resist. The Italians
found the resistance much stiffer in the mountainous area of
Cyrenaica than in Tripolitania, but the war with the Porte came
to an end not so much due to striking victories on battlefields as
to the Porte's difficulties at home and pressure from other direc-
tions. Peace with the Porte was made on October 17, 1912, the
hostilities having been initiated by Italy's declaration of war on
September 29, 1911.

Under pressure from native leaders, the Ottoman Porte issued
a firman (decree) on October 15, granting full autonomy to
Tripolitania and Cyrenaica, the protection of Ottoman interests

[13] The Italian force consisted of 34,000 men, 6,300 horses, 1,050 wagons,
48 field guns, and 24 mountain guns. When the occupation began, the
Turks had a garrison made up of some 5,000 men in Tripolitania and 2,000
men in Cyrenaica. Reinforcements were sent by both Italy and the Ottoman
Porte. Italy's forces in Libya shortly before she entered World War I were
about 60,000 soldiers.

being entrusted to the Sultan's representatives. However, Sayyid Ahmad al-Sharif and the Tripolitanian leaders regarded this action as a declaration of their country's independence and were determined to continue the war. Italy had approved of Libyan autonomy on the understanding that it would mean that the King of Italy would later regulate the conditions of autonomy on the basis of Italian sovereignty and define the status of the Sultan's representative. This arrangement was embodied in the Treaty of Lausanne, which terminated the war between Italy and Turkey. But there was an ambiguity in this treaty. The Sultan's representative was to fulfill the functions both of diplomatic representation and of religious liaison between the Caliph and his Libyan followers. The Sultan-Caliph was also to appoint the Qadi of Tripoli and indirectly control religious affairs of the country. Thus the Sultan of Turkey could have indirect political influence in Libya because, in Islamic countries, religious and political affairs are inseparable. This arrangement was made partly to satisfy the Italian government, which was anxious to come to an agreement with the Turks, but mainly to demonstrate to the Muslims that the Sultan-Caliph had not surrendered his religious authority over Muslims. Italy contended that the Sultan's secular authority could be separated from the Caliph's spiritual authority in Libya—a European conception of the feasibility of separating the secular from the spiritual power which was not feasible in orthodox Islamic legal theory.[14] But this arrangement proved unworkable and the problem was not resolved until the peace settlement of Lausanne (1923), in which Turkey surrendered all of her sovereign powers over Libya.

Resistance Movement in Tripolitania and Cyrenaica

Peace with the Ottoman Porte, which ended hostilities between Italy and the Sultan within a year after Libya was invaded by Italy, did not end the Italian war with Libyans. Italy had to

[14] For a discussion of the implications of the Lausanne Treaty of 1912, see Evans-Pritchard, *op. cit.*, pp. 113–15.

face a long colonial war with the natives before she could claim to have brought the country under her control.

When the news of peace between Italy and the Ottoman Porte reached Libya, the Tripolitanian leaders were divided at the outset as to whether they should continue the war or enter into negotiations with Italy on the basis of independence granted by the Sultan. The war party, headed by Sulayman al-Baruni,[15] prevailed on the assumption that Italy was not going to recognize Tripolitania's independence without war. But Baruni, though a daring leader, was unable to unite the people behind him, and the Italians were able to overrun the country without much difficulty. Baruni left for Istanbul in March, 1913.

To occupy the country by force, however, was one thing and to control it was another. Thus when World War I began in July, 1914, the Italians began to face difficulties. The tribes in Fazzan and in Sirte rose in rebellion and the Italians replied with force. Their dependence on friendly tribal chiefs such as 'Abd al-Nabi Bilkhayr did not help; for Bilkhayr's rival, Ramadan al-Suwayhili,[16] lured the Italians into an attack against Sirte, in which he inflicted a crushing defeat on them and captured substantial munitions.[17] In the meantime, a Sanusi force under the command of Sayyid Safi al-Din, Sayyid Ahmad's brother, attacked from Cyrenaica and joined hands with Ramadan al-Suwayhili. It looked then as if Italy's position had become untenable, for had Tripolitanian leaders co-ordinated their activities with Sayyid Ahmad, the outcome of events might have been totally different.

Tribal feuding and Tripolitanian opposition to Sanusi leadership weakened Libya's resistance movement. For Suwayhili's victory over his rivals tempted him to impose his leadership over the whole of Tripolitania and he was not prepared to share

---

[15] One of the Tripolitanian leaders who belonged to the Berber community. Born in 1870, he studied Arabic literature and composed poetry. After the collapse of opposition, he went into exile and died in 1940, shortly before the liberation of his country. For his life, see Abu al-Qasim al-Baruni, *Hayat Sulayman Pasha al-Baruni* (Cairo, 1948).

[16] He was also called al-Shutaywi.

[17] This was a battle known as the battle of al-Qurdabiya (June, 1915). See al-Tahir Ahmad al-Zawi, *Jihad al-Abtal Fi Tarablus al-Gharb* (Cairo, 1950), pp. 151–60; and Muhammad al-Akhdar al-'Issawi, *Kitab Raf' al-Sitar 'Amma Ja'a Fi Kitab 'Umar al-Mukhtar* (Cairo, 1936), pp. 28–33.

authority with Sanusi leaders. He first warned Sayyid Safi al-Din
to withdraw and then defeated him in battle in 1916. In order
to avoid further bloodshed, Sayyid Safi al-Din, by order of Sayyid
Idris, withdrew to Cyrenaica.[18] The political activities of the
Sanusis henceforth were confined to Cyrenaica.

The resistance movement in Cyrenaica, despite its lack of
resources, proved to be more effective due to Sanusi leadership.
Sayyid Ahmad al-Sharif, as head of the Sanusi order, supplied
leadership with the assistance of a few army officers who had been
in the Turkish Army. Chief among those officers was 'Aziz
al-Misri, who visited Sayyid Ahmad at Jaghbub when Sayyid
Ahmad declared that he was going to continue the war as the
Sultan's representative. But neither the Ottoman Porte nor other
Muslim countries could offer substantial help, although resistance
against Italy aroused great enthusiasm throughout the Muslim
world.

During 1913-14, the Italians moved systematically to occupy
Cyrenaica; Sayyid Ahmad's forces, unable to offer organized
resistance, resorted to a guerrilla warfare which gave the Italians
no respite. Sayyid Ahmad himself took the field, offering his
followers great moral encouragement. In several instances the
tribes defeated the enemy in surprise attacks, and the Italians
suffered heavy losses. Nevertheless, the Italians were able to hold
the coast and urban centers, while the tribes, in areas where they
could harass the enemy, remained in control.

When World War I broke out, internal conditions in Cyrenaica
had greatly deteriorated because of continued warfare: the population declined, resources dewindled, and plagues and other epi-
demics, bringing famine in their wake, demoralized the people.
No less damaging in weakening the resistance was the disagreement between Sayyid Ahmad and 'Aziz al-Misri which resulted
in the latter's leaving the field, taking back to Egypt most of
the artillery.[19] These circumstances might have led to complete

[18] Muhammad al-Akhdar al-'Issawi, *op. cit.*, pp. 36–47; Evans-Pritchard,
op. cit., pp. 122–23.

[19] In an interview with the present writer in Cairo (April 13, 1958), 'Aziz
'Ali pointed out that Sayyid Ahmad was an old-fashioned leader whose
manner of prosecuting the war was unacceptable to him. 'Aziz 'Ali, a
dynamic officer, left Libya because he was not permitted to carry on the
war in his own way.

internal collapse and to Italian pacification of Cyrenaica, but the Ottoman Porte's involvement in the war drew Cyrenaica into the struggle between the Great Powers. The Sanusi leaders, who cared only to continue the struggle against Italy, were unwillingly drawn into the conflict.

Renewal of fighting followed Italy's entry into the war in May, 1915. The Ottoman Porte had been trying to urge Sanusi followers to attack the British in Egypt, but Sayyid Ahmad, as his correspondence with the British authorities in Egypt indicates, tried to maintain peaceful relations with them.[20] When Cyrenaica was included in the area under British blockade, Sayyid Ahmad became more dependent on Ottoman supplies. The Sayyid was forced—some say he was tricked—into the war with the British, although he had no desire to be involved in a war with them while he was fighting Italy.[21] The Sanusi force, under Turkish command, crossed the Egyptian frontier in November, 1915, and advanced as far as Sallum; but the British forces counterattacked in January, 1916, and the Sanusi army was forced to withdraw from Egypt. After this retreat, Sayyid Ahmad turned Cyrenaica over to Sayyid Idris, who was at Ajdabiya, and left for Jaghbub. From there, believing that his presence in the country might embarrass Sayyis Idris' handling of public affairs, he left for Sirte and was taken therefrom in a German submarine to Istanbul. Never again did he return to his country; he spent the war years in Turkey and the greater part of the interwar years in Damascus and the Hijaz, until his death in Madina on March 10, 1933.[22]

[20] For text of correspondence see Arabic material by Amir Shakib (Chekib) Arslan to Stoddard, the New World of Islam, translated by 'Ajaj Nuwayhid (Cairo, 1933), Vol. II, pp. 129–35.

[21] The Ottoman Porte dispatched two army officers—Ja'far al-'Askari, an 'Iraqi by origin, and Nuri, brother of Enver—who brought pressure to bear on Sayyid Ahmad and forced him into the war with the British. See Amin Sa'id, al-Dawla al-'Arabiya al-Muttahida (Cairo, 1938), Vol. III, pp. 21–23.

[22] For his life, see Arslan's account in the Arabic translation of Stoddard's New World of Islam, Vol. II, pp. 140–65; Vol. III, pp. 374–76; Vol. IV, pp. 396–408.

Sayyid Idris and the Peace Settlement

Internal conditions in Cyrenaica, it will be recalled, had increasingly deteriorated following Italy's entry into the war, and there was general dissatisfaction with Sayyid Ahmad's involvement with the British in Egypt. A few Cyrenaican leaders began to speak their minds openly to Sayyid Idris, who was opposed to the war with England but who kept aloof at Ajdabiya, and urged him to intervene on their behalf to save Cyrenaica from a difficult situation.[23]

This situation was known to the British authorities in Egypt. In 1914, on his way to pilgrimage, Sayyid Idris stopped in Cairo and thereafter was in contact with the British. " He seems," as Evans-Pritchard stated, " to have made it clear to the British authorities that his view of the situation did not entirely agree with that of his cousin, and from this time the British favored his pretentions to the leadership of the Bedouin of Cyrenaica." [24]

Two episodes supported Sayyid Idris' approach to the handling of the situation. Sayyid Ahmad's defeat at the hands of the British made him realize that negotiations had become a necessity. He therefore transferred Sanusi leadership to Sayyid Idris and withdrew from the field. Moreover, Italy's defeat at the hands of the Austrians, especially at Caporetto (1917), prompted the Italian government to end military operations in Libya and come to terms with Sayyid Idris. In this negotiation the British authorities in Egypt acted as intermediaries.

Preliminary negotiations, between a British and an Italian mission on the one hand and Sayyid Idris and his counsellors on the other, began at al-Zuwaytina in 1916. No final agreement was reached, due mainly to distrust between Sayyid Idris and the Italians, but a *modus vivendi* was sought to enable both sides

[23] Sayyid Idris was nominally the head of the Sanusi order by legitimate right, being lineally the grandson of the founder of the Sanusi order, but upon his father's death he was a minor. Thus his uncle, Sayyid Ahmad al-Sharif, took over the leadership until Sayyid Idris came of age. For an account of the Cyrenaican leaders' approach to Sayyid Idris, see al-'Issawi, *op. cit.*, pp. 62–63.

[24] Evans-Pritchard, *op. cit.*, p. 126.

to continue the negotiations. Early in 1917, the negotiations were resumed at 'Ikrima, at the outskirts of Tubruq. Despite divergences of view between Sayyid Idris and the Italian mission, the persuasion of the British mission brought the two sides to agree on a number of specific terms. The agreement provided for an end of hostilities, freedom of movement between the zone of Cyrenaica held by Italy and the zone held by the Sanusis, each party's responsibility for security in its own territory (neither was to create new military posts or encroach on the territory of the other), and the disarming of the tribes. Other clauses dealt with the restoration of property to the Sanusis and the appointment of shaykhs of Sanusi zawiyas (lodges), to be paid by the Italians. Muslim law and the Islamic creed were to be observed in the zone under Italian control.

Agreement with the British presented no difficulty, for Sayyid Idris returned all prisoners to them and commercial relations, via the coast of Egypt, were resumed. No Sanusi zawiyas were allowed in Egypt, but alms were collected from Sanusi followers in Egypt. The Jaghbub oasis, though in Egypt, was to be administered by Sayyid Idris. To the Italians, the 'Ikrima agreement meant peace during the war and an opportunity to establish themselves more firmly later. It was by no means, however, a final settlement; for, as subsequent events demonstrated, both sides desired ultimately to rule the country to the exclusion of the other.[25]

The Native Regime in Cyrenaica and the Agreement of Al-Rajma

Following the war, Italy found herself exhausted at home and unable to dispatch further reinforcements for the assertion of her effective control over Libya. "In view of these facts," said Carlo Schanzer, Italy's Foreign Minister, "it seemed to our government that the time was ripe to try direct co-operation with the native population, granting them civil and political rights

[25] For a full discussion of the origins and terms of the agreement, see Evans-Pritchard, *op. cit.*, pp. 134 ff.

that formerly were limited by the discretion of both the central and the local government." [26] This policy, in line with the Wilsonian spirit that had become widespread following World War I, was intended to satisfy native demands for self-government and Italy's desire to govern Libya without resort to force.

On October 31, 1919, separate statutes were prepared for Cyrenaica and Tripolitania, adapted to their social conditions. Each province had a separate Parliament, a government council, and local councils intended to help the Italian administration govern the country in accordance with local traditions and customs. The Cyrenaican Parliament met in April, 1921, under the presidency of Sayyid Safi al-Din al-Sanusi. It was composed of some sixty members, mainly tribal shaykhs elected by their followers, and only a few members from the cities. There were three Italian members, representing the Italian community. It approved all orders concerning the application of the statute before such orders were issued, considered the direct taxes, and discussed such public utilities as were provided for in the budget. Parliament also had the right to address questions to the Italian administration concerning administrative matters. Altogether it held five sessions until March 1923, when, as a result of the rupture of relations with Sayyid Idris, it was disbanded.

This liberal policy, inspired by the socialist government in Rome, was entrusted to Giacomo di Martino, Governor of Cyrenaica, who had been acquainted with Libya since 1907. Di Martino trusted Sayyid Idris and believed that Italy could govern Cyrenaica indirectly through the Sayyid's influence. Di Martino's adviser on native affairs, 'Umar Mansur al-Kikhya, the son of a native dignitary who had represented Cyrenaica in the Ottoman Parliament, acted as a liaison between Sayyid Idris and the Italian administration. To put friendly relations into words it was decided that the 'Ikrima agreement, which left much to be desired, was to be replaced by a new agreement designed to define the new political and military relations between Italy and Cyrenaica. This was done in the agreement of al-Rajma (October 25, 1920).

[26] Carlo Schanzer, " Italian Colonial Policy in North Africa," *Foreign Affairs*, Vol. II (1924), p. 451.

By virtue of this agreement Sayyid Idris was given the hereditary title of "Amir" and recognized as the head of the self-
governing regime of the interior of Cyrenaica, comprising the
oases of Jaghbub, Awjila, Jalu, and Kufra, with the right of
residing at Ajdabiya as the seat of his administration. Sayyid
Idris was granted a personal monthly allowance, as well as one
for his family, was allowed his own flag, a salute of guns on
official visits, and the use of an official steamer. The Sayyid was
also promised subsidies to meet his general expenses and subsidies
to tribal shaykhs. All native personnel, qadis and others in
various capacities, were placed on the Italian payroll. It was
also agreed that the Sayyid would be consulted on appointments
and given the right to move freely; his people were allowed to
keep their arms and send representatives to the local Parliament,
while Sanusi lands were exempted from taxation. Sayyid Idris,
on his part, agreed to co-operate in the application of the statute,
to limit his army to 1,000 men (subject to increase by mutual
agreement), to encourage trade and communications, and to
liquidate within eight months the adwar (Sanusi bands) and all
military and political organizations connected with them in the
zone outside his administration. He also agreed that he was
entitled to the zakat (alms tax), but not to any other.[27]

This agreement, which might have created a working arrangement between the Sanusi followers and Italy, was not intended
to give much power or political recognition to Sayyid Idris,
although it tacitly recognized him as a secular ruler in addition
to the head of a religious order. The Sayyid, on his part, failed
to disperse the adwar within the time limit specified. He gave
as his reason for not doing so the need to maintain order within
his own territory. Di Martino, who accepted Sayyid Idris' reason,
explained to his government the Sayyid's good intention; but he
was in an unenviable position when the adwar continued undis-
persed. Di Martino suggested to his home government that it
make a display of force to impress the Sanusis with the necessity
of living up to their promises; but his advice, though accepted in
principle, was not translated into action.

Under the circumstances, Di Martino sought the implemen-

[27] Rodolfo Graziani, *Cirenaica Pacificata* (Milano, 1932), pp. 6–9.

tation of the Rajma agreement by another instrument, known as the Bu Maryam [Abu Maryam] agreement (November 11, 1921), through which a new compromise was reached. It was agreed that the adwar were to be held jointly, although in principle they were to be ultimately dissolved. Moreover, the Italian administration agreed to place the jointly held army on its payroll.

Di Martino, who died shortly afterward, was succeeded by a governor who enjoyed neither the confidence of Sayyid Idris nor could his Italian supporters tolerate his policy of appeasement. It became clear, even before the Fascist regime decided to reverse this policy, that hostilities were bound to break out again. The coming of Mussolini to power, which opened a new chapter in Italy's colonial history, put an end to the conciliatory policy toward the Sanusis and heralded a policy of pacification by military conquest. On March 6, 1923, the Italians dissolved the jointly held army and by surprise took half the Sanusi army prisoners. On May 1, the newly appointed Governor, General Luigi Bongiovanni, declared null and void all the instruments that had been agreed upon between Italy and Sayyid Idris. The latter, who had then reached Cairo, was formally informed of the action taken by Italy's Minister in Cairo. Sayyid Idris, who never again returned to Cyrenaica until it was emancipated from Italian control, remained in exile to guide those who had taken up arms against Italy.

After Sayyid Idris left the country, the Italian authorities arrested 'Umar Mansur al-Kikhya, who had served under Di Martino as a native adviser, and brought him to trial on the ground that his duplicity had misled the Italian government to sign the Rajma agreement. It was held that 'Umar Mansur, who urged the Italians to come to an agreement with Sayyid Idris, advised the Sayyid not to carry out its terms. 'Umar Mansur's trial, both in Banghazi and Rome, resulted in his detainment and imprisonment for over sixteen years, but after World War II he reappeared to play his role in the politics of his liberated country.[28]

[28] The writer's interview with some of Sayyid Idris' personal advisers, especially 'Umar Mansur al-Kikhya and Muhammad Saqizli, and with Di Martino's assistant, Giuseppe Daodiachi, whom he met in Rome in April, 1958. See also Evans-Pritchard, *op. cit.*, pp. 147 ff.

Before Sayyid Idris left Cyrenaica he had been proclaimed Amir over their country by Tripolitanian leaders—an action which complicated further his relations with the Italians and brought matters to a head. This action and the culmination of events that had taken place in Tripolitania following World War I will be dealt with following our discussion of the internal situation in that province.

The Tripolitanian Republic

Italy's control of Tripolitania during World War I hardly extended beyond Tripoli city. Sulayman al-Baruni, who had gone to Istanbul, returned in 1915 as his country's new Governor and continued the struggle against Italy to the end of the war. When the war was over, Baruni and Suwayhili, who proclaimed their country's independence, agreed to continue the war if Italy refused to recognize their independence. A national convention was held in November 1918, attended by a Council of Four.[29] Italy was formally notified of the establishment of the republic and there was preparedness on both sides to negotiate.

In line with her conciliatory policy in Cyrenaica, Italy agreed to recognize this regime and a statute was issued on June 1, 1919.[30] Like Cyrenaica, Tripolitania had a Parliament and the Italians agreed to govern the country in co-operation with native authorities.

The internal situation, however, was far from satisfactory; for Italy's weak position in Tripolitania, as in Cyrenaica, greatly tempted the native leaders to insist on independence, while the Italians aimed at controlling the country through native leaders. Nor was the position of native leaders strong enough to carry on a resistance movement, for rivalry among leaders weakened the movement. The Italians well understood this situation and never agreed to give in as they had in Cyrenaica.

[29] Owing to rivalry among the leaders, it was decided to appoint a council composed of Baruni, Suwayhili, Murayyid, and Bilkhayr, assisted by 'Abd al-Rahman Azzam, instead of one head of state.

[30] For text of the statute, see *Legge Fondamentale per la Tripolitania,* 1 Giugno 1919 (Tripoli, 1919); and Amin Sa'id, *op. cit.,* Vol. III, pp. 51–59.

As a result, Tripolitanian leaders held a conference at Gharian (November, 1921) at which it was decided to negotiate directly with the Italian government. A delegation headed by Khalid al-Qarqani went to Rome, but no agreement seems to have been reached and Qarqani went to Moscow to attend an Islamic conference held in 1921.[31]

In the meantime, the Gharian resolutions, which included an agreement to offer the leadership of Tripolitania to Sayyid Idris, were unacceptable to Italy and war broke out. The new Governor of Tripolitania, Giuseppe Volpi, who proved to be an energetic man, addressed a letter to Tripolitanian leaders inviting them to co-operate with him; upon their refusal, however, he began to pacify the country by force. It did not take long to recapture the area of disturbances, owing to the flatness of the country and the lack of effective native leadership.[32]

Proclamation of the Sanusi Amirate and Sayyid Idris' Departure for Egypt

Italian action to grant Sayyid Idris the title of Amir conveyed implicit recognition of his secular authority over Cyrenaica. It also tempted Tripolitanian politicians, quarrelling over the question of leadership, to offer him the leadership of Tripolitania. Tripolitanian leaders, finding themselves unable to secure from the Italians terms similar to those offered to Cyrenaica, decided at the Gharian conference to offer the Amirate of Tripolitania to Sayyid Idris, who then would be entitled to negotiate with Italy on behalf of Tripolitania.

At Gharian, a delegation headed by Bashir al-Sa'dawi was appointed and armed with a formal document dated July 28, 1922, signed by leading chiefs, investing Sayyid Idris with the Amirate over Tripolitania. A deputation had gone earlier (April, 1922) to Ajdabiya to sound out Sayyid Idris on the matter and

[31] Information supplied by 'Azzam and 'Abd al-Salam al-Busiri. See also Amin Sa'id, op. cit., Vol. III, pp. 346–50.
[32] Carlo Schanzer, op. cit., pp. 452–53; Amin Sa'id, op. cit., Vol. III, pp. 351–53.

was favorably received. But when the Sayyid was formally invested with the Amirate, he found himself in an embarrassing dilemma. His advisers, it seems, were divided on the matter. He could not possibly turn down the call to a patriotic duty and alienate the Tripolitanian leaders; on the other hand, he did not want an open conflict with the Italians on this particular point.

Due to the circumstances, Amir Idris delayed action. Extremists, who desired a rupture of relations between the Sanusis and the Italians, instigated a disorderly incident which prompted the Italians to complain to Sayyid Idris. The Sayyid, finding dissatisfaction growing on both sides, finally decided to accept the Tripolitanian offer, and pleading ill health, left by caravan for Cairo via Jaghbub in December, 1922. He was followed by a number of leading tribal chiefs; some remained with him in exile until the liberation of their country, while others returned to resist Italian control of the country.[33]

The 'Umar al-Mukhtar Resistance Movement

The collapse of Tripolitania's resistance to Governor Volpi's forces and the departure of Sayyid Idris from Cyrenaica gave the false impression that Libyan resistance to Italian occupation had at last been broken. Moreover, the Italians had brought into the country a more efficient and well-equipped army and could claim to have under their command a force numbering about 20,000 men, composed mainly of Eritrean troops. Finally, the Italian authorities had become so well entrenched in the towns that the native population under their control could not join the desert rebels.

In the desert and the mountainous area of the Jabal al-Akhdar (the Green Mountain) , the situation was different. From Ottoman times the tribesmen never really submitted to authority and rarely paid regular taxes. It was among these tribesmen that loyalty to the Sanusi house was at its height and, in the Sanusi

[33] al-'Issawi, *op. cit.*, pp. 56–61; Fu'ad Shukri, *al-Sanusiya Din wa Dawla* (Cairo, 1948) , pp. 221 ff.

name, the war against Italians was bitterly prosecuted. But a
war by tribesmen against an organized army could not last very
long; it was therefore guerrilla warfare, to which these tribesmen
were long accustomed, that kept the struggle against the Italians
going for more than nine years. This war, fought in the name
of the Sanusi order, needed a tribal leader devoted to Sanusism.
Such a leader was found in the person of Sayyid 'Umar al-
Mukhtar.

Sayyid 'Umar was born about 1862 in Cyrenaica. He belonged
to the Farhan family of the Minifa tribe and was educated in
Sanusi zawiyas—first at Zanzur and later at Jaghbub. He served
under Sayyid Ahmad al-Sharif and had fought against the Italians
since 1911. After the collapse of the resistance, he followed
Sayyid Idris to Cairo. But it was there, apparently in agreement
with the Sayyid, that he decided to return and lead the resistance
movement against Italy.

Having returned to Cyrenaica in 1923, 'Umar al-Mukhtar
gathered around him a number of able tribal leaders [34] and
reorganized a force essentially made up of those adwar that the
Italians had captured shortly before Sayyid Idris' exile. Sayyid
'Umar, who proved to be a courageous and skillful guerrilla
leader, supplied effective leadership for a small but mobile force
which kept the Italians busy pursuing him for almost a decade.

The tactics used by 'Umar's tribal force in attacking the
Italians were remarkable, for its swift withdrawal with captured
matériel gave the Italians neither the time to defend the population under their control nor the opportunity to engage the force
in a battle. When engaged in pitched battles, it is true that
'Umar's force suffered losses; but most of the battles took the
form of surprise attacks. At night 'Umar and his tribesmen could
move with greater freedom, so much so that his force constituted
the " nocturnal government " in the territory, collecting the zakat
(alms) and other contributions from their countrymen. It is
deemed outside the scope of this study to discuss the details of
the military operations dealt with elsewhere,[35] but it is significant

---

[34] Those who played a leading role were: Yusaf Abu Rahil, 'Abd al-Hamid
al-'Abbar, 'Uthman al-Shami, and others.

[35] Ahmad Mahmud [al-Tahir Ahmad al-Zawi], *'Umar al-Mukhtar* (Cairo,
1934) ; Graziani, *op. cit.*, pp. 58 ff; Evans-Pritchard, *op. cit.*, 157 ff; Shukri,

to note that these operations, though they eventually came to an end, were in the main responsible for Libyan defiance of Italian rule and refusal to come to terms with Italy. Sayyid 'Umar, whose name had become a legend, inspired young Libyans after World War II to work for the independence of their country through a political society bearing the name of 'Umar al-Mukhtar.

After a decade of resistance, the Italians learned how to cope with the situation. Supplies from Egypt and the Sudan were cut off by the erection of a barbed-wire barrier extending along the Egyptian frontier, and those natives who contributed to the resistance movement were ruthlessly dealt with. Finally, Sayyid 'Umar, in one of his encounters with the Italians, fell into their hands on September 11, 1931. Graziani, the Italian Governor, was then on vacation. He returned at once to put an end to a movement that was virtually the work of a single leader. Summarily tried and though old and wounded, 'Umar was hanged before a large crowd on September 16.[36] The resistance, already weakened by a lack of resources, broke down after 'Umar's death.

Exile

Sayyid Idris and a few of his followers decided to reside in Egypt; others sought residence in other Arab countries.[37] The Egyptian government, though it welcomed Sayyid Idris, made it clear that as a refugee he must give up his political activities, presumably in order not to antagonize the Italians with whom Egypt, especially the ruling dynasty, had friendly relations. The Sayyid agreed, though his advice on political matters was often sought by his followers.

op. cit., pp. 264–65; and Muhammad al-Tayyib al-Ashhab, 'Umar al-Mukhtar (Cairo, 1956).

[36] Graziani, op. cit., pp. 234 ff; Shukri, op. cit., pp. 312 ff. Abu Rahil, continuing the struggle, fell while fighting; Uthman al-Shami surrendered; and 'Abd al-Hamid al-'Abbar, the only one who was able to break through the barbed wire, went into exile. 'Abd al-Hamid al-Abbar told the present writer (August 1959) the story of his hazardous escape to Egypt by cutting the barbed wire, which cost the life of several of his followers who had engaged the Italian patrols.

[37] A few émigrés went to settle in Turkey, but the majority preferred to reside in Arab lands.

Most of the émigrés subsequently became too preoccupied in earning their living to take part in political activities. Very few could afford to continue the struggle against Italy, due to lack of material resources. Moreover, most of Arab lands then under European control could offer but little help to Libyans. A few committees were organized, notably the Tripolitanian-Cyrenaican Defense Committee in Damascus under the leadership of Sa'dawi and 'Umar Shinnib, but their activities were limited to occasional protests against the injustices of Italian rule in Libya. The émigrés co-operated with nationalists in other Arab countries and tried to influence Italy to modify her policy toward Libya. They carried on what was called a "war of the pen," whenever the press was permitted to agitate against Italy.[38] Perhaps one of the most intensive campaigns was carried on by Bashir al-Sa'dawi in Syria and by Amir Shakib (Chekib) Arslan, in his paper *La Nation Arabe*, in Geneva. In 1931, Sa'dawi went on a pilgrimage and made a speech to thousands of pilgrims in Makka against Italian injustices in Libya.[39]

A more serious effort to influence Italy to modify her policy towards Libya was the rapprochment between Mussolini and the Amir Shakib Arslan in 1935, which resulted in releasing several thousand Libyans confined in camps in the Sirte desert; but Arslan's relationship with Mussolini was unacceptable to the Libyans and was subsequently repudiated by most Arab leaders.[40]

Egypt's efforts to help Libyan émigrés were greatly appreciated, but her acquiescence to Italy's request to limit their political activities was a great disappointment to many of them. Most damaging was Egypt's agreement with Italy on December 2, 1925, in which the oasis of Jaghbub was given to Italy. Because of Sanusi attachment to this oasis, Egypt's action was criticized by Libyan émigrés. However, Egypt offered Libyans residing in her territory, especially those who had come from the territory

[38] The term "war of the pen," coined by Amir Shakib Arslan, was applied to nationalist agitation outside Libya against Italian occupation of that country.

[39] For text of the speech, see Fu'ad Shukri, *Milad Dawlat Libya al-Haditha* (Cairo, 1957), Vol. I, pp. 684–87.

[40] See Fu'ad Shukri, *op. cit.*, Vol. I, pp. 905 ff.

handed back to Italy, the right to acquire Egyptian citizenship. The position of the émigrés, however, remained precarious, because Italy often protested against their activities as harmful to the maintenance of order and stability within Libya.

It had become quite clear that unless Italy became involved in a war in which she were defeated, Libya had no chance of regaining her freedom. Such an opportunity, it was then held, presented itself in 1935, when Italy launched an attack on Ethiopia; but the success of Mussolini in defying the League of Nations and annexing Ethiopia put an end to such thoughts.[41] It was not until the crisis of 1938, when the clouds of war indicated that Italy might be involved in a conflict with other powers, that Libyans began to discuss the implications of the new circumstances for their country and the possibility of its being recovered from Italian control.

[41] Amir Shakib Arslan seems to have thought that collaboration with Mussolini might be advantageous to Libya and a number of Libyans were induced to fight in the Ethiopian campaign, but no appreciable effect followed that collaboration.

chapter II

War and Liberation

SHORTLY BEFORE THE WAR began, when the international situation became tense, the émigrés became active and began to speculate on how to take advantage of the new circumstances if Italy should become involved in a war with England. But the exiles had already been scattered and there were differences among Tripolitanians and Cyrenaicans as to whom their acknowledged leader should be. Some advocated the leadership of Sayyid Safi al-Din, younger brother of Sayyid Ahmad al-Sharif, but the majority agreed that Amir Idris, who had already played a significant role in Libyan politics, should be the leader.

When the war broke out in September, 1939, Tripolitanian and Cyrenaican leaders, who were genuinely willing to forget their differences, became very active and saw at once the need to co-ordinate their activities by an agreement on common leadership. They called for a conference to discuss the opportunity offered by the war for the recovery of their country. Meetings were held in Alexandria on October 20-23, 1939, in which, after a long discussion on how to reconcile personal differences among Tripolitanian and Cyrenaican leaders, it was decided to entrust their common leadership to the hands of Sayyid Idris, provided he agreed to appoint a joint committee of Cyrenaican and Tripolitanian leaders which would advise him on all future action that might be taken concerning the liberation of their

country.[1] The joint advisory committee, however, never functioned satisfactorily and personal differences continued to poison
relations between Tripolitanian and Cyrenaican leaders.

The Sanusi Force

When Italy entered the war in June, 1940, the Tripolitanian
and Cyrenaican leaders, despite their agreement at the Alexandria
conference to patch up their differences, failed to agree on a
policy of co-operation with Britain. Many Tripolitanian leaders
believed, in agreement with the then prevailing idea in the Arab
World, that the Axis Powers would win the war and that Britain
had no chance of survival. They accordingly did not want to
antagonize Italy, under whose control Tripolitania lay powerless,
by joining forces with her enemies. The Cyrenaican leaders,
sworn enemies of Italy, had no such inhibitions and their country
never reconciled itself to Italian rule. They welcomed Italy's
entry into the war and were anxious to resume their struggle
against her. " This opportunity," said King Idris to the author,[2]
" was regarded as our chance to shoot the last arrow against our
country's enemy. If we succeeded, the country would be recovered; if we failed, nothing would have been lost, since our
country was already in the hands of the enemy."

Thereupon Sayyid Idris, who had been in touch with the
British authorities in Egypt, approved the organization of an
Arab force to serve under the British command for the liberation
of his country, having been urged to form it by many of his
followers. Before Italy entered the war, the British had already
given thought to the possibility of enlisting the support of exiled
Arabs from Libya to organize an Arab force.[3] After Italy's entry

[1] A procès-verbal, signed by the leaders who attended the meeting on
October 23, 1939, was regarded as binding on all the Cyrenaicans and
Tripolitanians in exile. For text of the document see *The White Book
on the Unity of Tripolitania and Cyrenaica* (Cairo, 1949), p. 26 (Arabic).
[2] The writer's interview with King Idris in Tubruq (August 31, 1961).
[3] Major Jennings Bramley, who lived in a house in the desert west of
Alexandria and who had served with the Egyptian frontier's administration
during and after World War I, had been constantly in touch with Sanusi
leaders. General Wilson consulted Bramley on the possibility of Sanusi

into the war, General (later Field Marshal) Maitland Wilson, Commander of the British forces in Egypt, formally invited Sayyid Idris to ask his followers to participate in the formation of a Sanusi force and entrusted Colonel (later Major General) C. O. Bromilow with organizing it. In agreement with the British, Sayyid Idris issued invitations to Cyrenaican and Tripolitanian leaders calling for a meeting to be held in Cairo on August 8, 1940, to discuss the nature of the assistance to be given them. The text of the letter follows:

" To Shaykh —————:

Peace and God's mercy be upon you. We hope that you are in the best of health.

This is to inform you that the British government has decided to begin at once to organize battalions of the Sanusi Arab tribes in order to restore to them their liberty and emancipate their country from the hands of the Italian oppressors, and to secure their [country's] independence.

You are requested to come to Cairo on Thursday, August 8, 1940, [to a meeting to be held] at Nabatat Street, No. 6, Garden City, Cairo, in order to discuss the assistance to be offered, and the number of men who would be willing to undertake such an assignment. It is understood that your expenses will be paid by the British government.

August 3, 1940

> (signed) Muhammad Idris
> al-Mahdi al-Sanusi
>
> Colonel Bromilow
> Assistant Military Secretary
> British Troops in Egypt [4]

The meeting was held on August 7, 1940, one day before the appointed time, and Sayyid Idris made an opening statement in which he urged his countrymen to take part in the military

---

participation in the war and it was decided to consult Prince Muhammad 'Ali, Crown Prince of Egypt, to enlist the support of Sayyid Idris. Muhammad 'Ali's good offices resulted in opening conversations between Sayyid Idris and the British authorities in Egypt. See Field Marshall Lord Wilson, *Eight Years Overseas, 1939–1947* (London, 1948), pp. 31–32.

[4] A copy of the letter was supplied to the writer by Sayyid Mahmud Abu Hidma, Governor of Cyrenaica. See also, *The White Book,* p. 29.

operation for the final liberation of their country. A few of the Tripolitanian émigrés attended the meetings, but Ahmad al-Suwayhili and Tahir al-Murayyid, two of their principal leaders, arrived too late in the final session on August 9 to hear General Maitland Wilson and refused to take part in the discussion. When the text of the resolutions was presented to them for approval, they declined to sign it and withdrew with a few others from the conference. The Tripolitanian leaders, more sophisticated than their Cyrenaican compatriots, offered as justification for their action the idea that they wanted to obtain a definite commitment from Britain for the future independence of their country before they would take part in the war on her side. The Cyrenaican émigrés, including a few Tripolitanians, adopted the following resolutions:

1. Full confidence is placed in the British government, which stretched forth its hands to liberate the Tripolitanian-Cyrenaican country from the oppression of Italian colonization.

2. Full confidence is placed in the Amir Sayyid Muhammad Idris Bin al-Mahdi al-Sanusi, and the Sanusi Amirate is proclaimed over the two provinces [of Tripolitania and Cyrenaica].

3. A committee shall be appointed, composed of members representing Tripolitania and Cyrenaica who will act as an Advisory Council to the Amir.

4. Participation in the war with the British Army against Italy [is decided upon] under the banner of the Sanusi Amirate.

5. A provisional Sanusi government shall be established to manage [Libyan] affairs at the present time.

6. A recruitment committee shall be appointed under the [provisional] government.

7. A request through the Amir shall be put to the British government to provide the necessary expenses for recruitment and management of the [Sanusi] administration in the form of a budget prepared in accordance with the national and traditional life of the Arabs.

8. The Amir is empowered to enter with the British government into such political, financial, and military agreements as shall ensure for [our] country its liberty and independence.

These resolutions, composed of eight articles, have been publicly read and signed, by virtue of which we entered into a covenant

with God that we shall abide by them under the banner of the
Amir.[5]

The text of the resolutions, formally communicated to General
Wilson, established the basis of subsequent collaboration between
Libyans and Britain.[6] It was endorsed by Libyan émigrés in
Syria, the Sudan, and Tunisia, who offered to co-operate with
their compatriots in Egypt. A recruitment bureau was set up
under the command of Colonel Bromilow, assisted by Captain
(later Colonel) J. N. D. Anderson as liaison officer. Five battalions were organized, designed for guerrilla warfare in the
Jabal al-Akhdar (green mountain) as soon as circumstances
would permit. The Sanusi force, which was reorganized later as
a regular army, took its part in the Western Desert campaign.[7]
The Libyans in Tunisia and the Sudan were instructed to collaborate with the French authorities, although the scope of their
activities was much more limited. Some Libyans, who had been
forced to fight on the side of the Italians, surrendered at the
battle of Sidi Barrani and joined the British forces.

Finding that the initiative had been taken solely by Cyrenaican
leaders, the Tripolitanian émigrés were divided into two camps
on the matter. One group, consisting mainly of émigrés from
eastern Tripolitania, supported Sayyid Idris and joined the
Sanusi force. The other, under the leadership of Murayyid and
Suwayhili, acknowledged neither Sanusi leadership for the whole
of Libya nor co-operated in the formation of an army under

[5] The above document, signed by some 21 persons, is the writer's translation
of a photographic copy of the Arabic original supplied by Sayyid Mahmud
Abu Hidma. Cf. the text reproduced in *The White Book*, pp. 31–32; Fu'ad
Shukri, *Milad Dawlat Libya al-Haditha* (Cairo, 1957), Vol. I, p. 271.

[6] The principles included in the resolutions were endorsed at a national
convention held in Cairo on August 6, 1942, and the signatories renewed
their pledge to acknowledge Sayyid Idris as their leader.

[7] Since the desert campaign was a highly mobile operation requiring a
high degree of technical and mechanical skill, Libyan troops were in the
main employed to guard prisoners, installations, and lines of communications,
etc., thus relieving British troops for more active operations. However, one
battalion of Libyan troops took part in the fighting at Tubruq. See Wilson,
op. cit., p. 34; War Office, *British Military Administration of Occupied
Territories in Africa During the Years 1941–43* (London, 1945) Cmd. 6589,
p. 22; Lord Rennell of Rodd, *British Military Administration of Occupied
Territories in Africa During the Years 1941–1947* (London, 1948), p. 255.

the aegis of Sayyid Idris. As a result, they formed the Tripolitanian Committee and asked permission from the British authorities to form a separate Tripolitanian army.[8] The British authorities tried to reconcile the two opposing parties, but disagreement among the leaders made it exceedingly difficult to unite them. The Tripolitanian leaders reproached Sayyid Idris for misleading his countrymen into fighting with Britain before obtaining a definite pledge of independence, for his alleged failure to consult the Joint Advisory Committee prior to his decision to collaborate with the British, and for applying the term Sanusi to all those who desired to collaborate without prior agreement by them.[9] Since the Tripolitanian leaders offered to collaborate with the British on the basis of the same terms as those acceptable to Sayyid Idris without acknowledging his leadership, the opposition of the Tripolitanian to the Cyrenaican leaders was reduced in the last analysis to their objection to Sanusi leadership over Tripolitania.[10]

Great Britain's Pledge to Cyrenaica

On the basis of the power given him at the Cairo conference (August 9, 1940) to " enter with the British government into . . . political, financial, and military agreements," [11] Sayyid Idris wrote to Colonel Bromilow on August 27, 1940, proposing that:

1. Great Britain grant Libyans internal independence of their country.
2. Libya have its own government headed by a Muslim Amir acceptable to the British government.
3. Great Britain hold the protectorate over Libya and direct the organization of its financial and military affairs until it reached a higher social, cultural, and civil level.

[8] See *The Tripolitanian Committee: Its Origins, Policy, Principles and Actions* (Cairo, n. d.) ; and Shukri, *op. cit.*, pp. 296–307.

[9] Shukri, *op. cit.*, Vol. I, pp. 273–82; *The White Book*, pp. 32–37.

[10] In an interview with several Tripolitanian and Cyrenaican leaders who took part in the controversy over the Sanusi leadership, it was pointed out that Suwayhili and Murayyid had been reluctant to accept Sayyid Idris' leadership and were by no means ready to share all his views concerning collaboration with Britain. Cf. Shukri, *op. cit.*, pp. 287–96.

[11] See p. 31, above.

In conversations with the British authorities in Cairo, Sayyid Idris made it clear that his country was poor and small in population and that British assistance would be indispensable. It was tacitly agreed that Libya, like Transjordan, would be established as an Amirate which would enjoy self-government and be guided by British advisors, although no definite assurance concerning the future of Libya was given by the British government.

This tentative understanding was unacceptable to the more sophisticated Tripolitanian leaders who, having consulted 'Abd al-Rahman 'Azzam,[12] demanded a definite assurance of future independence. However, when General Wavell occupied Cyrenaica in the winter of 1940–41, Cyrenaican leaders too were disappointed that a Sanusi government was not established at once in their country. Moreover, the events in Ethiopia and the Levant during 1941, resulting in British recognition of Emperor Haile Selassie as the ruler of independent Ethiopia and the Free French declaration of the independence of Syria and Lebanon, prompted Cyrenaican leaders to demand the same treatment for their country. Thus, Sayyid Idris addressed a letter to Oliver Lyttelton, British Minister of State in Cairo, on September 10, 1941, demanding similar treatment as that offered to Ethiopia, namely, the granting of immediate sovereign independence. The Sayyid's letter, written at the suggestion of his followers, particularly 'Umar Shinnib who had taken active part in nationalist activities in Syria,[13] was unacceptable to the British authorities who were not prepared to commit themselves on the future of Libya before the end of the war. In his private conversations with the British authorities, however, Sayyid Idris was more moderate in his demands and showed his satisfaction with oral assurances.

Further correspondence between Sayyid Idris and the British authorities in Cairo dealt with the Sayyid's request to obtain a written pledge, public or confidential, which would satisfy his followers. Sanusi followers who co-operated with the British were warned, especially by Tripolitanian leaders, by what was called the futility of Perfidious Albion's pledges unless they

---

[12] 'Abd al-Rahman 'Azzam, it will be recalled, played an important role in Tripolitanian domestic politics and kept in touch with its leaders. See p. 21, above.

[13] See p. 26, above.

secured a written assurance promising independence after the war. Sayyid Idris echoed his followers' complaints to the British and, in one of his petitions, went so far as to demand that if they could not do something to make his personal position vis-á-vis his followers less difficult, he must retire from any active part in the collaboration movement with them.

During 1941, the British authorities in Cairo were busy in conversations with Sayyid Idris on the one hand and in correspondence with the Foreign Office on the other. The British Minister of State, after consulting the officers in charge of Sanusi affairs, impressed upon the Foreign Office the need for a public declaration assuring Sayyid Idris and his followers of the future independence of their country. Early in January, 1942, the Minister of State was able to inform Sayyid Idris that the Secretary of State for Foreign Affairs decided to make a statement in Parliament on the future of his country and communicated to him the text of the statement. In answer to a question raised in the House of Commons on January 8, 1942, Anthony Eden made the following statement:

> The Sayyid Idris al-Sanusi made contact with the British authorities in Egypt within a month of the collapse of France, at a time when the military situation in Africa was most unfavorable to us. A Sanusi force was subsequently raised from those of his followers who had escaped from Italian oppression at various times during the past twenty years. This force performed considerable ancillary duties during the successful fighting in the Western Desert in the winter of 1940–41, and is again playing a useful part in the campaign now in progress. I take this opportunity to express the warm appreciation of His Majesty's government for the contribution which Sayyid Idris al-Sanusi and his followers have made and are making to the British war effort. We welcome their association with His Majesty's forces in the task of defeating the common enemies. His Majesty's government is determined that at the end of the war the Sanusis in Cyrenaica will in no circumstances again fall under Italian domination.[14]

The Eden statement, making no definite promise that Cyrenaica would become independent after the war, was dis-

[14] *House of Commons Debates*, Vol. 377 (1942), cols. 77–78.

appointing to Sayyid Idris and some of his followers and was sharply criticized by Tripolitanian leaders. Sayyid Idris observed that the statement, though it promised the liberation of Cyrenaica from Italian oppression, was negative and devoid of any positive assurance of independence. He, accordingly, sent a note (February 23, 1942) to the Minister of State demanding that Britain:

1. Declare the complete independence of Libya in its internal affairs and recognize a Muslim ruler as its head of government;

2. Guarantee Libya against foreign attack;

3. Conclude a treaty with Libya, the terms of which would be agreed upon;

4. Appoint a joint Anglo-Libyan Committee to lay the foundation of a Libyan regime.

These specific proposals demanding immediate action were unacceptable to the British at a time when the Axis forces had not yet been driven out of North Africa. It was explained to Sayyid Idris that no specific promises could be given before the end of the war, although he was assured that his country would be given its freedom after the war. Despite Sayyid Idris' efforts to obtain a positive assurance of independence, he was reproached by Tripolitanian leaders not only because the Eden statement failed to include the promise that Tripolitania in addition to Cyrenaica would not fall again under Italian domination, but also because its reference to the Sanusi was taken to imply prior recognition of Sanusi leadership by the British government.[15]

Sayyid Idris, despite the dissatisfaction of extremists, took a more hopeful view of the situation and assured his followers that the oral pledges given to him for the independence of his country would be honored after the war. In an interview with King Idris (August 31, 1961), the present writer asked why the British were reluctant to give a written assurance of independence. "The British pointed out," said the King, "that they had given [written] pledges to King Husayn [of the Hijaz] during World War I which they could not fulfill; they accordingly did not want to give such pledges, but preferred to extend their utmost assist-

[15] *The White Book*, pp. 39–40.

ance to their allies after they had won the war." King Idris went on to say that he had acquainted the Cyrenaican leaders with the British assurances, and all agreed that their contribution to the war effort would be an investment in lieu of which they would demand the independence of their country after the war. Sayyid Idris was satisfied that collaboration with Britain would ultimately result in positive advantages to his country; for, as he pointed out, on what ground would his countrymen be able to ask for British support after the war, if they had failed to collaborate with them during the war?

British Occupation of Cyrenaica and Tripolitania

Although the Italian people were on the whole opposed to war and their military leaders were well aware of their country's weakness, Mussolini was greatly tempted to achieve his dream of a new Roman Empire on the ruins of what appeared to be the crumbling French and British Empires. Had Mussolini known that the British forces would destroy his empire before it could be saved by his Axis partners, he probably would not have taken the plunge and Libya (as well as the other parts of his African empire) would have had no chance to recover from Italian domination.

On June 10, 1940, Italy formally declared war on Great Britain. Her forces in Libya, made up of some nine divisions, were much greater in number than those of the British; but in morale and effectiveness they were inferior. The total strength of the Italian Air Force in Libya when the war began was approximately 250 aircraft, about 80 were stationed in the Dodecanese. These forces, placed under the general command of Marshal Balbo, had been organized as the Fifth Army in Tripolitania and the Tenth Army in Cyrenaica. Italy's geographical position in the Mediterranean gave her the initial advantage in the ability to reinforce any of these forces by air or sea without serious threat of interference by her enemies. However, from the very beginning the Italian fleet showed a reluctance to act and soon began to suffer heavy losses. The Italian Air Force showed both inefficiency and lethargy, which demonstrated that it was not ready for action.[16]

Before the fall of France, Marshal Balbo's Fifth Army was to defend the western frontiers of Libya against French forces in Tunisia, until the Tenth Army defended Cyrenaica against British forces in Egypt. During the first month of Italy's entry into the war, the British activities in the Western Desert, under the command of General (later Field Marshal) Archibald Wavell, were confined merely to defensive skirmishes and patrolling the area between al-Bardiya (Bardia) and Tubruq (Tobruk) and south to Jaghbub. After the collapse of France, Marshal Graziani, who succeeded Balbo as Supreme Commander in Libya,[17] began to make preparations to invade Egypt. Mussolini issued an order that whether the preparations were complete or not, Graziani should launch an attack on Egypt on the day the Germans set foot in England. Early in September, 1940, Mussolini issued another order, despite Graziani's complaint that he had not received the equipment necessary for motorizing two Libyan divisions, that an advance in Egypt should begin regardless of any German landing in England. Graziani had to change his plans and began his military operations on the Egyptian coastal frontier on September 14 and advanced as far as Sidi Barrani. This incursion into Egypt was regarded as the opening of the gates of Egypt to Italy. Before Graziani could finish his difficult task in the face of General Wavell's determination to resist it, Mussolini made his fatal mistake toward the end of October by attacking Greece.

The stiff Greek resistance came as a surprise to Mussolini, who expected an easy occupation of that country. Great Britain lost no time in sending reinforcements to Egypt and her naval forces in the Mediterranean inflicted heavy losses on the Italian fleet. Under the circumstances, Graziani could not proceed beyond Sidi Barrani, and General Wavell, taking the initiative

---

[16] Major General I. S. O. Playfair, *The Mediterranean and Middle East*, (London, 1954) , Vol. I, pp. 92, 95, 96–97.

[17] Balbo's death on June 29, 1940, aroused suspicion. " The anti-aircraft battery at Tobruk fired on his plane, mistaking it for an English plane, and brought it to the ground " (*The Ciano Diaries*, ed. Hugh Gibson, [New York, 1946], pp. 270–71) .

by counterattack, was able, early in December, to throw back
Graziani's forces beyond the Libyan frontiers. By the end of
December, eight Italian divisions had been completely destroyed,
and the Western Desert forces advanced toward al-Bardiya and
captured Tubruq on January 22, 1941.[18]

Italian reverses in the Greek campaign invited Hitler to come
to the rescue of his partner. Britain felt obliged to give Greece
all possible help, and some of her forces were diverted from the
Western Desert to the Balkans. Banghazi had already fallen into
the hands of British forces (February 6, 1941), when it was
decided that the advance into Libya must halt for the time being.
Graziani, defeated at the hands of General Wavell, had already
decided to withdraw to the vicinity of Sirte in the middle of the
coastal road between Banghazi and Tripoli, where he would
organize defenses. General Maitland Wilson was appointed Military Governor and Commander-in-Chief of Cyrenaica. The
British chiefs of staff decided that the British position in Cyrenaica should be temporarily defensive and the advance beyond
Banghazi should not take place, pending the outcome of the
Greek campaign.[19]

The German intervention in North Africa was at the outset
confined to bombing from the air, but later land forces were
also sent. On February 11, 1941, General Erwin Rommel went
to Rome and left for Tripoli to acquaint himself with the situation. German troops had already been dispatched to Tripoli
and antitank units had been pushed forward to Sirte. Hitler
announced that German forces under General Rommel would
be known as the Deutsches Afrika Korps, and the 15th Panzer
Division was to reinforce the Fifth Light Division which had
already been dispatched.

Before the German attack on Greece had even begun, the
British had lost a large portion of Cyrenaica. The decision to
keep a minimum force in Cyrenaica, presumably on the assump-

[18] At this campaign almost all Libyans in the Italian army were taken
prisoners. For an account of General Wavell's campaign in the Western
Desert, see Major General R. J. Collins, *Lord Wavell, A Military Biography*
(London, 1947), Chaps. 26–27; Playfair, *op. cit.*, Vol. I, Chaps. 6, 10, 11, 13,
14, 15; Churchill, *Second World War* (Boston, 1949) Vol. II, pp. 615–18.

[19] For General Maitland Wilson's role in the Cyrenaican campaign, see his
Eight Years Overseas, 1939–47, Chap. 2.

tion that there would be no serious threat to the British position, proved to be disastrous. Lack of air defense for Tubruq and Banghazi left these ports at the mercy of the Luftwaffe. Rommel lost no time in taking the initiative and began at once to enforce an offensive campaign on March 31. "The speed with which he overran Cyrenaica," says Rommel's biographer, "was impressive, even to professionals." [20] Under these conditions, Wavell ordered a withdrawal. Banghazi and Darna were evacuated early in April, and in the face of British quick retreat, Rommel drove his army ruthlessly after them into Egypt. When a British garrison held its position at Tubruq, supplied from the sea, Rommel surrounded it with adequate force and pursued the retreating British Army. The garrison at Tubruq proved to be a thorn in the side of the Axis forces until its fall in the following year.[21] On April 10, Rommel declared that the British forces were collapsing and let it be known that his objective was now the Suez Canal. Rommel's desert exploits brought not only General Wavell's transfer to another theatre of the war, but also a similar fate to his successor, General Auchinleck.[22] Rommel's ability was at once recognized by Hitler, who promoted him to Field Marshal directly from his headquarters, and inspired Winston Churchill to say in praise of him in the House of Commons (January 27, 1942): "We have a very daring and skillful opponent against us, and, may I say across the havoc of war, a great general." [23]

Failure to seize Tubruq induced the Italian command to urge the Germans to agree that a halt must be called before advancing into Egypt. Hitler regarded the capture of Tubruq as essential, and the German Chief of Staff, alarmed by lack of reports from

[20] See Desmond Young, *Rommel* (London, 1950), p. 94.

[21] Tubruq was important to the British because in it there were "large stocks of stores, a supply of water, and a port whose use would be invaluable to the enemy and should be denied to them" (Playfair, *op. cit.*, Vol. II, p. 33); Churchill, *op. cit.*, Vol. III, pp. 6, 396.

[22] It has also been argued that Churchill wanted to see a more aggressive policy adopted by the Commanders-in-Chief in the Middle East, although the Commanders-in-Chief were only too aware of the appalling problem of their lines of communications round the Cape.

[23] *House of Commons Debates*, Vol. 377 (1942), col. 598; Churchill, *op. cit.* Vol. III, p. 200.

Rommel, decided to send General Paulus, Deputy Chief of the General Staff, to examine the situation. General Paulus took part in the attack on Tubruq. Although this port resisted for another few months, the British garrison was weakened. General Paulus reported that the Afrika Korps was in difficulty and needed supplies. Rommel quickly reorganized his forces and, with recently arrived reinforcements, he renewed his attack in June. Wavell's last attacks on Halfaya Pass were repulsed and Rommel's offensive improved his position. General Wavell's plan of dislodging the enemy failed, and he was transferred in July, 1941, and replaced by General Claude Auchinleck. Between July and December, 1941, the German Afrika Korps was reinforced by the repair of damaged tanks.

Auchinleck's main contribution was the recapture of almost the whole of Cyrenaica. Rommel temporarily retreated, but he regrouped his army and attacked in January, 1942. He proved himself master of desert tactics and, outwitting British commanders, regained the greater part of Cyrenaica. While Auchinleck was still reorganizing, Rommel again struck the blow. He started toward the end of May and swept forward with his forces, intending to destroy the British forces at Sidi Raziq. Then he tried to capture Tubruq. The Free French were evacuated from Bir al-Hukayyim and Rommel attacked from the south. British casualties were very high. He attacked Tubruq and its garrison surrendered on June 20, 1942. These reverses not only caused the loss of the entire Cyrenaican province but also jeopardized the entire British position in the Middle East. As a result Winston Churchill and his Cabinet had to face a vote of censure in Parliament on June 25, 1941.[24]

Mussolini now wanted Egypt and made preparations to enter Cairo. Rommel crossed Egypt's frontier on June 24. The story of how Rommel's forces entered Egypt and were checked at al-'Alamayn does not fall within the scope of this book and has been told in detail elsewhere.[25] The help given by the United

[24] Churchill, *op. cit.*, Vol. IV, pp. 391–409.

[25] Field Marshal Viscount Montgomery, *El-Alamein to the River Sangro* (London, 1951) ; *The Memoirs of Field Marshal Viscount Montgomery* (London, 1958) , Chaps. 7–10; Desmond Young, *op. cit.*, Chap. 9; Playfair, *op. cit.*, Vol. III, Chaps. 12–14.

States in tanks and aircraft relieved the pressure on Egypt and
eventually forced Rommel to evacuate his forces from Libya.
After General Montgomery's victory at al-'Alamayn, Rommel's
forces were in full retreat. The recovery of Cyrenaica by the
British forces was not a very difficult task. Montgomery's forces
at al-'Alamayn began their counterattack on October 23. By the
end of this month the destruction of Rommel's forces was almost
complete, and the pursuit of the Axis forces had already begun.
On November 11, the Eighth Army entered Cyrenaica. Tubruq
was recaptured on November 13, Darna on November 15, and
Banghazi on November 20. Rommel received orders to hold
al-'Aqayla to the last man, but on December 13, he began to
retreat again. At Buwayrat, Rommel stayed from December 26,
1942, to January 14, 1943, and from here he retired slowly under
cover of a strong rearguard. Misrata was occupied on January
18, and Tripoli, in spite of attempts to defend it, fell on January
23.[26] A fortnight later the last of the Axis forces were evacuated
and the liberation of Libya was complete.

Military Administration in Cyrenaica

Cyrenaica changed hands three times before it was finally
occupied by the Eighth Army in November, 1942. General
Montgomery signed the proclamation of the British occupation
on November 11, 1942, and published the following message to
the people of Cyrenaica in which British policy during the military administration was outlined:

> Barqa has been conquered from the Italians by force of British
> arms in the course of the defeat of their army and will be admin-
> istered until the end of the war by a British military government.
> The end of the war means the conclusion of a peace treaty between
> the powers at war and does not mean the cessation of hostilities in
> Barqa or in North Africa only.
> The military government will not enter into questions relating

---

[26] Count Ciano notes in his diaries: " Today the communique announced
the fall of Tripoli. On many faces, the most humble, and the most sincere,
I saw deep lines of pain " (*Ciano's Diaries*, p. 574) .

to political affairs of the future but will endeavor to rule with firmness, justice, and consideration for the interests of the people of the country.

The population is called upon to behave peacefully and to obey my orders and the orders of my officers. Intrigue and discord between individuals or sections of the people will not be countenanced, and anyone making false accusations against others will be punished as a person likely to disturb the peace.

The British Army, during its period of rule in Barqa, wishes to see the people enjoy the benefits of peace that have been denied to them for many years. It does not wish to be obliged to take disciplinary action against them, since many individuals have helped British soldiers, and many have served in the British Army. But it will not hesitate to take such action, if its laws and orders are disregarded.

The object of the British Army is to pursue and defeat the enemy. The population must be patient and not make requests that will in any way hinder its operation. No supplies are available at present but they will be brought as soon as the requirements of the army permit. The British government has thanked Sayed Mohammed Idris el Senussi for the assistance he has given to the Allied cause and has promised that the Sanusis will not again be subject to Italian rule. While the British Army rules the country, it wishes to establish friendly and cordial relations with the people.[27]

After the first occupation, General Wavell suggested the establishment of military government in the occupied enemy territories under Major General Mitchell as Chief Civil Affairs officer. The War Cabinet decided on February 20, 1941, that the War Office should be responsible for the occupied territories, because the Foreign Office was not equipped to undertake the administration and the Colonial Office would be suspected of seeking to incorporate them into the British Empire. On January 29, 1941, General Wavell decided to detach Cyrenaica from the command of the headquarters in Egypt and appointed General Wilson as Governor and Commander-in-Chief of Cyrenaica, with a political officer responsible for the civil administration. Brigadier S. H. Longrigg served as the political officer in 1941–42.

[27] Lord Rennell of Rodd, *British Military Administration of Occupied Territories in Africa During the Years 1941–1947* (London, 1948) pp. 250–51.

Owing to the instability of the military situation, it was not until the third occupation that the headquarters of the British military government began to function in the territory. The seat of the administration was set up in al-Marj (Barce) in 1942, but moved to Banghazi in 1943. Brigadier (later Sir) Duncan C. Cumming, to whose hands the whole planning of the administration of Cyrenaica was entrusted, became the head of the Political Staff of the Eighth Army under General Montgomery. On March 10, 1943, the name of the British military government was changed to that of the British military administration.

After the third and final occupation of Cyrenaica, the Italian settlers had departed, leaving the territory virtually controlled by the British authorities. As early as May, 1942, Brigadier Cumming sent a memorandum to the Foreign Office recommending a more liberal treatment for Cyrenaica than other Italian colonies. He proposed that Italian sovereignty should be terminated, the Arabs of Cyrenaica should no longer be regarded as Italian subjects, and that Italian laws and courts should be abolished and replaced by new laws and courts suitable to an Arab community. The Foreign Office, though it approved Cumming's recommendations, stated that Italian sovereignty should continue in law and the Italian legal system should be enforced pending the termination of occupation by a peace treaty.[28] Thus, Italian law, purged of Fascist accretions, continued in force; but changes required by military necessity and the immediate needs of the inhabitants were made.[29]

Political officers had been appointed in Darna on November 1, in Shahhat (Cyrene) on November 23, in al-Marj (Barce) on November 24, in Banghazi on November 25, and in Ajdabiya on December 13, 1942. Thus by January 1, 1943, the basis of a

[28] The enforcement of the Italian legal system was required under the Hague Convention (see Article 43 of Convention IV). In reply to a letter sent by Sayyid Idris (January 25, 1943) to the British government demanding that Cyrenaica should not be treated as occupied enemy territory but should be given immediate independence, the British Minister of State reiterated a statement that had been made on the occasion of the capture of Tripoli in which it was stated that the future of the country would be settled at the peace conference at the end of the war.

[29] Lord Rennell, *op. cit.*, pp. 251–53; D. C. Cumming, " British Stewardship of the Italian Colonies," *International Affairs*, Vol. XXIX (1953), p. 13.

military administration was set up to fill the vacuum created by the disappearance of the Italian administration. Under the Italian regime, Cyrenaica was composed of the Banghazi and the Darna *perfetturas*, directly controlled by the authority of the Libyan government in Tripoli. Reconstituted as a separate unit, Cyrenaica was divided into seven, later regrouped into three, districts, and it was administered directly under the control of the British military administration. The seven districts were: al-Marj (Barce), Ajdabiya, Shahhat (Cyrene), Darna, Tubruq, Kufra, Banghazi Town, and Banghazi Rural.

The British administration began to create a native civil service in 1943, and this policy was pursued to encourage Arabs to fill responsible positions. The service of those who had worked under the Italian administration and of political exiles who returned was sought. The senior posts consisted of mudirs, qadis, and a few high departmental ranks. The post of qa'imaqam, chief of a district, to work directly under a civil officer, was revived. By the end of the war there were approximately 350 native officials in the districts and over 100 in the towns. The number of native officials grew steadily when young men began to return from educational missions sent to study in Egypt and England.

Sayyid Abu al-Qasim al-Sanusi, a cousin of Sayyid Idris, was first appointed as Qa'imaqam of Banghazi and later Secretary of Interior. Husayn Maziq, Fathi al-Kikhya, 'Ali al-Jirbi, and 'Abd al-Raziq Shaqluf served as secretaries for Interior, Justice, Public Works, and Finance. A municipal council was set up, composed of native dignitaries, which proved to be the most vocal organ in Cyrenaica for the expression of urban political opinion.[30] 'Abd al-Hamid al-Dibani was its Deputy Chief and 'Ali al-Fallaq, its secretary. A municipal council proclamation was issued in 1948 which extended native authority from the executive to the policy level. The declaration defined the powers and jurisdiction of the local authorities with a view to developing financial authority. Additional powers and responsibilities were later progressively transferred.

A public information office, headed by John Reid and assisted

[30] al-Tayyib al-Ashhab, *Barqa al-'Arabiya* (Cairo, 1947), pp. 540–43.

by Sulayman al-Jirbi, was established in Banghazi in March 1943, and an Arabic newspaper, called *Jaridat Banghazi*, was edited first by 'Abd al-Jawad Furaytis and later by Salih Mas'ud Buwaysir. The staff of the information office included Mahmud Abu Hidma and 'Abd-Allah Sakta, assisted by Mahdi al-Mutardi and Mahmud Makhluf, who promoted cultural and educational activities.

Although the Italian administration had difficulty in dissolving the tribal system, its disintegration had gone further than appeared on the surface. The authority of the shaykhs and tribal chiefs had declined, and only the two tribes of al-'Ubaydat and al-Bara'sa continued to possess recognized heads. The other tribes had split into numerous subdivisions. The administration tried to revive the traditional tribal authority and to encourage, to the dissatisfaction of the sophisticated younger generation, tribal chiefs to settle tribal disputes. The British military administration found this system to be useful and practical in carrying on the business of government in the tribal community.

The exodus of the Italian settlers presented a real problem for the administration; [31] for Cyrenaica had not merely faced a change of masters but the utter disappearance of a complete agricultural and economic system. This was most severely felt in the towns, where there was a noticeably sharp decline in the standard of living, and where the Arab population had become accustomed to certain modern conveniences. Such towns as al-Bardiya and Tubruq had been completely destroyed, and Banghazi suffered severe damage. The people had seen their country overrun by invading armies three times in two years. They had experienced two British withdrawals and had to face Italian revenge for their friendly attitude to the British forces. A few had been shot for the flimsiest reasons.

In the country the Bedouins, who were accustomed to living at a subsistence level and to periodic privation, were just able to survive while the campaign was going on. After the departure of the Italian settlers, the British administration invited the tribes to occupy, under short leases from the Custodian of Enemy

---

[31] The Italian settlers left Cyrenaica on the orders of the Italian government immediately after Rommel's defeat at al-'Alamayn.

Property (but the tribes took it for granted that they returned to their lost land), the abandoned Italian farms of the *Ente per la Colonizzazione della Libia.* The Bedouins were at first encouraged to safeguard the crops already sown by the Italians and then to sow the fields which had not yet become productive when the Italian farmers left. The most important agricultural area was al-Marj, where the Italians had expropriated more than 30,000 acres. The farms were entrusted to Arab tenants, supervised by a British officer. The cultivation of the farms of the Green Mountain made Cyrenaica almost self-supporting at a time when there was no available shipping space.[32]

Due to repeated occupation and evacuation of forces, the Cyrenaicans not only suffered material damage, but also their morale was shattered. While the war was still going on, many Cyrenaicans had given assistance to the British in dangerous situations, particularly in sheltering and guiding back to the British lines soldiers and airmen cut off by the enemy. For such services many a Cyrenaican suffered severe punishment inflicted by the Italians. However, Cyrenaicans benefited not only by the liberation of their country by the British, but also indirectly by gaining more personal liberty, the restoration of lands to former tenants, and some material progress achieved. Moreover, many families were reunited, émigrés returned to take active part in public affairs, and the threat—almost a nightmare to Cyrenaicans—that the Italian government was going to exterminate the natives to make room for Italian settlers disappeared.

Military Administration in Tripolitania

British military administration came formally into existence on December 15, 1942, when General Montgomery, at his Eighth Army headquarters near Ajdabiya, issued several proclamations, the first of which declared Tripolitania to be under British occupation. The other proclamations dealt with the methods by which the occupation was to be implemented. The occupying power can, under the Hague Convention, exercise such legislative,

---

[32] Lord Rennell, *op. cit.*, pp. 257–60.

judicial, and administrative powers as are needed during occupation. These powers were exercised by an operational commander, with the advice of a Deputy Chief Civil Affairs Officer who was responsible for the administration of the territory. When operational control was no longer necessary, the Deputy Chief Civil Affairs Officer was appointed as Chief Administrator responsible for the whole administration of the territory. Brigadier M. S. Lush was appointed as the first Deputy Chief Civil Affairs Officer in 1942 and was succeeded by Brigadier T. R. Blackley as Deputy Chief Civil Affairs Officer first and then, from 1944 to the end of military administration, as Chief Administrator. The garrison troops remained under the District Commander until their withdrawal, while the civil police and gendarmerie were responsible to the Chief Administrator.[33]

The administration under an occupying power enforces existing law; and the British, following this practice, enforced Italian law, modified either for military necessity or to meet the immediate requirements of the inhabitants. The Italian civil servants who remained in the territory after the withdrawal of Italian forces remained to serve in conjunction with the British authorities. Native Tripolitanians were soon to enter the service and their number steadily increased.

Under the Italian regime the territory was divided into two *Prefetturas*; Tripoli and Misrata; under the British administration it was divided into three provinces: Tripoli, Misrata, and Gharian. Each province, placed under the command of a Civil Affairs Office, was divided into several districts. The whole territory was divided into 21 districts and a number of municipos (a form of local government in control of public utilities).[34]

The ravages of the war had relatively little effect on Tripolitania and the population suffered much less devastation than in Cyrenaica. The Arabs welcomed the British occupation no less because of their expectation of a future Arab government than because of their dislike of Italian rule. The Italians, although regretting the disappearance of Italian rule, were

[33] The police and gendarmerie were recruited from natives and a police school had been opened at Tarhuna to train them.
[34] Lord Rennell, *op. cit.*, pp. 267–68.

anxious to return to normal life. The military administration from the start made it clear that its purpose was primarily to maintain peace and order and that, as a wartime administration, it would administer the territory in accordance with international law. When, however, the people found that British military administration had continued and their prospect for self-government was less favorable than in Cyrenaica, they became restless. They soon began to claim that Libya was but one country and they could see no reason for differentiation between the two provinces. Their reaction to British control was reflected as early as August, 1943, when a demonstration in Tripoli City took place culminating in the presentation to Blackley of a petition voicing certain grievances.[35]

Economic and social conditions were naturally disturbed by the war, but Tripolitania was better off than Cyrenaica since Italian peasants stayed on their farms and settlements and many of their compatriots remained in the towns. The total number of Italians was temporarily increased by several thousand who fled from Cyrenaica, but soon after the war the number of settlers gradually dwindled. Trade with Italy almost came to a standstill, but other markets had been found and British expenditure during the war eased the financial situation. Social services, temporarily suspended, were quickly restored. Although the Italians paid considerable attention to educational institutions, the schools were suspended during the war and the buildings, converted into barracks, were damaged. It took the British administration some time to reconstruct old buildings and build new schools for the Arabs.[36]

[35] Lord Rennell states: " The petition lamented the fact that Tripolitania was still treated as an enemy territory and that high Italian officials were working in departments dealing with native affairs: it asked for the employment of more native officials and equal salaries for them and Italians. It went on to ask for wider concessions of a peacetime nature, such as commerce with neighboring countries, the provision of transport and the granting of permission for pilgrims to go to Mecca, and the opening of primary schools for Moslems. Lastly the petition pointed out that certain taxation was a burden in that, whereas the lire had been devalued five times and direct taxes had been increased by the same amount, wages had not undergone equivalent change " (Lord Rennell, *op. cit.*, p. 288) .

[36] For the educational system under the British administration see A. J. Steele-Greig, *History of Education in Tripolitania: From the Time of the*

Although both Tripolitania and Cyrenaica had been under British military administration, the movement of people from one province to the other was restricted and trade was subject to customs. On March 16, 1943, the Cyrenaica administration recommended the adoption of a customs union between the two provinces, in which the same customs tariffs would be applied at all points of entry in both provinces, but without collection of custom duties at the land frontier between them (such as Ajdabiya or Sirte), where a statistical check would be sufficient. An agreement between the representatives of the two provinces was reached and it became the basis of their subsequent integration.

The Fazzan

By an agreement between General Alexander and General Leclercq de Hautecloque on January 26, 1943, the Free French forces were to advance from Lake Chad and to occupy the Fazzan oases of the southern Tripolitanian Sahara. It was also agreed that the French control would extend as far north as lat. 28° and as far east as long. 18°. Three days later, General Leclercq informed General Alexander that French forces had occupied Ghadamis, Darj (Derg), and Sinawan (near the Tunisian border) and it was agreed that they should administer this area also.[37] The French administration followed that adopted in the southern Algerian Sahara, consisting mainly of a direct military administration with the officers commanding the local garrison acting as political and administrative officers. The Free French forces entered this area, whose negroid population was hardly more than 40,000, in the hope that they might retain it permanently as part of the African region that included North and Equatorial Africa.

Fazzan was administered by the French military authorities

Ottoman Occupation to the Fifth Year under British Military Occupation (Tripoli, 1948).

[37] French forces had already occupied Kufra in the winter of 1940–44. A small French post remained there, although the oasis was primarily used by British raiding forces operating from Banghazi.

through the intermediary of a local ruling family, the House of Sayf al-Nasr, and Fazzanese officials. A French Resident, posted at Sabha, exercised authority over the whole of Fazzan; but responsibility for the territory was divided between three local administrations under two ministries in Paris. However, the regions of Ghat and Ghadamis for administrative purposes were attached to the military authorities of the neighboring French territories: Ghat to the southern military territories of Algeria, and Ghadamis to the southern military territories of Tunisia.[38]

National Stirrings

No sooner had the two provinces been liberated from Italian rule than the politically conscious public in both provinces began to agitate for participation in the administration and demanded the formation of political parties, although the British military authorities made it clear that such activities should be postponed until the war was over. Some of the political parties had their origins either in groups formed during the early period of Italian occupation or in societies founded by the émigrés while in exile. When Italian rule ended, the return of émigré leaders and the relative freedom enjoyed under British administration prompted the leaders to resume political activities. Nationalism, though confined to the few and articulate, became the dominating force, and the masses were stirred to agitate for the transfer of authority from foreign to native hands as the national aspiration of the entire nation. This spirit, though awakened by the events of World War II, was by no means new, for it was part of a larger wave of political consciousness that swept the whole of North Africa following the war.

While in exile many Libyans took an active part in the political activities of neighboring Arab countries, partly in sympathy with their coreligionists in their struggle to liberate their countries, but mainly, perhaps, because such a struggle was directed against Western colonial rule generally. In their participation with such

[38] See Lord Rennell, *op. cit.*, pp. 292–93; United Nations, *Annual Report of the United Nations Commissioner in Libya*, 1950, p. 9.

activities, they had not only learned at first hand the technique of nationalist agitation as practiced in Cairo, Beirut, and Damascus, but also the tactics employed in opposing foreign influence. Some of them took active part in nationalist agitation and participated in public meetings and street demonstrations. After their return to Libya, the émigrés were prompted to stage similar performances against foreign rule when circumstances permitting the expression of political opinion became more favorable.

In the meantime, a new generation had arisen within Libya itself during the thirty years of Italian domination. Although Italian policy aimed at keeping these young men immune from nationalist contamination, the tide of nationalism in neighboring Arab lands during the interwar period was so high that its influence was bound to be felt in Libya. Some young Libyans had been able to study abroad and were exposed to nationalist influences as were their exiled compatriots, although, upon their return home, they had to be discreet about their nationalist aspirations. Libyan nationalists, determined never to give their Italian rulers a respite, learned how to master the technique of stirring up opposition by clandestine methods, although many of them had to do so at the risk of death on the gallows. While such activities seemed futile to many outside observers at a time when Italy was successfully carrying out its colonial venture, Libyan nationalists hoped that the time might eventually come when Italy would pay the price of its uncompromising policy.

chapter III

Cyrenaica:
From British Military Administration to the Sanusi Amirate

THE BRITISH OCCUPATION of Cyrenaica in 1943 saved her people not only from extinction at the hands of their former Italian rulers, but also from worries that their lands might again be overrun by Axis forces. The émigrés and political exiles began to return, and the British administration made an effort to improve the social and economic conditions, especially to relieve acute distress and supply shortages during the war. Very soon political consciousness was awakened and the agitation for self-government under the Amirate of Sayyid Idris al-Sanusi became the chief preoccupation of the public.

Political consciousness was aroused partly by Allied declarations and partly by the general wave of Arab nationalism that had already reached a high pitch during and after the war. Above all, Cyrenaica was endowed with wise and balanced leadership in the person of Sayyid Idris, who enjoyed high prestige among the British and could voice with confidence the genuine aspirations of his people for self-government. Unlike Tripolitania, which for a long time was torn with factional rivalries, Cyrenaican political activities very quickly centered on impressing Great Britain with the need for transferring authority from British to Sanusi hands at the earliest possible moment.

53

Sanusi Leadership

Sayyid Idris derived his power partly from the traditional loyalty enjoyed by his family, and partly from his diplomatic activities during World War I and II, which resulted in his recognition as the Amir over his people after World War I and in the final expulsion of the Italians from his country after World War II. In tribal areas, where the Sanusi order was widespread, Sayyid Idris' authority was supreme; but in the towns, where nationalism began to gain ground, Sanusi leadership was admittedly acknowledged as a political expediency. Thus Sayyid Idris' leadership was acknowledged by all, and there was at the outset almost universal enthusiasm for his proclamation as the Amir of Cyrenaica.[1] Even after his return from exile, when he listened more often to older than to younger men, there was no question as to whom the future head of state should be.

Sayyid Idris also realized that British help and sympathy were essential for his country. Cyrenaica, it will be remembered, was liberated by the British with the help of the Sanusi forces and he seems to have genuinely believed in the value of British friendship and in the fact that British interests and his country's national aspirations were not essentially irreconcilable. It was thus that he was capable both of securing British sympathy and of controlling the nationalists. It was due to the prestige he enjoyed among his people that the British sought his advice while governing his country during and immediately after the war and consulted him on all matters affecting British policy toward his people. It was also clear to the British that he was the natural candidate for rulership and they were ready to acknowledge him as head of Cyrenaica, when the fate of the former Italian colonies was decided.

Sayyid Idris, however, preferred to remain outside his country so long as it remained under temporary foreign administration. He was confident that when the British military administration

---

[1] See Muhammad Abu Bakr, " al-Watan wa al-Amir," *Majallat 'Umar al-Mukhtar*, Vol. I (1943), pp. 3–4; and a leading article in Vol. I (1944), No. 12, pp. 2–3. This magazine represents the opinion of the new generation.

came to an end he would be entrusted with civil control of his country, but he did not want to be responsible while the military authorities were governing. He agreed to use his influence to impress on the people the necessity of showing patience for discomforts of preserving peace, and of co-operating with the British authorities during and immediately after the war, but he did not associate himself directly with the conduct of the military administration.

Suggestions were made to Sayyid Idris to visit Cyrenaica in the summer of 1943; but the Sayyid decided to send first a deputation of six members of the Sanusi family, led by Sayyid Safi al-Din, to convey to the people a message to keep hope high, to impress on them the need to keep order, and to co-operate with the British authorities. The party arrived in Banghazi on November 29, 1943, and made an extensive tour during November and December. They were received by the people with enthusiasm, expressing loyalty to the Sanusi family, but the party itself preserved a calm and correct attitude.

Greater enthusiasm was expressed when Sayyid Idris, after an exile of 22 years, himself visited Cyrenaica in July, 1944, accompanied by a few leading émigrés. The Sayyid received a tumultuous welcome, and speeches demanding independence and voicing loyalty to him as " the Amir " of the country were repeated in almost every town.[2] He addressed large gatherings in several towns and tribal centers, calling for unity and high moral conduct. When he visited Banghazi city on July 28, 1944, after an absence of almost a quarter of a century, he was presented with a sword, representing the country's struggle against Italian domination for more than thirty years. Two days later he gave an address in which he thanked the people for their welcome, promising a prosperous future and urging them to unite as one family and avoid dissension. Finally, he paid high tribute to

[2] He was officially addressed as " The Sayyid," but the people insisted on calling him the Amir. Brigadier Cumming recommended that it should be given general currency as an honorific title, but to avoid any suspicion that Britain was making a change in the status of the country before peace settlements, the administration addressed him " as His Eminence " while the people called him " the Amir." See Lord Rennell, *British Military Administration of Occupied Territories in Africa During the Years 1941–1947* (London, 1948), p. 254.

Great Britain and called for co-operation with her until the country received independence.[3] He returned to Cairo on August 6.

Sayyid Idris subsequently made several similar visits, which brought him into more intimate touch with the internal situation of his country, but declined to reside there during the military administration mainly because of the anomalous position he would occupy if regarded as Amir by his people, while he possessed no officially recognized status or authority. He preferred, accordingly, to remain in Cairo, despite the appeal of both his people and the British authorities to reside in Cyrenaica, and to collaborate with the authorities in essential matters. However, he was in constant touch with his followers in Cyrenaica, guiding them as to how the internal situation should be managed.

The Sayyid's followers had already been active in Cyrenaica, demanding his return as the acknowledged head of the country. Both tribal chiefs and influential men set themselves to work toward that objective. The return from exile in February 1945 of 'Umar Mansur al-Kikhya,[4] who was deported during the war to Italy by the Italian authorities, gave an impetus to Sayyid Idris' followers to renew their efforts to induce Sayyid Idris to return as head of the country. While in exile, 'Umar Mansur addressed a letter to Winston Churchill (October 4, 1944) in which he stressed his country's opposition to Italian rule and demanded the liberation of his country. A year later he was brought back by the British Army to Banghazi to resume his political activities. On February 25, 1945, only four days after his return, he appeared at the Mosque, on the occasion of the celebration of the Prophet's mawlid (birthday), and made a speech in which he expressed the country's aspirations for independence and read the letter he had sent to Mr. Churchill. In a dramatic manner, he called on the people to proclaim Sayyid Idris as Amir of Cyrenaica and asked Sayyid Abu al-Qasim al-Sanusi, the Qa'imaqam of Banghazi, formally to receive the people's homage on behalf of Sayyid Idris

---

[3] For text of the speech, see *Majallat 'Umar al-Mukhtar*, Vol. II, No. 1 (1944), pp. 2–4.

[4] See pp. 18 and 20, above.

and to communicate it to him.[5] 'Umar Mansur's proposals concerning the future status of his country were set forth in an article published in *Jaridat Banghazi*,[6] in which he advocated self-government under the Amirate of Sayyid Idris, a representative assembly elected freely by the people, and an administration assisted and guided by British advisers. The proposals became the subject of discussion by the public and the press.[7]

'Umar Mansur and his circle of elder politicians were in close touch with Sayyid Idris, who was still in Cairo, and kept him informed of their activities. Mansur had already communicated to the Sayyid a copy of the letter he had sent to Winston Churchill, for which the Sayyid thanked him in a letter dated April 7, 1945, and endorsed the contents of Mansur's letter to Churchill. In June, Mansur paid a visit to Cairo and, after consultation with Sayyid Idris, he addressed a letter to Sir Edward Grigg, British Minister of State in Cairo, dated June 18, 1945, in which he submitted a more elaborate plan for the establishment of an independent Cyrenaican government under the leadership of Sayyid Idris, to be assisted and guided by Great Britain. The fundamental points of his plan may be summed up as follows:

1. Great Britain to recognize Sayyid Idris as the Amir of Cyrenaica;
2. Cyrenaica to be recognized as an independent country. Her government should be representative and democratic, assisted by British advisers;
3. Great Britain to assist Cyrenaica in organizing an army, constructing a railway along the coast, and extending financial assistance;

[5] For text of Mansur's speech and a brief account of the meeting, see *Jaridat Banghazi*, February 27, 1945. The proclamation of the Amirate elicited a lively discussion in the press on whether the proclamation had not been made over twenty years before. Thus the welcome given to Sayyid Idris on his visit to Cyrenaica in 1944 may be taken to constitute an endorsement of that proclamation. See Mahmud Makhluf's article in *Jaridat Banghazi*, April 1, 1945; Saqizli's reply, *ibid.*, April 13, 1945; and Buwaysir's rejoinder, *ibid.*, April 24, 1945.
[6] *Jaridat Banghazi*, March 23, 1945.
[7] See *Jaridat Banghazi*, May 15, 16, and 17, 1945.

4. Great Britain will be given rights of stationing forces on Cyrenaican territory for a fixed period, provided that Britain will turn over all her barracks and establishments to Cyrenaica upon her evacuation.
5. Cyrenaica will be an ally of Great Britain.[8]

On the same day, Sayyid Idris addressed a letter to Sir Edward Grigg in which he endorsed the proposals set forth by 'Umar Mansur and stated that Mansur's letter was " in conformity with our desires and the desires of our Cyrenaican nation." Some of Mansur's proposals, including an alliance with Great Britain, had already been mentioned by Sayyid Idris in his public speech in Banghazi on July 30, 1944.

Upon his return to Banghazi, Mansur reported to his countrymen his efforts in Cairo on behalf of Cyrenaica.[9] The elder politicians were in full agreement that Cyrenaica was in need of foreign assistance and administrative advice, but it was hoped that the period of guidance would not be too long or indefinite.

Al-Jabha al-Wantaniya

Despite all attempts to induce Great Britain to respond to Cyrenaican demands, nothing on a subject of the greatest importance to the people was mentioned after the cessation of hostilities, beyond private assurances of turning over authority to Sayyid Idris when the fate of the former Italian colonies was decided in a peace treaty. When the Sayyid revisited Cyrenaica in 1945, there was an apparent disappointment that no statement was made concerning the future of the country. Further disappointments were voiced when the Council of Foreign Ministers, meeting in the Spring and Summer of 1946, failed to arrive at a decision on the Italian colonies and postponed the question for another year. Ernest Bevin, the British Secretary for Foreign Affairs, expressed the real feeling of the Libyan people on April 29, when he said that they did not want to return to Italian

---

[8] A copy of the letter was supplied to the writer by 'Umar Mansur.
[9] *Jaridat Banghazi*, August 7, 1945.

rule; but subsequent suggestions for a United Nations or Egyptian trusteeship for Cyrenaica were not favorably received.[10] Although some town dwellers and young nationalists may have favored a closer association with Egypt, the claim for an Egyptian or an Arab League trusteeship produced unfavorable reactions among the tribes and elder politicians who aspired to unconditional independence under the leadership of Sayyid Idris. On the suggestion for an Egyptian trusteeship, Sayyid Idris is reported to have said that Cyrenaica was in need of an alliance with a country strong on land and sea and in the air, not with a country that did not possess the power to defend herself.[11]

Under the circumstances, the politically conscious public became impatient to wait any longer for a decision on the future of their country. It was argued that the arrangement made with Britain in 1940 to participate in the war against Italy constituted an agreement with Britain for the future independence of the country. "Why should it be necessary then for the Council of Foreign Ministers to decide the future of Cyrenaica?", it was queried. Some elder politicians said that Cyrenaican independence was a matter between Sayyid Idris and Britain, and it should be proclaimed without further delay. Thus some doubt was cast, especially by young nationalists such as the 'Umar Mukhtar group, as to whether Britain really wanted to give Cyrenaica independence at all. They criticized Britain's alleged desire to maintain control of Cyrenaica for imperial purposes.

Sayyid Idris visited Cyrenaica again in July, 1946. Complaints were made to him about British reluctance to hand over authority to native leaders before a decision of the Great Powers concerning the Italian colonies was reached, and he allowed the country's leaders to send representations to the British authorities demanding self-government. In one of the representations (July 10, 1946), the leaders demanded:

> The fulfillment of the promises given by Britain to our Amir, [namely,] the full freedom and independence of the country for which our people participated in the war and contributed valuable services for the benefit of their allies.[12]

---

[10] See pp. 117–118, below.
[11] *The White Book*, p. 42.
[12] *Barqa al-Jadida*, Banghazi, July 14, 1946.

When the news reached Sayyid Idris that the Council of Foreign Ministers, meeting in Paris, was considering the fate of the Italian colonies, he suddenly returned to Cairo to confer with the British authorities and to keep himself informed of what would be the outcome of the Paris meetings. However, Sayyid Idris' sudden return to Cairo, misunderstood by his country's leaders to imply a protest against British reluctance to transfer authority to him, prompted the Sa'adi tribal chiefs to hold a meeting in al-Bayda' (July 26, 1946) in which it was decided to address a manifesto to the British authorities regretting the departure of Sayyid Idris and demanding the fulfillment of the country's national aspirations.[13] The manifesto included the following demands:

1. Acknowledgment of independence and the formation of a constitutional government.
2. Recognition of the Sanusi Amirate under Sayyid Idris.
3. Immediate transfer of the administration to the Cyrenaicans.

After consultation with the British authorities, Sayyid Idris returned to Cyrenaica on July 29. The seventh anniversary of the formation of the Sanusi Force on August 9, celebrated as a national holiday in Banghazi for the first time in 1946, was the occasion for Cyrenaica's leaders to reiterate their anxious desire to proclaim the country's independence as well as for Sayyid Idris to explain the purpose of his recent visit to Cairo. At a large gathering in Municipality Square attended by Sayyid Idris, representatives of the British administration, and the leading dignitaries of the country, 'Ali al-Fallaq, Secretary-General of the Municipality, welcomed the Sayyid in an opening speech. 'Umar Mansur, on behalf of the Municipality Council, expressed the country's national aspirations and said:

---

[13] The tribal chiefs surrounded the house of Sayyid Idris in al-Bayda' and requested his family not to return to Cairo. Among those present in the meeting were: 'Abd al-Hamid al-'Abbar, Sulayman Ruqruq, Khalil al-'Arida, and others. Salih Buwaysir, as a correspondent of *Jaridat Banghazi*, attended the meeting and wrote the manifesto for the tribal chiefs. The author acknowledges the courtesy of Buwaysir for letting him see the original text of the manifesto and other relevant documents.

All the small countries that had collaborated with Britain [during the war] have realized their aspirations except Barqa which is still anxiously awaiting and hoping [to realize her aspirations].[14]

Sayyid Idris gave an address, received with tumultuous acclamation, in which he explained the reasons for his visit to Cairo and described the difficulties encountered in the negotiation over the Italian colonies. He also urged the people to be patient, united, and prepared for the day, which would not be long delayed, when the country's national aspirations would be realized. He then went on to say:

> I have taken the opportunity to give the authorities concerned advice as to the ways in which the administration should be developed and the country prepared during this year for the responsibility to be undertaken in the near future.
>
> Upon my return I have found that the leading tribal chiefs have been thinking of forming a National Front (al-Jabha al-Wataniya) representing all the elements in the country. . . . [I have approved of] this organization, for it will support me in achieving the country's aspirations and lighten the burden of my efforts in the pursuit [of the country's goal]. . . . I hope that all will co-operate and support [this organization] so that its efforts will bear fruit in achieving our goal, namely, [the country's] freedom and independence.[15]

It was also announced that the scope of the Jabha was broadened by the inclusion of representatives of other tribes and town dwellers. Further additions to this body in November increased its membership to seventy-five, including an inner working committee of nineteen. The immediate purpose of the creation of the Jabha was to present the Cyrenaican case to the international commission of inquiry which was sent to ascertain the wishes of the people as to their future,[16] but it also served as the agency co-ordinating the activities of "elder politicians" in the face of the rising influence of younger nationalists.

[14] *Barqa al-Jadida*, Banghazi, August 11, 1946.
[15] *Ibid.*
[16] For this reason no Cyrenaican employed by the British military administration was included in this body.

On November 30, 1946, the Jabha made its first official declaration of policy in a manifesto, addressed to the British authorities, asserting the following demands:

1. Recognition of the Sanusi Amirate under Sayyid Idris;
2. Permission to form a national government to administer the country in preparation for complete independence.

This manifesto, though regarded by the British authorities as lacking in proportion due to its silence on how Cyrenaica would maintain her independence, was, in fact, both moderate and reasonable in tone. Cyrenaican elder leaders were prompted to take that step because they had sensed that Italian interests in Tripolitania were still strong and might succeed in getting the upper hand. If Cyrenaica were to join a scheme of unity with Tripolitania, as suggested in certain international councils, Cyrenaican leaders wanted first to insure their independence before they should join a scheme of unity with Tripolitania.

When Great Britain showed willingness to transfer powers from British military to Cyrenaican hands, the whole question of Libyan unity became the subject of controversy in Cyrenaica and led to an internal struggle between younger and elder politicians. While both old and young were agreed on the Sanusi Amirate, the insistence of the young on unity with Tripolitania under Sanusi leadership supplied a more attractive platform which compromised and weakened the position of the elder politicians. What were the ideas and aspirations of the young nationalist?

The 'Umar al-Mukhtar Group

In opposition to the group of elderly men and tribal chiefs, there were a few enthusiastic young men who felt keenly that elder politicians had been too much preoccupied with Cyrenaican parochialism to pay proper attention to the interests of the Libyan nation at large. Most of these young men had been influenced by the idea of nationalism as expounded and diffused by the Arab press. Some had studied in Egypt and were greatly influenced by the political ideas of her leaders. While in Egypt they witnessed the establishment of the Arab League and hoped that Libya would be re-established as an independent state to play her role in this newly created Arab organization. But these young men, though full of enthusiasm, had not yet been organized into a formal group and therefore were weak and impotent. The idea that young men should play an increasing role in the future shaping of their country was acknowledged by many leaders, but it was particularly prevalent among those who had been in exile when their country was still languishing under foreign domination.

The man who first broached the idea of organizing a society bearing the name of 'Umar al-Mukhtar was As'ad Bin 'Umran. As'ad, with a few other young men,[17] were then in Egypt and had just joined the Sanusi force. They began to organize the society early in 1942. Finding the conditions of war not quite favorable for a political organization composed of men who were still in the service, it was decided to call it " the 'Umar al-Mukhtar Sporting Society," but privately the members met to discuss political questions. The founders were men who had been watching the political development in Arab lands with a keen eye and hoped that once their country was liberated from foreign control, she would take her place in Arab political circles, while they themselves aspired to take an active part in public life. Sayyid Idris approved the idea of the society and became its patron.

After the expulsion of Axis forces from Cyrenaica, the Mukhtar group and other émigrés began to return to their country. The group, believing that the time had come to begin life anew, formally declared the formation of the society in Banghazi on April 4, 1943. They sought the support of a few elder men in order to widen its appeal to the public and elected as its head Shaykh Khalil al-Kawwafi, a highly respected man but one lacking in forcefulness, who was assisted by an executive committee.[18] The society was formally registered as a " club," the main purpose

[17] Such as 'Ali al-Fallaq, Mahmud Makhluf, and Mahdi al-Mutardi.
[18] The committee consisted of such personages as Yusuf Lanqi, Shaykh 'Abd al-Hamid al-Dibani, Husayn al-Bisaykiri, 'Abd al-Jalil al-'Unayzi, 'Abd al-Jawad al-Furaytis, Salim Bin 'Amir, and others.

of which was allegedly to promote cultural and sporting activities, but it was quite apparent from the very beginning that its ultimate objective was political. In July, 1943, the club began the publication of *Barqa al-Riyadiya*, a sports review, and in August, *Majallat 'Umar al-Mukhtar*, a monthly literary magazine.

The club was not opposed at the outset to the British administration, since its members were quite aware that they owed their country's liberation to the British and some of them, such as al-Fallaq, al-Mutardi, and Makhluf, held positions under the British administration. Very soon, less than a year after the establishment of the club, its press began to criticize the British authorities and the younger members posed as the spokesmen of the nation, demanding in no uncertain terms the fulfillment of their country's national aspirations. *Al-Watan*, which appeared as a private paper, voiced the viewpoint of the younger members of the club and indulged in arousing public opinion against the British administration. *Al-Watan* demanded that Sayyid Idris should be acknowledged as Amir. The British authorities replied that they were quite prepared to recognize Sayyid Idris as the Amir of Cyrenaica when the time came, but the Mukhtar group insisted on the immediate proclamation of such an Amirate, because it implied recognition of Cyrenaica's right to independence.

During 1945–46, the club underwent a change. It became avowedly political, its original structure already having been altered. Khalil al-Kawwafi, the club's president, resigned and was replaced by Mustafa Bin 'Amir. Bashir al-Mughayribi, a young but promising poet and an able speaker, became secretary. Older members of the executive committee were replaced by younger men, and the club became, to all intents and purposes, a youth movement. The club, indifferent to older leaders, issued political statements and indulged in criticizing the Jabha. On September 26, 1946, the British military administration suspended *al-Watan* on the ground that it aroused public opinion. Bin 'Amir, President of the club, asked to see E. A. V. de Candole, Chief of the British administration, who permitted the reissue of the paper on condition that Bin 'Amir would write a letter stating that the club was faithful to Amir Idris with no implied criticism to his authority. The paper, publishing Bin 'Amir's letter, reappeared on October 26. But the club, dominated by young nationalists, remained uncompromising toward the British authorities and those who co-operated with them.[19]

On December 7, 1947, Sayyid Idris proclaimed the dissolution of all political parties and expressed the hope that all political activities would be channeled through a National Congress which was to replace the Jabha. The club, obeying the order, reappeared as a sports organization after Bin 'Amir had seen the Sayyid. It ostensibly refrained from political activities, but its members continued to take part in politics on their own. Very soon, when the Four Power Commission [20] arrived in Libya and the Palestine question became the subject of public discussion, the club issued manifestos expressing its opinions on these questions. Its members participated in such activities as organizing a demonstration on the occasion of the United Nations resolution declaring the independence and unity of Libya, and greeting the Cyrenaican delegation upon its return from Lake Success. The name of 'Umar al-Mukhtar was dropped by the club upon the protest of the Mukhtar family against the use of the name, and the laws of association and the press, issued on January 10 and 11, 1950, forced the club to separate its cultural and sporting from its political activities. Due to circumstances, the Mukhtar group applied (January 14, 1950) for permission to form, under the association law, a new political organization called the National Association, but the new organization continued unofficially to be called the Mukhtar Club.

When Tripolitanian leaders, who had been given no assurance of independence and were fearful that their country might revert to Italian control, called for unity with Cyrenaica, the Mukhtar group, believing in the advantages of unity between the two provinces, proved to be more receptive to the Tripolitanian call than the elder politicians and became Cyrenaica's most outspoken advocates for national unity. The call for national unity gave the Mukhtar group a wider national appeal, but it accentuated its differences with the advocates of Cyrenaican parochialism.

The plan for unity with Tripolitania, however, caused a split

[19] Due to its uncompromising attitude, the club lost such personalities as Khalil al-Qallal, 'Abd al-Hamid al-Dibani, al-Fallaq, Shaqluf, and 'Ali al-Jirbi.

[20] See page 120 below.

between the Banghazi and the Darna branches of the Mukhtar club. The Darna branch accepted the absolute and unconditional unity between the two provinces which the National Congress of Tripolitania advocated, while the Banghazi branch, more interested in the concept of unity than its form, was willing to compromise by accepting federalism. More specifically, the disagreement between the two branches centered on the question of the competence of the Constituent Assembly raised by certain critics. Fearful that the controversy over the legal competence of the assembly might endanger Libyan independence, the Banghazi branch supported federalism as a necessary immediate step to achieve Libyan unity. This moderate stand, which pleased elder politicians,[21] resulted in a complete break between the Banghazi and the Darna branches. The Banghazi branch accepted federalism because (as Bashir al-Mughayribi told the author) it believed that the form of government was an internal matter that could be corrected in the future, but that the question should not endanger the creation of one Libyan state.[22]

When Cyrenaica was declared an Amirate in 1949 and the elder politicians were vested with authority, the Mukhtar group had to face stronger opposition. An account of the struggle between this group and its rivals will be given in the following pages, but it is significant to note that, although the Mukhtar group offered no constructive plan of reform, it remained perhaps the most potent political force in Cyrenaica.[23]

Recommendations of the War Office Working Party

It was during this time of uncertainty and clash of loyalties that Great Britain decided to concede to Cyrenaica certain measures of self-government, placing Sayyid Idris at its head,

[21] *Al-Taj*, Banghazi, January 22, 1951.
[22] See *Al-Watan*, Banghazi, December 26, 1960; January 23, 1951.
[23] Information on the Banghazi branch of the Mukhtar club supplied by Bashir al-Mughayribi, Mahdi al-Mutardi, and Mahmud Makhluf, on the Darna branch by 'Abd al-Hamid Bin Halim. 'Abd al-Mawla Lanqi and Mahdi al-Mutardi supplied the author with some of the club's publications.

before Cyrenaica joined a scheme of unity with Tripolitania as proposed in international councils. Until 1947, Sayyid Idris had shown great reluctance to reside permanently in Cyrenaica before he was recognized as its head, and the elder politicians were anxious to secure a position of power before accepting the scheme of unity with Tripolitania. Due to circumstances, the British government decided on September 26, 1946, to appoint a commission called the Working Party, under the direction of the War Office, to visit Cyrenaica and report its recommendations to the government through the Secretary of War. The Working Party was composed of five members, presided over by Lt. Col. Sir Bernard Reilly, and assisted by Sir Herbert Stewart, J. A. de C. Hamilton, and F. C. Newton. Denis A. Greenhill acted as secretary to the commission. The Party visited the territory toward the end of 1946 and submitted its recommendations in January, 1947.

The functions of the commission were to outline certain practical recommendations for the termination of British military administration and the transfer of power from British to Cyrenaican leaders. The ultimate objective of the recommendation was to " promote goodwill in the territory toward Great Britain," which would help to emphasize British policy toward Libya as a whole.

While the commission recommended in principle the granting of independence to Cyrenaica and recognition of Sayyid Idris al-Sanusi as the obvious candidate for the position of head of state, it recommended that such an objective should be achieved gradually, because without guidance the immediate withdrawal of British personnel and financial support following the period of British military administration would disrupt the management of many public services. The Commission accordingly recommended that the territory should pass through three stages of development:

1. The British military administration to remain for a short time.
2. The establishment of an Arab state under British trusteeship. Adequate financial assistance should be given for not less than ten years, including the rendering of administrative training and promoting educational and technical development.

3. The establishment of a fully independent state. During the second and third stages, Cyrenaica might be connected with Tripolitania in a unified Libya, as the creation of a such a state is consistent with the specific recommendations for Cyrenaica. A treaty of alliance with a major power is also recommended.

Sensing a feeling of disappointment that the country had not been given a measure of independence after four years of military administration, the Commission recommended that the period of tutelage should be short and that British policy should aim at ultimate independence. "We consider," the Commission recommended, "that British policy should now work openly to this end. By doing so it may dispel the feeling of frustration which is beginning to beset the people, and the British may recover the initiative in leading the country toward its goal, retaining at the same time for themselves the goodwill of the people and their own special position in the area."

Furthermore, the Commission recommended that Sayyid Idris, who had been hitherto paying only occasional visits to Cyrenaica, should reside permanently in the country. The Commission, in discussing this matter with Sayyid Idris, urged him to reside in the country, but the Sayyid, who wanted to reside permanently only after he was proclaimed head of the country, agreed only on certain specific conditions while the country remained under British military administration. His conditions emanated from his desire that he should be closely informed regarding British policy in Cyrenaica and that his advice be followed by the military administration in regard to consultations concerning bestowal of British honors and the appointments and promotions of local staff. He also demanded that one of the descendants of al-Mahdi al-Sanusi be recognized as his successor. Although some of the demands were unacceptable, such as that the military administration should follow his advice while it remained responsible to the British government and that a guarantee be given for Sanusi succession, the British authorities were able to persuade him to reside in Cyrenaica before he was formally proclaimed as Amir.

The Commission also recommended the reactivation and enlarging of the Executive Committee of the Jabha and that Sayyid

Idris should be invited to appoint five ex-officio members working under the British administration. The enlarged Executive Committee, which had only consultative power, eventually would constitute a Council of Ministers. Sayyid Idris approved the idea of an advisory council but suggested that its members should not remain in the Jabha, as this body should remain unconnected with the administration in order that it might express its views freely to the international commission of inquiry.

Finally, the commission recommended certain changes in the administrative organization, creating four secretaries in charge of Finance, Interior, Development, and Legal Affairs; the gradual appointment of natives to responsible positions and training them in the discharge of their duties; the acceleration of public works to help in the rehabilitation of the country; the development of education and the expansion of medical and other services; and assistance in the agricultural development of the country.

National Congress

In accordance with the recommendation of the War Office Working Party, Sayyid Idris agreed to take up his permanent residence in Cyrenaica in November, 1947. The British authorities allowed him to exercise certain powers, which had a calming effect on the internal situation, but due to the close association of elder politicians with the military administration, the Mukhtar group took a more critical attitude toward the British. The Jabha, consisting mostly of tribal chiefs, displayed a reactionary and unconstructive attitude which prompted the Mukhtar group to advocate a democratic form of government with safeguards against despotic tendencies.

The elder politicians, in an effort to break the power of the Mukhtar group, lured some of the moderate elements to form a dissident national association known as the Youth League (Rabitat al-Shabab). It was formed early in 1945, and the dominating figure in its executive committee was Salih Buwaysir; but the league failed to attract public attention. An attempt to merge with the Mukhtar club did not materialize, because the

League wanted to wield more effective influence in the central committee of the club. After the establishment of a native Cyrenaican administration, the League supported the elder politicians, in particular their parochial propensities, although the League advocated the broad concept of Libyan unity and joining the Arab League.[24] The creation of the League added confusion to the already existing political tension, which made Sayyid Idris feel uneasy about internal dissension.[25]

The first step taken by Sayyid Idris after his return was to order the dissolution of all existing political parties on December 7, 1947, and to call for their fusion in a new united front, composed of the representatives of all the parties. Although the Mukhtar group reluctantly agreed to close their headquarters, all other parties readily obeyed the Sayyid's order.

At a meeting of leading tribal chiefs, elder politicians, and conservative young men, it was agreed to form a National Congress (al-Mu'tamar al-Watani) early in January 1948. An executive committee, under the leadership of Muhammad al-Rida al-Sanusi, brother of Sayyid Idris, was elected on January 10 to draw up a program for the future of the country on the basis of the two principles of unity and the Sanusi Amirate.[26] The Congress demanded an independent sovereign state under the Sanusi headship. The aim of this program, it was then contended, was to impress the outside world with the determination of the people to have the principal voice in the settlement of their own future. When the Four Power Commission of Investigation visited Cyrenaica in April, 1948, the National Congress submitted its proposals, on behalf of the Cyrenaican people, as follows:

1. Complete and immediate independence of Cyrenaica.
2. Recognition of Amir Idris as King of a constitutional Cyrenaican state.

---

[24] *Barqa al-Jadida*, Banghazi, April 17, 1946.

[25] Owing to internal dissent, the League's activities were often suspended before it was dissolved. It reappeared in 1949 and supported the first Cyrenaican cabinet, but it came into conflict with the second cabinet and was dissolved in 1951.

[26] The other members of the committee were: Sayyid Siddiq al-Rida al-Sanusi, Sayyid Abu al-Qasim al-Sanusi, 'Ali al-Jirbi, and Khalil al-Qallal. See *Al-Watan*, Banghazi, January 13, 1948.

3. With regard to Cyrenaica's relation with Tripolitania, it was stated: "thereafter, if our Tripolitanian brothers wish to come under the Sanusi Crown, this will enable the unification of the Libyan countries in our state; otherwise Cyrenaica will retain her own full independence." [27]

The wishes of the tribesmen who were questioned by the Commission were tersely expressed as independence under Amir Idris, but when asked about trusteeship, Great Britain was the only acceptable trustee.[28] Young nationalists often expressed their views in terms of association with Egypt or the Arab League, and the Egyptian press, widely read in the country, stressed the need for Libyan unity and association with the Arab League.

The announcement of the Commission's findings that Cyrenaica, in common with other former Italian colonies, was unfit for independence caused bitter resentment. The people were anxiously awaiting the decision of the United Nations General Assembly, meeting then in Paris, on the future of the country. News that the Libyan Liberation Committee in Cairo was sending Bashir al-Sa'dawi, its head, to represent Libyan aspirations to the Assembly inspired Amir Idris to send his own delegation led by 'Umar Mansur, Chief of the Diwan, to plead the Cyrenaican case. But no decision was reached by the General Assembly at that session.

The Amirate of Cyrenaica

The failure of the Council of Foreign Ministers to settle the question of the Italian colonies exhausted the patience of the Cyrenaican leaders who had been waiting impatiently to take

[27] *Four Power Commission of Investigation for the Former Italian Colonies*, Vol. III: Report on Libya, pp. 7–8.

[28] An article in *Barqa al-Jadida* on "trusteeship," inspired by the British authorities with the object of enlightening the public on the meaning of the concept of trusteeship, was challenged by another in *al-Watan* warning the people not to be deceived and stating that trusteeship simply meant colonization and the "replacement of the Italian tyrants by benevolent Englishmen." For the controversy over Britain's role in Barqa, see a leading article by Tawfiq Nuri al-Barqawi in *al-Jabal al-Akhdar*, Banghazi, December 2, 1948.

charge of the country's administration at the earliest possible
moment. Sayyid Idris and the National Congress often impressed
upon the British the need for an immediate transfer of power
to Cyrenaican hands. A deputation, headed by 'Umar Mansur
al-Kikhya, left for London on November 23, 1948, to negotiate
with the British government over the establishment of a separate
regime in Cyrenaica. He also went to Paris to plead for the independence of Libya as a whole. If it were not possible to achieve
independence for Libya, 'Umar Mansur declared in a public
statement, Cyrenaica should proceed to declare her own separate
existence.[29] Owing to differences among the Great Powers regarding the disposal of the Italian colonies and the uncertainty
about the future status of Libya as a whole, Britain moved
quickly to grant Cyrenaica self-government under Sayyid Idris
as a first step in preparing this province for a possible link with
other Libyan territories. This decision was in agreement with
the recommendations of the War Office Working Party.

On June 1, 1949, at a meeting of the National Congress held
in the Manar Palace, Sayyid Idris proclaimed the independence
of Cyrenaica. A large crowd, including the Mukhtar group, had
assembled in the square in front of the Palace to listen to the
Amir's address. In his speech, Amir Idris said that he had asked
Great Britain and other powers, including the Arab and Islamic
countries, to recognize the independence of Cyrenaica and his
assumption of all functions of government. Loud applause and
cheers were heard both inside and outside the walls of the Palace.
When, however, he added that he wished his brethren in Tripolitania to achieve what Cyrenaicans had achieved, and, if they so
desired, to unite with Cyrenaica under one united leadership, the
leaders of the Mukhtar group outside the Palace cried: "No
independence [for us] before unity [with Tripolitania] is achieved;
we do not rejoice while Tripolitania is weeping; down with
sham independence." The Amir, though he was interrupted by

---

[29] *Barqa al-Jadida*, Banghazi, December 22, 1948. Mansur's statement, which
was construed by nationalist circles to imply an ignoring of the aspirations
of Tripolitania, aroused controversy in the press, but the elder politicians
supported Mansur's position. See *Sawt al-Sha'b*, Banghazi, December 25, 1948;
Barqa al-Jadida, Banghazi, December 31, 1948, and January 9, 1949; *al-Watan*,
Banghazi, January 11, 1949.

cries outside the Palace, went on to declare his intention to form a national government and to call a Parliament elected by the people.[30]

De Candole, the British Chief Administrator, replied in a statement to the Congress that:

> The British government recognizes the Amir, the freely chosen leader of his people, as the head of the Cyrenaican government; they formally recognize the desire of the Cyrenaicans for self-government and will take all steps compatible with their international obligations to promote it; they agree to the formation of a Cyrenaican government with responsibility over internal affairs; and they invite the Amir to visit London for discussions on this matter; in taking these steps they wish to emphasize that nothing will be done to prejudice the eventual future of Libya as a whole.

Upon leaving the Palace the Amir told the leaders of the Mukhtar group, who gathered around him, that " matters [concerning unity] would be achieved by patience and wisdom." In the evening when the group called on the Amir to congratulate him on his assumption of authority, they impressed upon him the need for unity with Tripolitania and reminded him that the Sanusi Amirate had already been acknowledged by all Tripolitanians. They requested him to send a cable assuring the Tripolitanians that he was still working for the unity of Tripolitania with Cyrenaica. The National Congress, by the Amir's order, sent a cable to that effect, and the Tripolitanian National Front, on its own initiative, sent a deputation to congratulate the Amir and request his support in achieving the unity of the two sister provinces.[31]

Amir Idris immediately began to discuss the question of forming a government with Cyrenaican leaders. Because of intense competition among rival groups, he looked for a neutral head who would rise above partisan rivalry. His choice fell on Fathi al-Kikhya, son of 'Umar Mansur al-Kikhya, who was then practicing law in Alexandria. Fathi had no idea that he was going to form a government when invited by the Amir to visit

---

[30] For text of the Amir's address, see *Barqa al-Jadida*, Banghazi, June 2, 1949.

[31] Information supplied by Bashir al-Mughayribi.

Banghazi, but his father had explained to him the Amir's intention. He was named as Premier-designate on July 5, 1949,
pending the formal transfer of powers from British to Cyrenaican
hands. The Amir was formally invited to visit England and to
discuss the future relations of his country with Britain. He left
Banghazi with Fathi on July 9, visiting Tripoli on his way, where
he was enthusiastically received, and spent two months in England and France. He returned to Banghazi on September 7,
1949, and began immediately to implement the declaration of
June 1, while Prime Minister Fathi al-Kikhya stayed on in Paris
for medical treatment on his way back.

On September 16, de Candole, the Chief Administrator, issued
a proclamation entitled the Transitional Powers Proclamation,
empowering the Amir to enact a constitution and defining the
powers to be exercised by the Cyrenaican government and the
powers reserved to the Chief Administrator, who was to be known
as the British Resident. The Cyrenaican government was to
exert power over all internal affairs, but on certain legal and
financial matters the British authorities were entitled to employ
some authority through their advisers. The reserved powers
under which the British Resident might legislate by decrees
included foreign affairs, defense (including public order if the
national government were unable to maintain it), and matters
relating to Italian property, pending the settlement of the future
of the Italian colonies. British advisers for legal and financial
matters were to be appointed by the Amir with the approval of
the British Resident. The constitution was not to be suspended
or amended without the approval of the British Resident who,
until full independence was achieved, reserved full power to
revoke, alter, or amend the Proclamation.

On September 18, while Fathi al-Kikhya was still in France,
the Amir issued a decree appointing the other members of the
Cabinet.[32] A draft constitution, which had been prepared by a

---

[32] The other members of the cabinet were: Sa'd-Allah Bin Sa'ud for
Interior and Deputy Premier, Muhammad Abu Dajaja for Finance and
Commerce, 'Ali al-Jirbi for Public Works and Transportation, Husayn Maziq
for Agriculture and Forests, and Khalil al-Qallal for Health. In addition
to the Premiership, Fathi assumed the portfolios of Defense, Education, and
Justice.

constitutional committee in consultation with the British authorities, was promulgated by the Amir as the constitution of Cyrenaica on October 11, 1949.[33] The constitution provided a bill of rights for the people and a Cabinet appointed by and responsible to the Amir, who was both the head of state and Commander-in-Chief of the armed forces. Parliament, composed of partially elected and partially appointed membership (the number of each fixed by a decree), was unicameral and had the power to initiate legislation subject to the Amir's veto. Every male subject who had reached the age of twenty-one had the right to elect deputies for Parliament, but the deputy had to be thirty years old in order to qualify for election. By a decree the number of deputies was fixed at sixty, ten of whom were to be appointed by the Amir from men who had distinguished themselves in the service of the country. The judiciary, which was designed to be independent of the excutive, was composed of civil and religious courts and a court of appeal. Finally, the Amir was given the right to declare a state of siege and suspend any article of the constitution, if circumstances were to warrant such action.

Fathi al-Kikhya, who was expected to return to Banghazi and assume his powers as Prime Minister, tendered his letter of resignation from Paris and returned to Alexandria to resume his law practice. In an interview with the author shortly before his death (1958), Fathi said that he found that his powers would be greatly restricted and was reluctant to be a Prime Minister in name only. He accordingly decided to resign, pleading that his Egyptian wife did not want to live in Banghazi. Nor was there an adequate body of civil servants who could run the administration without considerable dependence on British advisers. The Amir, accepting Fathi's resignation on November 7, 1949, invited his father, 'Umar Mansur, to form a government on the same day. Mansur completed the formation of his government on November 9.[34]

[33] For text of the constitution, see *Official Gazette of Cyrenaica*, October 11, 1949.
[34] In addition to the Premiership, Mansur assumed the portfolios of Interior, Foreign Affairs, Defense, and Education. Muhammad Abu Dajaja was given Finance; 'Ali al-Jirbi, Transportation and Public Works; Muhammad al-Saqizli, Justice; Husayn Maziq, Agriculture and Forests; and Khalil al-Qallal, Health.

Mansur, a man of forceful personality and great vigor, began immediately to reorganize the internal structure of the administration. On November 14, 1949, a decree was issued organizing the Municipality of Banghazi and appointing Yusaf Lanqi as Mayor. Other decrees, issued on November 29, dealt with the internal structure of the various governmental departments, appointing Sayyid Abu al-Qasim al-Sanusi, the Qa'imaqam of Banghazi, as Director-General for Interior, and a number of British advisers as civil servants in the Cyrenaican government. Relinquishing his post as Chief of the Royal Palace (Diwan), Mansur appointed in his place 'Abd al-'Aziz al-Hamzawi, legal adviser to the Amir, as Deputy Chief of the Royal Diwan on November 23.

Despite the support of elder politicians, Mansur immediately came into conflict with the Mukhtar group, because he was regarded as representing reactionary elements and issued restrictive measures on the activities of young men. Thus when the news of the United Nations resolution concerning Libya's independence and unity (November 21, 1949) reached Banghazi, and the scouts (Kashshaf) of the Mukhtar group staged an unauthorized demonstration to commemorate the occasion, Mansur dissolved the scouts. The Mukhtar group greeted the Cyrenaican delegation to the United Nations upon its return, which annoyed the elder politicians who hoped for a declaration that would recognize a separate independent Cyrenaica. The government's policy was severely criticized in the press, but Mansur retorted by issuing repressive measures. The depressed economic situation and a growing sense of frustration rendered Mansur's task in carrying on the business of government difficult.

Matters came to a head when the National Congress, already divided among itself, voted lack of confidence in 'Umar Mansur's government. Opposition within the Congress was led by Sayyid Abu al-Qasim, Vice President of the Congress, who was also serving as Director-General of Interior. Sayyid Abu al-Qasim, an ambitious member of the Sanusi house, was suspected of having been strengthening his position through tribal connections. He was accordingly reappointed by Mansur as Director-General for Civil Affairs, separating tribal affairs into another department under Sayyid Siddiq al-Rida, on December 20, 1949.

This move, which was interpreted as intended to curb Sayyid Abu al-Qasim's influence, incited the Sayyid to lead an opposition campaign in the National Congress.[35] On March 5, 1950, Abu al-Qasim made a speech in the Congress in which he attacked the Mansur government. Mansur advised the Amir to dissolve the Congress, but the Amir, realizing that the Prime Minister had lost confidence, asked for his resignation. 'Umar Mansur tendered his letter of resignation on March 9, and this was accepted two days later.

The Amir, at 'Umar's suggestion, invited Muhammad al-Saqizli, Minister of Justice, to form the new government on March 18.[36] Saqizli, a self-made statesman and a man of great personal integrity, had been too closely associated with the elder politicians to command respect among the younger generation. He proved to be, as subsequent events showed, a man of greater honesty and single-mindedness than they had anticipated, but he suffered from certain inflexibility, which disrupted many a measure of reform he had intended to carry out. The strongest opposition to his government, as in the case of his predecessor, came from the Mukhtar group, who attacked him as reactionary and opposed to national unity.

Saqizli further infuriated the Mukhtar group when preparations were being made for the opening of Parliament. An Electoral Law, issued on April 21, 1950, divided Cyrenaica into three electoral districts: Banghazi, Darna, and the Jabal al-Akhdar. Each one was subdivided into urban and tribal electoral districts. The Banghazi urban district was to elect six representatives, al-Marj (Barce) one, and Darna two. The tribal districts were to return the following: Banghazi, 15 representatives; the Jabal,

[35] I have it on 'Umar Mansur's own authority that Amir Idris, suspecting Sayyid Abu al-Qasim's political activities, ordered Mansur to reappoint the Sayyid as Director-General of Civil Affairs. Amir Idris, Mansur went on to say, had seen in a British Public Information pictorial (dated January 5, 1949) a statement to the effect that Sayyid Abu al-Qasim might succeed Amir Idris as ruler of Cyrenaica. The statement appeared without prior knowledge of Amir Idris and aroused suspicion as to Abu al-Qasim's activities.

[36] The other members of the government were: 'Ali al-Jirbi for Transportation and Public Works, Husayn Maziq for Interior and Education, Abu Dajaja for Finance, 'Abd al-Qadir 'Allam for Agriculture and Forests, and Sa'd Allah Bin Sa'ud for Health. Saqizli took over Justice in addition to Premiership.

15; and Darna, 11. Thus a total of 51 representatives were elected, 41 of whom were tribal representatives, with 10 others appointed by the Amir. This distribution, giving a greater representation for tribal districts, was construed as weakening the influence of the Mukhtar group, whose influence was limited to the two urban districts of Banghazi and Darna.[37]

Registration for voting began on April 17, 1950, and the elections were completed on June 5. The election returns showed that the Mukhtar group had won 10 seats known to be sympathetic to the group out of a total 60,[38] but the majority supported the government. The elections demonstrated that the Mukhtar group was influential in urban districts, and it attacked the government for restricting urban representation in order to curb its influence in Parliament.

Parliament met on June 12, presided over by Rashid al-Kikhya, and the Amir attended the opening meeting. Saqizli, on behalf of the Amir, read the Speech from the Throne. In it the nation was congratulated for having for the first time a freely elected Parliament. Plans for social and economic reconstruction were prepared, and it was promised that negotiations with Tripolitania for the abolition of trade barriers between the two territories would soon begin. The Speech paid high tribute to Great Britain for the friendship and assistance that had been extended to Cyrenaica.[39]

There was lively debate in Parliament; but its short term, which lasted barely a year, rendered its deliberations inconsequential. The United Nations resolution of November, 1949, providing for the independence and unity of Libya, predetermined that Cyrenaica's internal structure was subject to a drastic change. The Mukhtar representatives, although a minority in

---

[37] For text of the Cyrenaican Electoral Law, see *Official Gazette* (new series), supplement to No. 5, April 21, 1950.

[38] Only three members of the Mukhtar group were actually elected, namely, Mustafa Bin 'Amir, President of the club, from Banghazi; and Ibrahim Usta 'Umar and 'Abd al-Raziq Shaqluf from Darna. The other seven, who were regarded as sympathetic, included 'Abd al-Salam Bisaykiri, Salih Buwaysir, 'Ali Zuwawa, 'Abd al-Hamid Najm, and 'Abd al-Qadir al-Badri. (Information supplied by Bashir al-Mughayribi).

[39] For text of the speech, see Government of Cyrenaica, *Speech From The Throne* (Banghazi: Office of Publications and Information, 1950) (Arabic).

Parliament, were very articulate and their opposition, which on one occasion defeated a government measure, prompted the Prime Minister to suspend the session (April, 1951). Parliament was later prorogued *sine die.*

The defeat of government was on the questions of a charcoal monopoly and trade with Israel. Mustafa Bin 'Amir, representative of Banghazi and President of the Mukhtar Club, raised the issue by addressing a question to the Prime Minister. It was a year of drought and the government was negotiating an agreement with Israel. Bin 'Amir, seeking to force the government to boycott Israel in line with other Arab governments, was engaged in a verbal duel with the Prime Minister. To close the issue, the meeting was declared adjourned by the Speaker of the House. However, Bin 'Amir was able to report to the government that he had secured approval of the majority of the House by securing signatures to a petition demanding that the government should stop negotiating with Israel.

Saqizli had yet to face further opposition from the Mukhtar group before he moved to suppress the organization. On July 7, 1951, the group, already frustrated by the government, exploited the incident of a man who had died at the government hospital four days earlier and who had not been buried within three days in accordance with Islamic practice. The Mukhtar leaders incited the relatives of the deceased person to complain directly to the Prime Minister. On their way, they met a crowd that joined in staging a demonstration down Banghazi's main street. When one of the demonstrators shouted: "To Saqizli's house," the mob, already excited, went to the Premier's house and shattered the windows. When another shouted: "To the British Residency," the mob, defying the police who rushed to defend the Residency, assaulted the British flag and shattered the Residency's windows.[40]

Depressed economic conditions, resulting mainly from the drought and from deterioration in the administration following the British transfer of power to Cyrenaicans, were in large part responsible for a growing dissatisfaction and sense of frustration, but Saqizli was made the scapegoat for them. The government

[40] For an account of the incident, see *al-Watan,* Banghazi, July 10, 1951.

retorted by arresting the principal leaders of the Mukhtar group who, after a trial, were either thrown into prison or fined.[41] While the trial was going on, the government issued a decree on July 8, 1951, dissolving the Mukhtar organization and confiscating all its assets. Street demonstrations were organized to bring pressure to bear on the government to release the leaders, but to no avail. The suppression of the Mukhtar club by no means ended the agitation, since the group resorted to clandestine activities and the rift between the old and the new generations was widened.

Meanwhile, the focus of attention of the people was gradually turning from limited Cyrenaican issues to the more important problems before the National Constituent Assembly which was framing the constitutional foundation of the Libyan state. Libyans in the three territories of Cyrenaica, Tripolitania, and Fazzan were anxiously awaiting the approaching hour of the proclamation of independence on December 24, 1951. It was hardly more than half a year before Cyrenaica's regime would be adapted to fit the new Libyan constitutional structure. On December 24, 1951, the Saqizli government was reduced to a provincial administration and the Mukhtar group, hoping to participate in the national government, turned its attention to a wider horizon.

[41] Mustafa Bin 'Amir and 'Ali Zuwawa received three years at hard labor, Mahmud Makhluf a year and a half or a fine of £50, and Mughayribi six months or a fine of £35. Makhluf and Mughayribi paid the fine and escaped imprisonment.

chapter **IV**

Political Activities in
Tripolitania and Fazzan

N O SOONER had Tripolitania been liberated from Italian
rule than a meeting in Tripoli, on January 25, 1943, was
called by leading Arab dignitaries to discuss the internal situation
of the country and request the British authorities to grant permission for organizing political parties. When a petition was
submitted to the Military Administrator, Brigadier T. R. Blackley, it was rejected on the ground that the war was still going
on and that the opportune time to engage in political activities
would be when the future of the country had been decided by a
peace treaty. Further petitions were submitted, stating that the
Arabs of Tripolitania had welcomed the British plan to give
them freedom and that the internal conditions were not less
favorable for nationalist activities than in Cyrenaica, where their
compatriots had been allowed to organize a club. It was indicated
that Tripolitania and Cyrenaica were but one country and that
Tripolitanians could see no reason for discrimination. Dissatisfaction culminated in a demonstration in Tripoli city in August,
when a petition was presented to the British authorities enumer-
ating the city's grievances. Due to the circumstances, Blackley
allowed the reopening of a Literary Club (July 30, 1943) which
had been in existence under the Italian administration.[1] The

---

[1] The club, founded in 1919 and suppressed by the Italians in 1921, served
as a rallying point for nationalists to oppose Italian rule. Among those who

membership of the club included dignitaries from Tripoli city as well as representatives from the interior of the country. Ahmad al-Faqih Hasan, a notable belonging to a family that had distinguished itself as a great opponent to Italian rule, was elected President of the club. Although the club's purpose was outwardly literary, like the Mukhtar Club, it soon found itself engaged in political activities, for in Islamic lands, politics could hardly be separated from other ways of life.

The Italian settlers were at the outset anxious to return to normal life and showed little or no opposition to the British authorities; but when the Arabs demanded the ultimate restoration of authority to their hands, the Italian settlers began to express their desire to the British that Italian rule should be restored in the form of Italian tutelage. Still sympathetic to Fascism, some of them formed the Republican Fascist Party in January, 1944. The activities of this organization were by no means confined to Tripoli city. Its leaders, who proved to be opposed to the British authorities, were arrested and the movement was suppressed. It was natural that Italian settlers, who had been in the ascendancy under Italian rule, could not easily adapt themselves to new conditions of life when they found that authority had suddenly passed to another power which was favorable to the elements that had been suppressed under Italian rule. Some of the settlers tried desperately to perpetuate their ascendancy, which alarmed the politically conscious Arab public. As a result, the Arabs showed their concern about the future of their country and staged a demonstration in October, 1944, culminating in the presentation of a petition to the British administration demanding that Tripolitania should never again return to Italian control.

The visits of Sayyid Idris to Cyrenaica provided the Tripolitanian leaders an opportunity to arouse public interest in politics. Some advocated Sanusi leadership for Tripolitania and Cyrenaica, not because they were followers of the Sanusi order, but because they realized that Sayyid Idris was perhaps the only person capable

---

participated in reopening the club included Ahmad al-Faqih Hasan, who was elected President, Muhammad al-Mahruk, 'Abd al-Rahman al-Qalhud, 'Abd al-'Aziz al-Zaqalla'i, Mustafa al-Sarraj, and others.

of bringing about unity between the two provinces. Others either were opposed or reluctant to submit to Sanusi leadership. Still others presented a petition to the Chief Administrator asking that their country be placed under British tutelage after the war, but asserting that under no circumstances would they want the country to revert to Italian control. The nationalists protested to the Chief Administrator against those who asked for British tutelage and said that they did not represent the majority of the people. Thus the public was divided among itself and several groups had already been formed, each gravitating around a certain leading personality.

Lack of an assurance as to the future status of Tripolitania, in contrast to the promise given to the Sanusis in Cyrenaica that their country would not revert to Italian domination, caused a feeling of frustration among the politically conscious public, who complained that the absence of a free press and political parties deprived the country of essential means to enlighten the people concerning their rights and the national interests. The demand to organize political parties was the principal reason for agitation, although four clubs had already been in existence, ostensibly devoted to history and literature, sports and charity, but in reality functioning as political parties.[2] The military administration had set up an Advisory Council, headed by the Chief Administrator and composed of such notables as the Mufti of Tripoli, Salim al-Muntasir, Mustafa Mizran, and others. This Council represented the conservative elements in the country, but the political elements of opposing groups often resorted to street demonstrations. When, on October 7, a petition regarding the future of the country was presented to the Chief Administrator, the extremist elements led a crowd of several thousand people who, while parading down the streets, tore down Italian street signs and replaced them by others in Arabic.[3]

The cessation of hostilities brought about further political agitation. Uneasiness as to the future was expressed by all communities. The burning question of the day was the fate of the

[2] The four clubs were: The Literary Club, Sporting Club, Worker's Club, and The Reform Club of Misrata.

[3] A few of the leaders were detained and one of them, Mansur Bin Qadara, was exiled to Egypt.

country and in favor of what community the decision of the powers would be. The Italians, upset by a variety of difficulties— separated from families, depressed economic conditions, and un- certainty about the future—criticized Britain and her allies for not fulfilling their promises; but their position was weak and no support could be expected from a regime at home which had been weakened by the war. On one occasion the Bishop of Tripoli, Rev. Facchinetti, in a public address affirmed the right of Italy to her North African colonies which, he stated, she had purchased with " blood and tears " and at a great sacrifice. The immediate reaction was Arab threats and a protest to the Chief Administrator. Since the Bishop had spoken as a private person, he was advised to apologize to satisfy the Arab leaders. These political tensions were mainly due to the uncertainty of the country's future, the rising tide of nationalist feeling in neigh- boring Arab countries which had its repercussion in Tripolitania, and depressed economic conditions resulting from shortage of essential commodities during the war. As a result demonstrations, often aroused by trifling incidents, became almost a daily affair, and the mob frequently caused damage and widespread destruc- tion. The Jews were the subject of several mob outbursts during 1945, the first of which was caused by false rumors that the Qadi of Tripoli, whose office was in the Jewish quarter, was alleged to have been attacked by the Jews.

Political Parties

Upon the cessation of hostilities, political consciousness re- ceived further impetus when political exiles and students who had studied abroad returned home. When these were not given posts or their patriotic activities were not recognized, they joined the ranks of malcontents. This situation coincided with the rising tide of nationalism in the Arab world, which had already reached a high pitch of excitement after the war.

Oppressed for a long time under Italian rule and denied the right to organize political associations, Tripolitanian leaders quickly took advantage of the freedom given to organize political parties when the war was over. Unlike Cyrenaica, where Sayyid

Idris provided a balanced leadership, Tripolitania had long suffered from the lack of organized leadership and from factional differences which reduced the country to a state of virtual anarchy. Feudal and family loyalties continued to play significant roles in the shaping of political groups; nationalism, which had not yet taken root in the country, could not supersede these traditional loyalties. As a result, numerous political groups emerged and their leaders, vying for recognition, failed to co-ordinate their activities.

The Nationalist Party (al-Hizb al-Watani), a secret body at first, was organized by a few nationalists under the leadership of Ahmad al-Faqih Hasan in 1944 and presented itself as the party representing the national aspirations of the country at large.[4] It offered its help to the administration in the maintenance of law and order, as long as the aims of the administration did not conflict with the party's program. This qualified offer of help was declined and permission for the party to operate was refused. The party continued to conduct operations underground until the military administration officially recognized it on April 8, 1946.

The party's program, though asserting the ascendancy of Tripolitania, stood for complete independence of a united Libya; but if that was not possible, then a trusteeship for a united Libya under the Arab League. A few advocated an Egyptian protectorate. It was on this matter that dissension ensued within the party and the leader, Ahmad al-Faqih Hasan, withdrew to form another party. Mustafa Mizran, a conservative, replaced Ahmad al-Faqih as the leader of the party, and several other leading dignitaries joined the party and enhanced its prestige. The party claimed to have opened more than fifteen branches in various localities with a registered membership of 15,000.[5]

[4] The other persons who participated in the founding of the party were: 'Abd al-Rahman Duqduq, Mustafa Hasan, 'Abd al-Razzaq al-Bishti, al-Hajj Mahmud al-'Arabi, Yusuf al-Sa'idi, and al-Hadi al-Mushayriqi. Those who participated from Misrata were: Shaykh Khalifa al-Walda, al-Hadi Bin Huqayq, Mustafa Mahmud Badi, and Mahmud 'Abd al-Latif.
[5] Four Power Commission of Investigation for the Former Italian Colonies. Vol. III: *Report on Libya*, p. 11. For text of the party's program, see Mahmud al-Shunayti, *Qadiyat Libya* (Cairo, 1951), pp. 255–56.

While the Council of Foreign Ministers was discussing the question of the disposal of the former Italian colonies in Paris, rumors were circulated that Tripolitania might revert to Italian rule in the guise of trusteeship. This prompted a few leaders to request British rather than Italian trusteeship, while others, protesting against any form of trusteeship, called for the formation of a United National Front (al-Jabha al-Wataniya al-Muttahida), which would have a wider popular appeal because of the inclusion in its membership of the leaders of the National Party as well as conservatives. The leadership of the party was offered to Salim al-Muntasir, a dignitary belonging to one of Tripolitania's leading families, and the party's membership included such personages as Muhammad Abu al-Isʻad al-ʻAlim (Mufti of Tripoli), ʻAwn Sawf, Tahir al-Murayyid, and Ibrahim Bin Shaʻban. The party was officially formed on May 10, 1946. It advocated the independence and unity of Libya under Sanusi leadership in an effort to enlist the support of Sayyid Idris so that he might include Tripolitania in addition to Cyrenaica under his Amirate, against Italian claims.

The Jabha's advocacy of Sanusi leadership aroused factions which had been opposed to the extension of Sanusi influence in Tripolitania. ʻAli al-Faqih Hasan and his brother, Ahmad, led the dissident elements of the National Party to form the Free National Bloc (al-Kutla al-Wataniya al-Hurra) on May 30, 1946. The Kutla rejected Sanusi leadership and advocated the calling of a constituent assembly to plan the future form of government. The party's inclination was known to have been in favor of republicanism. ʻAli al-Faqih Hasan, though an eloquent speaker and a man of integrity, showed an uncompromising attitude toward moderate elements, which confined the appeal of his party to extremists. The party claimed that it had 70,000 members, but the British authorities put the figure at 800. It held public meetings and circulated leaflets calling for complete independence, unity of Libya, and membership in the Arab League. It asked also for the Arabization of the administration and complained of the number of Italians who were still employed in it.

On December 16, 1946, two members of the Free Nationalist

Bloc, 'Ali Rajab and al-Hajj Yusuf al-Mushayriqi, left the Bloc to form the Egyptian-Tripolitanian Union Party. 'Ali Rajab, who was the secretary of the Bloc, assumed leadership of the new party. He advocated a union under the Egyptian Crown provided Tripolitania (which, to him, included Cyrenaica) maintained its internal autonomy.[6] Neither in Egypt nor in Tripoli did the program have a widespread appeal. Still another dissident group formed a Labor Party in September, 1947, led by Bashir Bin Hamza after his summary expulsion from the Free National Bloc. This party advocated a united Libya under the Sanusi Amirate. Finally, a Liberal Party, led by an ex-Vice President of the Nationalist Party, was formally organized on March 11, 1948. Its membership was limited to moderate elements and advocated the establishment of a united Libya under the Amirate of Sayyid Idris.[7]

Apart from the Sanusi Amirate, all the parties were agreed on the fundamental principles of unity and independence; they demanded:

1. Complete independence;
2. Unity of the country (composed of the three provinces of Tripolitania, Cyrenaica, and Fazzan);
3. Membership in the Arab League.

Attempts had been made by many a party leader as well as by independent politicians to unite the three leading parties, but personal rivalry and family feuds disrupted any possibility of rapprochement.

As time passed, with no agreement among the Great Powers on the future of the country, the leaders naturally became

[6] For an exposition of the party's program and aspirations, see an address given by 'Ali Rajab in Cairo on May 23, 1947 at the Press Club: " The Desire of the Tripolitanian People to Enter Into a Union with the People of the Nile Valley " (Cairo, 1947) .

[7] Information on political parties supplied by leading figures who participated in political activities such as Salim al-Muntasir, Mustafa Mizran, 'Ali and Ahmad al-Faqih Hasan, The Mufti, Shaykh 'Abd al-Rahman al-Qalhud, 'Abd al-'Aziz al-Zaqalla'i, al-Hadi al-Mushayyiqi, 'Ali Rajab, and Muhammad Badi. See also the report on Libya by the Four Powers of Investigation; al-Shunyti, pp. 253–59.

increasingly impatient and less willing to compromise. They all had been under the influence of nationalism that was sweeping the Arab World, while the Great Powers were trying to find a satisfactory solution for the question of the former Italian colonies. To the Tripolitanians, the problem was not as complicated as it appeared to the Great Powers: they had acquired the right for self-government under the Atlantic Charter, the Italian forces had been defeated and expelled by force, they had never ruled with the consent of the native people, and therefore their return, in the guise of trusteeship or otherwise, was regarded as a breach of the war declarations and promises made by the Powers. They held that independence was a right belonging to the nation and that unity was a matter to be decided by its representatives. They expected the Powers, meeting in Paris, to recognize these inherent rights. Thinking along these lines was the chief preoccupation of the politically conscious public; as to the rest of the population, their pattern of life was hardly affected by the nationalist agitation.

Controversy over the Sanusi Amirate

From the time when Cyrenaican and Tripolitanian leaders were in exile, it will be recalled, their disagreement on Sanusi leadership kept them from collaborating in the liberation of their country. When the émigrés returned home they carried with them their differences, despite the new compelling reasons to unite against foreign intervention. Nor were the internal conditions conducive to harmony between the two provinces. Cyrenaica, owing to her small tribal population and meager economic resources, would become dependent on Tripolitania if the two provinces merged. Moreover, Cyrenaican tribesmen were unwilling to accustom themselves to agriculture and improve the backward economy of the country. These were important considerations in favor of asserting a Tripolitanian leadership if the two provinces were to merge, had there been no political rivalry involved.

Tripolitania, however, had always been torn internally by

tribal and factional feuds, which made it exceedingly difficult for its politicians to acknowledge a common leader. Nor were the religious and tribal loyalties strong enough to enable a tribal or a religious chief to impose his authority on the people. The Sanusi order, predominating in Cyrenaica, had relatively few followers among the tribes of Tripolitania and almost none in urban areas. Even if Sanusi followers were more numerous in tribal areas, the tribal system itself has been broken in Tripolitania and the majority of the tribes had become semisedentary. As a result, lack of cohesion and the absence of common leadership proved to be Tripolitania's greatest weakness and the quarrels among lesser leaders had enabled the Italians to bring about submission in this province more effectively than in Cyrenaica.

Although poor and wretched, the Cyrenaicans have taken pride in the fact that they resisted unrelentingly and without regard to sacrifice for almost twenty out of thirty years of Italian rule over their country. Continuous warfare and Italian retaliations drained the country. And this accounts, Cyrenaicans maintain, for the economic backwardness and poverty of the region. Their opposition, both at home and abroad, ultimately contributed to the weakening of Italian hold over the country. Above all, Cyrenaica was endowed with a balanced and wise leadership which spared the country the curse of tribal and feudal conflicts. Still attached to religious symbols and practices, the majority of the tribes conform to the Sanusi order as the true version of Islam. The Sanusi family, moreover, had played an acknowledged patriotic role in the country's resistance to Italian rule. Sayyid Idris, grandson of the founder of the Sanusi order, had distinguished himself as a statesman who commanded the respect of British and other European statesmen and his leadership was unanimously acknowledged by Cyrenaicans. His negotiations with the British in 1940, which bore fruit in the liberation of Cyrenaica from Italian rule, caused him to be held in high esteem among his people.

It became quite clear to many a Tripolitanian patriot that Libyan unity would not be achieved unless Sanusi leadership were acknowledged in Tripolitania. Nor were the Tripolitanians unaware of the significance of Sanusi leadership when their country was in danger of again falling under foreign domination if they did not receive the support of a leader who had already enjoyed high prestige in international councils. Under these conditions, it was natural that leading Tripolitanian statesmen again took the initiative, as their predecessors had done more than a quarter of a century before, in offering to Sayyid Idris their homage (bay'a) and acknowledging Sanusi leadership.

The United National Front (al-Jabha), it will be recalled, was formed to arouse the public to the danger of the country's reversion to Italian rule and to enlist support for acknowledging Sanusi leadership. To achieve this, the Jabha took the initiative by opening negotiations with Sayyid Idris, who was still in Cairo, and by sending a deputation to him to discuss the plan for unity between the two provinces under his leadership. The deputation, composed of Mahmud al-Muntasir and Tahir al-Murayyid, went to Cairo in June, 1946, armed with a letter explaining the Jabha's program, and presented to Sayyid Idris a plan for unity based on the following proposals:

(a) Any offer of independence or trusteeship made by the Great Powers to one of the two provinces without regard to the wishes of the other should be rejected;

(b) The Sanusi Amirate should be confined to the person of Sayyid Idris and was not to become hereditary in his family;

(c) The form of government should be parliamentary and constitutional.

A discussion on the basis of these proposals lasted for several days; a number of Tripolitanian and Cyrenaican leaders residing in Cairo participated, and Sayyid Idris, agreeing in principle to these proposals, issued a letter to the Jabha, dated June 14, 1946. The text of the letter follows:

To the Members of the Tripolitanian National Front (al-Jabha), Salim al-Muntasir, and his brethren . . .
Peace be upon you and God's mercy and blessings.
I have received with delight your letter, carried by Mahmud Bey al-Muntasir and al-Tahir Bey al-Murayyid, who were entrusted with

a mission to explain the principles of the Jabha's [program], namely, the achievement of the independence and unity of the country and her entry as a member into the Arab League. It is with pleasure that I declare my subscription to these high principles, which I have myself been trying to achieve with all my strength. Discussion concerning the future of the country and the principles [i. e., form] of government has been made with your deputation. God knows that if you have not yourself opened this subject, I would not have entered into such a discussion. For the ultimate goal that we all try to achieve is the [country's] independence and her national aspirations, so that the nation will enjoy the freedom for which she had for long endeavored to achieve. I hope that this goal will be reached, by God's help and the efforts of the country's sincere sons.

I have been asked to give my opinion on the following matter:

1. What would be the principles [i. e., the form] of government? I believe that the government should be constitutional. That the nation should elect a constituent assembly which would enact a constitution, by virtue of which a parliamentary system might be established along the lines followed in other Arab countries.

2. [The deputation] discussed with me the question of succession and the choice of the capital. My opinion is that these questions, despite the fact that they are prematurely raised, should be for the representative assembly, which would be elected by the people, to decide.

3. You have expressed the desire to form a joint committee representing the two provinces for the purpose of co-ordinating their activities and promoting these common interests, and that it should be connected with us as the only agency to voice the aspirations of the people to the outside world. I have no objection to the setting up of such an agency. I should also welcome the idea of sending [another] deputation representing you for the purpose of carrying on further discussion with us.

I want to thank you and thank the deputation for the satisfactory performance of the mission for which it was sent.

I am, etc. .

(signed) Muhammad Idris
al-Mahdi al-Sanusi [8]

---

[8] Information on the background of this correspondence, as well as a copy of Sayyid Idris' letter, was supplied to the present writer by Salim al-Muntasir (the author's translation) .

Encouraged by Sayyid Idris' reply, especially his approval of the unity and independence of the two provinces under his leadership, the Jabha held a meeting on November 21, 1946, at which the preliminary agreement with Sayyid Idris was discussed. A delegation of ten, under the leadership of Muhammad Abu al-Is'ad al-'Alim, the Mufti of Tripoli,[9] was appointed to negotiate with Cyrenaican leaders in Banghazi on the ways and means of implementing the preliminary agreement arrived at with Sayyid Idris.

The Jabha informed Sayyid Idris concerning the formation of the deputation and requested his presence in Banghazi at the time when Tripolitanian and Cyrenaican leaders would meet. Sayyid Idris sent word that he would arrive in Banghazi on January 13, 1947. On January 15, the Tripolitaian leaders had an audience with Sayyid Idris and the Sayyid appointed a Cyrenaican delegation led by 'Umar Mansur al-Kikhya, selected from the Cyrenaican National Front.[10] Upon the Sayyid's request, the Tripolitanian delegation submitted proposals made up of seven points as the basis of negotiation on the following day. The proposals may be summed up as follows:

1. Libyan unity within its natural frontiers, as they existed before World War II, and the rejection of any proposal dividing or separating any portion of the country.

2. Complete independence for all Libyan territories.

3. Acknowledgment of the leadership of Sayyid Muhammad Idris al-Sanusi, the proclamation of his Amirate over Libya, and the establishment of a constitutional, democratic, and parliamentary form of government.

4. The entry of the country into membership in the Arab League after independence.

5. The establishment of a joint committee for the purpose of

[9] The other members of the delegation were: Mahmud al-Muntasir, 'Awn Sawf, Shaykh Muhammad al-Hinqari, Shaykh 'Abd al-Rahman al-Qalhud, Muhammad al-Mayyit, Salim al-Murayyid, Ibrahim Bin Sha'ban, 'Abd al-Majid Ku'bar, Ishaq (Zakkino) Habib.

[10] The other members of the delegation were: Husayn al-Bisaykiri, Shaykh 'Abd al-Hamid al-Dibani, 'Umar Shinnib, Shaykh 'Abd al-Hamid al-'Abbar, 'Awad Lanqi, 'Abd al-Raziq Shaqluf, Munir al-Ba'ba', Renato Tshuba.

promoting the common interests of the country under the Amir's guidance.

6. The two parties undertake to carry out the principles agreed upon, to defend them with all possible means, and to reject any arrangement inconsistent with those principles.

7. This agreement, having been duly signed, will become binding upon both parties after the Amir's approval.

Two days passed, during which the Cyrenaican leaders were busy studying the proposals, before the two delegations met for discussion. On January 18, 'Umar Mansur, head of the Cyrenaican delegation, welcomed the Tripolitanian delegation in an opening speech and expressed Cyrenaica's desire for unity; but, he added, his delegation was not prepared to accept the latter part of the sixth proposal without reservation, i. e. " to reject any arrangement [for Cyrenaica or Tripolitania] inconsistent with those principles." He explained that Cyrenaica would continue to ask for unity, but could not bind herself unconditionally, for if she were offered a special status, she should accept it and ask for unity with Tripolitania. This reservation became the subject of a heated discussion during the morning session, for the Cyrenaican leaders held that the promise of independence given by the British authorities should not be rejected if Tripolitania were unable to achieve a similar status. The Cyrenaican delegation, rephrasing some of the proposals, suggested that the first point should read: " to work for Libyan unity." To the third point, following the clause " the proclamation of his [Sayyid Idris'] Amirate over Libya," the reservation " without any condition or stipulation," was added. Finally, the last part of the sixth point, which reads " to reject any arrangement, etc.," was deleted and replaced by the clause " if such an arrangement should be impossible to achieve, they should save what can possibly be saved, and then to try to save the remaining portion," on the ground that Cyrenaica should not suffer the same fate if Italy returned to rule over the country under the guise of trusteeship. The delegation also suggested deletion of the last sentence of the sixth point which required the Amir's approval of the proposals.

These reservations, unacceptable to the Tripolitanian delegation, were submitted in the form of three counterproposals to
the Cyrenaican delegation as follows:

1. The achievement of the unity and independence of Libyan
territory within its natural frontiers without dismemberment,
the proclamation of Sayyid Idris as an Amir over Libya, the
establishment of a constitutional, democratic, and parliamentary government, and the entry into membership in the Arab
League.

2. Same as point 5.

3. Same as point 7.

The sixth point, which caused much controversy, was dropped,
as it was implied in point 1. Nevertheless, these proposals were
unacceptable to the Cyrenaican delegation because Cyrenaica was
not given freedom of action in case Tripolitania were placed
against her will under trusteeship. The deadlock was complete,
and Sayyid Idris left the next day for Cairo. Attempts were made
during the following two days, mainly by the Mukhtar group,
to resume negotiations by rephrasing certain clauses of the final
Tripolitanian proposals, but the Tripolitanian delegation was
confronted with new proposals such as a demand that the joint
committee be composed of an equal number of Tripolitanian
and Cyrenaican members. This was entirely unacceptable to the
Tripolitanian leaders, who left for Tripoli dissatisfied with what
they denounced as Cyrenaica's extravagant demands.[11]

The failure of the two delegations to agree on a working plan
for unity became the subject of discussion in the press and in
political circles both in Tripoli and Banghazi. The extremists
in Tripolitania, such as the Free United Bloc (al-Kutla), criticized the members of the delegation for their concession on the
Sanusi Amirate, while the Mukhtar group of Cyrenaica charged
its Cyrenaican compatriots with lack of patriotism in emphasizing
local particularism.[12] The breakdown of the negotiations, which

[11] Information on the Banghazi negotiations supplied by 'Umar Mansur
and Shaykh 'Abd al-Rahman al-Qalhud. See also Shukri, *op. cit.*, pp. 335–51.
[12] *al-Watan*, Banghazi, January 28, 1947.

prompted some Tripolitanian leaders to reproach Sayyid Idris for not impressing upon the Cyrenaican leaders the need to compromise with the Tripolitanian delegation, demonstrated that the two provinces still felt strongly about their separate existence. However, Sayyid Idris himself was obliged to take into account the views of his Cyrenaican followers.

The Libyan Liberation Committee

The breakdown of the negotiations between Tripolitanian and Cyrenaican leaders displayed lack of internal agreement at a time when the Four Powers had just signed a peace treaty with Italy providing for the sending of an Investigation Commission to find out the wishes of the people of the former Italian colonies before a decision was taken on their future status. The representatives of the Arab countries and the Secretary General of the Arab League, it is true, had often expressed their views on Libyan unity and independence; [13] but Cyrenaican and Tripolitanian leaders had often given divergent, if not conflicting, views as to their national aspirations. Under the circumstances, it seemed necessary for Tripolitanian leaders to co-ordinate their activities and to reformulate their fundamental national aspirations in broad enough terms to be acceptable to all. To achieve this purpose a Libyan Liberation Committee was set up in Cairo in March, 1947, under the leadership of Bashir al-Sa'dawi, supported by the Arab League. Sa'dawi, who had just resigned from his position as one of Ibn Sa'ud's principal advisers, became the driving force behind the Liberation Committee.

Sa'dawi, it will be recalled, had taken an active part in the resistance movement against Italian rule. From early experience in politics, he had realized that the inherent weakness in his country's affairs was lack of leadership. He accordingly had been in favor of Sanusi leadership ever since Sayyid Idris was proclaimed as the Amir of Cyrenaica in 1921. After Italy's subjugation of Tripolitania, Sa'dawi went into exile and began to agitate

[13] Arab League, *The Libyan Question* (Cairo, 1950) (Arabic).

against Italian domination over his country. When the fate of Libya became dependent on the decision of the Great Powers, Sa'dawi felt that the time had come to resume the struggle for his country's independence. He took leave from the Sa'udi monarch, whom he had accompanied to Cairo in 1946, and began to contact Tripolitanian and Cyrenaican leaders, upon whom he impressed the need to subordinate local differences to more important national interests. Since he was not in Cairo when the negotiation for collaboration between Cyrenaican and Tripolitanian leaders broke down, he was still on good terms with both parties and tried to effect a reconciliation between them. He was horrified to find that the country's national interests had been subordinated to local jealousies and tried to focus the attention of Libyans on the goals of unity and independence. He returned just in time to impress upon his Tripolitanian compatriots in Cairo that unless Sanusi leadership were acknowledged by Tripolitanians and Cyrenaicans, Libya would probably never again be re-established as one state. Sa'dawi appealed to the Tripolitanian Committee, which was still active in Cairo, to put an end to its quarrels with Cyrenaican leaders and to acknowledge Sayyid Idris' right to be the future head of a united Libya. In the meantime, he impressed upon Sayyid Idris and his followers Tripolitania's need to unite with Cyrenaica. This was no easy task to accomplish in a frustrated country, torn with personal and factional differences. He was denounced as lacking in patriotism by extremist factions, and he was, perhaps, never able to win the confidence of those genuinely working for unity. However, he contributed greatly in paving the way for the acknowledgement of Sayyid Idris as head of state in Tripolitania, before succumbing to the influence of his Tripolitanian supporters and rejecting the federal compromise which was the only plan for Libyan unity acceptable to Cyrenaica and Fazzan.

   The breakdown of the negotiations between the Tripolitanian and Cyrenaican leaders at Banghazi (January, 1947) marked the beginning of Sa'dawi's frustration. Although he never abandoned his advocacy of Sanusi leadership, he, perhaps unwittingly, allowed himself to be swayed by the prevailing opinion among Tripolitanians that since Sanusi leadership had become the bone of contention between the two provinces, the decision on the future form of government should be postponed until the country had first won its unity and independence. This new formula, which was intended to rally all the parties and groups and to demonstrate to the outside world the unity of will and purpose in the country, satisfied only those Tripolitanian leaders who proved to be the sworn enemies of Sanusi leadership. However, contrary to Sa'dawi's own intentions, it was construed to mean by both Sayyid Idris and his Cyrenaican followers that Sa'dawi was no longer in favor of Sanusi leadership.

At this time, Sa'dawi began to organize the Liberation Committee, calling for Libyan unity and independence, without an express declaration concerning Sanusi leadership. This new move, however, was regarded by Cyrenicans as an affront to their leader. It is true that Sa'dawi continued to assure Sayyid Idris that the throne of Libya would eventually be offered to him, but his words carried with them no conviction to Cyrenaicans. Thus when he requested that Sayyid Idris participate in the Liberation Committee, the Sayyid demanded that a letter of invitation should be sent to him. When the letter arrived, dated August 22, 1947, Sayyid Idris referred it to the Cyrenaican National Front. Upon considering the matter closely, the Front rejected the invitation on the basis that there had been no prior consultation with Cyrenaican leaders and that the committee's program lacked any reference to Sanusi leadership.[14] Thus the Liberation Committee was composed only of Tripolitanian leaders, although its purpose was to defend Libyan rights generally. A year later, the headquarters of the Liberation Committee were moved to Tripoli.

The news concerning the formation of the Libyan Liberation Committee was not received with much enthusiasm even in Tripolitania at the outset, partly because Tripolitanian leaders had no prior intimation of it, but mainly because they did not know what Sa'dawi's real intentions were. When, however, 'Abd al-Rahman 'Azzam, Secretary-General of the Arab League, issued a statement to Tripolitanians inviting them to support the

[14] For text of Sa'dawi's letter and the reply of the Cyrenaican National Front, see Shukri, *op. cit.*, pp. 380–81.

Committee,[15] and Sa'dawi himself paid a visit to consult with the country's leaders, the Tripolitanians began to see in the Liberation Committee a forceful instrument for the defense of Libyan rights.

The arrival, in March, 1948, of the Four Power Investigation Commission gave Sa'dawi an opportunity to impress upon the leaders the need to subordinate their personal to national considerations. Sa'dawi, who arrived in Tripoli before the Commission, made such a dramatic appearance and his speeches were so impressive that his leadership was at once acknowledged by the public.[16] Under his influence, all parties except the Labor Party agreed to unite, and a memorandum calling for the unity and independence of Libya, with membership in the Arab League, was submitted to the Commission. Due to the breakdown of the Banghazi negotiations, the memorandum contained no statement about Sanusi leadership, a matter which was taken as further evidence that Tripolitanian leaders were not interested in Sanusi leadership and which resulted in a sharp disagreement between the Nationalist Party and the United National Front in Tripolitania.

Sa'dawi, satisfied that his efforts in Cairo and Tripoli had borne fruit in the display of a united public opinion before the Four Power Investigation Commission, left Tripoli for Cairo at a critical time; for, shortly after his departure in April, the rift between the Tripolitanian leaders over Sanusi leadership became more acute. While in Cairo, Sa'dawi tried to reconcile the differences by issuing an avalanche of declarations in favor of Sayyid Idris and by making an appeal to Tripolitanian leaders to acknowledge Sanusi leadership, but to no avail. He returned in July to reunite the parties (except the Labor Party) by suggesting the formula of a " united independent Libya under the Sanusi Amirate." This constructive plan which should have met Cyrenaican demands was rejected by the Cyrenaican National

---

[15] For text of 'Azzam's statement, see Arab League, *The Libyan Question*, pp. 34–35.

[16] The public may have also been influenced by the consideration shown to the Committee, especially to Sa'dawi, its leader, by the officials of the British Military Administration. See *The Report of the Four Power Commission of Investigation*, Vol. III (Libya), p. 10.

Congress; but Sa'dawi, hoping that the new formula would eventually bring about the reconciliation of Cyrenaican leaders, concentrated on winning his battle against Tripolitanian sensitivities.
However, the disagreement between Sa'dawi and Salim al-Muntasir, caused mainly by personal differences, discouraged Sayyid
Idris from entering into an agreement with any party.

Further Split in the Party System

The immediate cause of the disagreement between Sa'dawi and
Muntasir was a trifling matter. While in Egypt, Sa'dawi sought
the aid of the Egyptian Prime Minister to persuade Sayyid Idris
to accept the formula of Libyan unity and independence under
Sanusi leadership. However, his efforts, which reflected an earnest
desire to bring about unity between the two provinces, resulted
in further splits in Tripolitania's party system. For, having
brought the parties to agree on unity and independence, Sa'dawi
reverted to his earlier formula of Libyan unity and independence
under Sanusi leadership. Muntasir, leader of the Jabha, wanted
himself to sponsor the idea of Sanusi leadership and asked Egypt
to offer her friendly guidance to Sayyid Idris; but Sa'dawi, who
regarded his efforts on Libya's behalf as transcending personal
and partisan lines, overlooked procedural matters and negotiated
with the Egyptian Prime Minister without prior consultation
with Salim al-Muntasir. 'Abd al-Rahman al-Qalhud, Secretary
of the Jabha, held a meeting in which the issue was decided in
favor of Sa'dawi.[17] Salim al-Muntasir, regarding the decision as
a personal slight, tendered his resignation, and the Jabha elected
Tahir al-Murayyid as its new leader. Given a mandate by the new
leader, Sa'dawi officially requested the Egyptian Prime Minister
to negotiate with Sayyid Idris. To end further complications of
the issue, Sayyid Idris wisely suggested that decision on this matter
should be postponed until Libya had won her independence.

Salim al-Muntasir, with a few other dissenters, formed a new
political party known as the Istiqlal (Independence) Party. Its
followers were mainly from the segment of the people who had

[17] The author's interview with Qalhud.

been opposed to Sa'dawi and to the Arab League, which had lost prestige after the Palestine war, and advocated the independence of the country and unity with Cyrenaica without reference to the Arab League.

Meanwhile, the idea of independence, which remained the ultimate objective of all political parties and groups, seemed remote to a few leaders who began to look, under foreign influence, for outside guidance. They argued that to achieve independence " we must have help." If Great Britain did not offer help, on the ground that she was interested only in Cyrenaica, Tripolitania must seek help elsewhere. " We must arrange an interim deal with some power," the leaders argued, " even an unpopular deal, which safeguards our aspirations." This power, they contended, must be a Western Power. The Arab League had become unpopular, Russia was an anathema, France was unacceptable as a North African imperialist power, and the United States was not interested. A joint trusteeship was regarded as impracticable. There remained only Italy. Although disliked and distrusted, she still had a number of supporters and had become active in seeking United Nations trusteeship. These leaders showed readiness to deal with Italy, with a view to achieving the ultimate independence of the country, and they were wholeheartedly supported by the Italian settlers. Thinking along these lines was naturally inspired by the project which Ernest Bevin and Count Sforza, the British and Italian Foreign Secretaries, had arrived at by virtue of which Cyrenaica and Tripolitania would be placed under temporary British and Italian trusteeships before they achieved final independence.

Upon his return to Tripoli in February, 1949, Sa'dawi was alarmed to find these " defeatist " arguments gaining ground in the country. He had already approached the British Foreign Office in January, while in Europe leading the Tripolitanian delegation to the United Nations, to extract from the British government support for Tripolitanian national aspirations and abandonment of the attitude of silence and " unsympathetic spectator." The Foreign Office would not commit itself and, perhaps due to Bevin's agreement with Sforza on the plan of an Italian trusteeship over Tripolitania, made it clear to Sa'dawi that Britain did not wish to accept any long-term responsibility for Tripolitania. Returning empty-handed to Tripoli and confronted with a movement in favor of an Italian return to the country, Sa'dawi began actively to rally the leaders against this new Italian move and went to Cairo to discuss the situation with the Arab League for the financing of a Tripolitanian delegation to the forthcoming meeting of the United Nations Assembly. While a good deal of argument centered on whom the delegates should be, Sa'dawi suddenly fell ill and could not go. It was finally decided that 'Ali al-'Unayzi, a Cyrenaican in the Secretariat of the Arab League, and Mansur Qadara, assisted by Fu'ad Shukri, an Egyptian, would form the delegation. They arrived at Lake Success in April. This was the meeting in which the Bevin-Sforza plan, providing for a British and an Italian trusteeship over Cyrenaica and Tripolitania, was introduced.[17a] Sa'dawi was still hoping for an understanding with the British, but his personal quarrels with Brigadier Blackley, the Chief Administrator, and the announcement of the Bevin-Sforza plan, put an end to any such hope. He now could rely only on the support of the Arab League, and in his speeches to the public he indulged in attacks on all foreign powers.

National Congress

The radio announcement of the Bevin-Sforza Plan on May 8–9 was the cause of intense political agitation directed mainly against Italy for her desire to return to Tripoli in the guise of a United Nations trustee, and against France for her support of Italy. There was also widespread resentment against Britain for what was felt to be a betrayal of the country's national aspirations. On May 11, the Tripolitanian leaders announced that a general strike would take place on that day, to be followed by a peaceful demonstration of protest against the Bevin-Sforza Plan in which the Arab officials of the British military administration were asked to participate. During the demonstration, anti-British slogans were shouted and anti-British banners were

[17a] See pp. 128–132, below.

carried, denouncing Britian for her support of an Italian trusteeship over Tripolitania. A petition was presented to the British
authorities in which demonstrators gave notice of their intention
to stage a civil disobedience campaign which would continue
until the danger of an Italian return to the country had receded.[18]

The leaders of the Nationalist Party and the United National
Front (al-Jabha), who were in agreement as to their national
demands, met on May 14 to co-ordinate their activities by forming
a single body called the Tripolitanian National Congress. The
leadership of this body, which all other parties were invited to
join, fell naturally on Sa'dawi, who had become a national hero
in Tripolitania. His long struggle against Italian domination
of the country and his rich experience in Arab politics well-fitted
him to be the leader of the new organization.

The Congress quickly set to work, conducting a widespread
campaign against the Bevin-Sforza Plan. It was decided that
schools and shops should be closed, that a civil disobedience
movement should be launched, and that the public should
withold payment of taxes and other levies. Disturbances and
demonstrations became almost a daily affair until May 17, when
news was received that the Bevin-Sforza proposal had been
rejected. On the following day, the general rejoicing throughout the country induced a large crowd to assemble outside the
headquarters of the National Congress where the Mufti, in the
absence of Sa'dawi, addressed the crowd on one of Tripoli's
happiest occasions since its liberation in 1943. Celebrations of
various kinds continued for the next two days until May 19. The
leaders of the National Congress were convinced that the rejection of the Bevin-Sforza Plan had been directly brought about
by the impression of the protest made on the members of the
General Assembly. When, however, further reports from Rome
and public statements by Sforza and other Italian statesmen
showed that Italian designs to perpetuate Italian influence were
still alive, the Tripolitanian leaders felt the weakness of their
position. In a statement made in the House of Commons on July
9, 1949, the British government tried to assure the Tripolitanians
that it did not consider itself any longer bound by the proposals

[18] *Tarablus al-Gharb*, Tripoli, May 12, 1949.

embodied in the Bevin-Sforza plan,[19] but public opinion remained fearful of Italian designs until the General Assembly voted in favor of Libyan independence.

The National Congress was aware of the difficult task that lay ahead of the country, especially in achieving internal unity. It was felt that the time had come to dispatch a delegation to Banghazi to congratulate Amir Idris on the occasion of the declaration of Cyrenaican independence (June 1, 1949) and to discuss with the Cyrenaican leaders the question of Sanusi leadership.

The Tripolitanian delegation was cordially received at Banghazi, and Amir Idris was invited to visit Tripoli on the way to his state visit to England. The Amir's visit to Tripoli on July 19, 1949, was on the whole successful, for the National Congress, under Sa'dawi's influence, made every effort to impress the Amir with Tripoli's loyalty to the Sanusi house.[20] An atmosphere of cordiality was evident when the Amir again passed through Tripoli in August on his return to Banghazi. Although decidedly pleased during his two visits and expressing his sympathies with the country's national aspirations, the Amir did not commit himself to any definite expression of opinion on the future of Tripolitania. In August, 1949, the National Congress held several meetings in which the party's program, calling for a united and independent Libya under Sanusi leadership, was affirmed.[21]

The other question with which the National Congress was preoccupied was the organizing of a delegation to the forthcoming meeting of the United Nations in September. Attempts were made to send a joint delegation of the National Congress and the Independence Party, but the personal rivalry between Sa'dawi and Salim al-Muntasir wrecked any possible co-operation on the matter. Therefore two delegations were sent to Lake Succcess, accompanied by an official of the Arab League to act as their liaison officer and adviser. The National Congress delegation

---

[19] *House of Commons Debate*, Vol. 466 (1949) cols. 2128–29.

[20] The press referred to the visit as a " historic day," and Sa'dawi welcomed the Amir in the name of " the Libyan nation " (*Tarablus al-Gharb*, Tripoli, July 11, 1949).

[21] *Tarablus al-Gharb*, Tripoli, August 21 and 25, 1949.

was composed of Sa'dawi, Mustafa Mizran, and Fu'ad Shukri; the delegation of the Istiqlal Party was composed of Ahmad Rasim Ku'bar, 'Abd-Allah Sharif, Mukhtar Muntasir, and 'Abd-Allah Bin Sha'ban. Fortunately, the representatives at Lake Success rose above factional differences when the two rival parties in Tripoli refused to co-operate. Both the National Congress and the Independence Party celebrated Independence Day on November 21, but the rejoicing public, paying no attention to factional differences, celebrated the occasion for several days.

Political Activities of the Italian Settlers

In the early twenties, the policy of Italy under Count Volpi, Governor of Tripolitania, was to encourage capitalists to develop the country by granting them development concessions. The policy of businesses during the governorships of De Bono and Badoglio was to encourage the employment of cheap native labor rather than Italian immigrants. Later, the immigrants arrived through a plan instituted by Marshal Balbo which aimed at mass demographic colonization in both Tripolitania and Cyrenaica. The immigration plan began in 1932, under the auspices of the *Ente per la Colonizzazione della Libia,* and had as its aim the colonization of the Fourth Shore (as Libya was known) with large numbers of peasants from Italy. It was thus that agricultural centers were created between 1933 and 1939 in several areas in Tripolitania and Cyrenaica. When World War II broke out, it was just at the time when the Italian government had begun to enlarge its demographic colonization into a five-year plan.

The Italian settlers hardly had begun to cultivate their newly acquired lands when the war interrupted their endeavors. Thus when the British forces occupied Tripolitania, they were anxious to return to normal life as quickly as possible. Although they suffered the loss of their ascendant position, their relations with the Arabs remained on the whole cordial.

After the war the Italian settlers began to revive their activities, hoping that some form of Italian authority over Libya might be restored. Such hopes became high when the Italian government itself began to spread propaganda in Libya. In 1947, following the signing of the peace treaty, the *Ministro dell'Africa Italiana* became extremely active in propaganda for the restitution of the colonies. This propaganda took the form of press articles sent both to Italians and Libyans. The main points of emphasis were that Fascist acts in Libya under Mussolini should be ignored, and that Italy was the only Mediterranean Power capable of exercising and willing to accept tutelage over Libya. The press also discredited the British administration and called attention to the deterioration in the agricultural and commercial life of the country. Although the great majority of the Libyans did not like Italian rule, Italian propaganda claimed that the Arabs had been fond of Italians and that only the Sanusis, who had fallen under Brtish influence, were anti-Italian.

In October, 1947, Signor Brusasco, the Italian Secretary for Foreign Affairs, made a statement in Rome to the effect that Italy had asked for the restitution of her colonies. This statement caused an adverse reaction among the Arabs, who threatened to oppose it by armed force if necessary. Their attitude caused considerable consternation among the Italian settlers and inspired many of them to come to an understanding with Arab leaders regarding the independence of Libya.

Four main groups were formed among the settlers after the war.

1. *The Italian Representative Committee.* Its principal leaders were Admiral Fenzi and Count Sottocasa. This committee was formed in 1947 to provide an Italian Advisory Council for the Chief Administrator in place of the Provincial Commissioner's Council, which had exhibited left-wing leanings and was felt by the settlers to be unrepresentative. The committee, because of unsatisfactory election results, could hardly claim to represent the whole community, and the British authorities were unwilling to accord it any official advisory status. However, the committee enjoyed a large measure of support among a group of the Italian settlers, and shortly before the arrival of the Four Power Commission, it was granted qualified permission to express views on behalf of its supporters. The committee, composed of former Fascists, was right-wing in sympathy, and in an uncompromising manner demanded Italian trusteeship over Libya.

2. *The Italian Association for the Progress of Libya.* This was a left-wing group, composed mainly of Italian intellectuals sympathetic to Communism, and led by Enrico Cibelli, a member of the former Italian Advisory Council to the Provincial Commissioner. The association, formed in 1948, was in favor of Libyan independence and was strongly opposed to the attitude of the Representative Committee. Under the influence of the latter, the association agreed to recommend to the Four Power Commission that, if independence was considered impossible, an Italian trusteeship should be preferred.[22]

3. *The Popular Democratic Front.* This was another left-wing group, following the line of the Popular Democratic Front in Italy (although not formally affiliated with it) and led by Alvaro Felici. The front appealed to the working classes of all communities, not only to Italians. It favored the independence of Libya and many of its supporters were sympathetic to communism.

4. *The Libyan Economic Front.* This was essentially a nonpolitical body, mainly concerned with the economic development of the country, led by Domenico Cattiti. It was loosely organized, and its schemes were grandiose and impracticable.

The intense activities of these groups, especially the Representative Committee which had the support of the Italian government, strained Italo-Arab relations, and when it appeared that the Great Powers were favoring Italian trusteeship, the Arabs displayed resentment at Italian attempts to reinstate authority over the country.

In April, 1949, the Italians were able to arrange for two pro-Italian Arabs to appear at Lake Success to oppose the Libyan Liberation Committee delegation. The rejection of the trusteeship proposals at the United Nations came as a surprise to many an Italian, but the majority began to realize the importance of Arab feelings. Enrico Cibelli, leader of the Association for the Progress of Libya, tried to unite the various Italian groups under his leadership in a program of full recognition for Arab aspirations. The settlers, however, were sharply divided into right-

[22] Cf. Report of the *Four Power Commission of Investigation for the Former Italian Colonies*, Vol. III, pp. 16–17.

and left-wing groups and no one seems to have been able to unite them. Signor Alessandrini, who visited Tripoli in July, 1949, was able to explain the Italian government's new policy to his compatriots, and a gradual recovery of confidence among the settlers seemed to follow. The main objective of Italian propaganda was then concentrated on the encouragement of the Arab Independence (Istiqlal) Party, while Cibelli, pursuing an independent line, tried to cultivate relations with the National Congress. The settlers, following such a moderate course of action, greatly improved the friendly relations between Arabs and Italians, both on the personal and the communal levels. Their parties declined in importance and, although many of them left the country, the majority abandoned political in favor of economic activities.

Fazzan

The French occupation of Fazzan, carried out by the Free French forces in agreement with the British forces that occupied Cyrenaica and Tripolitania,[23] was intended to be temporary, pending the decision of the Great Powers as to the fate of the Italian colonies. However, the French authorities, hoping that Fazzan might be united with French Equatorial Africa, began to discourage Fazzanese relations with other Libyan territories by diverting their trade relations to Algeria. They had, it will be recalled, already tied up Fazzan administratively with southern Algeria.[24] Sayyid Ahmad Sayf al-Nasr, who had co-operated with the Free French forces in the occupation of Fazzan, became the chief instrument through which the French intended to administer the territory.

When, after the war, a few Fazzanese leaders expressed a desire for the establishment of an autonomous regime, the French began to tighten their control over the territory. Meanwhile, Fazzanese leaders had already been in touch with Tripolitanian

[23] See pp. 50-51, above.
[24] See p. 51, above.

leaders who encouraged them to oppose the French authorities. As a result, the leaders began to discuss the possibility of organizing a resistance movement, and a secret Fazzanese Society was formed toward the end of 1946. Shaykh 'Abd al-Rahman Bin Muhammad al-Barquli was elected President of the Society, and Muhammad Bin 'Uthman al-Sayd its Vice-President. Bin 'Uthman, who proved to be one of the most active opponents of the French, began to conduct clandestine relations with Tripolitanian leaders and with Amir Idris of Cyrenaica. Ahmad Sayf al-Nasr, who outwardly collaborated with the French, gave his blessings to the society, as Bin 'Uthman has told the author.

In 1947, the French authorities uncovered the society's activities and arrested a few of its members. As a result, the society suffered a temporary setback. When, however, the Four Power Investigation Commission arrived in Fazzan in 1948, the society openly denounced the French administration and demanded the unity of Fazzan with other Libyan territories under Sanusi leadership.[25] Soon after the departure of the commission, Bin 'Uthman was arrested and thrown into prison, presumably owing to his hostile activities against the French administration. He remained in prison for six months and then was under police surveillance for a short while until he was released at the request of the United Nations Commissioner, Adrian Pelt, when he visited Sabha in February, 1950.

When the United Nations passed a resolution (November 21, 1949) enabling Libya to be constituted as one state, the French prepared a plan to establish an autonomous Fazzanese government along the lines followed in Cyrenaica. At Pelt's suggestion, the plan was not carried out; instead an administrative regime was set up under French supervision until Fazzan could be associated in one form or another with other Libyan territories.

In 1950, the French authorities decided to establish a Fazzanese Representative Assembly and install a chief of the territory of Fazzan, who was to be elected by the Assembly. Elections for an Assembly of fifty-eight representatives were held in early February, 1950, in accordance with local election practice, and on February

---

[25] For Fazzanese national aspirations as stated before the Investigation Commission, see p. 122, below.

12, the Assembly elected Ahmad Sayf al-Nasr as Chief of Fazzan.[26] On February 13, the chief of the territory chose three principal advisers from among the members of the Assembly. The portfolios of Justice and Interior were given to Hammuda Taha, Finance and Agriculture to Nasr Bin Salim, and Health and Education to Mahdi Ahmad.[27] The chief also chose eight assistant advisers. The French Resident held the executive powers. Ahmad Sayf al-Nasr, who already had been in touch with the Amir of Cyrenaica, welcomed the decision of the United Nations to re-establish Libya as one state, and he declared to Adrian Pelt, who visited Sabha in May, 1950, that Fazzan would recognize the Amirate of Sayyid Idris over the whole of Libya. He expressed the view, on behalf of Fazzan, that Libya should be established on a federal basis of the three provinces of Fazzan, Tripolitania, and Cyrenaica, and that under this arrangement the Fazzanese should continue to manage their own internal affairs. These views formed the basis of the instructions given to Fazzanese representatives who took part in laying the constitutional foundation of the United Kingdom of Libya during 1950–51.

Retrospect

Before the three sister provinces of Tripolitania, Cyrenaica, and Fazzan were united because of compelling external forces, they had passed through long and bitter experiences of rivalry and disunity, which had made them appreciative of the new opportunity for unity. Cyrenaica and Fazzan, it is true, could not match Tripolitania in population and resources, but their attachment to the Sanusi house, which supplied leadership for the whole country, laid the foundation for self-governing institutions. Cyrenaican tribal leaders took pride in the fact that they had carried on a relentless struggle against Italian rule until

[26] Although no candidate was proposed in opposition, the followers of Barquli suggested the incorporation of Fazzan into Tripolitania and saw no reason for the elections of a chief for Fazzan. The representatives of Ghat refused to take part in the elections for the Assembly. (See Pelt's *First Annual Report*, 1950, p. 12).

[27] Cf. *ibid.*, p. 12.

eventually their Amir, Sayyid Idris, was able to join the Allied forces in 1940 and emancipate the country.

Tripolitania, on the other hand, lacking organized leadership and the happy circumstances which enabled Cyrenaica to assert her independence, looked to Sayyid Idris as the natural candidate for the position of chief of a united Libyan state. Motivated by political considerations, Tripolitania wanted Sayyid Idris to become secular head of the state—not as religious head in his capacity as the leader of the Sanusi order—and wished him to be a constitutional monarch. However, since Tripolitania was the more developed economically and its population more than double that of Cyrenaica, it was felt that full unity of the provinces would inevitably shift the center of political gravity to Tripolitania, and that Cyrenaica and Fazzan would either lose their identities or become junior partners in the union. " Cyrenaica," said 'Abd al-Hamid al-'Abbar [28] to the author, " does not want to be dissolved in a union with Tripolitania." In a province in which such a feeling is still strong, the scheme of unity, in order to be acceptable to its people, must take into consideration the sensitivities of the people no less than material considerations.

When, therefore, the opportunity for achieving unity presented itself under favorable external conditions, the scheme of unity was bound to be in the nature of a compromise plan. Before we discuss the nature and form of the internal structure of the Libyan state as framed by the representatives of the three provinces, let us first turn to a study of the external forces that helped to bring the three provinces together and create the Libyan Union.

[25] See p. 25, above.

chapter V

The Making of a State

WHILE THE THREE Libyan territories—Cyrenaica and Tripolitania in particular—had been reluctantly debating the ways and means by which they would achieve unity, the external forces involved proved to be more constructive than the most optimistic elements working for unity had expected. Rarely in the life of a nation did external forces prove to be so helpful in overcoming centrifugal forces, for the experience of history demonstrates that internal dissension often invites foreign powers to extend their control over the country rather than to discourage internal discord. Weak and divided internally, Libya otherwise could scarcely have aspired to a place among the newly independent nations of the world. Her Arab supporters tried in international councils to secure for her a short-term tutelage under the aegis of a friendly power. But Libyan leaders who opposed tutelage were not discouraged and eventually won the case for their country's independence. They tried to enlist the support of all nations and rejected any form of foreign control. But Libya's greatest asset in achieving unity and independence, without having to pass through a transitional stage of tutelage, was the conflicting policies of the Great Powers. Not only had the cold war between the Eastern and Western Powers just begun, but the Western Powers themselves could not agree on a plan for the future of Libya, although several of them had cast covetous eyes on Libyan territory. Discord among the powers proved to be Libya's greatest advantage and her leaders played their cards cleverly by exploiting international rivalries.

111

We have already studied Libya's political development by analyzing internal forces. Let us now look at this development from a different perspective—the international angle.

Libya's Position After the War

Libya's position after the war was closely tied with the fate of other Italian colonies in Africa because Italy was still legally the possessor of sovereignty over all her former colonies. Thus when Libyan leaders demanded self-government after their country had been liberated from Italian control in 1943, they were told that a decision concerning the future of the country would have to await the signing of a peace treaty with Italy. Not until Italy had given up sovereignty over her colonies could Libya raise her voice as to what her future should be.

Libyans in exile began to work for the freedom of their country from the time when Italy entered the war against Britain, but after the war they became more active in international circles in order to insure that their country would not revert to Italian rule. Libyan leaders impressed upon the Great Powers their passionate desire for independence and showed unusual ability in exploiting the differences among the powers to secure their country's freedom. When a peace treaty was finally signed with Italy in 1947, Libyans had to await a decision on the larger question of the disposal of the Italian colonies, because the Italian treaty left the matter to be decided upon by the Big Four Powers, the signatories of the peace treaty with Italy. However, a decision on the disposal of the Italian colonies was not reached and Libya had to wait another two years before independence was secured through the United Nations in 1949. Two more years had to elapse before a national government was established and authority finally passed from foreign to Libyan hands. It was perhaps the combination of favorable circumstances—Mussolini's ill-advised entry into the war, traditional British support for the Sanusis, and discord among the Great Powers—that gave Libya the chance to rise quickly to statehood, before any other North African country could aspire to a similar position.

The Disposal of the Italian Colonies

Italy hoped to keep her colonial empire by placing the responsibility of her participation in the war on Mussolini. Thus upon Mussolini's fall from power in 1943, the new Italian government under Signor Bonomi made an effort to save part of its empire by renouncing claims to all territorial acquisitions made since Mussolini's rise to power. Libya, formally occupied in 1911, thus would have remained in Italian hands if the Great Powers had agreed to make such a concession. Great Britain, it is true, had promised Sayyid Idris in 1942 that Cyrenaica would not again fall under Italian control; [1] but this declaration was by no means intended to cover the entire Italian North African territory and Italy seemed to have entertained the desire to regain control of Tripolitania. Thus when Anthony Eden made a statement in the House of Commons on October 4, 1944, implying that Great Britain would oppose Italy's return to all of the colonies, the Italian Premier requested clarification. He was informed that the Eden statement was misunderstood.[2] So Italy remained hopeful that after the war her North African colonies might be restored to her.

Although Libya and all other Italian colonies had been touched upon at various international conferences, Potsdam in particular, no serious attempt was made to settle colonial questions until the Council of Foreign Ministers met in London in September, 1945, to consider the larger problem of drawing up a peace treaty with Italy. The Soviet government had indicated its desire to receive trusteeship for certain territories at the San Francisco Conference (1945), and a Soviet proposal for a specific trusteeship over Tripolitania was submitted at the Potsdam Conference (1945). The Italian government demanded the restoration of the entire Libyan territory, conceding certain rights to some powers, presumably Great Britain and the United States, to station forces there for security purposes.[3] The Great Powers ma...

[1] See p. 35, above.
[2] The *Times*, London, October 7, 1944.
[3] Prime Minister di Gasperi wrote to the Secretary of State of the United States on August 22, 1945: ". . . We gather that while no objection re...

tained that proposals relating to colonies should be a matter for the Council of Foreign Ministers to discuss.

The Council of Foreign Ministers seems to have agreed that, in principle, the Italian colonies should be brought under the trusteeship system of the United Nations, but there was considerable disagreement as to the form of the trusteeship and the country or countries to whom the administering authority should be entrusted. The United States submitted a plan for a " collective trusteeship " under the United Nations which, in the case of Libya, would last for ten years, at the end of which time that country would become independent.[4] The Soviet Union, on the ground that it had " wide experience " in " establishing friendly relations between different nationalities," proposed to take over the administration of Tripolitania and suggested to the council that ten years would be adequate to prepare the country for independence. Molotov, the Soviet Foreign Minister, assured the council that the " Soviet system " would not be introduced " into this territory, apart from the democratic order that is desired by the people." He explained that the Soviet Union desired to have a sea outlet on the Mediterranean and demanded such bases in Tripolitania.[5] However, neither France nor Great Britain was prepared to accept the Soviet proposal. Great Britain, on the other hand, was prepared to support the American proposal of

---

raised against Italian sovereignty in Tripolitania, strategic guarantees are being sought in Cyrenaica in order to afford full security to the bordering countries and to the international sea routes. We believe that such a security could be obtained through the establishment of "strategic areas," air and naval bases and other guarantees in the Tobruk sector and in Marmarica, without depriving Italy of the sovereignty on the Cyrenaica plateau, which she has already partly transformed into a suitable territory for her agricultural emigration " (*Department of State Bulletin*, Vol. XIII (1945), pp. 764–65).

[4] Opinion in the State Department concerning the Italian colonial question remained divided, and the American delegation, in presenting the proposal of collective trusteeship, was ready to agree to whatever compromise was necessary to all parties. Cf. James Byrnes, *Speaking Frankly* (New York, 1947), p. 98. See Vernon McKay, " The Future of Italy's Colonies," *Foreign Policy Reports* (January 1, 1946), pp. 273–74; and Benjamin Rivlin, *Italian Colonies* (New York, 195), pp. 9–10.

[5] Byrnes, *op. cit.*, p. 96. For the thesis that Russia needed an outlet on the Mediterranean, see Maurice Vernet, " The Soviet Union and the Mediterranean," *The Fortnightly* (December, 1945), pp. 363–68.

"collective trusteeship" subject to qualifications, but France was not willing to accept it even in principle, fearing the possible impact of such independence on her African possessions.

When the Council of Foreign Ministers reconvened in Paris six months later (April, 1946), more specific proposals had been formulated, but none of them met with the approval of the Council. To resolve the impasse, Great Britain proposed the immediate granting of independence to Libya. Finding that this proposal would eliminate the Soviet Union, Molotov modified his plan of individual trusteeship to that of a joint trusteeship. Under this plan the Italian colonies would be divided into four units, in each of these Italy would jointly exercise authority with one of the Big Four Powers, at the end of which the colonies would become independent. Tripolitania, Molotov suggested, would be jointly administered by the Soviet Union and Italy. His proposal was rejected.

The next step taken by the Soviet Union was to support the claim of Italy for a sole trusteeship over Tripolitania. To this proposal, both Britain and the United States, showed willingness to agree. Britain, however, was prepared to accept it only on condition that Cyrenaica would not be included under the Italian trusteeship and suggested that it should be placed under British trusteeship. The United States declared her readiness to accept the proposal provided that a definite date for the independence of Libya was fixed.[6] As a result no final agreement was reached nor had this impasse been resolved when the Council resumed its meeting on June 15. It was finally decided to insert in the peace treaty a provision deferring the question of the disposal of the Italian colonies for a year after the peace treaty with Italy became effective, during which time the Four Powers were to reach an agreement on the colonies. If an agreement was not reached, the matter would be referred to the United Nations General Assembly for a final decision. At the Paris Peace Conference, the Powers finally agreed on the wording of the article concerning the Italian colonies, the text of which reads as follows:

---

[6] Department of State, *Paris Meeting of the Foreign Ministers* (Publication No. 2537, Conference Series 86), pp. 4–5; Benjamin Rivlin, *op. cit.*, pp. 12–13.

Article 23. (1) Italy renounces all right and title to the Italian territorial possessions in Africa, i.e ., Libya, Eritrea, and Italian Somaliland.

(2) Pending their final disposal, the said possessions shall continue under their present administration.

(3) The final disposal of these possessions shall be determined jointly by the governments of the Soviet Union, of the United Kingdom, of the United States of America, and of France within one year from the coming into force of the present treaty, in the manner laid down in the joint declaration of February 10, 1947; issued by the said governments, which is reproduced in Annex 10.

The declaration of Four Powers, which was incorporated as Annex 11 of the Treaty of Peace, reads:

1. The governments of the Union of Soviet Socialist Republics, of the United Kingdom of Great Britain and Northern Ireland, of the United States of America, and of France agree that they will within one year from the coming into force of the treaty of peace with Italy bearing the date of February 10, 1947, jointly determine the final disposal of Italy's territorial possessions in Africa, to which, in accordance with Article 23 of the treaty, Italy renounces all right and title.

2. The final disposal of the territories concerned and the appropriate adjustment of their boundaries shall be made by the Four Powers in the light of the wishes and welfare of the inhabitants and the interests of peace and security, taking into consideration the views of other interested governments.

3. If, with respect to any of these territories, the Four Powers are unable to agree upon their disposal within one year from the coming into force of the treaty of peace with Italy, the matter shall be referred to the General Assembly of the United Nations for a recommendation, and the Four Powers agree to accept the recommendation and to take appropriate measures for giving effect to it.

4. The Deputies of the Foreign Ministers shall continue the consideration of the question of the disposal of the former Italian colonies with a view to submitting to the Council of Foreign Ministers their recommendations on this matter. They shall also send out commissions of investigation to any of the former Italian colonies in order to supply the Deputies with the necessary data on this question and to ascertain the views of the local population.[7]

---

[7] United Nations, *Treaty Series*, Vol. 49 (1950) , pp. 139, 214–15.

The function of the Paris Conference concerning the Italian colonies was merely to approve the proposals presented by the Four Powers in the treaty of peace. Certain doubts were raised concerning the competence of the General Assembly to make a decision on the matter, but the satisfactory settlement reached left no doubt as to the wisdom of referring the question to that Assembly.

Egypt and the Libyan Question

Egypt took keen interest in the Italian colonies, especially Libya and Eritrea, because of their geographical propinquity and the historical connections between her and these colonies. Thus, no sooner had the Four Powers met in London to discuss the question of a peace treaty with Italy than Egypt promptly submitted a memorandum (dated September 12, 1945) in which she expressed her interest in Libya and Eritrea and asked that she should be consulted on the final disposition of these colonies. The memorandum stated that Egypt and Libya were bound by common bonds and that Libya had been in the past either independent or united with Egypt, except during the relatively short Italian rule. Thus Egypt suggested that a plebiscite should be held in Libya to determine whether its people would prefer to attain independence or unite with Egypt. If Libya desired independence, Egypt would respect her desire and she could join the Arab League as an equal member with the other Arab states. Finally, the memorandum stated that if the Council of Foreign Ministers decided against holding a plebiscite and placed Libya under a sole trusteeship, the trusteeship should either be entrusted to Egypt or to the Arab League.[8]

Since no agreement had been reached at the initial meetings of the Council of Foreign Ministers, Egypt submitted another memorandum in January, 1946, in which she asked to be represented at the forthcoming peace conference in which the Italian peace treaty would be drawn up. Although Egypt was not invited

[8] The latter part of the memorandum dealt with Eritrea. For full text, see F. Shukri, *Milad Dawlat Libya al-Haditha* (Cairo, 1957), Vol. I, pp. 30–32.

as a participant, she was given assurance that her representative would be invited to submit the Egyptian viewpoints on the Italian colonies as an interested party. Thus, on August 21 and 23, 1946, the Egyptian representative at the Paris Conference made statements, which were later put in writing (August 30, 1946), in which the Egyptian views were presented. With regard to Libya, the Egyptian representative reiterated Egypt's demands as stated in earlier memoranda. More specifically, Egypt's desire to modify the Egyptian-Libyan frontier and to include within Egyptian territory the oasis of al-Jaghbub, the town of Sallum, and several other minor places was stated.[9] Since it seemed quite clear that Egypt had little chance of obtaining trusteeship over Libya, her demand for frontier rectification constituted the chief points stressed in subsequent memoranda.

The Arab League and the Libyan Question

The Arab League showed no less concern about the future of Libya than did Egypt, partly because the League regarded itself as the custodian of Arab interests generally,[10] and partly because it sought to place Libya, if she failed to obtain independence, either under the sole trusteeship of Egypt or under the collective trusteeship of the League itself. No less interested in Libyan affairs was 'Abd al-Rahman 'Azzam, the Secretary-General of the Arab League. He had been following the course of events in that country with a keen eye since his participation in its internal politics in World War I,[11] and he seems to have aspired to exercise personal influence over the country through some form of League tutelage. Thus, as early as September, 1945, he circulated a memorandum to the members of the Arab League in which he expressed views similar to those stated in the Egyptian memorandum to the Council of Foreign Ministers, and called upon the Arab states to press the Great Powers either to grant Libya independence on the basis of a plebiscite or to allow her

[11] See p. 21, above.
[10] The Arab League Pact states that the League considers in a general way " the affairs and interests " of all the Arab countries (Article 2).
[11] See p. 21, above.

to unite with Egypt.[12] 'Azzam submitted a memorandum to the Council of Foreign Ministers (September 28, 1945) in which he expressed views identical with those stated in his memorandum to the League members. In private conversations with the chiefs of delegations, he reiterated more emphatically his concern about the future of Libya lest she should fall again into the hands of Italy or any other colonial power.

The Libyan question was placed on the agenda of the Council of the Arab League for the first time on December 4, 1945. In that meeting the Council voted to endorse the proposals embodied in the memoranda presented by various Arab states in support either of Libyan independence or trusteeship under Egypt or the Arab League.[13] The matter was taken up again by the Council in its meeting on April 6, 1946, and a resolution was adopted calling upon the League members to impress upon the Great Powers consideration of the national aspirations of the Libyan people.[14] 'Azzam followed up this resolution by a circular sent to the League members in which he reiterated his views on the Libyan question and called upon the Arab states to support Libya's national aspirations.[15] 'Azzam brought the matter again before the Council of the League on June 9 and 10, 1946, and the Council adopted resolutions in support of Libyan national aspirations.[16] In its meeting on June 11, 1946, the Council endorsed a resolution taken by the heads of the Arab states at a meeting held in Inshas, Egypt, on May 30, 1946, in which the heads of states declared themselves in favor of Libyan independence.[17] The League Council, in subsequent meetings, expressed its support for Libya whenever the Secretary-General brought the matter to the attention of the members.[18]

[12] The Arab League, *The Libyan Question*, (Cairo, 1950), pp. 3–9.
[13] *Proceedings of the Council of the Arab League*, Second Session, 1945, pp. 179–81.
[14] *Ibid.*, Third Session, 1946, pp. 133–35.
[15] The Arab League, *The Libyan Question*, pp. 15–18.
[16] *Proceedings of the Council of the Arab League*, Fourth (Extraordinary) Session, 1946, pp. 24, 35.
[17] For text of the Inshas communique, see *ibid.* pp. 17–18.
[18] *Ibid.* Fifth Session, 1947, pp. 108–109, 348–50, Sixth Session, 1947, pp. 22–23, 39–40, 79–80, 82–83; Seventh Session, 1947, pp. 64, 191; *The Libyan Question*, pp. 27–32.

The personal views of 'Azzam concerning the Libyan question had become well known in Arab circles and his efforts in international councils in support of Egypt's claim to trusteeship aroused the criticism of many a Libyan patriot. Ever since he submitted the League's first memorandum to the Council of Foreign Ministers in September, 1945, he said in strongly worded statements that any attempt to place Libya under the control of a single European power would be entirely unacceptable to the Arabs. He declared to many a Western statesman that some form of an international administration in which Egypt participated would merit consideration, but he contended that the most satisfactory arrangement would be to place Libya under the trusteeship of the Arab League, with Egypt assuming the major responsibility due to common geographical consideration and Egypt's familiarity with the problems of that country. 'Azzam also expressed himself in favor of the unity of Cyrenaica and Tripolitania; but he said that if the unity and independence of the two territories were not possible, then Cyrenaica might be incorporated into Egypt.[19]

The Four Power Commission of Investigation

Upon the enforcement of the Italian Peace Treaty (September 15, 1947), the Deputies of the Council of Foreign Ministers began to work on the implementation of the provisions concerning the Italian colonies. The work of the deputies, which began on October 3, 1947, consisted in dispatching a commission of investigation to the Italian colonies, consulting with other "interested governments," and preparing recommendations to the Council of Foreign Ministers for a final decision on the disposition of the Italian colonies. Meanwhile, the Four Powers were considering other factors relevant to the colonial question, especially the Italian general elections of 1948, which both the Soviet and the Western Powers tried to exploit to their advantage.

The Peace Treaty provided that the decision on the disposition

[19] The writer's interview with 'Abd al-Rahman 'Azzam. See also *The Times*, London, June 18, 1946; and *The Spectator*, London, June 14, 1946.

of the Italian colonies should take into account the wishes and welfare of the inhabitants no less than considerations of peace and security. The Four Powers accordingly decided to dispatch a Commission of Investigation, composed of a representative from each,[20] to find out what the wishes of the people were and to report on the internal conditions of the territories. The Commission, appointed by the Deputies on October 20, 1947, was instructed to confine its report to facts and to refrain from making recommendations on the final disposition of the territories. The instructions were intended to insure that the Commission should go out to the colonies with an open mind, in search of the real wishes of the inhabitants. There were, however, differences of opinion among the representatives as to "what constituted a fact," owing to a different national approach to colonial questions.[21] These differences were copiously embodied in memoranda, brackets, and footnotes.

The Commission spent seven months in the colonies, from November, 1947, to May, 1948. It arrived in Libya on March 6, 1948, and left on May 20, 1948, having spent forty days in Tripolitania, ten in Fazzan, and twenty-five in Cyrenaica. On the way back, the Commission stopped in Rome to hear the views of several former Italian personnel.

When the Commission arrived in Tripoli, the people were naturally in a state of intense political excitement concerning a question which was to them most important concerning their future life. The leader of the Free National Bloc, 'Ali al-Faqih Hasan, was arrested by the Military Administrator in order " to ensure the free expression of opinion " as it was then stated.[22] The Commission was preceded by the arrival in Tripoli of Bashir al-Sa'dawi, head of the Libyan Liberation Committee, whose influence on the political parties resulted in the demand for a

[20] The chief representatives were: John E. Utter (United States), F. E. Stafford (Great Britain), Burin des Roziers (France), and first, Artemy Fedorov and later, N. I. Klinov (Soviet Union).

[21] See the remarks of the chief British representative, F. E. Stafford, " The Ex-Italian colonies," in *International Affairs*, Vol. XXV (1947), pp. 47–55.

[22] 'Ali al-Faqih Hasan told the present writer that he was arrested by the British authorities in order to enable Sa'dawi, who was at the outset on good terms with the British authorities, to rally all the parties together and present views acceptable to the British.

united independent Libya. Thus, in spite of rivalries among leaders, the political parties had been able to pose as a unified national front. They presented a declaration of policy embodying three principal points, namely, complete and immediate independence, the unity of Libya (comprising all provinces), and membership in the Arab League. The members of the Commission sought to interview people who were outside the influence of political parties and some who were picked at random. They were impressed by the fact that practically all those who had been interviewed asked for immediate independence. Although the claim for the unity of Libya and membership in the Arab League was neither unanimous nor properly understood, it was clear that all leaders wanted independence and did not want foreign rule. Strong opposition was voiced against Italian rule, and only a small minority expressed itself in favor of Italy. The political parties expressed friendly feelings toward the Italian settlers and stated that they would give them complete equality of rights, once independence was attained. The Jews aligned themselves with public demand, and the Italian settlers made it clear that they would not welcome further Italian immigration. Nevertheless, the Commission, finding the country not self-supporting and its existence and future development dependent on assistance from foreign sources, was unanimous in reporting that it was not ready for independence.[23]

Fazzan was the next province to be visited by the Commission. Not only did the Commission find a vast area sparsely populated (50,000 inhabitants scattered in an area of about 125,000 square miles), but also backward in almost all aspects of life. Although it was not easy to find out what the real feeling of the people was, since many had only a vague idea about political views, they seemed in the main to have been content with the French administration. A few articulate leaders declared themselves in

---

[23] It was during the Commission's visit to Tripoli, on the eve of the Italian general elections, that the Soviet Union declared that it was in favor of entrusting Italy with trusteeship over all her former colonies. " Some local commentators," said Stafford, the chief British representative, " acidly remarked that this seemed to prejudge the issues which the Commission was investigating " (Stafford, " The Ex-Italian Colonies," *International Affairs*, Vol. XXV (1949), p. 53).

favor of the unity and independence of Libya.[24] Due to the poverty of the inhabitants and its meager resources, the Commission expressed serious doubt as to whether Fazzan could ever become an independent country.

Finally, the Commission visited Cyrenaica. The inhabitants, especially the tribes, wanted an independent Cyrenaica under Amir Idris, with any form of government he approved, even though the country was not self-supporting. The chief political organization that voiced an opinion on the future of the region was, of course, the National Congress, which had superseded all previous political parties (except, perhaps, the Mukhtar group), and its program was clearly defined in these terms: complete and immediate independence of Cyrenaica and constitutional government under Amir Idris and his heirs. Cyrenaican leaders showed a willingness to unite with Tripolitania only on these terms. Dislike of the Italians was deep-rooted in this area and rejection of them was more outspoken. The Amir told the Commission that he was in agreement with what the people had said and he desired to co-operate with Great Britain on the basis of an alliance. Owing to this unanimity of opinion, the Commission reached a greater measure of agreement on Cyrenaica than elsewhere. However, due to the deficiencies of the region, economic and otherwise, it was felt that foreign assistance would be essential for many years to come.

It was no easy task for an international commission to assess the facts in an area where the policies and interests of the Great Powers were conflicting. Since France and the Soviet Union—the latter changed its attitude only on the eve of the Commission's visit to Libya—favored the return of Italy to Libya, their representatives naturally were not inclined to sympathize with the national aspirations of the Libyan people. Although Great Britain and the United States were willing to support an Italian trusteeship over Tripolitania and British trusteeship over Cyrenaica, their representatives showed a willingness to accept the demand for independence as the genuine wish of the Libyan people.

Despite these divergences and preconceived notions, the findings

[24] See p. 108, above.

of the Commission indicated general agreement on certain fundamental questions. It is clear from the Commission's report that there was an almost unanimous sentiment on the part of the people for freedom from foreign rule and a genuine aspiration for independence, even though a full realization of the responsibility and its implications was perhaps lacking. A corollary of the desire for freedom was the lack of sentiment for a return to Italian rule. This feeling was expressed in terms varying from mere lack of sentiment for the Italians to violent denunciation of Italian oppression. However, due to the poverty of the country and its meager resources, concerning which there was full agreement, the Commission reached the inevitable conclusion that Libya was not self-supporting, that it would need foreign assistance for many years to come, and that it therefore was not yet ready for independence.[25]

The findings of the Commission, especially its reference to Libya's unpreparedness for independence, came as a surprise to the Libyan people. The desire of the French to keep Fazzan under their control, their support for an Italian trusteeship over Tripolitania, and the Soviet Union's new move in favor of the return of the Italian colonies to Italy created confusion and frustration throughout the country; but the leaders did not give up the struggle for their national ambitions and were counting on the support of the Arab states and the possibility that some of the Great Powers might change their stand in their favor.

Viewpoints of Other " Interested Governments "

The Italian Peace Treaty provided that the Council of Foreign Ministers, before making a decision on the disposition of the Italian colonies, should not only take into consideration the wishes of the population, but also consult with other " interested governments." The term " interested governments " was construed to include all the powers that signed the Italian treaty,

---

[25] See [Council of Foreign Ministers], *Four Power Commission of Investigation for the Former Italian Colonies*, Vol. III: *Report on Libya* (mimeographed).

with the addition of Egypt. Thus nineteen states had been invited to express their views on the question of the Italian colonies.[26]

Two states claimed Libya in part or as a whole. Italy asked that the whole of Libya, together with all other African colonies, should be returned to her in the capacity of an administering authority under the United Nations trusteeship system. In support of her claims Italy argued that after the fall of Mussolini, she became an ally and therefore no longer was an enemy. She was prepared to give up the colonies acquired under the Fascist regime, but Libya had been annexed by Italy before Mussolini came into power. Italy's principal motive in acquiring the colonies was to use them to absorb her surplus population, and not for imperialistic exploitation. It was for this reason that Italy wanted colonies and would be willing to undertake the trusteeship over Libya under the United Nations charter.

Egypt, motivated by cultural, geographical, and historical connections, supported Libyan unity and independence. However, if the Four Powers were not prepared to grant Libya immediate independence, Egypt felt that in view of her close proximity and the common cultural and historical heritage, she was entitled to be the administering authority under a United Nations trusteeship. Egypt also presented certain specific territorial claims, mainly on the Egyptian-Libyan frontier, for national security. At the outset Egypt claimed the plateau of Sallum and the oasis of Jaghbub, but later she demanded also the port of al-Bardiya and the oases of Arkinu, 'Uwaynat, and Sara. The area claimed by Egypt, extending from the Mediterranean to the Libyan-Sudanese frontier, was held to be part of Egyptian territory ceded by Britain to Italy when both Egypt and Libya were under foreign rule.[27]

The viewpoints of the other interested governments varied greatly, but no specific territorial claims were presented by any one of them. Most of these states were in favor of entrusting

---

[26] They were: Australia, Belgium, Brazil, Byelorussia, Canada, China, Czechoslovakia, Egypt, Ethiopia, Greece, India, Italy, Netherlands, New Zealand, Pakistan, Poland, Ukraine, Union of South Africa, and Yugoslavia.

[27] For the text of the various memoranda submitted by Egypt to the Council of Foreign Ministers, see Shukri, *op. cit.*, Vol. I, pp. 206–22.

Libya, whether united or divided, to an administering authority
under the United Nations Trusteeship Council. As to the administering power, the Soviet Union, Brazil, Byelorussia, Czechoslovakia, Netherlands, Poland, Ukraine, and Yugoslavia were in
favor of Italy. China proposed immediate independence; Egypt
and Pakistan proposed an Arab League state (i. e. Egyptian)
trusteeship if independence were not granted. Australia, Canada,
New Zealand, and the Union of South Africa proposed British
trusteeship; and India suggested a United Nations trusteeship
without naming a specific administering authority.[28]

Recommendations of the Deputies
and the Action of the Four Powers

Upon receiving the report of the Commission of Investigation
and hearing the viewpoints of other interested governments, the
Deputies submitted a set of recommendations to the Council
of Foreign Ministers concerning the disposition of the Italian
colonies. The Deputies were inclined to place Libya under the
trusteeship of one or two of the powers, but disagreed as to when
the country should be placed under trusteeship and under which
power. The Soviet Union proposed Italian trusteeship for the
whole country; Britain and the United States proposed British
trusteeship for Cyrenaica and postponement of a decision for
one year of Tripolitania and Fazzan; and France proposed postponement of a decision for a year for the whole country.

The stage was now set for the Four Powers to act. A meeting
was held in Paris on September 13, 1948, in which the recommendations of the deputies were considered. Not only did the
powers fail to agree as to what to decide about Libya, but also
about other colonies. The conflict between the Soviet and the
Western blocs had become so intense that it influenced the views
of the Four Powers on the future of the Italian colonies. The
Soviet Union, abandoning her support for Italian trusteeship,
now reverted to collective trusteeship, which was originally pro-

[28] For a summary of the views of the nineteen states, see Benjamin Rivlin,
op. cit., pp. 22–23.

posed by the United States and rejected by the Soviet Union.
Great Britain and France, while they had been in favor of
collective trusteeship, now rejected the new Soviet proposal.

It became quite clear that there was no common ground for
a final action and the question, in accordance with the provision
of the Peace Treaty empowering the General Assembly of the
United Nations to act as the final arbiter, was referred to that
Assembly, scheduled to hold its third regular session on September
15, 1948.

The Libyan Question Before the United Nations

1. *Preliminary Discussion.* Although the Libyan question was
placed on the agenda of the first part of the third session of the
General Assembly, then meeting in Paris, the delegates had
neither the time to study nor to consult with their governments
on the matter. The question was therefore deferred to the second
part of the session to be held at Lake Success in April, 1949.

The Italian colonies were the first item on the agenda of Committee I (Political and Security). The Committee decided to
invite Italy to send a representative to participate in the discussion without the right to vote and, at the suggestion of Sir
Zafrullah Khan, Foreign Minister of Pakistan, a hearing was
given to representatives of the principal native organizations
in the colonies. Libya, after a careful examination of the requests
of local organizations, was represented by the Cyrenaican National Congress, the Libyan Liberation Committee, The National
Association of Refugees, the Association of Libyan Ex-Servicemen,
and the Jewish Community. The representatives of these organizations were given hearings by Committee I and submitted
written statements. They were agreed concerning unity and independence, but their statements varied somewhat as to the form
of unity.[29]

The Committee's deliberations revealed divergent views on the
future status of the colonies. Referring specifically to Libya,
the Soviet representative stated that peace and security in that

---

[29] The writer's interviews with Mansur Qadara, 'Ali al-'Unayzi, and Khalil
al-Qallal.

region required the withdrawal of British forces and the establishment of a United Nations trusteeship over Libya. Great
Britain and the United States replied that peace in that area
could not be maintained through direct United Nations administration, and that British bases in Cyrenaica and Tripolitania
were necessary for peace. Egypt's representative supported the
view that Libya was ready for independence, while others raised
doubt as to its preparedness for immediate independence.

The Latin American bloc, hoping that an agreement might
be reached before the meeting of the Fourth Session of the
General Assembly, proposed to postpone action. A draft resolution was presented providing that independence would be
granted to Libya at the end of a ten-year period if the General
Assembly decided that such a step were appropriate, and that a
committee (composed of Egypt, Italy, Britain, and the United
States) should submit to the Fourth Session the terms and conditions under which Libya would be placed under trusteeship.

The debate in Committee I revealed no common ground for
action. The Latin American bloc declared itself to be in favor
of Italian trusteeship and the Arab-Asian bloc favored independence. No compromise—although several formulas were proposed—was able to obtain a sufficient majority for a decision. A
subcommittee was established to study and propose a resolution
based on the various viewpoints.[30] Hardly had the subcommittee
started to work when an agreement between Britain and Italy
was announced which provided a fresh topic for discussion.

2. *The Bevin-Sforza Plan.* On the day of its first meeting, the
Subcommittee was confronted with the unexpected news that
Ernest Bevin and Count Carlo Sforza, the British and Italian
Foreign Ministers, had come to an agreement in London on the
question of the Italian colonies. The agreement was a compromise plan, based on the one hand on the British war promise
that Italy would not be allowed to return to Cyrenaica, and on
the other, on the efforts of the Latin American bloc to support
Italy. The Bevin-Sforza plan satisfied both Italy, by promising

[30] Composed of Australia, Brazil, Chile, Denmark, Egypt, Ethiopia, France,
India, 'Iraq, Mexico, Poland, Union of South Africa, Soviet Union, United
Kingdom, and United States.

her a United Nations Trusteeship over Tripolitania, and Britain, by offering her a trusteeship over Cyrenaica. Moreover, France was to receive the trusteeship over Fazzan. The plan was also based on the principle that Libya would be re-established as an independent state at the end of ten years, if the General Assembly decided that such a step was appropriate. The Italian trusteeship over Tripolitania was to begin in 1951 upon the termination of British military administration.

Due to the compromise nature of the plan, it received the support of Great Britain, the United States, and the Latin American states, although it was repudiated by the Arab, Asian, and Soviet blocs on the ground that it ignored the national aspirations of the inhabitants of Libya. On May 13, the plan was approved by the Subcommittee and a resolution was presented to Committee I. Concerning Libya the draft reads:

> That Libya be granted independence ten years from the date of adoption of this Resolution, provided the General Assembly then decided that this step was appropriate:
>
> (a) That Cyrenaica be placed under the International Trusteeship System, with the United Kingdom as the administering authority, without prejudice to its incorporation in a united Libya;
>
> (b) That Fazzan be placed under the International Trusteeship System, with France as the administering authority, also without prejudice to its incorporation in a united Libya;
>
> (c) That Tripolitania be placed under the International Trusteeship System, by the end of 1951, with Italy as administering authority, also without prejudice to its incorporation in a united Libya. During the interim period, the present British temporary administration should continue, with the assistance of an Advisory Council consisting of representatives of Egypt, France, Italy, the United Kingdom, the United States, and a representative of the people of the territory. The Advisory Council should determine its scope and duties in consultation with the administering authorities.
>
> That the powers charged with the administration of the three territories take all necessary measures to promote the co-ordination of their activities in order that nothing be done to prejudice the attainment of an independent Libyan state, the Trusteeship Council to be responsible for supervising the execution of this provision.[31]

---

[31] United Nations Document (A/C. I/466); Rivlin, *op. cit.*, p. 36.

The resolution also provided that agreements to implement the recommendations be framed by the Trusteeship Council and the Interim Committee of the General Assembly (Little Assembly).

Before the Subcommittee's resolution was accepted by Committee I, it was subjected to sharp criticism, especially by Arab representations. The chief points of criticism were that the resolution was based on a compromise agreement reached outside the United Nations, that it satisfied the Great Powers but ignored the interests of the native population, and that it divided Libya into three political entities when the principle of unity had already been accepted. The criticisms of the Arab and Asian representatives were even more violent.

Several amendments to the draft resolutions were rejected; the only one adopted was a Norwegian amendment stipulating that independence for Libya would be automatic at the end of ten years, unless the Assembly decided otherwise. The resolution as amended was accepted by the Committee due to the strong support given by Great Britain, the United States, France, and the Latin American bloc. The vote was 34 to 16, with 7 abstentions; but the specific vote concerning the proposal to place Tripolitania under Italian trusteeship was only 32 to 17, with 8 abstentions, which raised doubt as to the possibility of the acceptance of the whole resolution by the General Assembly, since Italian trusteeship over Tripolitania was the principal reason for Latin American support of the plan. This initial lack of agreement on the whole resolution provided the Arab and Asian delegations with the opportunity of influencing a sufficient number of delegates so as to defeat the resolution for lack of the two-thirds vote necessary for its adoption by the General Assembly.

From the time when the news concerning the Bevin-Sforza plan reached Tripoli, disturbances and protests started and continued until the fate of the Bevin-Sforza plan was sealed at the General Assembly on May 17. It may have seemed to the Tripolitanians that the impression they made by violent protest dissuaded the Assembly from voting for its adoption. However, the Assembly's failure to adopt the plan was caused by dissension among the Great Powers rather than by street demonstrations in

Tripoli city. The Arab and Asian delegates, supported by the Soviet bloc, denounced the plan as based on "hegemony and domination." The Polish representative attacked it as "a stab in the back of the United Nations," and stated that it divided the Italian colonies "without regard for the inhabitants of those territories and their true economic interests or for geographical considerations." [32] Sir Zafrullah Khan, Foreign Minister of Pakistan, criticized the plan on the ground that it divided Libya, although he declared himself in favor of collective trusteeship:

> Instead of enjoying collective trusteeship under the United Nations, or trusteeship under one power, Libya was faced with the prospect of division into three parts, with three forms of administration using three different languages, which would ensure the further disruption of its economy and the indefinite postponement of its independence, despite the professions of those supporting the draft resolution.[33]

The Western Powers, the United States and England in particular, explained that this was the best solution that could be expected under the circumstances. Warren Austin, the representative of the United States, said:

> It had not been possible to find a solution which could completely reconcile the various proposals made. It was possible, however, to apply the trusteeship system of the United Nations. It was also possible to work out agreements designed to stabilize the rights of the populations concerned in accordance with the Charter and the peace treaty with Italy. [But] such measures did not constitute imperialism or colonialism, as it had been alleged.[34]

When the vote was taken, only 33 voted in favor of Italian trusteeship over Tripolitania, 17 against, with 8 abstentions—one vote less than the two-thirds majority necessary for its adoption. The Haitian delegate, Emile Saint-Lot, unexpectedly voted against the plan. As the resolution was acceptable to the Latin American countries only on condition that Italy was to obtain

[32] United Nations, *Official Records of the Third Session of the General Assembly*, Part II, p. 528.
[33] *Ibid.*, p. 534.
[34] *Ibid.*, p. 549.

trusteeship over Tripolitania, the paragraphs providing for British trusteeship over Cyrenaica were unacceptable to the Latin American bloc. The whole plan accordingly was overwhelmingly defeated by a combination of the Latin American, Arab-Asian, and Soviet votes. In the final vote only 14 were in favor; 37 were against, with 7 abstentions. The Libyan protests against the Bevin-Sforza plan exerted indirect influence by provoking the Arab delegates both to enlist the support of other interested delegates, and to persuade still others, especially the delegate of Haiti, to vote against it.[35] It was this combination of the Arab-Asian and Soviet blocs that was in the last analysis responsible for the defeat of the Bevin-Sforza plan.

The news of the Assembly's rejection of the plan was received with " painful surprise " by the Italian government. The plan, it was held, represented what Italy felt to be her minimum colonial ambitions. Count Sforza, co-author of the plan, regretted that " the sacrifices made by Italy in regard to her former African territories have failed to satisfy a majority composed mostly of delegations representing colored people and small nations." [36] Count Sforza, however, was aware of the growing anti-colonial movement and the fact that the days of colonialism, even if Italy had been reinstated as a colonial power, were numbered. In a speech at Chicago in June, 1941, he declared that " we must dismiss from our minds any colonialistic idea." [37] Thus when his plan was defeated, he showed Italy's readiness to support Libya's unity and he was the first to modify Italy's position toward Libya's independence—a prudent attitude which gained for Italy the support of the Arab bloc in obtaining the trusteeship over Eritrea and Somaliland. However, Count Sforza's failure to secure the trusteeship over Tripolitania aroused criticism by those who regarded Italy's defeat as a blow to Italian foreign policy.[38]

---

[35] 'Ali al-'Unayzi, a member of the Libyan delegation, proved to be instrumental in persuading Emile Saint-Lot to cast his vote in favor of Libya. Saint-Lot, after Libya's rise to statehood, was made an honorary citizen of Libya.

[36] Sforza's statement in *New York Times*, May 19, 1949.

[37] Count Carlo Sforza, " The Near East in World Politics," in P. W. Ireland, ed., *The Near East: Problems and Prospects* (Chicago, 1942) , p. 6.

[38] Needless to say, the rejection of the Bevin-Sforza plan led to general

3. *Compromise.* Failure to obtain the two-thirds majority necessary to place Tripolitania under Italian trusteeship prompted the Latin American bloc to withdraw its support for the resolution as a whole. This meant that the question of the Italian colonies had to be postponed until the fourth session of the General Assembly, and a resolution to this effect was proposed by the Polish delegation.[39]

It became clear, however, that any solution which would have a chance of adoption would have to be acceptable to the Latin American and the Arab-Asian blocs, since their lack of agreement, as demonstrated in the vote on the question of Italian trusteeship over Tripolitania, would result in a stalemate over the whole question of Italian colonies. An agreement between the two blocs, therefore, would have to be in the form of a compromise. The Arab-Asian bloc wanted self-government for the colonies in general and the Arab states insisted on independence for Libya. A compromise satisfactory to the Arab-Asian bloc would be a formula granting immediate independence to Libya and trusteeship over the other colonies. Thinking along this line gradually developed, and the Italian and the Latin American delegations moved in this direction. Meanwhile, Britain and the United States, having failed to obtain the necessary vote for placing Libya under trusteeship, quickly realized that an alternative to trusteeship would be independence. As a result, the formula of a united independent Libya gradually gained ground.

4. *The General Assembly's Resolution.* The Libyan question (as part of the larger question of the Italian colonies) was taken up at first by Committee I. Italy was invited to participate in the discussion and representatives of various national organizations (selected by a subcommittee) appeared before the Committee. Cyrenaica was naturally represented by the National Congress, and Tripolitania by the National Congress and the Independence Party. The Jewish community of Tripolitania was also invited to send a representative.

---

rejoicing in Tripolitania, while in England it was received with mixed feelings.

[39] United Nations, *Official Records of the Third Session of the General Assembly*, Part II, pp. 604-8.

When trusteeship over Libya was rejected, the agreement on independence became almost a foregone conclusion. Both Great Britain and the United States declared themselves in favor of independence, despite the "backwardness" of the country, but held that a transitional period of three to five years was necessary to prepare the country to stand alone. The Soviet Union, in the guise of championing the cause of colonial areas, called for "immediate" independence, the withdrawal of foreign forces, and the liquidation of all military bases within three months. France, although in favor of independence, was not in favor of the idea of Libyan unity. Italy's position, as stated by Count Sforza, had changed from that of coveting tutelage to that of favoring immediate independence. The Arab and Asian delegations were all in favor of immediate independence. A variety of proposals was presented, ranging from immediate independence, independence as soon as practicable, to Libyan independence at the end of three years. On October 11, a subcommittee of seventeen, which held meetings between October 11 and November 1, 1949, was appointed for the purpose of drafting a resolution.[40] A series of compromises having been reached, the subcommittee drafted a resolution to the effect that Libya was to receive independence as soon as possible, and in any case not later than January 1, 1952. Questions relating to Libyan unity, the role of the United Nations in achieving independence, and the withdrawal of foreign forces consumed most of the committee's time. After a prolonged discussion, however, a draft resolution was finally adopted by 49 votes to 1, with 8 abstentions.[41] The text of the draft resolution relevant to Libya follows:

1. That Libya, comprising Cyrenaica, Tripolitania, and Fazzan, shall be constituted an independent and sovereign state;

2. That this independence shall become effective as soon as possible and in any case not later than January 1, 1952;

[40] They included: Argentina, Australia, Brazil, Chile, China, Czechoslovakia, Denmark, Egypt, Ethiopia, France, Guatemala, India, 'Iraq, Liberia, Mexico, Pakistan, Poland, Union of South Africa, USSR, United Kingdom, and United States.

[41] For the work of the Subcommittee and the debate of the Committee I, see *United Nations Documents*, General Assembly, A/1089 (November 15, 1949), pp. 1–21.

3. That a constitution for Libya, including the form of the government, shall be determined by representatives of the inhabitants of Cyrenaica, Tripolitania, and Fazzan meeting and consulting together in a National Assembly;

4. That, for the purpose of assisting the people of Libya in the formulation of the constitution and the establishment of an independent government, there shall be a United Nations Commissioner in Libya appointed by the General Assembly and a Council to aid and advise him;

5. That the United Nations Commissioner, in consultation with the Council, shall submit to the Secretary-General an annual report and such other special reports as he may consider necessary. To these reports shall be added any memorandum or document that the United Nations Commissioner or a member of the Council may wish to bring to the attention of the United Nations;

6. That the Council shall consist of ten members, namely:

(a) One representative nominated by the government of each of the following countries: Egypt, France, Italy, Pakistan, the United Kingdom, and the United States;

(b) One representative of the people of each of the three regions of Libya and one representative of the minorities in Libya;

7. That the United Nations Commissioner shall appoint the representatives mentioned in paragraph 6 (b), after consultation with the administrative powers, the representatives of the governments mentioned in paragraph 6 (a), leading personalities and representatives of political parties and organizations in the territories concerned;

8. That, in the discharge of his functions, the United Nations Commissioner shall consult and be guided by the advice of the members of his Council; it being understood that he may call upon different members to advise him in respect to different regions or different subjects;

9. That the United Nations Commissioner may offer suggestions to the General Assembly, to the Economic and Social Council, and to the Secretary-General as to the measures that the United Nations might adopt during the transitional period regarding the economic and social problems of Libya;

10. That the administering powers in co-operation with the United Nations Commissioner:

(a) Initiate immediately all necessary steps for the transfer of power to duly constituted independent government;

(b) Administer the territories for the purpose of assisting in the establishment of Libyan unity and independence, co-operate in the formation of governmental institutions and co-ordinate their activities to this end;

(c) Make an annual report to the General Assembly on the steps taken to implement these recommendations;

11. That upon its establishment as an independent state, Libya shall be admitted to the United Nations in accordance with Article 4 of the Charter.[42]

The draft resolution having been adopted by an overwhelming majority in Committee I, the granting of independence by the General Assembly became almost certain. The report of the Committee, prepared by the representative of Panama, was submitted to the General Assembly on November 19, 1949. The debate lasted till November 21.

The representative of 'Iraq opened the discussion by declaring his government's support for the Committee's proposal. The British representative declared his country's support of the proposal, although he expressed doubt concerning its details; he went on to say that his government " would cheerfully and fully co-operate with the Commissioner and his Council in their assigned task." [43] Sir Zafrullah Khan, Foreign Minister of Pakistan, expressed the feeling of all those who favored Libyan independence when he said:

[The] resolution regarding the disposal of the former Italian colonies had not met with the approval of all delegations. His delegation was, however, gratified that considerable progress towards an ideal solution had been made during the current session, and that the draft resolution represented fair compromise between what each delegation might regard as ideal and what was practicable from every point of view. . . . The proposal with regard to Libya commanded a more nearly unanimous support in the General Assembly than the proposals with regard to the other two former

---

[42] *Ibid.*, pp. 22–23.
[43] United Nations, *Official Records of the Fourth Session of the General Assembly*, 1949, pp. 266–67.

colonies. It was a matter of very great satisfaction that the United Nations had given practical proof of wise statesmanship in handling the problem of Libya. . . .[44]

In spite of doubts raised by the French delegation as to the wisdom of the short time limit for independence, and the protest of the Soviet Union delegation that Libya should be granted immediate independence, the resolution was adopted by a vote of 48 to 1, with 9 abstentions.

Having succeeded in resolving the question of the former Italian colonies in a relatively short period, the United Nations demonstrated the possibility of the decisiveness of collective action at a time when the Four Powers failed to agree on a settlement for almost four years. The final settlement of this question enhanced the prestige of the United Nations and supplied a precedent for resolving political issues by having recourse to an international body.

Implementation of the General Assembly's Resolution

In accordance with the General Assembly's resolution, the United Nations was to keep a watchful eye on the internal development of Libya and was to be fully informed by reports presented by its Commissioner. Furthermore, in any question that might arise in consequence of the Commissioner's discharge of his powers, whether with regard to the interpretations of his terms of reference or in his relations with other interested powers, the United Nations was the final arbiter.

On December 10, 1949, the General Assembly appointed Adrian Pelt, Assistant Secretary-General of the United Nations, as the United Nations Commissioner in Libya.[45] The Council which

---

[44] Ibid., p. 279.
[45] Adrian Pelt, a former member of the League of Nations Secretariat, had had long experience with the working of international organizations before he joined the United Nations. Before he assumed his position as United Nations Commissioner in Libya, Pelt served as Assistant Secretary-General for conference and general services. He was born in 1892.

was to advise Pelt consisted of representatives of the powers
named by the General Assembly.[46] Pelt went to Libya for a
preliminary study of the situation. He arrived in Tripoli on
January 18 and visited the three provinces. In a statement issued
in Tripoli, he outlined the purpose of his mission as follows:

> I should like to take this opportunity to tell you in general terms
> the purpose of my mission. My terms of reference are clear: they
> state that the United Nations Commissioner will assist the people
> of Libya in the formulation of their constitution and in the estab-
> lishment of an independent government. The Commissioner is also
> instructed, after consultation with the administering powers, the
> members of the Council, and the leaders and representatives of the
> political parties and organizations in Libya, to appoint the repre-
> sentatives of Libya in the Council. It is not my function to govern
> your territory; that remains within the competence of the admin-
> istering powers until you assume it for yourselves.[47]

Pelt spent three weeks in Libya. In order to set up the Advisory Council, he concentrated his major effort on consultation
with the administering powers, the Amir of Cyrenaica, and the
principal political parties and leaders of the three provinces. He
requested Libyan leaders to submit to him the name of one
agreed candidate for each of the four seats specified in the United
Nations resolution. Only Fazzan submitted the name of an
agreed candidate, selected by the Assembly of Representatives.
After a prolonged discussion and consultation, the Amir of
Cyrenaica on March 28 submitted eight names and invited Pelt
to select one of them. In Tripolitania the political parties submitted seven names, and the minorities four names. From these
Pelt selected four representatives, after consultation with the
administering powers and the representatives of the six powers
named by the General Assembly. The Advisory Council for

----

[46] These were appointed by their governments as follows: Egypt, Muhammad Kamil Salim; France, Georges Balay; Italy, Baron Giuseppe Vitaliano
Confalomiri; Pakistan, Abdur Rahim Khan; United Kingdom, Sir Hugh
Stonehewer Bird; United States, Lewis Clark.
[47] United Nations, [First] *Annual Report of the United Nations Commissioner in Libya*, 1950, p. 39 (hereafter referred to as Pelt's *Annual Report*).

Libya, composed of ten members, was duly established on April 5, 1950.[48]

The Advisory Council of Ten

In addition to the United Nations Commissioner, the resolution of the General Assembly provided that "a Council to aid and advise him [the Commissioner]" should be appointed, and the Commissioner, in consultation with this Council, submit to the Secretary-General an annual report (paragraphs 4–5). The resolution also provided that in the discharge of his functions the "Commissioner shall consult and be guided by the advice of the members of his Council, it being understood that he may call upon different members to advise him in respect to different regions or different subjects" (paragraph 8).

The Council was organized soon after the Commissioner had accepted his assignment; six members were appointed by the powers named in the General Assembly's resolution and four by the Commissioner in consultation with Libyan leaders. Consisting of ten members, it was often referred to as the Council of Ten.

The United Nations Commissioner, it is clear, was under an obligation to consult the Council, but was he under an obligation to accept the advice of the Council? Could the Council exercise a veto power over the Commissioner? These were matters of principle which the Council was bound to discuss when it began to work on April 25, 1950. The issue was raised in connection with a question asked by the representative of Pakistan as to whether the administering powers were prepared to transfer powers to the Libyan people. In the Commissioner's opinion, the General Assembly's resolution did not provide for any transfer of power to the people of Libya during the transitional period, but only to "a duly constituted independent government." [49]

---

[48] The Four Libyan representatives were as follows: Cyrenaica, 'Ali al-Jirbi (replaced later by 'Ali al-'Unayzi); Tripolitania, Mustafa Mizran; Fazzan, Ahmad al-Hajj al-Sanusi (replaced later by Muhammad Bin 'Uthman); the Minorities, Giacomo Marchino.

[49] Pelt's *First Annual Report*, 1950, p. 17.

The representatives of Pakistan and Egypt insisted that the
Council, under paragraph 8 of the resolution, must be consulted
by the Commissioner "on any matter in which he might co-
operate with the administering powers," and the representative
of Egypt went so far as to add that "the Commissioner was
indeed bound by paragraph 8 of the resolution to accept and to
follow the advice of the Council in all cases." The Commissioner,
supported by other representatives,[50] stated his view on the question of his relationship with the administering powers, saying
that he was "solely responsible" for his actions to the United
Nations, although he had often "consulted them," and that he
had kept the Council duly informed.[51]

Of the ten members, the representatives of Pakistan and Egypt
often gave dissenting opinions on matters relating to the role of
the administering authorities and the constitutional form of
the Libyan state. The representative of Egypt, acting upon
instructions from his home government, often echoed the political
aspirations of the National Congress of Tripolitania, especially
on the question of federalism vs. unity, and the representative
of Pakistan supported the views of the representative of Egypt.[52]

Having taken the preliminary steps, Adrian Pelt proceeded
to construct his plan for shaping a constitutional framework
for Libya by the formation of a National Assembly. He followed
a practical approach in the discharge of his task and, within the
short span of less than two years, was able to announce the
fulfillment of his mission.

---

[50] He also consulted his legal adviser (see *ibid.*, pp. 64–69).

[51] *Ibid.*, p. 17.

[52] In an interview with Muhammad Kamil Salim, representative of Egypt,
I raised a query as to why the representative of Pakistan had invariably
supported him. Salim replied that Abdur Rahim Khan, the representative
of Pakistan, was acting upon instructions from his government that he
should support the representative of Egypt. When I asked Sir Zafrullah
Khan, the Foreign Minister of Pakistan, whether he had given such instructions, he denied that such instructions had ever been given, but he candidly
said that he had told Abdur Rahim Khan to be guided by the representative
of Egypt, since Egypt was well-acquainted with Libya's problems.

chapter VI

Constitutional Evolution

N O ISSUE HAS STIRRED more controversy and excitement
among Libyans since the achievement of independence than
that of drawing up a constitutional framework for their country.
Even before Libya had obtained independence, Tripolitanian
and Cyrenaican leaders for a long time had debated the form of
the union they aspired to achieve, and their lack of agreement
on a formula acceptable to all proved to be such a stumbling
block that the issue was not resolved until compelling forces
brought the leaders of the two sister provinces to reason. Libya's
constitutional structure proved to be her perennial problem; for
even though the federal compromise had finally been adopted,
the present structure might well be endangered if the equilibrium
necessary to maintain it were disrupted. Thus, the basic problem
to which the architects of the Libyan constitution addressed
themselves was not so much one of harmonizing social classes,
protecting minority rights, or determining what constituted an
efficient government for the newly established state, but rather
the problem of how to maintain a balance among three provinces
vying for equality of status, despite the great disparity in resources, population, and cultural levels. The ultimate success
or failure of any constitutional experiment would, therefore,
depend on how Libya's continued problem of unity was solved.
This and the following chapter, which will be devoted to a study
of Libya's constitutional issues, will provide the necessary background for an appreciation of this problem.

Preliminary Steps

Adrian Pelt's principal task, after his arrival in Libya, was the implementation of paragraph 3 of the General Assembly's resolution, providing that a constitution should be drawn up by representatives of the people of Libya. After consultation with the administering powers, the Amir of Cyrenaica, the Chief of the territory of Fazzan, and the leaders of Tripolitania's political parties, Pelt decided that a Preparatory Committee should be formed, in which the three provinces would be equally represented, as a step toward the preparation of the constitution by a National Constituent Assembly. To achieve this purpose, Pelt submitted to the Advisory Council a plan in which he outlined the steps necessary for the drafting and promulgating of the consituation. The text of the plan follows:[1]

a. Election of local assemblies in Cyrenaica and Tripolitania during June 1950;

b. Selection of a Preparatory Committee of the National Assembly not later than July 1950 for the purpose of recommending the method of election, including composition of the Libyan National Assembly, and of drafting a constitution;

c. Election and convening of the Libyan National Assembly during the fall of 1950;

d. Establishment, by the National Assembly, of a provisional Libyan government early in 1951;

e. Adoption of a constitution, including the form of government for Libya, by the National Assembly during 1951;

f. Proclamation of independence by Libya and formation of a definitive Libyan government before January 1, 1952.

The plan was endorsed in principle by the Advisory Council in its meeting on May 4, 1950, but it was criticized on the specific points concerning the composition and functions of the proposed Committee. Under the influence of Tripolitania's political parties, especially the National Congress, the representatives of

[1] Pelt's *First Annual Report*, 1950, p. 19.

Egypt and Pakistan objected to the establishment of an elected Preparatory Committee on the ground that an election in Tripolitania under British military administration would select representatives likely to be swayed by British influence. They also objected to the proposal that the Committee prepare a draft constitution for the consideration of the National Assembly, on the basis that such an action might delay the calling of a National Assembly and that " the National Assembly would have to create its own Preparatory Committee to study and formulate a draft constitution." [2] Pelt, in accepting these various suggestions, pointed out that the Preparatory Committee would have to prepare an electoral law if the National Assembly were to be an elective body.

Pelt's plan of establishing the Preparatory Committee, however, was postponed due to divergent views on the subject. The representatives of Egypt and Pakistan, with the concurrence of the representative of Tripolitania, Mustafa Mizran, maintained that elections in Tripolitania should not be held because they might lead to disturbances in the country, and instead, suggested an appointed body. Nor did the resolution of the General Assembly specify the method by which the National Assembly was to be established. After a prolonged discussion, in which the representative of France advocated the method of election, it was finally agreed to select the Tripolitanian representatives by consultation with the party leaders, since Tripolitania had a number of established political parties.

On June 14, 1950, a draft resolution, submitted by the representative of Pakistan, was adopted by six votes to none with three abstentions, and one representative of Fazzan was absent.[3] The text of the resolution reads:

> The Council advised the Commissioner by this resolution to take the following action:
>
> (a) Request the Amir to propose the names of seven representatives from Cyrenaica;

---

[2] *Ibid.*, p. 22, n. 48.
[3] The representative of Fazzan, under French influence, was in favor of electing the Tripolitanian representatives.

(b) Consult the political leaders in Tripolitania, and, after obtaining their views on the subject, propose, for the advice of the Council, the names of seven outstanding personalities of Tripolitania to be invited by the Commissioner to join the representatives of Cyrenaica;

(c) Request the Chief of the Territory of Fazzan to nominate seven representatives from Fazzan who should consult the representatives of Cyrenaica and Tripolitania, meeting in Tripoli not later than July 1, and prepare a plan whereby the representatives of the inhabitants of Cyrenaica, Tripolitania, and Fazzan should meet in a National Assembly for the purposes stated in paragraph 3 of the resolution of the General Assembly.[4]

The Preparatory Committee of Twenty-One

The next step was to form the Preparatory Committee, composed of twenty-one members, in accordance with the resolution of the Advisory Council. However, two problems had arisen in connection with the composition of the Committee. First, was the Italian community in Tripolitania to be represented? Secondly, in what manner should Pelt, after consultation with the leaders of political parties, appoint the seven representatives of Tripolitania? After negotiation, the Tripolitanian parties agreed to include among their representatives one Italian and one Jewish representative as an indication of the spirit of tolerance which they wished to show to these communities upon achieving independence. Some doubts were expressed in Cyrenaica and Fazzan concerning the wisdom of this action, for it was found that it might have serious consequences for the future of the country. The matter was therefore referred to the Advisory Council on June 24, 1950, and the Council expressed the following opinion:

> Italian participation in the Committee of Twenty-One or in the National Assembly would not prejudice the settlement of the legal status of the Italians after the promulgation of the Libyan constitution and the attainment of Libya's independence.[5]

---

[4] Pelt's *First Annual Report*, 1950, p. 22.
[5] *Ibid.*, p. 23.

This opinion, regarded as satisfactory to both the Amir of Cyrenaica and the Chief of Fazzan,[6] settled the question of minority representation and Pelt at once began his consultations with those in control of Tripolitania's political parties and its leading personalities concerning the choice of the seven representatives. Before the parties could reach an agreement, prolonged negotiations were conducted in which Bashir al-Sa'dawi used his persuasiveness. It was not until July 11 that Pelt was able to submit his findings to the Council. He stated that five political parties had presented identical lists of Arab candidates and four of them had included the name of an Italian as a representative of the minorities. The leaders of two other parties, the Independence Party and the Free National Bloc, did not oppose the inclusion of a representative of the minorities among the Tripolitanian representatives, although there was much disagreement concerning the inclusion of a minority representative, especially an Italian, on the Committee. The Independence Party and the Free National Bloc refused to present lists of candidates on the premise that representation on the Committee should be based on the size of the population of each territory, thereby repudiating the principle of equal representation of the three provinces.

Pelt's chosen list of seven representatives was carefully scrutinized by the Advisory Council. The representative of Pakistan objected to the inclusion of the Mufti of Tripolitania because he had not been suggested by the party to which he belonged,[7] and the Mayor of Misrata because he held positions under the British administration and his own party objected to his nomination.[8] The representative of Egypt, though in agreement with the representative of Pakistan, accepted the nomination of the Mufti, but suggested the substitution of the leader of the Egypto-Tripolitanian Union, 'Ali Rajab, for the Mayor of Misrata. This

[6] The Amir of Cyrenaica had deferred the question of Italian participation in the National Assembly to the Committee of Twenty-One.

[7] The Mufti of Tripolitania, Muhammad Abu al-Is'ad al-'Alim, was the Vice-President of the National Congress Party of Tripolitania.

[8] The Mayor of Misrata, Salim al-Qadi, was a member of the National Congress of Tripolitania. He was a member of the Ahliya Court and of the Administrative Council.

was supported by the representative of Tripolitania, Mustafa Mizran, and Pelt accepted it as a compromise. The Council, by a vote of six to none, with four abstentions, approved Pelt's list of candidates.

On July 25, 1950, Pelt invited the persons approved by the Advisory Council to sit on the Committee of Twenty-One. The Committee, so formed, held its first meeting on July 27 and adopted its rules of procedure. As its Chairman, it elected Muhammad Abu al-Is'ad al-'Alim, the Mufti of Tripolitania, and two secretaries—Khalil al-Qallal of Cyrenaica and Muhammad Bin 'Uthman al-Sayd of Fazzan. The work of the Committee consisted of the following principal decisions.[9]

First, what should be the number of members in the National Assembly? Some expressed the opinion that Tripolitania should have a larger representation due to its superiority in population. However, after some discussion, the principle of equal representation was accepted. It was also decided that the National Assembly should be composed of sixty representatives, twenty from each province. The decision, made on August 7, 1950, was carried by seventeen votes, with three abstentions and one absent member.

Secondly, should members of the National Assembly be elected or selected? The representatives of Fazzan and one representative from Tripolitania, 'Ali Rajab, supported the principle of election because an election was in conformity with the democratic principles followed by civilized nations, and it was the only way of finding out what the wishes and aspirations of the inhabitants were. The representatives of Cyrenaica and Tripolitania upheld the principle of selection, believing that it would take a long time to make the necessary preparations for holding elections and that " in their opinion elections in Tripolitania would be premature " since " there was as yet no national government in the territory and the British administration, could, if it so wished, influence the result of the elections." [10] However, neither

[9] The writer's interviews with the Mufti of Tripolitania, Qallal, Zaqalla'i, and 'Ali Rajab. For a summary of the work of the Committee, see Pelt's *Second Annual Report*, 1951, pp. 71–74.

[10] *Ibid.*, p. 71.

proposal prevailed when the number of votes required was totaled. The representatives of Fazzan, under instructions from Ahmad Sayf al-Nasr, Chief of Fazzan, insisted on their viewpoint. They were accused, especially by the Tripolitanian representatives, of disrupting the work of the Committee under pressure from France.[11] When further discussion on the question did not resolve the issue, the matter was brought to the attention of Adrian Pelt. Pelt began to consult the leading personalities in the country, including the Amir of Cyrenaica, the Chief of Fazzan, and the heads of political parties, with the object of persuading, as he stated, " the political leaders of Tripolitania to agree upon a list that would be truly representative and could be submitted to the Committee of Twenty-One with reasonable chance of gaining approval." [12] Moreover, 'Umar Shinnib, a representative of Cyrenaica, went to Fazzan with instructions from the Amir of Cyrenaica and tried to persuade its chief, Ahmad Sayf al-Nasr, to change his position. The Cyrenaican " good offices " and the Pelt consultations bore fruit in the Fazzanese representatives' acceptance of the principle of selection on condition that " the main political parties of Tripolitania, as also that portion of the population that did not belong to any political party, were represented in the Assembly." Thereupon a resolution was passed on October 12, proposing that the Tripolitanian members should be appointed to the National Assembly by selection on condition that " the national political parties, politically independent persons, and the various regions of Tripolitania were represented in the National Assembly." In the same meeting, the Committee, on the basis of a proposal made by 'Ali Rajab, adopted a resolution to the effect that nonnational minorities could not participate in the National Assembly, but that the resolution " did not mean that the Libyans were not prepared to safeguard the social, religious, and economic rights of minorities and foreigners."

At its meeting on October 13, the Committee considered the manner in which the members of the National Assembly should

---

[11] The writer's interview with Zaqalla'i. See also al-Taj, Banghazi, November 20, 1950.
[12] Pelt's Second Annual Report, 1951, p. 72.

be selected. It had already been agreed that the Amir of Cyrenaica and the Chief of Fazzan would select the representatives
of Cyrenaica and Fazzan, and it was decided that the Mufti of
Tripolitania would select the Tripolitanian representatives. The
text of the resolution reads:

> His Highness, Sayyid Muhammad Idris al-Sanusi, will select the
> representatives of Cyrenaica; Ahmad Sayf al-Nasr will select the
> representatives of Fazzan; in accordance with the unanimous wishes
> of the Tripolitanian representatives on the Committee of Twenty-
> One, the representatives of Tripolitania will be selected by His
> Eminence the Mufti, who will hold the necessary conversations and
> consultations and will then draw up a list and submit it to the
> Committee of Twenty-One not later than October 26, 1950.[13]

Finally, at its meeting on October 15, the Committee discussed
the date and place of the first meeting of the National Assembly.
It was agreed that the date of the opening session should be
November 25 and that the headquarters of the Assembly should
be in Tripoli, but that the Assembly would be free to decide
where to meet later. The final text of the resolution, embodying
all the decisions taken by the Committee, was unanimously
adopted as follows:

(1). The National Assembly will be composed of sixty members.

(2). The representation of the three territories of Cyrenaica, Tripolitania, and Fazzan in the National Assembly will be on a
basis of equality; namely, twenty representatives of each territory.

(3). Representation in the National Assembly will be by means
of selection, consideration being given to the equitable representation of the National Arab parties in the various areas, as
also of independent individuals and leading personalities, particularly where the territory of Tripolitania is concerned.

(4). The selection of the representatives of Cyrenaica will be made
by His Highness the Amir Muhammad Idris al-Sanusi, and
the selection of the representative of Fazzan will be made by
His Excellency Ahmad Sayf al-Nasr. In accordance with a
proposal put forward unanimously by the Tripolitanian repre-

---

[13] *Ibid.*, p. 72.

sentatives in the Committee of Twenty-One, the selection of the representatives of the territory of Tripolitania will be made by the Chairman of the Committee, His Eminence Mahammad Abu al-Isʻad al-ʻAlim who, after the necessary consultations and conversations, will draw up a list of candidates and submit it to the Committee of Twenty-One not later than October 26, 1950. Copies of this resolution will be sent to His Highness the Amir and His Excellency Ahmad Bey.

(5) Nonnational minorities will not be allowed to participate or to be represented in the National Assembly. There is, however, a genuine intention and a general feeling that all civil, religious, and social rights of all minorities and foreigners should be fully safeguarded in the future constitution of Libya. The Committe is confident that this principle will be taken into consideration by the National Assembly when it draws up the constitution, in accordance with the practice of all civilized nations.

(6). The National Assembly will hold its first meeting in the city of Tripoli on November 25, 1950, after which it may decide to hold its subsequent meetings elsewhere.[14]

At the same meeting, after the vote on the final resolution, the Cyrenaican delegation presented a proposal on the form of the future government of Libya, specifying that the form should be federal and monarchical, with the Amir of Cyrenaica as King. They added that this proposal " was not intended to be more than a recommendation to the National Assembly." [15] The proposal, to which there was an objection by the Tripolitanian and Fazzanese delegations, was dismissed as beyond the competence of the Committee because it belonged to the National Assembly, although no objection was raised to the idea that the Amir of Cyrenaica should be the King of Libya.

The Mufti of Tripolitania, due to lack of agreement on the list of candidates, was unable to submit the list on October 26. The time limit was extended more than once. On October 30, the Mufti finally presented a list which was criticized by ʻAli Rajab and Zaqallaʻi by reason of his failure to consult all political parties and independent personalities. However, the list was

[14] *Ibid.*, p. 73.
[15] *Ibid.*, p. 73.

approved by a vote of sixteen to one ('Ali Rajab), with one
abstention (Zaqalla'i) and three absent (Marchino, al-Baruni,
and Rashid al-Kikhya).

Consideration of the Commissioner's
First Annual Report by the General Assembly

In accordance with the General Assembly's resolutions of November 21, 1949, providing that an annual report on the implementation of its recommendations must be presented, Pelt submitted his first report early in September, 1950, shortly before
the meeting of the General Assembly. The report was first considered by the Political Committee on October 9, 1950. Criticism
was levelled at the manner in which the National Assembly was
established and at the slowness shown by the administering
authorities in transfering powers to the Libyan people. Three
proposals were made at first. The first, which was later reintroduced by the Soviet delegation to the General Assembly, provided
for the unity of Libya and the withdrawal of foreign forces; the
second, stressed the formation of governmental institutions in
accordance with the wishes of the people; and the third, in which
the Arab-Asian bloc participated, emphasized the unity and the
early transfer of powers to an independent Libyan government.
The three proposals, incorporated into one draft resolution,
provided that:

> The Commissioner, aided by the Council of Libya, would take
> the necessary steps toward the achievement of the independence and
> unity of Libya, in co-operation with the administering powers, to
> ensure the early, full, and effective implementation of the General
> Assembly resolution of 1949.

The draft resolution, having been discussed by the Political
Committee, was passed on October 19 by fifty-three votes to one
(Ethiopia), with five abstentions (Soviet bloc).

When the resolution was debated by the General Assembly on
November 16, 1950, criticism was again levelled at the way in
which the Libyan National Assembly was formed. The Soviet

delegation remarked that Britain and France failed to give effect to the General Assembly's resolution and charged them with a deliberate attempt at " the dismemberment of Libya." For this reason, the Soviet delegation stated, they submitted a draft resolution providing for the unity of Libya and the withdrawal of foreign forces.

The Arab delegations concentrated their attack on the undemocratic character of the Libyan National Assembly and the separation of the three provinces into autonomous units. The British, American, and several Latin American delegations supported the draft resolutions of the Political Committee and pointed out that, although the Libyan National Assembly was not an elective body, the steps taken in establishing it were in conformity with the General Assembly's resolution of 1949. In view of these divergent viewpoints, it was decided to invite Adrian Pelt to give his observations on the matter. Pelt said:

> While listening to the various speeches made in the course of this debate, I have noted with particular interest a pronounced note of criticism concerning the establishment and composition of the National Assembly which is going to convene on November 25. . . .
>
> . . . I feel that I should be wasting the time of the General Assembly by entering into the details of the case, except to point out that the National Assembly was appointed and not elected, very much against my own advice and that equality of representation as between the three territories had to be incorporated into the National Assembly's set up as a matter of unavoidable political expediency. Both Cyrenaica and Fazzan having made this equality of representation a *sine qua non* for their participation both in the preparatory Committee of Twenty-One and in the National Assembly, neither of those two bodies would have been able to meet on a different basis, and the first essential step toward Libyan unity would not have been made if this condition had been rejected. . . .
>
> With regard to this National Assembly which is to convene on November 25, I feel bound to say that since it is an appointed and not an elected body, there are grave doubts in my mind as to whether it will have the necessary moral and political authority to elaborate a final and definite constitution for Libya.
>
> I have always envisaged the future independent Libya as a democratic state. Hence the future parliament of Libya should preferably

be an elected body, that is to say, a body to be elected by the Libyan people as a whole. At the same time, we have to recognize conditions in Libya as they are. As a result of historical and geographical circumstances, Libya is composed of three territories which, although they have a great deal in common—more than enough to constitute a nation united in a single state—they have their own local peculiarities, outlooks, and interests to which they are attached and which they want to safeguard. This is particularly true with regard to Cyrenaica and Fazzan.[16]

Pelt went on to describe the internal situation and pointed out that the Libyan provisional government, which was to assume control of the administration in place of the administering powers, should not be made responsible to the National Assembly for the simple reason that " it would be virtually impossible to organize the new state for independence in the short time left." He stated that upon his return to Libya he intended to present to the Advisory Council a suggestion which would be communicated to the Libyan National Assembly. The suggestion would include the following points:

First, that the constitution to be prepared by the National Assembly should be considered as a draft to be enacted in a provisional form, but which will require final approval and, if necessary, may be amended by a parliament to be elected by the Libyan people as a whole. Even at the cost of a certain loss of time, I feel this to be an absolutely essential precaution if the Libyan state is to be founded on a stable political basis.

Secondly, that in order to reconcile the two tendencies existing in the country, that is to say, the unitary concept and that of territorial particularism, parliament should consist of two chambers—a small senate composed of elected representatives of the three territories on a basis of equality, and a popular chamber to be elected by the people as a whole. In my opinion, that popular chamber should have among its competencies the sole competence over the state budget.

Thirdly, that the Libyan government should be responsible to the popular chamber.[17]

---

[16] United Nations, *Official Records of the General Assembly*, Fifth Session, 1950, Vol. I, pp. 411–12.

[17] *Ibid.*, p. 412.

Despite Pelt's cogent argument, which persuaded several delegations to support the Political Committee's draft resolution, the Egyptian delegation presented an amendment in which it expressly stated that the Libyan National Assembly should be an elective body. Pelt remarked that if the National Assembly, as provided in the draft resolution, were to convene before January 1, 1951, the period from November, 1950, to the end of the year would be forty-four days only. " It is absolutely out of the question," he added, " to have a National Assembly elected within that short time." He warned that:

> If the General Assembly . . . were now to suggest that the National Assembly, which is going to convene on November 25, must be elected, there would be no National Assembly until far into next year, and in that case I must point out that the possibility of achieving independence by the end of next year would become a dream. The date of December 31, 1951, for independence would in that case be out of the question.[18]

Not withstanding Pelt's warning, the Egyptian delegation, supported by the Arab bloc, insisted that the National Assembly should be an elective body. It was pointed out that Pelt himself suggested that the proposed constitution would not be a final one and that a truly democratic parliament should be convened later to reconsider the constitution. " Our aim," said the Egyptian representative, " is to simplify this unusually complicated procedure and to save both time and labor. . . . We merely ask for a duly elected and representative National Assembly."

Upon the suggestion of the Turkish representative, who requested Pelt " to give the General Assembly the benefit of his opinion as to whether it would be possible to hold normal elections within the time limit proposed in the amendment," Pelt replied:

> What has happened up to now in Libya, whether one does or does not like it . . . is the result of a carefully worked out compromise among the Libyans of the three territories. To upset this compromise would not only mean considerable loss of time . . . but also

---

[18] *Ibid.*, p. 416.

it would have the most serious political consequences . . . one must even take into account the possibility of a breakdown of the Libyan unity which has so far been achieved.

I should like to impress upon the representative of Egypt, who knows so well what conditions are in Libya, that if he presses his amendment, he risks rendering the greatest possible disservice to Libya.

The representative of Turkey has asked whether elections could be held within the time limit now proposed. . . . My reply must definitely be in the negative. . . .[19]

When the vote was taken the Egyptain amendment was rejected, having failed to obtain the necessary two-thirds majority, and the draft resolution as a whole was adopted by fifty votes to none, with six abstentions. The representative of Turkey had perhaps expressed the feeling of the majority of members who supported the resolution, when he said that his delegation was not opposed to the principle of election enshrined in the Egyptian amendment, but abstained because of the " complexity of the problem " which might delay the independence of Libya. By adopting this resolution, the General Assembly put an end to the controversy concerning the legality of the National Assembly and approved the constitutional steps taken in Libya for which Adrian Pelt had become the target of attack. The resolution encouraged Pelt to continue his constructive work, despite the trenchant attack against the assembly made by opposing elements within and outside Libya.

Consideration of the Work of the Committee of Twenty-One By The Advisory Council of Ten

Before the Libyan National Assembly set to work, Pelt had yet to face another storm of criticism instigated in the Advisory Council of Libya. On December 15, 1950, he presented to the Advisory Council a memorandum on the work of the Committee of Twenty-One which was discussed on March 10–11, 1951.

[19] *Ibid.*, p. 421.

Mustafa Mizran, the representative of Tripolitania, opened the discussion by questioning the competence of the Committee of Twenty-One to go beyond " the preparation of a plan for bringing into being the National Assembly." The crucial point was, of course, the composition of the National Assembly, because the selection of the Tripolitanian members by the Mufti of Tripoli was unacceptable to the National Congress Party. Mizran was supported by Kamil Salim and Muhammad Khan, the representatives of Egypt and Pakistan. At the outset Kamil Salim focused his attack on procedural matters. He pointed out that the Committee of Twenty-One had not only " deviated " from its terms of reference but also acted in " flagrant violation " of them. He added that the plan prepared by the Committee should have first of all been examined by the Commissioner and the Advisory Council before it proceeded to set up the National Assembly. By adopting its own rules of procedure, such as that all decisions of the Committee were to require a two-thirds majority and that fifteen members should constitute a quorum, the Committee made decisions of far-reaching significance. Its rules of procedure guaranteed that:

> No decisions could be taken without the support of the Cyrenaican and Fazzanese members of the Committee, who together represented less than one-third of the inhabitants of Libya. Thus, the minority would be able to dominate the majority, which was, to say the least, undemocratic. The provision that fifteen members of the Committee should constitute a quorum meant that the Committee could not meet in the absence of the Fazzanese members; in effect, less than five per cent of the inhabitants of Libya had been given what amounted to a right of veto which had paralyzed the Committee's work for many weeks.[20]

The Egyptian representative charged the Committee with " flagrant irregularity " and cited ten examples, ranging from procedural to specific decisions. The most important was the selection of the Tripolitanian members of the National Assembly by the Mufti. Because the Mufti had selected members unacceptable to the National Congress, headed by Bashir al-Sa'dawi, the

---

[20] Pelt's *Second Annual Report*, 1951, p. 2.

selection was denounced as "irregular," although Sa'dawi at the outset had approved both the principle of selection and entrusted the Mufti with the power of choosing members. The Egyptian representative added:

> The Mufti, assisted by the British administration, had drawn up a list of twenty Tripolitanians and had submitted it to the Committee of Twenty-One. Of the six Tripolitanian members of the Committee, three had supported that list. Thus, thirteen Cyrenaican and Fazzanese members of the Committee had ensured that the Mufti's appointments were accepted, despite objections from some of the Tripolitanian members; while Cyrenaica and Fazzan were each free to appoint their own twenty members of the National Assembly, the Tripolitanian members, representing two-thirds of the population, had been selected by the other third.[21]

The criticisms levelled at the Committee of Twenty-One were challenged by the representatives of the United States, France, Great Britain, Cyrenaica, and Fazzan. 'Ali al-Jirbi, the representative of Cyrenaica, stated that no objection had been raised to the work of the Committee of Twenty-One " until the names of the Tripolitanian members of the National Assembly were announced, and it was therefore permissible to wonder whether the present objections were not based on personalities rather than on principles."[22] The representative of Fazzan, Muhammad Bin 'Uthman, in endorsing the viewpoint of the representative of Cyrenaica, observed that:

> Since he had been a member of the Committee of Twenty-One, he was able to testify that the outcome of its work represented a compromise in the interests of Libyan unity and that concessions had been made on all sides. He could find no record of opposition to the Committee in the General Assembly, nor had the General Assembly moved to modify or nullify the decision to convene the National Assembly. The Tripolitanian members of the Committee had represented all shades of opinion, though the National Congress Party had had the greatest number of representatives.[23]

The discussion on the work of the Committee of Twenty-One ended without any formal vote being taken, but Pelt requested

[21] *Ibid.*, p. 3.   [22] *Ibid.*, p. 4.   [23] *Ibid.*, p. 6.

the advice of the Council on several proposals he had made at the General Assembly (November 16, 1950),[24] the presentation of which was intended to be an advice to the Libyan National Assembly. He pointed out that his proposals had been informally discussed with Libyan political leaders and with the governments of the United States, France, Italy, Egypt, and the Secretary-General of the Arab League between December 21, 1950 and January 16, 1951. Serious misgivings were expressed as to the opportuneness of giving such advice to the National Assembly unless it was requested. He also pointed out that:

> . . . to advise that the Constitution should be ratified by a parliament to be subsequently elected would undermine the authority of the National Assembly and create instability where, above all things, stability was needed.[25]

On January 23, 1951, Pelt, after consultation with various leaders, submitted to the Council a letter to be communicated to the National Assembly as advice, the text of which reads:

1. The constitution to be prepared by the National Assembly should be enacted in a provisional form, would require final approval and amendment, if necessary, by a parliament to be elected by the Libyan people as a whole.
2. Provisions should be made in the constitution for a parliament consisting of two chambers, a small senate composed of elected representatives of the three territories on a basis of equality and a popular chamber to be elected by the people of Libya as a whole.
3. The popular chamber should have amongst its competencies the sole control over the state budget.
4. The Libyan government, that is the Libyan Cabinet, should be responsible to the popular chamber.[26]

Pelt's letter was discussed by the Council on March 12 and 13, 1951. It was subjected to sharp criticism by the representatives of Tripolitania, Pakistan, and Egypt. The first denounced as illegal the action taken by the Committee of Twenty-One in

[24] See p. 152, above.
[25] Pelt's *Second Annual Report*, p. 6.
[26] Pelt's *Second Annual Report*, 1951, p. 78.

establishing an appointed National Assembly, and the second
levelled his attack at the change in the text of the Commissioner's
letter from that which he had presented to the General Assembly.
The most devastating criticism, made by the representative of
Egypt, centered around the federal system as implied in Pelt's
letter. He said:

> Federation was the keystone of that draft resolution and of the
> Commissioner's memorandum. . . . Federation, too, was the reason
> why there had been so much insistence on the principle of equality
> of representation between the three territories regardless of the
> number of their inhabitants. . . . The Egyptian delegation had felt
> it advisable temporarily to accept the principle of equal representa-
> tion in order to bring the representatives of the three territories
> together to perform one simple task, namely, to prepare a plan. . . .
> It had thought that once the Libyans could meet together, in any
> shape or form, it would be for them to decide the matter. It had
> never realized at the time that federation was the fundamental
> policy of the United Kingdom, France, and the United States; that
> dramatic truth had only become apparent in the light of subsequent
> events. . . . Four facts were outstanding: first, federation was desired
> by the administering powers; secondly, the majority of Libyans
> condemned federation, otherwise there would be no need for the
> fears which the Commissioner had mentioned; thirdly, democratic
> principles favored the majority of the population, but, fourthly,
> those principles must be sacrificed to make way for federation.[27]

Two alternative draft resolutions were offered by the representatives of the United States and Fazzan in which certain
elements of compromise were offered. However, Pelt's draft
resolution was adopted by a vote of six to three, with one abstention. The same votes secured the adoption of the draft resolution of the United States' representative. Pelt stated that " he
reserved the right to change or amend at his own discretion
the advice he had received." [28]

On April 3, 1951, Pelt addressed a letter to the President of
the National Assembly, which had been convened on November
25, 1950, in which he embodied the advice adopted by the

[27] *Ibid.*, p. 9.
[28] For a summary of the Council's discussion, see *ibid.*, pp. 7–12.

Council as well as his own observations.[29] He pointed out that this letter was essentially the same as that he had submitted to the General Assembly, but that he had deleted, concerning the constitution, the words: it "should be considered as a draft." He explained that:

> The reason for this deletion was that on my return to Tripoli I had noted that in circles in and outside the National Assembly the use of the word "draft" was considered as a diminution of the National Assembly's authority to determine a constitution for Libya in accordance with the United Nations resolution of November 21, 1949.[30]

Pelt's letter consisted of certain specific suggestions concerning each of the four fundamental points he had presented to the Council of Libya.

(1) Since the National Assembly had adopted the federal system he suggested that not only the lower chamber but also the upper chamber should be established on the basis of election. However, he advised that a limited number of members in the upper chamber should be appointed by the head of state in order to include public men of experience as well as representatives of ethnic and religious groups.

(2) Two different methods for changing the constitution had been suggested by the Council of Libya: one by amendment, which required a two-thirds majority; and one by review after a fixed period. The amendment procedure was the one by which most constitutions are normally changed. However, Pelt felt that the National Assembly of Libya might consider the general review procedure as useful for the following reasons:

> Firstly, the fact that the constitution now being elaborated will be the work not of an elected but of an appointed body; secondly, that Libya, having no precedent of constitutional government in the modern sense of the word, might wish to give itself an opportunity, after a fixed number of years, to look back over its recent experiences and to determine through a democratic procedure whether the state requires structural changes.

---

[29] For text of the letter, see *ibid.*, pp. 71–80.
[30] *Ibid.*, p. 78.

(3) He suggested the adoption of the principle of political responsibility of ministers before Parliament. He warned that too rigid an application of the principle might lead to instability. He therefore suggested the adoption of a formula of ministerial responsibility with a " wise restraint " against governmental instability, specifying that the cabinet should be made responsible only to the lower chamber.

(4) He had suggested in his statement at the General Assembly (November 16, 1950) and in his request for advice to the Council of Libya (January 23, 1951) that the lower chamber should have the sole control over the state budget. The discussion of the Council of Libya indicated that approval of the upper chamber should be left open, although all financial bills should be submitted first to the lower chamber. " The Commissioner holds the view that," Pelt's letter finally added, " while in principle the lower chamber should have the last word in financial matters, the question of the competence of the upper chamber in such matters will have to be considered, since the National Assembly decided on December 2, 1950 that Libya will be a federal state."

Provisional Administration

Prior to the establishment of a Libyan national government several preliminary steps had been taken to transfer provincial administration from foreign to native control. In June, 1949, an Arab administration had already been authorized in Cyrenaica which gave this province a self-governing regime; [31] but no such institutions were possible in Tripolitania and Fazzan under foreign military rule. Only municipal councils were allowed to develop in Tripolitania under British administration, and these had been granted only a limited amount of self-government after 1948.[32] In Fazzan the French administered the territory under a French military administration till 1950, when an As-

---

[31] See pp. 71 ff., above.

[32] For texts of the regulations concerning municipal councils, see Pelt's *First Annual Report*, 1950, pp. 71–74.

sembly of Representatives elected Ahmad Sayf al-Nasr as Chief of the Territory; but the administration remained in French hands.

When the United Nations General Assembly passed a resolution (November 21, 1949) granting Libya independence, Amir Idris impressed upon Bashir al-Saʻdawi the need of establishing a prototype Arab self-governing regime in Tripolitania. Saʻdawi seemed to have agreed with the Amir at a meeting in Banghazi (February 2, 1950) and promised to discuss the plan with Tripolitanian political leaders.[33] However, after his arrival in Tripoli on February 7, Saʻdawi changed his mind. Tripolitanian leaders, who had heard that Cyrenaican leaders had presented to Adrian Pelt a memorandum demanding that the Libyan system of government should be federal,[34] warned Saʻdawi that the establishment of a separate Tripolitanian regime would be a prior acknowledgment of the federal system by Tripolitania. Thus when the Tripolitanian National Congress met at Tajura on March 25, 1950, and passed several resolutions, including the implementation of the United Nations resolutions, no mention was made of the formation of a Tripolitanian government.[35] Meanwhile, the controversy over the legality of the National Constituent Assembly and the federal form of government had occupied the public for the remainder of the year, and the conservative elements began to realize that only a federal system would insure the unity of the country, although extremists continued to denounce it as inconsistent with national interests.[36] Thus when the Libyan National Assembly met in November, 1950, it was keenly felt that steps should be taken to integrate the three provinces before a provisional national government was established.

The initiative for forming separate regimes in Tripolitania

[33] *Tarablus al-Gharb*, Tripoli, February 3, 1950.

[34] It was announced that Sayyid al-Siddiq al-Rida al-Sanusi, President of the Cyrenaican National Congress, presented a memorandum to Pelt demanding that Cyrenaica would join a Libyan union only on a federal basis (*Tarablus al-Gharb*, Tripoli, February 2, 1950).

[35] For text of the Tajura resolutions, see *Tarablus al-Gharb*, Tripoli, March 28, 1950.

[36] See *Tarablus al-Gharb*, Tripoli, April 14 and May 5, 1950 (in favor of federalism); and December 12, 1950 (against federalism).

and Fazzan was taken by the National Assembly itself. On February 21, 1951, the Assembly adopted a resolution inviting the King-designate, who had been proclaimed the future King of the country on December 2, 1950, to select the members of local provisional governments in Tripolitanian and Fazzan and to request the administering powers to enable these governments to exercise their powers as a preliminary step toward the establishment of the Libyan federal government. The local provisional governments were created in March, 1951, under councils of regencies, pending the final adjustment of these regimes when the Libyan constitution was enforced.[37]

Steps for the establishment of a provisional government of Libya, however, proved to be more complicated. Adrian Pelt discussed the question with the King-designate, the various provisional governments, Sa'dawi, and other influential leaders. It was agreed that the General Assembly of the United Nations had given sole authority in the matter to the Libyan National Assembly, since the King-designate had not yet assumed his constitutional powers. However, when the Assembly discussed the matter (March 17–24), it decided to name a committee (composed of three members from each province, presided over by the President of the Assembly) to proceed to Banghazi and discuss with the King-designate the establishment of a provisional government before April 1, 1951.

The King-designate, having consulted the leaders of political parties and influential dignitaries on the composition of the provisional government, communicated his opinion to the Committee. Thus, upon the Committee's return to Tripoli, the National Assembly met on March 29 and adopted a resolution embodying the names of the provisional federal government. The resolution reads:

---

[37] For the composition of the Fazzan government, see p. 107, above. The Tripolitanian government, nominated by Brigadier Blackely, was as follows:
   Prime Minister: Mahmud al-Muntasir
   Minister of Finance: Mansur Qadara
   Minister of Education: Fadil Bin Zikri
   Minister of Agriculture: Salim al-Qadi
   Minister of Transportation: Ibrahim Bin Sha'ban
   Minister of Public Works: Muhammad al-Mayyit.

The National Assembly decides:

(1) To establish as from this day (March 29, 1951) the provisional federal government, whose functions shall include the following:

(a) To establish contact with the United Nations Commissioner regarding the preparation of the plan provided for by the United Nations General Assembly's resolutions of November 17, 1950, concerning the transfer to it of the powers from the two administering powers in Libya:

(b) To receive the powers progressively transferred from the two administering powers in Libya in a manner that will ensure the transfer of all powers from the two existing administrations before January 1, 1952, in accordance with the United Nations General Assembly's resolution of November 17, 1950, provided that its exercise of such powers would be in conformity with the provisions of the constitution, with particular regard to the distribution of powers between the federal government and the local governments, when that matter has been determined by the National Assembly.

(2) To appoint the following persons, whose consent has been obtained, to the offices of State as given below:

Sayyid Mahmud al-Muntasir—Prime Minister, Minister of Justice, and Minister of Education.

Sayyid 'Ali al-Jirbi—Minister of Foreign Affairs and Minister of Health.

Sayyid 'Umar Shinnib—Minister of Defense.

Sayyid Mansur Qadara—Minister of Finance.

Sayyid Ibrahim Bin Sha'ban—Minister of Communications.

Sayyid Muhammad Bin 'Uthman—Minister of State.

(3) That His Eminence, the President of the National Assembly, shall communicate this resolution to the authorities concerned.[38]

The provincial government's function was to plan and co-ordinate the work of the various administrations and to co-operate with a co-ordinating committee created to prepare the administrative and budgetary plans for the transfer of powers from the administering authorities to the Libyan government.

---

[38] Government of Libya, *Proceedings of the National Assembly*, pp. 55–58. On April 17 the National Assembly passed another resolution by virtue of which the Ministry of Justice was entrusted to the Minister of Foreign Affairs, and the Ministry of Health was placed under the Minister of State. *Ibid.*, p. 66.

The National Constituent Assembly

The composition of an assembly designed to prepare a constitution for the newly created state of Libya became the subject
of a heated controversy both in national and international circles.
The Advisory Council of Libya, it will be recalled, had discussed
the manner in which the National Assembly would be composed
and it was on the recommendation of the leaders of political
parties, including the National Congress Party, that of the principle of appointing, rather than electing, the Tripolitanian members was adopted. The National Congress Party, under the
leadership of Bashir al-Sa'dawi, was satisfied that since four out
of the seven Tripolitanian members of the Committee of Twenty-
One were members of the National Congress, the appointment of
the Tripolitanian representatives in the National Assembly
would meet with the prior approval of the National Congress
Party. When, however, the Mufti of Tripolitania submitted a
list of representatives to the Council of Twenty-One which did
not meet the approval of the National Congress Party, the National Assembly was denounced on the premise that it was appointed rather than elected. The representatives of Egypt and
Pakistan, it will be recalled, had already questioned the legality
of the National Assembly at a meeting of the Committee of
Twenty-One,[39] and the National Congress Party aroused the
people to demonstrate against the alleged illegal action of the
Committee in accepting the members of the National Assembly.[40]

The head of the National Congress Party went so far as to
appeal to the United Nations and the Arab League, disputing
the competence of the National Assembly to draw up a constitution for Libya. The alleged incompetence of the National Assembly became the principal theme of the campaign of the
National Congress during the spring and summer of 1951, and

[39] See p. 154, above.
[40] The demonstration paraded the streets on January 23, 1951, and proceeded to the United Nations Office and its leaders submitted to Adrian
Pelt, United Nations Commissioner, three demands: dissolution of the
National Assembly, the unitary system of government, and proportional representation. See *Tarablus al-Gharb*, Tripoli, January 24, 1951.

Sa'dawi made a number of rash statements in which he declared that the whole question of Libyan independence should be reconsidered by the United Nations General Assembly " so that a fresh decision compatible with the wishes of the people of Libya could be obtained." [41]

'Abd al-Rahman 'Azzam, Secretary-General of the Arab League, was no less violent than Sa'dawi in his criticism of the legality of the National Assembly. Since the National Congress Party, representing sources in Libya friendly to Egypt, had lost its influence in the National Assembly, 'Azzam advised the political committee of the Arab League to refuse recognition of the new Libyan state.[42] In an interview with the editor of the Italian newspaper *Tempo*, 'Azzam said:

The constitution of the new state [of Libya] must be proclaimed by a freely elected Assembly representing the Libyan people in numerical proportion. Otherwise the new state would be based on a false foundation and we would be unable to recognize it. The Libyan [National] Constituent Assembly in the manner in which it has been set up, without popular nomination and without a representation from the various regions which is absolutely out of proportion to the number of inhabitants, can only represent an assembly of private persons, and we cannot recognize it as a representative organ of the Libyan people, in the same way as we will be unable to recognize the legality of its decisions. It is an illegal assembly, and I have recently informed Washington—the American Department of State—that the Arab League cannot tolerate a state in its midst which has been founded on an illegal basis.[43]

---

[41] See *Shu'lat al-Hurriya*, Tripoli, March 18, 1951; and the *Sunday Ghibli*, Tripoli, August 5, 1951. See comments on these statements in *Proceedings of the National Assembly*, pp. 76–77.

[42] For text of 'Azzam's recommendations to the League's Council, see Arab League, *Proceedings of the Council of the Arab League*, Fourteenth Session, 1951, pp. 6–7. 'Ali al-'Unayzi, a Libyan in the Arab League Secretariat, resigned from his post on January 26, 1951, in protest against the League's attitude concerning the legality of the National Assembly. 'Unayzi had been sent by 'Azzam to Libya in the latter part of 1950 to report on the Libyan attitude toward the National Assembly. He submitted a report dated January 11, 1951, in which he advised the Arab League to recognize the National Assembly. When the League paid no attention to his views, he returned to Libya and was appointed a member of Pelt's Advisory Council (information, and a copy of the report, supplied by 'Unayzi).

[43] *Il Tempo*, Rome, January 5, 1951.

'Azzam's statement aroused sharp criticism in many Libyan quarters, particularly in Cyrenaica and Fazzan. Since his statement appeared in an Italian newspaper, it gave the impression that 'Azzam was seeking a rapprochement with Italy against Libyan interests.[44] Upon the recommendation of the political committee, the Council of the Arab League passed a resolution (March 17, 1951) recommending that the Arab States not recognize the constitutional regime created by the National Assembly.[45] This attitude disappointed not only Cyrenaican and Fazzaneze leaders but also conservative Tripolitanian elements who regarded the recommendation as obstructing Libya's constitutional development. Thereupon the National Assembly, in its meeting on January 17, 1951, decided to send a delegation, headed by the President of the National Assembly, to explain the Libyan viewpoint to the Council of the Arab League. The delegation, during its visit in Cairo from January 22 to February 8, protested the appearance of 'Azzam's statements in the press and explained to the Egyptian Foreign Minister, Muhammad Salah al-Din, and Arab delegations the state of the internal situation in Libya. Salah al-Din was willing to accept the legality of the National Assembly, but he insisted on the viewpoint suggested by Adrian Pelt that the draft constitution should be approved by an elected Libyan Parliament. Other Arab delegates, especially the 'Iraqi and the Lebanese, supported the Libyan viewpoint and contended that the Libyan constitutional issue was a domestic question in which the Arab League had no right to interfere.[46] The Libyan delegation explained also the Libyan viewpoint to the Egyptian press, which had been acquainted only with the viewpoints of the Arab League Secretariat and the Libyan National Congress Party.[47] This seems to have ended any further action by the

[44] *The Cyrenaica Mirror*, Banghazi, January 21, 1951; *al-Watan*, Banghazi, January 9, 1951; *Al-Taj*, Banghazi, February 5, 1951.

[45] Arab League, *Proceedings of the Council of the Arab League*, Fifteenth Session, 1951, pp. 84–85.

[46] See text of the report of the delegation to the National Assembly in *Proceedings of the Libyan National Assembly*, pp. 33–35.

[47] Bashir al-Sa'dawi, leader of the National Congress Party, arrived in Cairo on January 27, 1951, to influence both the Arab League and the press; but the 'Umar al-Mukhtar group, though in sympathy with Sa'dawi's viewpoint on Libyan unity, opposed his attack on the National Assembly and dispatched

League's Council, although 'Azzam continued to make statements unfavorable to the National Assembly.

The question of the legality of the Assembly became the subject of national discussion. The critics pointed out that its appointment by the Committee of Twenty-One on the basis of equal representation of the three provinces was incompatible with the resolutions of the United Nations General Assembly (November 21, 1949, and November 17, 1951), which stipulated that the National Assembly should be "duly constituted and representative."[48] The critics also stated that Adrian Pelt himself doubted the "moral and political authority" of the National Assembly to draw up a final constitution for Libya, although Pelt advised against reversal of the action of the Committee of Twenty-One in appointing the members of the National Assembly and recommended the acceptance of the principle of equal representation as the only possible way of linking the three provinces together. The National Assembly, in discussing the question of the legality of its composition on January 18, 1951, declared that the two members of the Advisory Council (the Egyptian and the Pakistani representatives), who objected to the principle of appointment, had already approved of it in correspondence with the Amir of Cyrenaica.[49] Nor was the principle of appointment, as in the case of Tripolitania, inconsistent with "a duly constituted and representative" body, since all the important leaders and dignitaries of Tripolitania had already been consulted on the list of candidates before it was presented to Adrian Pelt, who in turn submitted it to the Committee of Twenty-One for appointment. Needless to say, the resolution of the General Assembly did not specify that such representation should necessarily be made on the basis of popular election. The principle of proportional representation suggested by the Congress Party, which might have been adopted if the three provinces had agreed to join the union on unitary basis, was obviously irrelevant. Cyrenaica and Fazzan

Mahmud Makhluf to counteract Sa'dawi's influence (The writer's interviews with Makhluf; see also *al-Taj*, January 26, 1951).

[48] See *Shu'lat al-Hurriya*, Tripoli, March 8, 1951.

[49] For text of the letters, see *Tarablus al-Gharb*, Tripoli, January 19, 1951; and *Barqa al-Jadida*, Banghazi, January 21, 24, 26, 1951. See also *Proceedings of the National Assembly*, p. 26.

agreed to join the union on the basis of the principle of equal representation, without which the calling of a National Assembly would have been impossible.

Declaring itself competent to draw up a constitution for the country and supported by both the United Nations Commissioner and the majority of the Committee of Twenty-One, the National Assembly proceeded to carry out its task with confidence. The agitation of the opposition elements and the press grew steadily less violent and the moderate elements prevailed.[50]

Adoption of the Federal System and the Proclamation of the Amir of Cyrenaica as King of Libya

Before the National Assembly began to consider the steps necessary for the drafting of the constitution, two fundamental laws were enacted at the outset, because these were deemed necessary to determine the future of the Libyan state. The first, stipulating that Libya should be a federal state, was supported by Cyrenaican and Fazzanese representatives and only reluctantly accepted by Tripolitanian members, in the hope that such a system would be a step toward a more perfect union.

The selection of the federal system, which had already been opposed by the representatives of Egypt and Pakistan at the Advisory Council, presented another opportunity for the National Congress Party to attack the National Assembly and denounce it as illegal. Federalism was attacked by extremists as a scheme designed by the imperialists to divide Libya into three states.

From the time when the National Assembly met, the press debated the question of federalism and pointed out its advantages and disadvantages for the country. The Cyrenaican and Fazzanese leaders made it crystal clear that they were not prepared to agree to any form of unity unless it was on a federal basis with equal representation, fearing that a unitary system might lead to the

[50] Munir Burshan, " Ayn al-Akthariya al-Sahiqa? " *Tarablus al-Gharb,* Tripoli, May 5, 1950.

domination of Cyrenaicans and Fazzanese by Tripolitanians.[51]
In a country like Libya, with its extensive area and vast desert
stretches, federalism is perhaps the most suitable system. The
Mukhtar group, who had been in favor of a unitary system, began
to press for moderation as a reaction to Sa'dawi's agitation against
federalism and conceded that there were circumstances which
"made it essential that the form of government of the Libyan
state should be federal," and that "federalism is not contrary
to the principle of one state." [52] The case for unity was defended
on the ground that a country as small in population as Libya
could not afford to dissipate its resources on an elaborate system
of government, although it was conceded that a decentralized
system of administration was advisable. The extremists denounced the system as an instrument by which Britain and
France sought to perpetuate their influence in Cyrenaica and
Fazzan and organized street demonstrations against it in Tripoli
city.[53] They even argued that it was inconsistent with Islamic
principles of government and that no other Arab country had
been willing to adopt it.[54] It was not difficult to meet such an
objection, since some form of federalism had existed in early
Islam and Syria had adopted the federal system during the
interwar period.[55]

A quieter debate was conducted within the National Assembly.
It was pointed out that the federal system was the only practical
measure which would enable the three provinces to be linked
together and eventually lead to full unity. A case in point was
the form of government which the United States had chosen in
order to achieve unity. Convinced that federalism was but a
transitory system, the Assembly adopted it without further ado.[56]

[51] See al-Istiqlal, Banghazi, December 16, 1950; Barqa al-Jadida, Banghazi,
December 17, 1950.

[52] Al-Watan, Banghazi, January 16, 1951.

[53] Tarablus al-Gharb, Tripoli, December 29, 1950; al-Libi, Tripoli, August
30, 1951.

[54] Sadiq Bin Zarra', "al-Fidiraliya Dakhila fi al-Islam," Shu'lat al-Hurriya,
Tripoli, February 11, 1951.

[55] Tarablus al-Gharb, Tripoli, December 20, 1950; January 23, 1951.

[56] See Proceedings of the National Assembly, pp. 9–10. When the King-
designate visited Tripoli in May he made a speech in which he tried to rally

Federalism having been accepted, it did not take long to pass the law proclaiming the form of government to be monarchical and offering the throne of Libya to the Amir Idris of Cyrenaica. This law was unanimously adopted, amid the applause and acclamation of the National Assembly, on December 2, 1950. It was resolved that a message should be sent to the Amir to inform him of the decision taken by the Assembly and that it considered him King as of that day. The Amir thanked the Assembly for offering him the throne, but preferred to postpone the proclamation of his acceptance until the constitution was promulgated, which would enable him to exercise his royal prerogatives. He was therefore known as the King-designate. On December 4, 1950, the members of the Assembly decided to appoint a delegation to proceed to Banghazi and present, on behalf of the Assembly, the text of its historic resolution. The members of the Assembly expressed the desire that they should all share the honor of presenting this historic document to the King. Thus the delegation was composed of all the members of the National Assembly. It proceeded to Banghazi and presented the Assembly's resolution on December 17, 1950, in the presence of Saqizli, the Prime Minister of Cyrenaica, Bashir al-Sa'dawi, leader of the National Congress Party, and other dignitaries.[57] The Amir, in a short speech, thanked the delegation; but one of the Tripolitanian members, 'Abd al-'Aziz al-Zaqalla'i, made a statement in which he reiterated his reservation at the Assembly's meetings that while he shared the honor of proclaiming the Amir as King of Libya, he was still in favor of the unitary—not the federal—form of government. The King replied that full unity was the ultimate objective of all. Feeling that his task was fulfilled by the proclamation of the monarchy, Zaqalla'i tendered his letter of resignation; for, as he told the author, he did not want to

support for the federal principle which the National Assembly had just adopted. He said: " We consider that the attacks of certain countries which inveigh against this system are the result of immaturity and lack of knowledge as to the true state of affairs of Libya and the wishes of its inhabitants " (*Sunday Ghibli*, Tripoli, June 3, 1951). For full text of the speech, see *Tarablus al-Gharb*, Tripoli, May 31, 1951.

[57] For a short account of this historic meeting, see *al-Taj*, Banghazi, December 18, 1951.

participate in drawing up a constitution based on the federal principle.[58]

Drafting of the Constitution

The monarchical and federal systems having been proclaimed (December 2, 1950), the National Assembly proceeded in the following meeting (December 4) to appoint a drafting committee known as the Committee of the Constitution, composed of 18 members, to prepare a draft constitution.[59] To speed up the work, the committee formed a subcommittee composed of six,[60] known as the working group, to draft the various parts of the constitution and present them to the Committee.[61]

From the very beginning, Adrian Pelt conveyed to the National Assembly the advice given by the United Nations Advisory Council [62] and placed at its disposal all the legal and other technical assistance that he was able to provide. Pelt, moreover, made available the services of his own legal adviser who gave the Committee and the working group assistance whenever requested.[63]

On December 6, 1950, the Committee held its first meeting; the working group, which prepared the actual draft, held its first meeting on December 11.[64] The working group began first to study the question of the distribution of powers between the federal and the provincial governments. Copies of a dozen

[58] The National Congress Party decided that all its representatives in the National Assembly should resign in protest against the Assembly's adoption of the federal system. Only one, Ahmad al-Sari, tendered his letter of resignation. Thereupon the National Congress Party passed a resolution dismissing those who did not resign. See *Shu'lat al-Hurriya*, Tripoli, March 3, 1951.

[59] 'Umar Shinnib acted as Chairman of the Committee and Sulayman al-Jirbi as secretary. The Committee was given legal advice by 'Umar Lufti and 'Awni Dajani.

[60] Two from each province.

[61] *Proceedings of the National Assembly*, pp. 12–14, 153.

[62] See p. 157, above. For a discussion on Pelt's message to the National Assembly, see *Proceedings of the National Assembly*, pp. 62–64, 65–66.

[63] Pelt's *Second Annual Report*, 1951, pp. 15–16.

[64] For a summary of the proceedings of the drafting committee, see *Proceedings of the National Assembly*, pp. 153–200.

constitutions of federal systems were translated and circulated among members of the committee to acquaint them with federal constitutional structures. Having read the texts, the working group, with the help of the legal adviser, proceeded to draw up the articles concerning the distribution of powers. Some members wanted to specify the powers of both the federal and the provincial governments, leaving all residual powers to the federal government; others thought that the powers of the federal government should be specified, leaving residual powers to the provinces. The latter viewpoint prevailed, and the working group decided that in principle all matters concerning foreign affairs, national defense, finance, communications, justice, public education and health, and various other important matters, which generally fall within the jurisdiction of a central government, should be handled by the federal government. The draft plan on the distribution of powers was completed on March 19, 1951, and was sent to the committee for study. This draft was approved on May 17. The committee reserved its opinion on certain financial and economic subjects, pending the advice of the United Nations experts.

The working group then continued to prepare the clauses concerning fundamental rights and freedom. A Bill of Rights was drafted on the basis of the relevant parts of the constitutions of Egypt, 'Iraq, Syria, Lebanon, Transjordan, and the Universal Declaration of Human Rights.

The King's prerogatives were in the main based on several Arab constitutions, the constitution of 'Iraq in particular.[65] The King's approval of laws was particularly stressed. A law which did not receive the King's assent might be referred to Parliament for reconsideration. The working group also prepared the draft concerning the Cabinet. Some members expressed the opinion that the Cabinet should be responsible to the King, while others thought Parliament should be responsible. In the end the Cabinet was made responsible only to the House of Representatives, with the restriction that in the case of votes of censure a two-thirds majority should be required.

There was a difference of opinion as to how members of Parlia-

[65] The author's interview with 'Awni Dajani.

ment should be selected, especially the Senators. Some insisted that the Senators should be appointed by the King. The first viewpoint was based on the assumption that Libya had no experience in constitutional matters and that it would be more advantageous to leave to the King the right to appoint persons who had not been elected to the lower chamber and whose experience would be useful to Parliament. The decision in this matter was left to the Committee on the Constitution.

The method of choosing members to the lower house elicited several viewpoints. Some thought that the provincial legislators should elect deputies to the federal Parliament from among its members. It was pointed out that such a parliament would essentially represent the provinces. Others suggested that each province should elect its deputies, in accordance with the electoral law of the province. This meant that there would be three different electoral laws, instead of one federal electoral law, and that representation in Parliament would still remain provincial in spirit. A compromise was finally adopted which reads: " The House of Representatives shall consist of members elected in the three provinces in accordance with the provisions of a federal electoral law." [66]

The working group, against the advice of Pelt, adopted a rigid method of amending the constitution, like that of most federal constitutions. Pelt had suggested that a country like Libya, without previous constitutional experience, might feel the need to reconsider its constitution after a few years and suggested a method, to be fixed by the constitution itself, for revision after a number of years. The choice of the capital was left to the Committee, because of basic disagreement on the subject. The chapter on finance was quickly disposed of, since the group followed the suggestions given by the experts, except with regard to the income tax. The group decided to give the federal government the right to legislate on this matter, and to leave to the local administrations the enforcement of the law and disposition of the revenue produced by that tax. This was completed and transmitted to the Committee on August 23.

The draft concerning the transfer of powers had already been

[66] Pelt's *Second Annual Report*, 1951, p. 18.

drawn up by Pelt, as Chairman of the Co-ordination Committee, and the National Assembly made its decision on the distribution of powers between the federal government and local administrations in principle. When the Working Group and the Committee of the Constitution had approved the distribution of powers concerning finance, the whole chapter on the distribution of powers was referred to the National Assembly and was approved without modification on August 18.[67]

The working group, which held ninety-six meetings, forwarded each chapter drafted to the Committee on the Constitution for approval. The Committee, which held twenty-five meetings, made no important changes in the draft prepared by the Working Group.

It was in the National Assembly that some of the controversial clauses were finally adopted. The discussion on the draft constitution began on September 10, 1951, and after Sulayman al-Jirbi, Secretary of the Assembly, read the first four chapters, no decision at all was reached for a week. The secretary read the other chapters on September 17 and again no decision was made, the reason being that the Assembly was subjected to constant pressure from the opposition in Tripoli city, which virtually paralyzed its work. It was deemed necessary, therefore, to move the Assembly to Banghazi—a quieter place—to enable its members to debate the articles of the constitution with relative freedom.[68] On September 17, the President of the National Assembly received a message from the King-designate inviting the members to meet in Banghazi. A copy of the draft constitution had already been presented to the King-designate and the Assembly resumed its meetings in Banghazi on September 29. With the influence of Adrian Pelt, who often discussed controversial points with important members, common grounds of agreement were found. The King-designate also discussed informally certain controversial points and helped to bring about agreement.

The Assembly reopened its debate on the draft constitution on October 2, 1951. It had already approved the chapter concerning

[67] *Proceedings of the National Assembly*, pp. 80–84: Pelt's *Second Annual Report*, 1951, p. 19.
[68] The writer's interview with Khalil al-Qallal and Sulayman al-Jirbi.

the distribution of powers on August 18; but certain points concerning immigration were discussed again, because the Cyrenaican members proposed that the future federal law concerning immigration into a province should be authorized only with the prior consent of the province concerned. The question was resolved by an agreement to add an article which satisfied the Cyrenaican demand entitled " General Provisions." [69]

A more important issue which elicited an animated discussion had to do with the prerogatives of the Crown. The Cyrenaican members contended that too little power had been given to the King and too much to Parliament. They pointed out that Libya was still inexperienced in politics and a completely democratic system of government was not in the national interest. This viewpoint, reflecting the political theory of a patriarchal society, was contested by the Tripolitanian members. They explained that without reflection on the personality of the King, for whom they had the highest respect, they felt that a democratic parliamentary regime was essential for Libya in order to conform with the spirit and purposes of the United Nations' resolution as well as with the future interests of the country.[70] Having agreed on this general principle, the National Assembly approved the first ninety-two articles with only minor alterations.

Meanwhile, the working group, in consultation with Pelt, had again considered Article 87, concerning the ministerial responsibility, in the form it had appeared in the draft constitution. The commissioner explained that:

> Instead of ensuring ministerial stability, the text would render the government of the new State less stable, since the King would be obliged to intervene to solve conflicts which would inevitably arise between the House of Representatives and the government whenever the government had not the confidence of the majority of the House.[71]

Upon Pelt's recommendation, the working group agreed to replace the phrase " a two-thirds majority " by the phrase " a majority of the members of the House." In its meeting on Octo-

[69] *Proceedings of the National Assembly*, pp. 103–104.
[70] *Proceedings of the National Assembly*, pp. 105-107.
[71] *Second Annual Report*, 1951, p. 20.

ber 3, the National Assembly, upon the suggestion of Khalil al-Qallal, decided to accept the clause as revised.[72] The National Assembly proceeded quickly to adopt in the same meeting the remaining articles, except those concerning the distribution of customs revenue, the naming of the capital, and the articles concerning succession to the throne.

The working group, in consultation with Pelt, again discussed the clauses concerning the distribution of federal revenues, including customs revenues, which the National Assembly had accepted in principle, stating that customs should be under the jurisdiction of the federal government. Despite some objections from Cyrenaican members, the clause was adopted as it appeared in the draft constitution.

The question of the capital, on which there was divided opinion, was finally resolved. Two proposals had been put forth: One, that Tripoli and Banghazi should be the two capitals of the State; and the other, that the seat of the federal government would normally be in Tripoli. The first was supported by Cyrenaican members and the second by Tripolitanian and Fazzanese members. The debate, in which unofficial consultations had been offered by the King-designate and Pelt, ended by approving the first proposal.[73]

On October 7, the National Assembly completed the adoption of the articles still in abeyance, especially those concerning succession to the throne, the distribution of revenues, and immigration. Before the Assembly completed the debate, Qallal proposed an amendment to Article 67 concerning the ratification of treaties. He stated that the King did not want to take full responsibility of ratification and proposed: " The King shall declare war and conclude peace and enter into treaties which he ratifies after the approval of Parliament."

The proposal was approved with loud acclamation as a more democratic clause than the one which had existed before.

Having completed the adoption of all the articles one by one, the National Assembly unanimously passed a resolution to adopt the whole constitution, and entrusted its President and the two

---

[72] *Proceedings of the National Assembly*, p. 109.
[73] *Ibid.*, pp. 119 and 196.

Vice-Presidents with its promulgation, its communication to the King, and its publication in the official gazette.[74]

While the unanimous vote was being taken, and while one of the members was about to speak, the King-designate and Prime Minister Mahmud al-Muntasir paid the National Assembly an unexpected visit. Expressing optimistic approval, the King congratulated the Assembly on the completion of the constitution and the President of the Assembly welcomed the King in a short speech.[75]

The remaining session of the National Assembly was devoted to enacting an electoral law. Some members, under pressure of time, thought that the matter might be left entirely to the provisional government; others held that it was the duty of the National Assembly to approve and promulgate the law in order to insure that it was in conformity with the newly enacted Constitution. The latter opinion was finally accepted, with the proviso that the provisional government prepare the draft law.[76]

On October 21, 1951, the provisional government presented a draft electoral law, based on the provisions of several Arab electoral laws, to the National Assembly. A working group was set up to study the draft and submit a report before November 1. Bearing in mind that Libya did not yet possess traditions concerning elections, the working committee did not intend to propose, as it was pointed out to Adrian Pelt, " a law as perfect as those which existed in more advanced countries with more democratic experience." [77] The Committee took into account certain special conditions, particularly the existence of tribal communities. On October 31, Pelt met with the working group and called its attention to certain shortcomings in the report,

[74] The official proclamation of the Constitution took place on the same day (October 7), but the United Nations was not informed of this fact until October 18.

[75] *Ibid.*, pp. 120–121.

[76] Article 204 of the Constitution stipulated that " The provisional federal government shall draw up the first electoral law for Parliament, provided it is not contrary to the provision laid down in this Constitution. The law shall be submitted to the National Assembly for approval and promulgation. The said law must be promulgated within a period not exceeding thirty days from the date of the promulgation of this Constitution."

[77] Pelt's *Supplementary Report*, p. 4.

such as giving too much power to the supervisors of elections and the registering officers, and the distinction between electoral procedures in rural and in urban districts. The working group assured Pelt that his observations would be taken into consideration in the report to the National Assembly.

The draft electoral law was discussed by the National Assembly in seven meetings, from November 1 to 6, 1951. The law was essentially the same as that submitted by the provisional government. However, several changes were made, based in the main on Pelt's suggestions, such as the establishment of committees competent to take certain final decisions originally entrusted to supervisors.[78] Certain other amendments, based on the electoral law of Iraq,[79] were made; but the distinction between rural and urban districts, which subsequently aroused criticism, was maintained. As to the supervisor-general's power to invalidate an election, the National Assembly, on the recommendation of the working group, interpreted this power as meaning that it could only be exercised during the holding of elections. After the elections, Article III of the Constitution would apply. The electoral law provided likewise for petitions protesting against the validity of elections to be submitted to the House of Representatives within ten days from the time the House began its meetings. The electoral law was adopted unanimously by the Assembly at its forty-third meeting on November 6, 1951.[80] The Assembly remained in session until the proclamation of independence, although no business meetings were held in the interim.[81]

In retrospect, the work of the National Assembly can be looked upon as a successful experiment in producing a constitutional framework for the newly-created state of Libya. The viewpoints of the three component provinces were divergent on almost all fundamental points, and dissident groups made it exceedingly difficult for the Assembly to work in an atmosphere free of

[78] *Ibid.*, p. 5.
[79] *Proceedings of the National Assembly*, p. 131.
[80] *Ibid.*, pp. 128–150. For text of the electoral law, see *Government Gazette*, Vol. I, no. 3, November 6, 1951; and for subsequent amendments see *ibid.*, Vol. V, no. 10, November 22, 1955.
[81] For a survey of Libya's constitutional development, see Ismail R. Khalidi, *Constitutional Development of Libya* (Beirut, 1956), Chaps. 4–6.

confusion and personal rivalries. The members of the Assembly, however, showed remarkable self-restraint in matters on which there was much hard feeling. Rarely did any member register a protest against any other, nor was there any complaint about rules of order.[82] The President of the Assembly conducted the meetings in a businesslike and orderly fashion. His wisdom and dignity impressed all and proved to be a moderating element; for whenever he sensed that the debate was leading to a sharp conflict or emotionalism, he intervened to bridge personal differences and bring harmony by suggesting a short recess during which he reconciled the conflicting viewpoints.[83]

Nor was the National Assembly unprepared to listen to the criticism of opposing groups or to the advice of experts. Some members often voiced the opposing views of critics and tried to influence the Assembly, especially on such matters as the relationship between federal and provincial powers, the composition of parliament, and the choice of the capital. But the Assembly also considered the advice of experts, especially the Commissioner's helpful suggestions, and accepted several of them with satisfaction. The King-designate, who preferred not to interfere in the Assembly's deliberations, often exercised a moderating influence in cases of sharp conflict.

Adrian Pelt, in his report to the General Assembly of the United Nations, registered his satisfaction with the work of the National Assembly and its willingness to be guided by his advice and the advice of the Council of Libya. Pelt remarked that, generally speaking, the National Assembly acted on his advice " in the spirit if not in the letter." He added, " Only on the question of the revision of the Constitution, did the National Assembly not follow [his] advice. . . . On all other points, and particularly on the question of the composition of the Parliament, of ministerial responsibility, and of control of the revenue and expenditure the decision of the National Assembly followed the recommendations of the Council of March 13, 1951 and of the Commissioner." [84]

---

[82] A case in point was Furaytis' complaint against other's intolerance of his viewpoints, although Furaytis had full freedom in expressing his often parochial position (*Proceedings of the National Assembly*, p. 102) .

[83] *Ibid.*, pp. 113–114.

[84] Pelt's *Second Annual Report*, 1951, p. 21.

chapter VII

The Machinery of Government

THE PROMULGATION of the constitution marked the crowning effort of Libyan leaders to bring the three sister provinces together to form one state. The constitution is an instrument capable of further development and in its present form it is a milestone along the road of ultimate national unity. The study of it will therefore unfold not only the long struggle to overcome centrifugal forces, but also the will and purpose of the Libyan people to achieve a more perfect union.

Constitutional Instruments

A constitutional government for Libya had been envisaged for some time before the National Assembly met to draw up a constitution. The resolution of the General Assembly of the United Nations (November 21, 1949), which affirmed the legal basis for the establishment of an "independent and sovereign state," stipulated that a constitution should be drawn up by the representatives of the Libyan people meeting in a National Assembly. When the National Assembly met in November, 1950, its members declared that Libya's system of government should be monarchical and its form federal. The Amir Idris, who was proclaimed King of Libya by the National Assembly (December, 1950), had already made public a constitution for Cyrenaica in July, 1949, and promised Tripolitanian leaders that if ever the two sister provinces should be united, the form of government would be constitutional and parliamentary. Thus the function of the National Assembly of drafting a constitutional framework for Libya was essentially to work out the details of a form of government that had already been accepted in principle on earlier occasions. Nor was the constitutional structure dealt with by the National Assembly alone, for under the federal form of government, which presupposes the existence of national and provincial governments, several other constitutional instruments were to be drafted by state or provincial assemblies. These subsidiary instruments are no less important than the general or federal constitution for the study of the structure of government and the distribution of authority.

The constitution of Libya, if taken to mean all the instruments relating to the incidence and distribution of authority, is more than the document proclaimed by the National Assembly on October 7, 1951. During the relatively short period from the time when the United Nations resolution was adopted (November 21, 1949) to the declaration of independence (December 24, 1951), Libya passed through several stages before its constitutional structure was completed. From the viewpoint of constitutional history, therefore, the Libyan constitution may be regarded as including the following instruments:

(1) The Resolution of the United Nations General Assembly of November 21, 1949, as interpreted and endorsed by the resolution of November 1950.

(2) The Two Fundamental Laws of December 2, 1950, passed by the National Assembly proclaiming the adoption of the monarchical and federal systems of government.

(3) The Fundamental Law of December 4, 1950 (passed by the National Assembly) providing for the adoption of the Libyan flag (composed of red, black, and green bands with a white star and crescent in the center).

(4) The transitory laws passed by the National Assembly providing for the establishment of a provisional national government, a Council of Regency in Tripolitania, and a local government in Fazzan.

(5)   The "Constitution of Libya," promulgated by the National Assembly on October 7, 1951.

(6)   The three Organic Laws of the provinces, promulgated by the three provincial Legislative Assemblies.

(7)   The constitutional rules and traditions that have developed in practice and were accepted as binding in the working of the government.

The foregoing instruments are by no means ordinary laws or statutes; they are rather "fundamental" laws, for no legislative body has the power to alter or repeal them by the ordinary process of legislation. They cannot be superseded by statutes which, on the contrary, have to be enacted in a manner to conform with them. However, some of these documents are now only of historical value, since their provisions have either expired or were superseded by others when Libya became independent. Such are the resolutions of the United Nations General Assembly of November 21, 1949, and November 7, 1950. The Fundamental Laws of December 2,and 4, 1950, have been superseded by articles 1, 2, and 7 of the Constitution of October 7, 1951. The transitory laws passed by the National Assembly, except the electoral law of November 6, 1951, have expired upon the establishment of national and provincial governments. It may also be noted that the Constitution of October 7, 1951, contains a number of transitory and provisional articles that have become obsolete, due to the temporary nature of the functions for which they were provided.

The Libyan general and provincial constitutional laws may be classified among so-called "written constitutions." Unlike the British constitution, all the provisions which are now embodied in the general or provincial constitutions are "written," i. e., were enacted and issued at a certain specified time. The document known as the Constitution of October 7, 1951, is the most important of all the constitutional instruments, since it embodies the general constitutional principles applicable to the whole country, while each of the three provincial constitutional instruments is applicable only to one of the three provinces.

All the Libyan constitutional instruments fall in the category known as " rigid constitutions," in contrast to " flexible constitutions," because their provisions can only be amended by a special procedure. "A flexible constitution," says Dicey, " is one under which every law of every description can legally be changed with the same ease and in the same manner by one and the same body; while the rigid constitution," he continues, " is one under which certain laws generally cannot be changed in the same manner as ordinary laws." [1] The rigidity of the Libyan constitution, like all other federal constitutions, is the result partly of the requirement of a two-thirds majority for amendment and partly of the necessity of securing the approval of the provincial legislative asemblies.

One article of the Libyan Constitution is absolutely rigid, because no change is permitted in the substance of this article. Its text reads:

> No proposal may be made to review the provisions relating to the monarchical form of government, the order of succession to the Throne, the representative form of government, or the principles of liberty and equality guaranteed by this Constitution (Article 197).

While this article is intended to perpetuate the monarchical and democratic form of government, its wording deprives Parliament of its competence to amend the constitution. It seems unlikely that such a clause could prevent Parliament from using its power to repeal the whole of Article 197—as Barthelemy noted concerning a similar provision in the Constitution of the Third French Republic—as provided under Articles 198–199.

One result of a " rigid " constitution is that, as in the United States, the municipal (internal) laws of the country must necessarily be divided into ordinary and constitutional laws: the latter always predominate, and other laws must conform to them. The term " constitutional " is always used in countries whose constitutions are rigid in the sense that a particular law conforms to the provisions of the constitution; and the term " unconstitutional " means that it is contrary to them. The procedure for determining whether laws are constitutional or not is provided for in countries with rigid constitutions by special courts. The

[1] See A. V. Dicey, *Introduction to the Study of the Law of the Constitution*, 8th ed. (London, 1923) , pp. 122–123.

Supreme Court of Libya, like the Supreme Court of the United States, fulfills this function.[2]

Three steps are specified for the amendment of the federal constitution:

(1) Each of the two Houses of Parliament (by absolute majority of all members) must adopt a resolution stating the need for and specifying the subject of amendment.

(2) Discussion and voting in each House cannot take place unless two-thirds of the members are present. An amendment is adopted only by a majority of two-thirds of the members present in each House and it must be approved by the King.

(3) As to provisions relating to the federal form of government, amendments cannot become valid unless adopted by all the provincial legislative assemblies and steps taken concerning other provisions before they are presented to the King for approval.

No amendment has yet been made to the constitution, although serious thought has been given to amending certain provisions which might simplify the elaborate structure of the government. Many a Libyan contends that there is a pressing need for such an amendment, although those in authority seem to believe that the time has not yet come to propose such a thing.

The amending of any of the three provincial constitutions is, as a rule, by a two-thirds majority of all the members of the Legislative Assembly. Both the Tripolitanian and Fazzanese Organic Laws permit the amendment of any provision during the first session of the legislative assemblies by a simple majority of all the members. The two-thirds majority must apply after the first session. The Organic Law of Cyrenaica stipulates that before an amendment is adopted the need for and the subject of the amendment first must be discussed and adopted by a majority of all the members of the Legislative Assembly. The clause that no amendment is permitted concerning the monarchical system in the federal constitution is reiterated in the Organic Law of Cyrenaica.

[2] See pp. 200-201, below.

The Federal System

The federal principle, a compromise designed to preserve states' rights while at the same time yielding primacy in certain matters to a common political authority, is the product of Western thought and was accepted by Libyans not without hesitation under pressure of external circumstances. It proved to be a working compromise for a country whose provinces had for a long time been searching for a working scheme of integration. Although the elaborate administrative structure is often the subject of criticism, Libyan unity, as one keen observer said about the American Union, "was wrung from the grinding necessities of a reluctant people." The federal system permitted Libyans, in fuller form than was possible under any system of local government, to administer purely local affairs within each province separately. It also gave them the satisfaction that in common matters they appeared to the outside world as one Libyan nation. However, federal systems vary and each one operates in accordance with the internal conditions that made possible its establishment. What kind of a federal system has Libya adopted? Let us first examine the relevant articles of the Constitution.

"Libya consists of the Provinces of Cyrenaica, Tripolitania, and Fazzan,"[3] and "its form [of government] is federal and representative."[4] The federation is made of three "states" which Libyans, not unlike Canadians, preferred to call provinces rather than "states" for the simple reason that they desired to stress national unity. The national or common government is called the federal government. The powers of the Libyan government, like other federal systems, are enumerated; but all residual powers are left to the provinces.[5] Federal powers are divided into two categories: The first consists of matters which are all within the legislative and executive powers of the federal government, and the second consists of matters which are only within the legislative powers of the federal government, while the implementation of the legislation falls within the competence of the provinces

[3] Article 3.   [4] Article 2.   [5] Articles 36–39.

acting under the supervision of the federal government. The latter category is called " joint powers."

The legislative and executive powers of the federal government, specifically stated, are as follows: [6]

(1) diplomatic, consular, and commercial representation; (2) United Nations affairs and those of its specialized agencies; (3) participation in and implementation of decisions taken by international conferences; (4) all matters relating to war and peace; (5) the conclusion and implementation of treaties and agreements; (6) the regulation of foreign passports and visas; (10) immigration into and emigration from Libya; (11) admission to and residence of foreigners in Libya and their expulsion; (12) all matters relating to nationality; (13) all other matters relating to foreign affairs; (14) provision for the land, sea, and air forces, their training and maintenance and their employment; (15) all matters relating to defense industries; (16) all matters relating to military, naval, and air force arsenals; (17) the limitations of powers in cantonment areas, the appointment of personnel for these areas and determining their powers and the regulation governing their residence; [7] (18) arms of all kinds for national defense, including firearms, ammunition, and explosives; (19) all matters relating to martial law; (20) atomic energy and materials essential to its production; (21) all other matters relating to national defense; (22) air lines and all agreements relating to them; (23) federal roads and other roads which the federal government, after consultation with the provinces, decides do not belong to a particular province; (26) the construction and control of federal railways, after agreement with the provinces which they cross; (27) all matters relating to customs; (28) taxation necessary to meet the expenditure of the federal government, after consultation with the provinces; (29) federal banks; (30) currency, the minting of coins, and the issue of notes; (31) federal finances and public debt; (32) exchange and stock exchanges; (33) inquiries and statistics relating to the federal government; (34) all matters relating to

[6] Article 36.
[7] Boundaries, however, must be delimited in consultation with the provinces (Article 36 (17)) .

the officers of the federal government; (35) in consultation with the provinces, the promotion of agricultural and industrial production and commercial activities and the ensuring to the country of essential foodstuffs; (36) the acquisition, management, and disposal of properties of the federal government; (37) co-operation between the federal government and the provinces in the work of the criminal police and the establishment of a central bureau for the criminal police and the pursuit of international criminals; (38) all matters relating to the universities and other institutions of higher learning and the determination of academic degrees; (39) all other matters specified in the constitution to the federal government. Moreover, any provincial power delegated by the province to the federal government becomes a federal power as stipulated under Article 37:

> The federal government may, with the agreement of any province, delegate to it or to its officers the executive power concerning any matter which is within its competence under this Constitution, pro-vided the federal government will bear the expenses of the execution.

Joint powers, defined as those by which the federal government exercises the legislative and the provinces the executive, are described as follows:

> In order to ensure a co-ordinated and unified policy between the provinces, the legislative power relating to the following matters [below] shall be within the competence of the federal government, while the executive power in connection with the implementation of that legislation shall be within the competence of the provinces acting under the supervision of the federal government.[8]

The joint powers relate to the following matters: (1) com-panies; (2) banks; (3) organizations of imports and exports; (4) income tax; (5) monopolies and concessions; (6) subsoil wealth and mines; (7) weights and measures; (8) all forms of insurance; (9) census; (10) shipping and navigation; (11) major ports which the federal government considers to be of impor-tance with regard to international navigation; (12) aircraft and air navigation, the construction of airports, the regulation of air

[8] Article 38.

traffic, and the administration of airports; (13) lighthouses, including lightships, beacons, and other provisions for the safety of sea and air navigation; (14) the establishment of the general judicial organization subject to the provisions of Chapter 8 of the Constitution; (15) civil, commercial, and criminal law, civil and criminal procedure, the legal profession; (16) literary, artistic, and industrial copyright, inventions, patents, trade-marks, and merchandise marks; (17) newspapers, books, printing presses, and broadcasting; (18) public meetings and associations; (19) expropriation; (20) all matters relating to the national flag, the national anthem, and official holidays; (21) conditions for practicing scientific and technical professions; (22) labor and social security; (23) the general system of education; (24) antiquities and archaeological sites and museums, libraries, and other institutions declared by a federal law to be of national importance; (25) public health and the co-ordination of matters relating to them; (26) quarantine and quarantine stations; (27) conditions for licenses to practice the medical profession and other professions relating to health.

These powers having been distributed, it is evident that Libya presents an example of federalism in which the provinces continue to preserve essential powers, although they have accepted the delegation of certain specific powers to the national government. It should also be noted that the federal government is dependent to some degree upon the provincial governments for the implementation of some of its legislation. This is a matter which places the national government not on a level with, but dependent on, the provincial governments. Thus in such matters as the levying of taxes, immigration, and holding general elections, the national government does not deal directly with the people, but acts through the provincial governments only. This is an element of subordination which is characteristic of confederal, not of federal organization, because in true federal systems the national government must be able to act in direct contact with the people.[9] However, the provincial governments cannot, under any circumstances, nullify a federal law, which clearly indicates that the right of final determination rests within

[9] See K. C. Wheare, *Federal Government* (London, 1951), pp. 14–15.

the federal government.[10] Moreover, the Libyan national government is regarded as fully competent in legislative and executive powers and it possesses, in principle, the right of supervision over the provinces. This is an element which establishes the supremacy of the national government.

The Monarchical System

The Libyan monarchy, it will be recalled, was instituted before the Constitution was promulgated. It was predetermined by the role the Sanusi house had played in Libyan history, especially in Cyrenaica, and the support given to King Idris by the Great Powers. King Idris, long before he had been proclaimed Amir of Cyrenaica in 1949, had already been acknowledged as leader by Cyrenaicans and Tripolitanians in 1920 and 1921. His negotiations with the British authorites during World War II and the role he had played in the liberation of his country made him the natural candidate for the throne of his country. Libyan monarchy, as defined in a fundamental law passed by the National Assembly on December 2, 1950, was declared to be " constitutional, democratic, and representative." [11] The constitutional instrument passed by the National Assembly on October 7, 1951, confirmed the establishment of the monarchy and added, " the sovereignty of the United Kingdom of Libya is vested in the nation. By the will of God, the people entrust it to King Muhammad Idris al-Sanusi and after him to his male heirs, the oldest after the oldest, degree after degree." [12]

" The throne of the Kingdom is hereditary." [13] The King

[10] " Where it is constitutionally provided that," says Willoughby, " in case of alleged conflict between federal and state law, such conflict shall be considered by a federal tribunal whose decrees are enforceable by the federal executive, then, in such case, a Bundesstaat [federation] certainly exists " (W. W. Willoughby, *Fundamental Concepts of Public Law* (New York, 1931), p. 202.

[11] *Proceedings of the National Assembly*, p. 10. Cf. a similar decision that had been taken in Iraq in 1921 concerning the Iraqi monarchy (M. Khadduri, *Independent Iraq* [London, 1960], p. 19.).

[12] Article 44. Cf. Article 19 of the Iraqi Constitution of 1925.

[13] Article 45.

attains his majority on completing his eighteenth year. " If the King is a minor, or if any circumstances prevent or delay him from exercising his constitutional powers and he himself is unable to appoint a deputy or deputies, the Council of Ministers shall with the consent of Parliament appoint a Regent or a Council of Regency to perform the duties of the King and to exercise his right and powers until such time as he becomes of age or is capable of exercising his powers." [14] In the event of a vacancy on the throne, Parliament should hold a joint meeting of the two Houses without convocation to appoint a successor within ten days, " three quarters at least of the number of members of the two chambers shall be present and the voting shall take place openly by a majority of two-thirds of the members present." [15]

The King is the supreme head of the state and the supreme commander of the Libyan armed forces.[16] He approves laws and orders their enforcement. He may also proclaim martial law, subject to the conditions stated in the constitution.[17] He issues orders for the holding of general elections and for the convocation of Parliament. He opens Parliament, adjourns, prolongs, or dissolves it.[18] When Parliament is not in session, and the necessity arises for urgent measures, the King issues decrees which have the force of laws, provided they are not contrary to the constitution and they must be submitted to Parliament at its first session.[19] However, the King is not responsible; he is " inviolable " and " shall be exempt from all responsibility." The King acts through his Ministers and " responsibility rests with them." [20]

The King selects the Prime Minister and appoints the other

[14] Article 50.
[15] Article 46.
[16] Articles 58 and 68.
[17] Article 70.
[18] Articles 65–67.
[19] Article 64. " If they are not submitted to Parliament or if they are not approved by either of the Chambers they shall cease to have the force of law." Cf. Article 26 of the Iraqi Constitution.
[20] Articles 59–60. These articles express the doctrine of the perfection of judgment in English Constitutional Law. " The King," says Blackstone, " is not only incapable of doing wrong, but of thinking wrong." Since the Ministers countersign the King's orders, they are held responsible for him. In a truly constitutional monarchy " the King," as Thiers has it, " reigns, but does not govern."

ministers on his recommendation; he also may dismiss the Prime Minister or may dismiss any minister on the recommendation of the Prime Minister.[21] The King exercises similar prerogatives with regard to the appointment and dismissal of provincial governors.[22]

The King, on the recommendation of the Prime Minister, confers ranks, titles, and decorations and can grant pardons and commute sentences. No death sentence is carried out without the King's consent.[23]

The Cabinet

The Cabinet is made up of the Prime Minister and a number of other ministers. They must all be Libyans, but none should be a member of the Royal Family, and a minister may or may not be a member of Parliament.

The Cabinet is responsible for the conduct of public affairs, both internal and external, in accordance with the powers given to the federal government. The ministers are jointly responsible to the Lower House for all the acts of the Cabinet, as well as being individually responsible for the policies of their own ministries. Should a majority of all the members of the Lower House pass a vote of no confidence in the Cabinet, the Cabinet must resign. If the decision in question relates to one minister only, the minister must resign. However, the Lower House " shall not consider the request for a vote of no confidence, whether such request be direct or implied, unless it has been presented by fifteen or more of the deputies. Such request may not be discussed except after eight days from the date of its presentation and shall not be voted upon except after two days from the completion of the discussion thereon." [24]

The ministers are not permitted to hold offices other than their own public offices, whether in the government or on the board of directors of any company. Nor are they permitted to purchase

[21] Article 72. Cf. Article 26 of the Iraqi Constitution of 1925.
[22] Article 180.
[23] Articles 71, 76–77.
[24] Article 87.

or rent any property belonging to the state, nor should they directly or indirectly be involved in undertakings transacted with the government.

The Cabinet meets under the chairmanship of the Prime Minister and all decisions are submitted to the King for approval before they are carried out.

If the Prime Minister resigns, or if he is dismissed, all the ministers are regarded to have resigned or been dismissed.[25]

Parliament

Legistlative power is vested in Parliament and the King. Parliament is composed of two houses, the Senate and the House of Representatives.

The Senate, like other federal systems, represents the provinces. It consists of twenty-four members, each province is equally represented by one-third of the members. The King appoints one-half of the senators; the other half are elected by the legislative assemblies of the provinces. The appointed senators are chosen from among Libyans who are prominent in public life and who are needed to serve the country in a legislative capacity. Members of the Royal Family may be appointed to the Senate, but may not be elected.[26] A Senator should not be less than forty years of age. The term of membership is eight years; half of each of the appointed and elected senators to be replaced every four years. A former Senator may be appointed or elected again.[27] The President of the Senate must be appointed by the King,[28] but the two Vice-Presidents are elected by the Senate and approved by the King. The President and the two Vice-Presidents serve for only two years, but are eligible for more than one period of service. The Senate meets and adjourns at the same time as the House of Representatives.

The House of Representatives is an elected and representative body of the whole population on the basis of one deputy for every 20,000 male inhabitants, provided that the number of

[25] Article 89.   [27] Article 98.
[26] Article 96.   [28] Article 87.

deputies of any of the three provinces not be less than five. The deputies must not be less than thirty years of age and are elected in the three provinces according to a federal electoral law by direct election through secret ballot. The term of members of the House of Representatives is four ordinary one year sessions, beginning in the first week of November.[29] If Parliament is not convened, it shall meet on the tenth day of the same month.[30] Unless dissolved, the duration of each regular annual session is five months, and the other seven are a parliamentary vacation.

The right of suffrage is not universal, because women do not vote, but it is universal " manhood " suffrage. Any person is eligible to vote (1) if he is a Libyan subject, (2) has completed his twenty-first year, (3) is not a lunatic or mentally defective, (4) has not been convicted of any crime, (5) is not an undischarged bankrupt, (6) is not a member of the armed forces or the police. Candidates are eligible for election if they (1) have completed their thirtieth year, (2) have not been sentenced for a period of six or more months or sentenced for an election irregularity in the past five years, (3) are able to read and write the Arabic language, (4) are not members of the Royal Family.[31]

Legislation can be initiated in the House of Representatives or the Senate or proposed by the government, except for financial laws, which must be initiated in the House of Representatives or proposed by the government. Neither House may discuss a draft law before it has been considered by the appropriate standing committee; if the law is adopted by either one of the two Houses, it is presented to the other. A draft law rejected by either House may not be reintroduced in the same session.[32] Draft laws are passed article by article, and then again as a whole. Draft laws, when passed by both Houses, become laws only after being confirmed by the King. The King " shall promulgate them

[29] Article 129 provides: " Elections for a new House of Representatives shall take place within the three months preceding the expiration of the period of office of the old House of Representatives. If it is not possible to carry out elections within the said period, the term of office of the old House of Representatives shall extend until they are held."

[30] Article 112.

[31] See *Federal Electoral Law of 1951*, revised in 1955, (see *Official Gazette*, November 6, 1951 and November 22, 1955) .

[32] Article 135.

within thirty days of the date of their communication to him." [33]
If the King does not want to confirm the legislation, he may send
back the law to Parliament for reconsideration and Parliament
must reconsider the law. However, if the law is passed again by
a two-thirds majority of the members composing each of the two
Houses, the King must confirm and promulgate it within the
thirty days following its communication to him. If the majority
is less than two-thirds, the law cannot be reconsidered during
the same session. "If Parliament in another session passes such
a bill again by a majority of all the members composing each
of the two chambers, the King shall sanction and promulgate it
within the thirty days following the communication of the decision to him." [34]

Every member of Parliament may put questions to and demand
explanations from ministers. "Discussion on an interpellation,"
states Article 122, "shall not take place until at least eight days
after it has been presented, except in cases of emergency and
with the consent of the person to whom the interpellation is
addressed." Meetings of both Houses of Parliament are open to
the public unless the government or ten members of either House
request that the debate should be *in camera*.

Members of Parliament have absolute freedom of speech and
enjoy parliamentary immunity. They are not liable to arrest,
nor can they be brought to trial while Parliament is in session,
unless they have been arrested in cases of *flagrante delicto*, or the
House of which they are members has authorized the arrest.

Control of Foreign Relations

Foreign relations are conducted in the name of the King, but
he acts under the advice of the federal government. He appoints
and dismisses all diplomatic representatives at the proposal of
the Minister of Foreign Affairs. He also receives foreign diplomatic missions.

The King declares war and concludes peace upon the recommendation of the Cabinet; but since he ratifies treaties only after

[33] Article 136.   [34] Article 121.

the approval of Parliament (Article 69), it follows that the conclusion of peace by a peace treaty requires the prior approval of Parliament. The Constitution makes no mention of the need for parliamentary approval if an agreement is signed with a foreign power. The practice ran that such agreements, if they were of technical nature or of minor importance, were concluded by the executive alone.

There are, however, some international obligations which qualify the King's powers with regard to foreign relations. First, there is the Anglo-Libyan treaty of 1953, which establishes " a close alliance " between the two countries and requires that each party should not adopt in its foreign relations " an attitude which is inconsistent with the alliance or might make difficulties for the other party." [35] Secondly, there are the rights given to foreign powers (England and the United States) which might compromise the position of Libya vis-à-vis other powers.

Finally, Libya is a member of the United Nations and the League of Arab States and is bound by the provisions of both the Charter and the Pact respectively of these world and regional organizations. Libya is also bound by a score of treaties with foreign powers which regulate her foreign relations. The rights and obligations of Libya under these instruments are exercised through regular diplomatic channels. Libya is represented in foreign countries by a number of permanent diplomatic missions, especially with members of the United Nations, and has received a few foreign missions.

Provincial Governments

Libya is made up of three provinces: Tripolitania, Cyrenaica, and Fazzan. These provinces, it will be recalled, decided to form the United Kingdom of Libya by a formal action taken at the third meeting of the National Assembly on December 2, 1950. They preserved their local self-government by agreeing to delegate only certain specific powers of general character to the national government, while the residual powers remained with

[35] See pp. 226 ff., below.

them. Each province laid down its own Organic Law within a year of the enforcement of the Constitution. They were meanwhile bound to enforce federal laws and observe the provisions of the Constitution.

Each province is governed by a Wali (governor), who is appointed or removed by the King. The Wali represents the King in the province and is responsible to him. He approves the laws passed by the Legislative Assembly and issues orders as the King's representative in carrying out the business of the administration. He opens, prorogues, and dissolves the Legislative Assembly in the King's name.[36] The Wali can at any time speak or take part in the discussion of the Legislative Assembly, but does not have the right to vote in that Assembly. The orders of the Wali must be countersigned by the Chief of the executive Council and the Nazirs, except for the (a) order appointing the Chief of the Executive Council, which must be signed by the King, and (b) the orders appointing the Nazirs, which must be signed by the King upon the recommendation of the Chief of the Executive Council. Finally, the Wali refers to the Supreme Court any law passed by the Legislative Assembly which is considered inconsistent with the Constitution. If the Supreme Court decides that the law is constitutional, the Wali must promulgate the law within thirty days following the Court's decision. Each province also has an Executive Council, composed of a Chief of the Council and a number of Nazirs [37] (department heads), who are appointed or dismissed by the King on the recommendation of the Wali. The Executive Council is responsible to the Legislative Assembly of the province on the specific actions of each department. A vote of no confidence by approximately two-thirds of the members of the Assembly [38] requires the Chief of the Council to resign, and a vote of the majority of all the members requires the Nazir to resign.

Each province has a Legislative Assembly for enacting leglis-

[36] See texts of the *Organic Law of Tripolitania*, Articles 51–56; *Organic Law of Cyrenaica*, Articles 8–17; *Organic Law of Fazzan*, Articles 43–48.

[37] Eight Nazirs are specified for Tripolitania and Fazzan.

[38] Specifically by 13 in Cyrenaica, 25 in Tripolitania, and 10 in Fazzan. In the latter a majority of 10 is required in a vote of no confidence in the Nazir.

lation dealing specifically with matters relating to the province. At least three quarters of the members of the Assembly must be elected. The Tripolitanian Assembly is made up of forty members, the Cyrenaican of twenty members, and the Fazzanese of seventeen members. Thirty members of the Tripolitanian and three-quarters of the Cyrenaican assemblies are elected. The Fazzanese members are all elected. The duration of the session is four years, and each Assembly meets for several months. Legislative procedures and debate in these Assemblies are not unlike those in the federal Parliament.[39] The Wali must approve legislation and can return it for reconsideration, stating reasons for so doing, but if the Legislative Assembly affirms its legislation by two-thirds majority, the Wali must approve and promulgate the legislation within thirty days of receiving it. The King can dissolve the Legislative Assembly on the recommendation of the Chief of the Executive Council and consultation with the Wali, but elections for a new Assembly must be held within ninety days from the date of dissolution. The Wali must give an opening address to the Assembly describing the state of affairs in the province and the plans of future development. Members of the Legislative Assemblies enjoy the same rights and immunities as members of the federal Parliament. Meetings are open to the public unless the representatives or the Executive Council request that the meeting must be *in camera*.[40]

The judicial system in the provinces is uniform and is established by a federal law. Decisions made in one province are accepted and enforced in all others.

The Administrative System

Under the Italian administration, Libya, when it became the Italian Fourth Shore, was united into one territory and divided into four provinces, namely, Tripoli, Misrata, Banghazi, and Darna. Each was subdivided into districts, and the provinces

[39] For certain variations see the Organic Laws of the three provinces.
[40] *Organic Law of Tripolitania*, Articles 11–50; *Organic Law of Cyrenaica*, Articles 26–58; *Organic Law of Fazzan*, Articles 9–42.

and districts were placed under the control of the governor, who was ultimately responsible to the Italian government in Rome.

Under the British military administration, the administrative system was slightly modified. Each of the three provinces was put under separate military administration, and each province was subdivided into a greater number of districts.

After the establishment of the national government a new administrative system, originally Ottoman, was adopted by the Italian and British administrations and was set up. Each of the three provinces was divided into a number of districts (*mutasarri-fiyyas*) governed by a *mutasarrif*, and each district was subdivided into *mudiriyas*, each governed by a *mudir* and *na'ib mudirs*. Tripolitania was divided into four large *mutasarrifiyyas*, each governed by a *Kabir al-Mutasarrifin*, and a number of other subdivisions. In each city there was a municipality (*baladiya*), headed by a *ra'is*, who was responsible to the mutasarrif of the district.

Appointments of Libyans in the administration began after the British assumed control of the country; but the number gradually increased when authority was yielded to the Libyan provisional government. The number of British personnel was reduced to only a few advisers to the various departments and very few were employed as technicians after the proclamation of independence. A civil service committee, composed of British and Libyan members, was set up to select civil servants from the provinces for federal administration.

In 1951 a civil service law was issued to regulate the employment of civil servants; but this law, which was intended to be temporary until the federal administration had been organized, was replaced by another more elaborate law in 1956 which specified the manner of employment, the privileges and duties of the civil servants, and disciplinary measures.[41] With this law as a model, provincial civil service laws were also issued in 1956 which regulated civil service in the provinces. A pension law and regulations implementing the civil service law were issued in 1957. Libyan young men who studied abroad, as well as the new graduates of the Libyan University, have been gradually filling

[41] *Official Gazette*, June 24, 1956.

responsible positions and are gaining experience which may well qualify them to raise the level of efficiency. However, the need for fully competent civil servants is still pressing.

The Judicial System

The judicial system is designed to be free in principle from interference by any other agency. " The judges shall be independent," states Article 142 of the Constitution, "and in administration of justice, they shall be answerable only to the law." Thus the Constitution recognized the doctrine of the separation of powers in order to insure justice (so far as it concerns the independence of the judiciary), as in every other modern state.

Under the Italian regime, as under Ottoman rule, there existed two types of courts, the civil and religious, since the Italian government did not want to encroach on the Islamic system of law relating to personal status. Under the regime created after independence, Libya took the revolutionary step, in line with other more developed countries like Egypt and Syria, of incorporating the Islamic law of personal status into a modern civil law and abolishing the religious courts as provided for in the Law of Judicial Organization of September 20, 1954. As a result the rank and file, who for centuries had been accustomed to the less sophisticated religious courts, found the new civil courts too complicated and too expensive for the settlement of disputes which previously had been disposed of more quickly and satisfactorily by the traditional religious courts. The dissatisfaction was naturally more outspoken in rural and tribal communities, mainly in Cyrenaica; this prompted the national government to reconsider the possibility of separating the existing courts into religious and civil courts. The government, after the whole matter was examined, decided to separate the courts into two types and enacted a new Law for Judicial Organization dated October 18, 1958.[42] It is unfortunate that Libya, having disposed of the traditional system of courts, reverted to it before trying

[42] For text of the law, see *Government Gazette*, November 10, 1958.

to adapt the new judicial system to its social conditions. Perhaps Libya had from the very beginning adopted too advanced a system, for it might take a very long time before she can again abolish religious courts.

There are three types of courts in Libya. They are: (1) civil courts; (2) religious courts; and (3) the Supreme Court. The jurisdiction of the civil courts extends to all matters of civil, commercial, and criminal law, and actions for or against the government, national or provincial, while the jurisdiction of the religious courts extends essentially to rural and tribal communities and deals with matters relating to the personal status of Muslims and pious foundations (Waqfs) in accordance with the Maliki school of law.

Judges are appointed by the Minister of Justice and the justices of courts of appeal by the King, on the recommendation of the Minister of Justice, but neither the judges nor the justices are liable to be transferred except by approval of the judicial council of the province. Justices of the courts of appeal are appointed for life and cannot be dismissed, but judges attain this immunity only after five years of service. There are judicial councils in the provinces, charged with the task of supervising and disciplining judges of various grades.

The Supreme Court

The Supreme Court, composed of a president and of a number of judges appointed by the King, is a federal agency and the highest judicial body in the country. The President of the Court presides, after taking an oath before the King; if the President is absent or unable to perform his duties, the King appoints a member of the court to replace him. If the office of a judge is vacant, or if the judge is absent or unable to perform his duties, the King, after consulting the President of the Court, appoints another judge in his place or someone to replace him during his absence. When the court was set up in 1953, the statute of the court permitted the appointment of foreign judges for a period of ten years until qualified Libyans could take their places.

The statute also specified that at least two well-qualified experts in Islamic law must be appointed as judges in the court; they were to be chosen from among Libyan judges who had graduated from certified institutions.

The judges of the Supreme Court enjoy full immunity and cannot be removed from office, nor can any reduction in their salary or allowances be made after they have been appointed. " If it appears that for reasons of health," states Article 147 of the Constitution, " or because of loss of confidence or respect which the office requires, one of them can no longer exercise his functions, the King, with the approval of the majority of the members of the Court excluding the member concerned, shall relieve him of his office." [43]

The Supreme Court is called " to hear disputes which may arise between the federal government and one or more provinces or between two or more provinces." The Court also decides on the constitutionality of any laws or constitutional and administrative questions referred to it, taking into account the provisions of the Constitution of the country.[44] Finally, the Supreme Court acts as the highest court of appeal in the country. "An appeal may be lodged with the Supreme Court," states Article 153 of the Constitution, " in accordance with the provisions of the federal law against any judgment by a provincial court in civil or criminal proceedings, if such judgment include a decision in a dispute concerning this constitution or the interpretation thereof." [45] All civil and judicial authorities, federal and provincial, should give the Court any assistance it may require, and any individual, if called by the Court to appear or present evidence needed, should do so.[46] The legal principles embodied in the decisions of the court are regarded as binding on all courts within the country.[47] Thus the Libyan Supreme Court, like the Supreme Court of the United States, can play an important role in the development of the federal system of the country.

[43] See also Article 11 of the statute of the Supreme Court, *Official Gazette*, November 18, 1953.

[44] *Ibid.*, Articles 14–25.

[45] *Ibid.*, Articles 15 and 17.

[46] *Ibid.*, Article 29.

[47] *Ibid.*, Article 28; Article 155 of the Constitution.

Working of the Government

On October 7, 1951, the Constitution was promulgated and on December 24, 1951, the independence of the country was declared; but an established monarchy, a federal government, and a provincial administrative system had already been in existence. To complete the form of a parliamentary government it remained necessary to order the holding of elections. The election of representatives was held in February, and that of senators in March, 1952. The first Parliament met on March 25, 1952.

Since the establishment of the monarchy only one sovereign, King Idris I, has occupied the throne of Libya. As the grandson of Muhammad b. 'Ali al-Sanusi, he has been the head not only of the Sanusi house but also of the Sanusi order ever since his uncle, Sayyid Ahmad al-Sharif, who acted as Regent of the order during Sayyid Idris' minority, died in 1933. In accordance with the Organic Law of Cyrenaica, in addition to holding the title of King of Libya, he is also the Amir of Cyrenaica.[48] The latter title, it will be recalled, was assumed in June 1949 when Cyrenaica was proclaimed a self-governing Amirate, although the title of Amir had been used since 1920.

Since King Idris had no living children—all his offspring having died in infancy—he appointed his brother Sayyid Muhammad al-Rida as heir apparent. Sayyid al-Rida, holding the title for a short period, died in the summer of 1955. A second marriage also failed to produce an heir, and the King again appointed another member of the Sanusi house, Sayyid Muhammad al-Hasan al-Rida, a nephew, as heir apparent on October 26, 1956.

From the establishment of the national government in 1951 to the time of writing (1961), Libya has had seven Cabinets. In other words, Libya has had an average of one new Cabinet every twenty months.[49] In contrast to other Arab countries, Cabinet changes in Libya have proved to be relatively infrequent, and there have been only two Cabinet crises of any importance. Since political parties, because of intense political strife between

[48] Organic Law of Cyrenaica, Article 2.
[49] See Appendix II.

the government and the parties, have been suppressed from the very beginning of Libya's independent life, one basic element of a truly democratic form of government has been eliminated, thus relieving the executive of a direct public pressure. There have remained only two other factors that might contribute to Cabinet changes, namely, the King, who has the right to dismiss a Cabinet, and Parliament, which can cause the fall of a government, by a vote of no confidence. The King seems to have been reluctant to dismiss his Prime Ministers except perhaps in the case of Saqizli,[50] and the Prime Ministers, so long as they enjoyed the King's confidence, tended to betray authoritarian tendencies in governing the country. Nor has Parliament been able to control the Cabinet, although it has the power of casting a vote of no confidence—which has been exercised only once—owing to the control of elections by the government. There has remained, therefore, one fundamental factor which has caused the fall of almost all cabinets—the conflict between Palace entourage and the Cabinet. In a form of government in which the Cabinet is responsible both to the King and Parliament, the Palace can indeed play a very effective role in Cabinet changes by indirect interference, even if the King proves to be reluctant to change Cabinets. A study of each Cabinet's rise and fall will be dealt with in the following pages.

Under a federal system it is neither good policy nor is it in the interest of stability for the Prime Minister to be chosen without regard to his local loyalties. Since the King was Cyrenaican, he chose for the the first Prime Minister a Tripolitanian. Thus, the Prime Minister of the provisional government and the head of the first Cabinet, who had headed the Tripolitanian local government under the British administration, was the Tripolitanian, Mahmud al-Muntasir. The second and third governments were headed by Cyrenaicans, Saqizli and Bin Halim; the fourth by a Tripolitanian, Ku'bar; and the present by Muhammad Bin 'Uthman, a Fazzanese. No strict rule can be said to have emerged from this practice, but the precedent has certainly been established that candidates for the Premiership should be sought from each one of the three provinces in a more or less alternate

[50] See p. 243, below.

manner. In each Cabinet the provinces must be represented by an adequate number of Ministers. In the first Cabinet there were three Tripolitanians, two Cyrenaicans, and one Fazzanese. This general proportion was continued, although by no means can it be said to have established a pattern, for the number of Cyrenaicans in the Saqizli Cabinet exceeded that of Tripolitanians, and in the Kuʻbar Cabinet the number of Tripolitanians was double that of Cyrenaicans.

Parliament has met regularly since 1952. The original senators, eight from each province, had all been appointed by the King in 1952, in the absence of the provincial Legislative Assemblies and remained in office until 1956. In 1956, the King appointed four senators from each province and the Legislative Assembly of each province elected four, for eight years. In 1960, lots were drawn for the retirement of half of the number, in accordance with Article 98 of the constitution, which requires the retirement of half of those who completed the eight years of their term, and the replacement of the other half by one-half appointed by the King and one-half elected by the Legislative Assemblies of the provinces. Thereafter, half of the senators were to be changed every four years, after having completed a term of eight years.

There have been three different Houses elected; the first in 1952, the second in 1956, and the third in 1960. No dissolution of Parliament has yet been made. From the very beginning there has been a noticeable eager desire on the part of political leaders to enter Parliament, especially when opposition parties were still in evidence, in order to influence government policy. After the dissolution of parties, most of the candidates in the second election were government nominees and the electorate showed less eagerness to go to the polls than in the first election, due to the rigid control exercised by the government. In the third election, there was a noticeably greater freedom, resulting in the victory of candidates who conducted vigorous campaigns on their own. Several candidates who held seats in the first two elections lost in the third, and new faces, including former members of opposition parties, for the first time won seats in the new Parliament. The new opposition elements proved to be instrumental in the fall of the Kuʻbar Cabinet. This is a significant phenomenon which may well mark the beginning of a new trend in Libyan politics by which Parliament may exert increasing influence over the government.

Tribal chiefs as well as city dwellers were represented; indeed it has always been the complaint, especially of the town dwellers of Cyrenaica, that the tribal chiefs were overrepresented. Another criticism is often made, both in Tripolitania and Cyrenaica, that the elections in the rural and tribal communities, especially in the first two elections, were rigidly controlled by the government, so much so that supporters of the government were always elected. While control of the elections by no means completely suppressed criticism in Parliament, the experience of Libya with parliamentary life has proved more rewarding than in many other Arab countries, due both to the relatively free elections and the reluctance of the King to order the dissolution of Parliament before the expiration of a parliamentary session.

The status of the provinces after independence has undergone a change since the constitution was enforced. Cyrenaica, which had become fully self-governing in 1949, was reduced to the status of a province on an equal level with the other two provinces. Her Prime Minister became a Wali, the Cabinet an Executive Council, and the Ministers Nazirs. Only three Walis have been appointed in Cyrenaica.[51] The provisional administrations in Tripolitania and Fazzan, which were instituted in March, 1951, came to an end and a Wali with an Executive Council and a Legislative Assembly, was established in each one of them. Seven Walis have been appointed in Tripolitania [52] and two in Fazzan.[53]

---

[51] Muhammad Saqizli (1952-54), Husayn Maziq (1954-61), and Mahmud Abu Hidma (1961-).

[52] The Tripolitanian Walis were: Fadil Bin Zikri (1952-53), Siddiq al-Muntasir (1953-1954), 'Abd Al-Salam al-Busiri (1954-55), Muhammad Jamal al-Din Bash Agha (1955-58), Tahir Bakir (1958-60), Abu Bakr Na'ama (1960-61), and Fadil Bin Zikri (1961-).

[53] The Fazzanese Walis were: Ahmad Sayf al-Nasr (1952-54) and 'Umar Sayf al-Nasr (1954-).

Political Parties

From the time Libya was emancipated from Italian control, there was keen interest in organizing political parties along Western lines in order to develop a democratic form of government. Before the war, political parties existed in the form of groups revolving around leading feudal or tribal chiefs, but they could hardly be called parties in the modern sense of the term. This traditional pattern persisted, although some of the parties that developed in Tripolitania showed a tendency to invite the public to participate in political activities. Six political parties in Tripolitania and three in Cyrenaica developed spontaneously after the war [54]—they all, it will be recalled, demanded independence and were opposed to Italian return to their country.

The programs of the Tripolitanian parties consisted of three basic principles: (1) complete independence; (2) unity of the three provinces; (3) and membership in the Arab League. The Cyrenaican parties, except perhaps the 'Umar al-Mukhtar group, stressed local self-government within the larger Libyan unity and demanded that Sayyid Idris be the head of state.

Although some of the Tripolitanian parties and the 'Umar al-Mukhtar group of Cyrenaica advocated the principles of democracy, all the parties were based on a traditional pattern in structure. Nor did they, except for the 'Umar al-Mukhtar Club, carry on any important social or cultural activities in the country. They could hardly be called popular, in the sense that they included the people, nor did the public outside the large towns have a clear understanding of the significance of party platforms. However, the parties, especially the 'Umar al-Mukhtar Club in Cyrenaica and the National Congress in Tripolitania, claimed that they enjoyed the support of the majority of the people. The leaders as a rule were either members of well-known families or wealthy city dwellers. Among the tribes, the chiefs spoke for the tribesmen and these, especially in Cyrenaica, were under Sanusi influence. The tribal and rural communities supported the authoritarian and patriarchal principles of government which

[54] For a discussion of the origin of these parties see pp. 58-66, 84-88, above.

have been the accepted pattern in the history of this part of the world.

After the promulgation of the constitution and the declaration of independence, the National Congress Party of Tripolitania was dissolved and the Mukhtar Club, even before Cyrenaica had joined the union, was closed. The remaining political parties failed to achieve their purpose and were dissolved shortly after independence. Thus the party system, that had been formed before independence, disappeared mainly because it had lost the *raison d'être* for which it had arisen. Since the achievement of independence was the principal reason for the establishment of the parties, there seems to be no chance for the reappearance of new parties unless new principles are formulated which will appeal to the politically conscious public. Although there are indications that new ideas are gradually spreading among the younger generation, the time has not yet come for expressing these ideas in the shape of party platforms. Nor does the ruling authority seem to be well-disposed to the reappearance of a party system. Thus political groups tend to work underground.

Conclusion

In viewing in retrospect the steps that led up to the establishment of the present regime, it will be noted that two features of Libya's constitutional framework have been stressed, namely, the federal type of unity and the democratic form of government. Both are novel features in the internal structure of the country and have been adopted in order either to overcome a particularly pressing difficulty or to meet the desire of a certain section of the public.

Federalism, as has often been reiterated, was adopted as the only means of achieving unity, for without it neither Cyrenaica nor Fazzan would have been prepared to surrender its fully self-governing status. As a political measure it proved to be the answer to Libya's internal dissension; but federalism, by its very nature, requires an elaborate constitutional structure which has proved to be too costly for so small a nation as Libya.

Federalism, however, should not be looked upon as a rigid system; as the historical experience of the United States has shown, it is a flexible legal framework which helps co-ordinate relations among the provinces until a strong central government can exercise an increasingly greater number of functions and responsibilities.

However, a federal system may have a compensating feature in that it requires some elements of democratic government, for it emphasizes representation, majority rule and minority rights, the co-ordinate existence of two sets of laws, two sets of public officers, and groups that can give cohesion to a complex of loyalties.[55] The constitution has provided a democratic framework of government which, as one member of Parliament has said, may be favorably compared with that of many other democratic governments in the East.[56] The actual operation of the government, however, will depend on how Libyan leaders want it to work. Some critics have cast doubt on the value of democratic governments in Eastern lands and have tended to regard them as " too much in advance of the requirements and political education of the country." [57] These critics assert that real progress can only be achieved by direct administration. Yet the significance of democratic institutions must depend on their possibilities for the future and not on the quantitative achievement of an efficient authoritarian regime.

[55] E. g., followers of the National Congress in Tripolitania and the Mukhtar group in Cyrenaica.
[56] See a statement by 'Ali al-'Unayzi in Parliament on March 30, 1953, in *Proceedings of the House of Representatives*, First Session, 1952, p. 23.
[57] Cromer, *Modern Egypt* (London, 1908) , Vol. II, p. 278.

chapter **VIII**

Trial and Error in Self-Government I:
From Muntasir to Saqizli

FROM THE TIME the United Nations passed a resolution (1949) to the effect that Libya should be constituted as an independent state, it was agreed among the powers that authority should be transferred from foreign to native control at the earliest possible moment. Since the three provinces had been administered as separate territories, it seemed then that the establishment of a national government was the natural step to be taken before the question of distribution of powers among the provinces was tackled. Cyrenaica and Fazzan, against Tripolitanian wishes, had already established separate administrative regimes. When Tripolitanian leaders were invited to establish a prototype regime, they declined to do so on the basis that such a move would compromise their national aspiration to achieve unity. Not until Libyan independence and unity had been recognized in principle and the National Assembly had adopted the federal form of government did moderate Tripolitanian leaders, to the dissatisfaction of the Congress Party, agree to organize a separate administrative regime in their province. Thus the foundation of the future structure of government was affirmed before authority was conveyed to Libyan management.

Transfer of Powers

On February 21, 1951, the National Assembly, having already adopted the federal system, passed a resolution to establish local governments which would " receive the powers to be transferred from the two Administering Powers." The King-designate was requested to appoint the personnel of such governments and to ask " the Administering Powers in Tripolitania and the Fazzan to enable those persons to receive and exercise their powers as a preliminary measure towards the establishment of the federal Libyan state by the appointed date, in accordance with the resolution of the United Nations." [1] Since the British administration, owing to local opposition, was unable to convoke an elected assembly in Tripolitania, the only practical course open to it was to set up a local government by a decree, called the Transitional Powers Proclamation, issued by the Chief Administrator. The King-designate approved of this procedure and such a government was set up in March, 1951. The Administrative Council, presided over by the Chief Administrator, in which the principal political parties (except the National Congress) were represented, formally approved the establishment of a Council of Regency, in accordance with the resolution of the National Assembly (March 8, 1951). The Transitional Powers Proclamation, by virtue of which powers concerning internal affairs were transferred to native control, terminated the existence of the Administrative Council, and the position of the Chief Administrator, who was head of the Council, was reduced to that of a British Resident.[2] Mahmud al-Muntasir, who served as Vice-President of the Administrative Council, became the head of the Tripolitanian government.[3] Adrian Pelt, who showed concern lest this

[1] *Proceedings of the National Assembly*, p. 40; Pelt's *Second Annual Report*, 1951, p. 83.

[2] For text of the Transitional Powers Proclamation, see his Majesty's Government, *Annual Report to the General Assembly of the United Nations Concerning the Administration of Cyrenaica and Tripolitania*, 1950–51, pp. 26–30.

[3] Muntasir, born in 1903, belongs to a distinguished family. He studied in Italy and worked for a long time in the Waqf Department. It was not until the British occupation of Libya that he began to take part in politics and

step should weaken the Libyan federal government, advised that the newly created local governments be called " administrations " rather than " governments." [4]

The Tripolitanian government, composed of departments headed by Libyan ministers, began to direct the administration and discharge functions previously exercised by the British administration in internal affairs. The powers were perhaps equally divided between the British Resident and the Council of Ministers (known as the Council of Regency) —the latter's powers included the administration of public utilities, the control of agriculture, education, and public health. It was rightly doubted that the partition of authority would be equal,[5] for the powers reserved to the British Resident included legislative and financial matters as well as the defense of the territory and the conduct of foreign relations.[6] However, each department was headed by a native director, assisted by several British advisers. If not viewed solely in terms of how much power the Libyan personnel actually exercised, the sharing of authority by Libyans and British was intended to insure a gradual assumption of responsibility and to allow Libyans to gain administrative experience during the transitional period.

Mahmud al-Muntasir, who showed remarkable ability in heading what was virtually a diarchy, served hardly a month when he resigned to form the provisional federal government. The Tripolitanian administration continued to exist as a temporary regime until December 24, 1951, when the first national (federal) government was formed and the three local governments of Cyrenaica, Tripolitania, and Fazzan were transformed into pro-

---

Blackley, who appreciated his ability and integrity, appointed him as head of the Tripolitanian government.

[4] Pelt pointed out that the selection of the members of the Tripolitanian government was perhaps not done in full consultation with the King-designate in accordance with the resolution of the National Assembly. See Pelt's *Second Annual Report*, p. 85. The selection of Muntasir, however, as head of the government, received the King's approval to the writer's best knowledge.

[5] Pelt's *Second Annual Report*, p. 85.

[6] The British Resident's report states: " In the discharge of the functions which have been retained during the past year, His Majesty's government was, of course, mindful of the needs and desires of the people of Libya " (British Government, *Annual Report . . . to the United Nations*, p. 4.) .

vincial administrations. During the period from the establishment of local governments to their transformation into provincial
administrations, the British authorities in Cyrenaica and Tripolitania, and the French in Fazzan, gradually transferred all internal
powers to the provinces. General powers and the powers of
defense and foreign relations, although exercised separately on
behalf of the provinces, were eventually transferred to the Libyan
federal government upon the formal declaration of independence
on December 24, 1951.[7]

Grants-in-aid, both to local and to central authorities, had
already been approved by the British and the French governments in order to enable the Libyans to assume their responsibilities. Such grants-in-aid proved to be essential not only during
the transitional period but also after Libya had assumed responsibility for herself, owing to her meager resources during the early
years of independence.

A co-ordination committee, under the supervision of Adrian
Pelt, was set up to advise on the ways and means by which
powers were to be transferred.[8] The work was particularly hard,
since the progressive transfer of powers could not easily be done
in a smooth and harmonious manner. Libyans, who for long
had been under foreign rule, were naturally anxious and perhaps
too impatient to wait long for the assumption of powers. Friction
and a certain delay in the transfer were perhaps inevitable; but
the process on the whole was completed with a great measure
of success. The final discharge of responsibility, as described in
the British report on the administration of Cyrenaica and Tripolitania, was made with the following concluding remark:

> In response to the wish of the Libyans that their country should
> achieve independence at the earliest possible date, the British ad-
> ministrations in Cyrenaica and Tripolitania have made every effort
> in preparation for this. In future it will be for the Libyan people,
> officials, and Ministers alone to man and steer the ship of state and
> to conduct their affairs with the wisdom and foresight of which they
> already shown promise.[9]

---

[7] For the proclamations of the transfer of powers from British to Libyan
hands, see the British Government, *Annual Report . . . to the United Nations,
Supplementary Reports* (Annexes).

[8] Pelt's *Second Annual Report*, pp. 88 ff; *Supplementary Report*, pp. 1–2.

[9] The British Government, *Annual Report*, p. 25.

Declaration of Independence and the Formation of the First National Government

The preliminary steps for the assumption of full responsibility having been completed by the provisional government during the nine months of its existence, the stage was now set for the formal proclamation of independence. On December 24, 1951, at the Manar Palace—formerly Graziani's—in Banghazi, King Idris, in the presence of the provisional government, foreign representatives, and native dignitaries, formally proclaimed the independence of his country and the enforcement of the Constitution. The King-designate, who on that day became by constitutional decree the first Sovereign of Libya, said:

> We joyfully proclaim to the noble people of Libya that in fulfillment of their endeavors and of the United Nations Resolution of November 21, 1949, our beloved country has, with the help of God, attained independence. . . .
>
> We formally proclaim that Libya had, from today, become an independent sovereign state, and, in compliance with the Resolution of the Libyan National Assembly of December 2, 1950, we take to ourself henceforth the title of " His Majesty the King of the United Kingdom of Libya."
>
> We welcome also the coming into force at this moment of the Constitution of the Country, as drawn up and promulgated by the National Assembly on the 6th day of Muharram in the year 1371 (October 7, 1951). It is our wish, as you well know, that the life of the country should conform to the constitutional principles, and we intend henceforth to exercise our powers in accordance with the provision of this Constitution . . . it is our duty one and all to preserve what we have gained at so dear a price, and to hand it down carefully and faithfully to our posterity.
>
> At this blessed hour, we are mindful also of our heroes of the past. We invoke the dew of God's mercy and reward upon the soul of our righteous martyrs, and we salute the sacred banner, the legacy of our fathers and the hard-earned symbol of our unity, in the hope that the new era which dawns today will be for our country an era of well-being and of peace. . . .[10]

---

[10] *Tarablus al-Gharb*, Tripoli, December 25, 1951; Pelt's *Supplementary Report to the Second Annual Report*, (1951) p. 25.

On the same day, immediately after the proclamation of independence, Muntasir, head of the provisional government, tendered his letter of resignation to the King in accordance with the terms providing for the establishment of the provisional government. The King invited Muntasir to form the first national government, the members of which were the same as those who served in the provisional government, with the exception of 'Umar Shinnib, the Minister of Defense.[11] Three of the Ministers were Tripolitanians, two Cyrenaicans, and one Fazzanese. The exclusion of Shinnib, who aspired to remain as Minister of National Defense, from the Cabinet proved to be a source of considerable trouble for the Prime Minister; for, after Shinnib's appointment as Chief of the Royal Diwan (Palace), the Prime Minister's opponent in his new position of power rendered the Prime Minister's task in his relations vis-à-vis the Diwan more difficult.

On the same day the King, upon the recommendation of the Prime Minister, issued decrees appointing the Walis for the three provinces. Saqizli, the Prime Minister of Cyrenaica, became its first Wali; Ahmad Sayf al-Nasr, Chief of the government of Fazzan, Wali of that province; and Fadil Bin Zikri, Minister of Education in the Tripolitanian Government, Wali of Tripolitania. The self-governing regimes of the three provinces were converted into local "administrations," and their chiefs of departments, who had been Ministers, a title now applied only to members of the national government, came to be known as Nazirs (chiefs or controllers). In accordance with Article 177 of the Constitution each province proceeded to draw up its own Organic Law, to be promulgated within a year of the enforcement of the Constitution, and to organize its own local administration. The Transitional Powers Proclamations of Cyrenaica and Tripolitania, the Constitution and Parliament of Cyrenaica, and the Councils of Regency of Tripolitania and Fazzan were terminated, and all powers under the Transitional Powers Procla-

[11] The composition of the government was as follows: Muntasir for the Premiership and Foreign Affairs; Fathi al-Kikhya for Deputy Premiership, Justice, and Education; Mansur Qadara for Finance and Economics; 'Ali al-Jirbi for National Defense; Ibrahim Bin Sha'ban for Communications; and Muhammad Bin 'Uthman for Health.

mations vested in the British Resident were now to be exercised by the King.

Upon his return to Tripoli (on the evening of December 24), the Prime Minister handed Adrian Pelt a note containing the official notification that Libya had become an independent country and requesting him to inform the President of the United Nations General Assembly of the declaration of independence. In the meantime an application for membership in the United Nations, which reflected Libya's earnest desire to join that organization, was communicated to its Secretary-General.

The work of Adrian Pelt was not terminated without due expression of the appreciation of the Libyan government. " Our thanks to the General Assembly," reads the Premier's letter to the President of the United Nations General Assembly, " must be directed above all to its agent, the United Nations Commissioner in Libya, Mr. Adrian Pelt. We have come to regard him not only as our beloved friend and wise counsellor, but as one who toiled without regard for personal convenience or health for our interest." [12] Pelt's work was gratefully acknowledged by associating his name with more than one public place in the country. The author heard many Libyans speak warmly of him; rarely was his name mentioned without praise. Libyans, moreover, acknowledged the work of all those who represented the United Nations during the difficult period of their country's rise to statehood.

First General Elections

No sooner had Libya's independence been proclaimed than the national government promptly began to implement the provisions of the Constitution. One of the first important acts was the holding of general elections. The Constitution provides that the first general elections were to be held within a period not exceeding three and a half months from the date of the promulgation of the electoral law.[13] Since the law was promulgated on

[12] Pelt's, *Supplementary Report to the Second Annual Report*, p. 3.
[13] Article 205: " The First elections to the House of Representatives must take place within a period not exceeding three and half months from the date on which the electoral law is promulgated."

November 6, 1951, the period was to expire on February 20, 1952. Therefore, the government had set February 19 as the polling day and the election results were to be announced on the following day. According to Article 211, the first Parliament was to convene within a period of not more than twenty days from the day the election results were announced—that is, not later than March 11, 1952; but actually the first Parliament was unable to meet until March 25.

The national government took pains to prepare all preliminary arrangements, registration of electors, issuance of writs, and nomination of candidates as well as all other necessary steps to complete and announce the election results. The government's task, in view of the counteraction of opposition parties in the elections, proved to be quite formidable, for at various times during the polling the opposition resorted to violence.

The first step taken was to divide the three provinces of Libya into urban and rural electoral districts. These districts were divided into constituencies or tribal units, and the constituencies into polling districts, each of which had a polling station.[14] On November 26, 1951, the Minister of Justice issued an electoral notice specifying the names and boundaries of the electoral districts, constituencies, and polling districts, assigning in the meantime distinguishng letters and numbers to constituencies and polling stations.[15]

Libya was divided into ten urban and rural districts.[16] These were subdivided into fifty-nine constituencies corresponding to the number of seats in the House of Representatives: thirty-five for Tripolitania, fifteen for Cyrenaica, and five for Fazzan.[17] The constituencies, except in Fazzan, were determined on the basis of one for approximately every 20,000 inhabitants.[18] The fifty-nine constituencies were subdivided into 226 polling stations.

The Minister of Justice issued further electoral notices in

[14] The Electoral Law, Article 7.
[15] *Ibid.*, Article 8.
[16] There were three electoral districts—one in Tripolitania, two in Cyrenaica (Banghazi and Darna), and one in Fazzan—and seven rural electoral districts: three in Tripolitania, three in Cyrenaica, and one in Fazzan.
[17] Article 206 of the Constitution and Article 6 of the Electoral Law.
[18] Article 101 of the Constitution.

November and December appointing a supervisor-general of elections and officers to perform the duties of registration. Notices were also issued in due course, calling upon eligible persons in urban and rural districts to have their names entered in the electoral registers of their respective districts. Three weeks were allowed for registration from the date of the notice. The registers included the names of all eligible persons, normally resident in their polling areas, who had applied for registration.[19]

On December 4, a notice was issued to the public concerning the preparation of the electoral registers and the steps which eligible voters should take to have their names entered in the register. The process of registration proved to be slow and tedious, and the Minister of Justice found it necessary to extend the period for registration more than once. In January, 1952, the Minister of Justice issued writs of election through the supervisor-general. These were explained to voters and included the date, time, and place of the nomination and election of candidates. Nominations were completed at the end of January, and each candidate completed and delivered his paper to the Returning Officer, including a declaration indicating that he possessed the qualifications required for his election. Polling was scheduled to take place on February 19, 1952, and the polling stations remained open for the whole day. Voting, in accordance with the law, was by secret ballot in urban districts and through the Registering Officer in rural districts.

The National Congress Party, believing that the majority was on its side, held a meeting on January 20, 1952, in which it was decided to participate in the elections. Sa'dawi, leader of the party, urged the public to go to the polls and support candidates who would be "the true and honest representatives" of the people. The party, following Sa'dawi's speech, passed resolutions which were communicated to the King and published in the press. These may be summed up in the following:

1. Loyalty to the King, the symbol of the country, and the embodiment of the national aspirations of the people.

---

[19] Article 13 of the Electoral Law also provides that the registration officer can register the name of any person who appears to him to be qualified for registration in his polling area, even if such person fails to apply.

2. Freedom of elections.

3. Neutral stand of the government during the elections.

4. The interference of some government officials in the elections in certain constituencies was apparent.

5. The government's transfer of several tribal chiefs indicates its partiality in the elections.

6. The government's prohibition of officials from joining certain parties, while it allowed them to join others, is illegal.

7. The government is requested to take into consideration the above proposals.

8. These proposals shall be communicated to the King.[20]

A delegation proceeded to Banghazi to submit these proposals to the King on February 28; and the King, to the satisfaction of the delegation, declared that elections should be held " in an atmosphere of freedom and justice." On February 4, 1952, the Congress announced its platform and the names of its candidates and urged the people to vote for them. The principal points of the platform were as follows:

1. Loyalty to the King

2. The achievement of Libyan unity

3. The realization of the country's true independence.

4. Preservation of the country's freedom and sovereignty

5. Preservation of the country's reputation abroad

6. Justice and equality among all the people

7. Promotion of education and its spread among the people

8. Improvement of health conditions

9. Promotion of the agricultural and industrial development of the country

10. Creating new jobs for workers and improving the conditions of labor.[21]

During January and February, the Congress Party conducted an active election campaign and had high hopes of winning a majority in Parliament, since two thirds (35 out of 55) of the seats in the House of Representatives would be held by Tripoli-

---

[20] *Shu'lat al-Hurriya,* Tripoli, February 21, 1952.

[21] *Shu'lat al-Hurriya,* Tripoli, February 4, 1952.

tanians. Since the federal form of government, against which the Congress Party had conducted an active campaign, was not popular in Tripolitania, it was conjectured that the victory of that party would inevitably lead to the revision of the constitution and the abandonment of the federal system. While Sa'dawi often reiterated his party's loyalty to the King, rumors were circulated that Sa'dawi was contemplating the overthrow of the monarchical system.

On February 19, the elections were completed, resulting in the victory of the Congress Party in Tripoli City,[22] and an overwhelming victory for progovernment candidates in the country. In Cyrenaica the elections were held on the same day as in Tripolitania, but the most important aspect was the tribal elections. Only in the city of Banghazi did family rivalry play a part in the elections.

The defeat of the Congress Party in the tribal area of Tripolitania came as a surprise to the Party's leaders who had expected an overwhelming victory. Believing that government officials had tampered with the elections, the tribes, inspired by Congress leaders, rushed to government buildings and destroyed public property, cut telephone wires, and interrupted transportation. Weapons were carried openly and there were indications that these disturbances might have developed into a widespread uprising against authority.[23]

The government reacted quickly to stop the threatened rebellion. The principal leaders were arrested and police surveillance of the area of disturbance was imposed. The influence of the Congress Party was confined to Tripoli city; but even here the government's decision to expel Sa'dawi, the moving spirit of the party, on the ground that he had held a Sa'udi passport, paralyzed its activities. The idea of banishing Sa'dawi from the country had already been discussed in the Cabinet, but the King, who advised moderation, had discouraged such a drastic measure. When, however, certain indications made it clear that the Con-

[22] The candidates for Tripoli City were the following: 'Abd al-Rahman al-Qalhud, 'Abd al-'Aziz al-Zaqalla'i, Mustafa Mizran, Mustafa al-Sarraj, and Muhammad al-Zaq'ar.

[23] See *Al-Libi*, Tripoli, March 24, 1952; *Al-Manar*, Banghazi, February 11 and 25, 1952.

gress Party was encouraging the tribes to seize power by force, the government, with the King's approval, decided to act on February 21. The Wali, Fadil Bin Zikri, was instructed to issue orders to the chief of police who, in the early hours of the following day, sent a police detachment to arrest and deport Sa'dawi. Escorted all the way to the Egyptian frontier, he tried, during the plane's stop at Banghazi and after his arrival in Cairo, to appeal to the King against the government's action, but to no avail. From Cairo Sa'dawi proceeded to Riyad to resume his post as one of Ibn Sa'ud's political advisers, a position that he held until his death. He died in Beirut, while on a visit, in January, 1957.

Viewed in retrospect, the expulsion of Sa'dawi as a short-term measure relieved the government of a powerful opponent; but his disappearance from the country, where factional rivalries had long dominated Tripolitanian politics, hastened the collapse of political parties. The immediate effect of the disappearance of an opposition party, which rendered Parliament an obsequious assembly, was to place the Cabinet in the position of facing alone the struggle with the provincial authorities. For under a federal form of government, and where parochial feeling is strong, the central authority always needs the support of elements sympathetic to unity. It may be remarked also that the expulsion of a man who had just returned from exile, having spent the greater part of his political career struggling for his country's liberation, was indeed harsh regardless of his personal failings.

Parliament

Elections having been completed, preparations for the opening of the first parliamentary session were made. The date for the opening of Parliament, which should have been not later than March 11, 1952,[24] was set on March 25.

Parliament met in a joint session at Banghazi, the eastern capital, presided over by 'Umar Mansur al-Kikhya, who had been appointed President of the Senate on March 23, 1952. In an

[24] Article 211 of the Constitution.

impressive ceremony the King attended the opening meeting, surrounded by members of the national government, leading members of the Sanusi House, and dignitaries of the country. The King, amid loud applause, read Article 47 of the Constitution before both Houses:

> I swear by Almighty God to observe the Constitution and the laws of the country and to devote all my efforts to the maintenance of the independence of Libya and to defending the safety of its territory.

Having thus taken the Constitutional oath, the King handed the Speech from the Throne to the Prime Minister, Mahmud al-Muntasir, who read it before the joint meeting. The King left immediately afterwards. 'Umar Mansur, who presided over the joint meeting, made a short speech in which he said with pride that the meeting of the first Parliament was one of the fruitful results of the long struggle for independence.[25] The two Houses then reassembled in separate chambers and the first meeting was devoted to the taking of the constitutional oath by the members of Parliament.

Henceforth Parliament met regularly. On the following day, the House of Representatives met to elect its first Speaker, 'Abd al-Majid Ku'bar, and both Houses elected standing committees. Two temporary committees were set up in each House; one for the preparation of the text of the reply to the Speech from the Throne, and the other for the internal regulations of each House.

It was not until the fourth meeting (March 31) that the discussion on the reply to the Speech from the Throne was initiated. The Speech, embodying the government's program, may be summed up as follows. After the usual thanks rendered to God, the King expressed his gratefulness for having lived long enough to see the fruits of his long endeavors in the struggle for the country's liberation. He congratulated the nation on the completion of the constitutional structure of the state and earnestly called upon the country's representatives to exercise their rights, reminding them of their responsibilities to enact legislation on

---

[25] *Proceedings of the Senate,* First Session, 1952, p. 9.

the basis of wisdom and past experience. He hoped that the administrative and financial systems would be strengthened in order to ensure the stability and independence of the country. In the realm of foreign affairs, he stressed the country's aspirations to co-operate with other nations and to establish firm and friendly relations with them. He paid high tribute to the United Nations representatives as well as to the representatives of other countries who rendered all possible assistance to Libya in achieving her independence. He also stressed his government's desire to protect the rights of foreigners living in the country.

In domestic affairs, the King dwelt more extensively on the measures which his government intended to lay down by enacting legislation based on the laws of other countries, Egypt in particular, adapted to the needs and social conditions of the country. These included educational, financial, health, and other legislation which were designed to speed up the development of Libya and place it on the same footing as other countries. He appealed to the members to co-operate with the government in carrying out this program.[26] In the reply to the Speech from the Throne, both Houses of Parliament endorsed the program embodied in the speech, stressing the items which were deemed most urgent for the country.[27]

The first year of the parliamentary session lasted until August 18, 1952, during which Parliament kept itself busy enacting laws, addressing questions to members of the government, and discussing matters brought to its attention. Owing to pressure of work, the government submitted a relatively small number of bills to Parliament. The number of laws enacted barely exceeded ten, including the budget concerning which there was a lively discussion, and the internal regulations of both Houses of Parliament. However, there had been addressed to the government a considerable number of questions designed to exercise parliamentary supervision as well as to afford the government an opportunity to explain its position on several matters of public concern.

[26] For text of the Speech, *Proceedings of the Senate*, First Session, 1952, pp. 3–8; *Proceedings of the House of Representatives*, First Session, 1952, pp. 3–9.
[27] See *Proceedings of the House of Representatives*, First Session, 1952, pp. 17, 20–23; *Proceedings of the Senate*, First Session, 1952, pp. 14–15.

There was a noticeable spirit of co-operation between Parliament and the government and an earnest desire to fulfill parliamentary functions satisfactorily. At the last sitting of the annual session (August 18), the Deputy Prime Minister, Fathi al-Kikhya, thanked Parliament for its diligent work and co-operation, and the two members of the House of Representatives, 'Unayzi and Buwaysir, remarked that the way in which their House had functioned demonstrated that the country possessed a number of able men who knew how to discharge their public responsibilities faithfully.[28] The meetings of Parliament were held partly in Banghazi (March 25–April 8, 1952), and partly in Tripoli (April 27–August 18, 1952), when the national government itself moved from the eastern to the western capital.

During its second year, which lasted from November 10, 1952, to November 17, 1953, without recess, Parliament devoted the greater part of its time to passing more than a dozen laws and debated and approved both a temporary and an annual budget. The Speech from the Throne, which reiterated a program of reform, similar to that of the first, stressed a policy of austerity in government expenditure, due to the need for economic reconstruction. The government promised to establish the Supreme Court, to organize a national army and, in foreign affairs, to join the League of Arab States and the Universal Postal Union.[29]

During the debate on some government measures, especially the budget, a small group of representatives organized themselves as a parliamentary opposition bloc (al-Kutla). The bloc included not only former members of the Congress Party, such as Mizran, Qalhud, Sarraj, and Zaqalla'i, but also others from Cyrenaica, such as Bisaykiri and Buwaysir, who joined in vocal criticism of the government's conduct in domestic and foreign affairs. It was pointed out that criticism was necessary,[30] and the government was severely censured on some specific measures.[31]

[28] *Proceedings of the House of Representatives*, First Session, 1952, pp. 316–17.

[29] *Proceedings of the Senate*, First Session, 2nd year, 1953, pp. 3–7; *Proceedings of the House of Representatives*, First Session, 2nd year, 1953, pp. 3–7.

[30] *Proceedings of the House of Representatives*, First Session, 2nd year, 1953, p. 54.

[31] *Ibid.*, pp. 79, 125–26, 168–71.

Sharper criticism was directed against the government's financial policy and one critic, Mustafa al-Sarraj, bluntly said that if the government could not pursue a sound policy it should resign.[32] The government, pleading lack of resources, was in a strong position to reply that it had done its utmost to accomplish what it had in a relatively short period.[33] Criticism in the form of questions was also made, including foreign affairs; but the debate on some of the crucial matters, especially the Anglo-Libyan Treaty, was carried on *in camera*.[34] From November 9 to November 17, 1952, Parliament debated the annual budget; but it was not approved without sharp criticism.[35] The debate in the Senate, though less trenchant, was in harmony with the criticism levelled against the government's financial policy. On several occasions, such as when enacting the Supreme Court law, the Senate took the initiative in making several changes in the draft law.[36] However, members of Parliament, in both Houses, demonstrated an ability to conduct parliamentary debate in a dignified manner and to fulfill their functions with a high sense of responsibility.

Libya's Admission to Membership in the Arab League

The desire to join the League of Arab States, at a time when the League was enjoying its greatest prestige, was almost unanimous among Libyans. When, however, 'Abd al-Rhaman 'Azzam, Secretary-General of the League, took sides in Libya's domestic issues and supported Sa'dawi in his attack on the National Assembly, Libya's moderate elements began to doubt the advantage of joining that organization, although the League's council by no means shared 'Azzam's personal views on Libya. Thus, when Libya's independence was proclaimed in December,

---

[32] *Ibid.*, see also statements made by Bisaykiri and Buwaysir, pp. 599–604, 860–62.
[33] See a statement made by the Minister of Finance, *ibid.*, pp. 565–566.
[34] *Ibid.*, p. 703.
[35] *Ibid.*, pp. 782 ff.
[36] *Proceedings of the Senate*, First Session, 2nd year, 1953, pp. 309–339.

1951, Muntasir, who sent an application to join the United Nations on the same day, made no such move with regard to the Arab League.

When 'Abd al-Rahman 'Azzam was replaced by a new Secretary-General in 1952, the reason for the opposition to 'Azzam personally disappeared, and those who had been anxious to join the League began to press for Libya's admission to that organization. In February, 1953, the Libyan Cabinet made a decision, with the King's approval, to apply for admission. The application, dated February 12, 1953, made no mention of Libya's reasons for staying out of the League from December, 1951, to February, 1953; it merely stated Libya's desire to co-operate with other Arab countries, with which she had shared the feeling of Arab brotherhood and common national aspirations, and to achieve the goals embodied in the Pact of the Arab League.[37]

Libya's application was the first item on the agenda of the Council for its meeting of March 28, 1953, and the President of the Council, Amir Mustafa al-Shihabi, presented the application before the Council. No discussion followed the presentation, and the voting for Libya's admission was unanimous. The members of the Libyan delegation, headed by Muntasir,[38] waiting in an anti-room, were immediately invited to take their seats and to participate in the Council's deliberations. Shihabi, on behalf of the League's Council as well as of his Syrian delegation—indeed all other delegations expressly shared his feeling—welcomed the Libyan delegation and Libya's admission in the most flattering terms. Muntasir, speaking on behalf of his country, replied with full appreciation of the warm welcome extended to him and his delegation, and assured the Council that all Libyans share that appreciation.[39]

Muntasir's words to the League's Council were not merely

[37] For text of the application, see the Arab League, *Proceedings of the Council of the Arab League*, Seventeenth and Eighteenth Sessions, 1952–53, p. 38.
[38] The other members of the delegation were Sayyid Ibrahim Ahmad al-Sharif al-Sanusi, Libya's Ambassador to Egypt; Abu Bakr Ahmad, Senator; Khalil al-Qallal, member of the House of Representatives; and Abu Bakr Abu Na'ama, member of the House of Representatives.
[39] Arab League, *Proceedings of the Council*, 1952–53, pp. 17–19.

lip service. Libya's admission by a unanimous vote of the League's Council was favorably commented on by Libya's press and in its political circles. "At last," one press commentator wrote, " Libya had joined the Arab League as its eighth member to participate in achieving the high ideals of the great Arab Nation." [40]

Treaty of Alliance Between Libya and Great Britain

The idea of concluding a treaty of alliance between Libya and Great Britain goes back to the time when Cyrenaica was under British military administration and Sayyid Idris, who had just returned from exile, declared that his country was in need of an alliance with a power strong on land, on the sea, and in the air.[41] Serious thoughts concerning the signing of such a treaty were expressed again when Cyrenaica was declared an Amirate in June, 1949; but since the whole question of the former Italian colonies was then taken up by the United Nations, it was deemed necessary to postpone the conclusion of a treaty until Libya's fate, whether independence or trusteeship, was decided. When the decision was made in favor of Libya's independence, Great Britain, in agreement with the United States and France, was the first to conclude a treaty with Libya. The broad outline of the treaty had been the subject of several conversations between Amir Idris and Britain's representatives in Cyrenaica, but the details of its provisions were not discussed until the first Libyan national government was formed.

One day before Libya's independence was proclaimed on December 24, 1951, Sir Alec Kirkbride, who had been Britain's Ambassador to Jordan, arrived in Banghazi to present his letters of credence on the day of independence as Britain's first Ambassador to that country. Kirkbride's first task was to open negotiations for a treaty of alliance between his country and the newly-created independent state of Libya. Since Libya's Prime Minister did not speak English and Kirkbride spoke Arabic

[40] *Barqa al-Jadida*, Banghazi, April 1, 1953.
[41] See p. 59, above.

fluently, the negotiations were conducted in Arabic. King Idris, who followed the negotiations with keen interest, was kept informed by the Prime Minister; but Kirkbride, as he told the author, on more than one occasion discussed matters relating to Cyrenaica directly with the King, since Muntasir, as a Tripolitanian, did not want to take responsibility for such matters.

Although there was common agreement on the fundamental provisions of the treaty, there were protracted negotiations before it was signed in 1953. The principal point of disagreement was Britain's demand to permit the use of the bases for stationing forces of powers friendly to Britain. While the Libyan government was willing to give Britain the right to station her own land and air forces, it was not prepared to permit other powers to use them. The Libyan government, on the other hand, demanded substantial financial compensation for use of the bases while the British government wanted to reduce the amount to a minimum. Another point of disagreement was the British request for a waiver of Libyan jurisdiction over members of the British armed forces both within and outside of the bases. The Libyan government, while it agreed to waive such jurisdiction within the bases, insisted that any criminal act commited outside the bases should be brought before national courts. These as well as other matters were finally resolved and the draft treaty was presented to the King. After carefully scrutinizing the text with his Ministers, he ordered Muntasir to sign it on July 29, 1953.

The treaty provides that " peace and friendship and a close alliance " between Libya and Great Britain are established and that each one of them " undertakes not to adopt in regard to foreign countries an attitude which is inconsistent with the alliance or which might create difficulties for the other party " (Article 1). Each party, whether in war or armed conflict, will come to the aid of the other as a measure of collective defense. " In the event of an imminent menace of hostilities involving either of the High Contracting Parties they will immediately concert together the necessary measures of defense " (Article 2). To insure mutual defense measures, each party " will furnish to the other all the facilities and assistance in his power on terms to be agreed upon." In return for facilities provided by Libya for British forces on conditions to be agreed upon, Britain pledged financial assistance to Libya on terms to be agreed upon. (Article 3). Neither Britain nor Libya undertakes in the present treaty any obligations that violate other obligations undertaken under the United Nations Charter or, in the case of Libya, the Pact of the Arab League (Article 4). The duration of the treaty was fixed at twenty years, subject to renewal or replacement by another.

In two separate agreements, signed on the same day, military and financial matters were dealt with in detail. Britain promised to supply arms, ammunition, and equipment for the Libyan army; but co-operation in military matters did not "obligate Libyan armed forces to serve outside Libyan territory." Libya, on the other hand, granted Britain " facilities within the territory of Libya for military purposes," provided that such facilities did not compromise Libyan sovereignty. Moreover, Libya afforded Britain the use of lands and buildings for military purposes, as well as all other technical facilities needed for the use of such lands and buildings. Britain was also given the right to supervise and control aircraft and vehicles and other means of transportation and communication. Finally, Libya granted the right of entry, passage, and movement within Libya of British land and air forces as well as the use of civil airports.

The jurisdiction clauses dealt in detail with civil and criminal offenses, the waiving of jurisdiction in matters concerning offenses committed by one member of the armed forces against another and in places devoted to the exclusive use of British forces.

The purpose of the financial agreement was " to assist Libya to enjoy conditions of financial stability and orderly economic development." To this end Britain promised to give financial assistance annually for the duration of the agreement. For the first five years, Britain promised to contribute one million pounds for economic development and £2,750,000 as financial assistance for the budget. For each succeeding five years, Britain promised financial assistance, the amount of which was to be agreed upon by the two governments.[42]

---

[42] *Treaty of Friendship and Alliance between the United Kingdom of Great Britain . . . and The United Kingdom of Libya* (London: Her Majesty's

The purpose of the treaty was obviously defensive, mainly to provide a substitute for British defense facilities in Egypt which Britain had already decided to move to another suitable location. Egypt, however, in order to obtain better terms in her negotiations with Britain tried to influence Libya to delay the signing of the treaty until the Egyptian negotiations were completed. Egypt went so far as to offer financial assistance to Libya if she delayed the signing of the treaty, but no long-term guarantee was offered. As a result, a press campaign, in which Bashir al-Sa'dawi and 'Abd al-Rahman 'Azzam participated, was directed against the Libyan government and Muntasir was denounced as a tool in the hands of the imperialists.[43]

Within Libya the press criticized the treaty in more moderate tones; but a few writers began to ask for more liberal terms even before the treaty was signed.[44] The politically conscious public was divided into three categories on the subject of the treaty. There were those who were opposed to any kind of a treaty with Britain; those who were in favor of the treaty but demanded greater financial aid; and those who approved of the treaty but were not in favor of granting large areas for the use of the British forces. The public, especially in Tripoli, was so incited by the foreign press and propaganda that on one occasion (August 22, 1953) demonstrations had to be suppressed by the police.

Stationery Office, 1953), cmd. 8914; United Nations, *Treaty Series*, vol. 186 (1954), pp. 185–283. See Appendix IV.

[43] Sa'dawi said in Cairo: " The signing of the Anglo-Libyan Treaty was an act that amounts to treason " (*al-Nida'*, Cairo, August 11, 1953); see also *Al-Ahram*, Cairo, September 1, 1953. 'Azzam made the following statement: " No one in Libya has the right to conclude a treaty with Great Britain allowing foreign troops to remain in Libya and thus restrict the complete independence which the United Nations decided for that country and which is a natural right for every people. It must be noted, however, that the Libyans have no constitution yet and that no Constituent Assembly, freely elected and duly representative of the people, has as yet elaborated a constitution. No one therefore has the legal right to conclude any agreement on behalf of that country; and every such agreement which provides for occupation by a foreign power or powers of Libya, or part of it, or which affects the complete independence approved for that country by the United Nations, shall be considered as opposed to the United Nations resolution and to Libya's natural rights " (*al-Ahram*, Cairo, September 20, 1951).

[44] See the editorial: " The Example of History: the ties and chains which are being shaped for Libya," *al-Basha'ir*, Banghazi, June 22, 1953; and Salih Buwaysir, " The Treaty," *al-Difa'*, Banghazi, June 18, 1953.

In August the treaty was sent to Parliament for approval. In the House of Representatives it was referred to the Defense and Foreign Relations Committee for recommendations. It was carefully scrutinized by that committee and a detailed report, embodying its points both of weakness and of strength, was submitted on August 13, 1953. The main points of strength centered on financial aid, defense, and the maintenance of independence. "The treaty fortifies Libya's independence," states the report, "and maintains it against external aggression and guarantees for it a state of economic stability through which it can carry out many projects for increasing its production and raising the standard of living of its people, without any interference in its financial, economic, and political affairs." The defects of the treaty, in the committee's opinion, centered on certain vague clauses such as that in Article 3, which failed to specify the area of land to be used by British forces, and on certain clauses in the military agreement that might appear to encroach on the sovereignty of Libya. Other minor points referred to lack of adequate compensation for the use of land and to customs exemptions and the employment of Libyans. The report criticized also the financial agreement, the limited assistance offered by Britain, and the division of the period of assistance into two phases without clear reason. Finally, the treaty did not provide that British forces should evacuate Libyan territory immediately upon the expiration of the treaty or in the event it was not renewed. However, the committee recommended its approval and hoped that the government would take into consideration the points raised by the committee when the Treaty was reviewed. A similar report prepared by the Senate Committee included nothing not covered by the committee of the House of Representatives. The treaty, approved by Parliament and ratified by the King on December 7, 1953, was enforced on the same day.

The significance of the treaty lies not only in the securing of British support for Libya's independence against any foreign encroachment, but also in the limitation of the size of the British military forces and the confining of the British military installations, which had been scattered about the country since the British occupation in 1943, to areas specified in the Treaty.

Nor was Muntasir unaware of the political advantages he derived, for the treaty secured British support for his country's participation in international councils and it rightly became the cornerstone of Libya's foreign policy following her independence until she was able to gain strength and confidence in her dealings with other nations.

Federal vs. Provincial Powers

No sooner had the federal system begun to function after independence than a serious conflict between the national and provincial governments developed. It has been observed that all federal unions have experieced in their early history some kind of conflict between state and national authorities until initial difficulties were ironed out and traditions for harmonious relations established. It was therefore natural that Libyan federalism should face similar difficulties when it began to operate.

There were, however, certain factors, both general and circumstantial, which complicated the federal experiment in Libya. To begin with, it is clear that Chapter 10 of the Constitution, which defines provincial powers, is too brief and often vague. These powers, more elaborately defined in the Organic Laws of the provinces, have been stressed at the expense of federal rights on the ground that Articles 39 and 176 specify that residual powers belong to the provinces.[45] More specifically, the legal position of the wali, who represents the King, has become a bone of contention between the Palace entourage and the national government. To whom should the wali be responsible—the King or the Prime Minister? Article 180 merely states that "the King shall appoint the wali and may relieve him of office," which may mean that the King, who is not responsible, shall appoint or relieve him upon the recommendation of the Prime Minister. However, the Organic Laws of the provinces specify that the wali represents the King and also is responsible to him only.[46]

---

[45] See also Articles 95 and 199 of the Constitution.
[46] Article 16 of the Organic Law of Cyrenaica; Article 54 of the Organic Law of Tripolitania; and Article 45 of the Organic Law of Fazzan.

No less important a matter is the question of the national government's supervision of the expenditure of public funds allocated to the provinces. The national government has argued that since the funds were allocated annually from its receipts, the expenditure of the funds must be subject to the supervision of the national government, although Article 174, which provides for such allocations, is silent on the matter. The provinces have refused to concede the right of supervision on the ground that they have exclusive control over the conduct of their administrations save in those matters specifically defined in the Constitution.

The circumstantial factors manifested themselves from the very beginning of Libya's rise to statehood. Upon the execution of the Constitution, the three provinces, which had been administered separately under foreign control or guidance, became the three constituent " administrative " units within the federal union, and their chiefs were reduced to the status of walis. The King, upon the recommendation of Muntasir, appointed Fadil Bin Zikri, Saqizli, and Sayf al-Nasr as walis of Tripolitania, Cyrenaica, and Fazzan on December 24, 1951. The three walis, especially those of Cyrenaica and Fazzan, who had been governing their territories as heads of governments, continued to regard their positions as heads of virtually self-governing provinces. Saqizli, who was Prime Minister of Cyrenaica from 1950 to 1951, tended to direct the administration as if no change had occurred in the status of Cyrenaica. He regarded himself as responsible only to the King, who was also the Amir of Cyrenaica,[47] and tried to interpret the Constitution in a manner which restricted federal powers. A case in point was the right of jurisdiction over real property given up by foreign powers. After her withdrawal from Cyrenaica, Britain desired to rent some of the buildings which she had returned to Libya. Muntasir rightly pointed out that Britain had given up her property rights to the national government and that any decision concerning the disposal of the property, whether in the form of rental or otherwise, must rest with the national government. Saqizli contested such rights on the ground that the national government, which possessed the right to negotiate with foreign powers, did so only on behalf of

[47] Article 2 of the Organic Law of Cyrenaica.

the province, and that the right of disposal must rest with the province. This, as well as other issues, created what came to be known as the legal controversy between the national and the provincial governments.

The King was inevitably drawn into this controversy. As head of the Sanusi house and recipient of great support from Cyrenaica, he naturally sympathized with Saqizli; but, as King of the newly-created Libyan union, and no longer merely the Amir of Cyrenaica, he fully appreciated the viewpoint of Muntasir. At the outset the King supported Muntasir, because of the prestige and influence of a Tripolitanian Prime Minister and the need for keeping the federal system from falling apart. Nor was Saqizli's position as Wali of Cyrenaica untenable, for he had involved himself in Sanusi quarrels, siding with one faction (Sayyid Abu al-Qasim) against another (Sayyid ʿAbd-Allah ʿAbid), which aroused the Palace entourage against him. To put an end to this quarrel, the King ordered his First Minister to take Saqizli into his government as Minister of Education. Saqizli's work in the national government from May, 1952, to September, 1953, proved to be in favor of federal authority, for it gave him the opportunity to appreciate the viewpoint of the Prime Minister when his own instructions as Minister of Education had not been carried out by the provincial Departments of Education. When Saqizli returned to Cyrenaica as Chief of the Royal Diwan in 1953, his views on the legal controversy between the national and the provincial powers had become more balanced.

No sooner had Muntasir won over Saqizli, a pillar of Cyrenaican parochialism, than he himself fell victim to Sanusi quarrels. Ibrahim al-Shalhi, Nazir of the Royal Household, who had been at the outset a supporter of federal authority, came to the rescue of his protégé, Sayyid ʿAbd-Allah ʿAbid, who had not won Muntasir's favor, by taking a stand against federal authority. In an effort to maintain a balance between federal and provincial authorities on the one hand and among rival personalities on the other, the King showed reluctance to subordinate the position of the Wali to the national government. He began to appreciate the value of his position as the balancing factor in the conflict between the federal and provincial governments and saw in the federal system a useful instrument for the maintenance of Libyan unity without sacrificing Cyrenaica's traditional parochialism. Thus, when Husayn Maziq was appointed Wali of Cyrenaica on May 14, 1953, replacing Saqizli, and Siddiq al-Muntasir was made Wali of Tripolitania on June 13, 1953, replacing Fadil Bin Zikri, the two decrees were issued neither in consultation with, nor over the countersignature of, the Prime Minister. Moreover, the two decrees were assigned to the Chief of the Royal Diwan, not to the Prime Minister, to be carried out.

Muntasir naturally protested to the King against both the issuance of an order without prior consultation with him and the entrusting of the execution of the order to a person who was not a member of his government. He made it crystal clear that the national government must possess certain elements of supremacy over provincial governments, whether in the appointment of walis or in financial supervision, if the federal system were ever to lead toward ultimate unity; for, as he explained to the King, the country might as well be governed directly through the walis without a national government. Under the present system, Muntasir went on to explain, the King could select a Prime Minister in whom he had confidence, and, therefore, no apprehension need be entertained if the wali's status were subordinate to the national government, since the King could always dismiss the Prime Minister at his pleasure.

On January 21, 1954, Muntasir addressed a letter to the President of the Supreme Court, which had just been established, requesting an advisory opinion on the legal status of the walis vis-à-vis the national government. More specifically, he asked the Court to give an advisory opinion on the validity of several Royal decrees, such as those dealing with the appointment of the new walis for Cyrenaica and Tripolitania, dated May 14 and June 13, 1953, without prior consultation with the national government. He also requested an advisory opinion on the validity of the direct delegation of powers to the wali by the King and the national government's right of supervision over the provinces. Muntasir's letter to the Court was supported by a memorandum, prepared by the legal bureau of the national government, in which the viewpoint that the Libyan national government is a parliamentary government responsible to Parliament for its exercise of powers of the head of state was stressed. The head of the Libyan State (the King), the memorandum stated, could not exercise his powers directly, because he is immune and not responsible. It follows that the King's powers, which the Libyan Constitution specifies, must be exercised by a responsible government. The same principle applies to the King in his relations with the provincial governments. As to the Wali, the memorandum explained that, although he is entrusted with powers given to him by the national government, he is essentially an official responsible to the national government, since his appointment and replacement must be made by the King, whose powers should be exercised by the national government. The wali's powers, derived from Articles 38, 178, and 181 of the Constitution, were to be exercised under the supervision of the national government. But despite article 54 of the Organic Law of Tripolitania, Article 15 of the Organic Law of Cyrenaica, and Article 45 of the Organic Law of Fazzan, the wali's powers could not be interpreted to exceed those powers given him under the Constitution.

The Royal Diwan, in order to resolve the issue between federal and provincial authorities, intervened in the matter. It devolved upon Saqizli, who had become Chief of the Royal Diwan on September 18, 1953, to try his hand in defense of provincial authority without prejudicing federal authority, since he now had become more appreciative of the viewpoint of the national government, having served as one of its members. He submitted to the King an able memorandum (dated January 31, 1954) in which he analyzed the legal position of the federal system and suggested that the issue could be resolved without recourse to the Supreme Court. He regarded the basic issue between the national and provincial governments as centering on the position of the wali, who was responsible to the King, while the latter was not responsible under the Constitution. Saqizli contended that this problem might be solved in the light of the experiences of other countries whose federal form of government resembled that of Libya. He stated that the Canadian and the Australian systems, which had not moved too much in the direction of centralization, might be helpful in Libya's problem. He observed that Canadian and Australian governors, who exercised their powers through provincial executive councils responsible to provincial legislative assemblies, were not themselves responsible. Similarly in Libya, if the provincial executive councils, presided over by an executive chief, became responsible, the walis, who represent the King, would be relieved of responsibility. He accordingly, recommended that the Organic Laws of the provinces should be revised so as to provide for the appointment of presidents for the provincial executive councils who would preside over the councils and become responsible for their actions before the King or the provincial legislative assemblies, thus relieving the walis of legal responsibility.

In an interview with the author, Saqizli pointed out that the Constitution was drawn up somewhat hastily by the National Assembly, leaving much to be desired in the way of clarification of a number of important provisions such as those concerning the distribution of powers. He pointed out that when he was Prime Minister of Cyrenaica he had suggested that the members of the committee drafting the constitution should be men well versed in constitutional law, and he recommended a number of able candidates for such work; but, for political reasons, most of his nominees were not appointed. Thus, no sooner had the national government begun to operate than the shortcomings of the Constitution became apparent.

Before the Saqizli proposals had been adopted, Muntasir, faced with a new difficulty arising from a decree affecting the composition of his government, tendered his resignation to the King in April, 1954. The proposals concerning the appointment of chiefs of executive councils, rendering the chiefs responsible both to the legislative assemblies and the King, were formally adopted when the revision of the Organic Laws of the provinces was carried out toward the end of the year.

Reshuffling of the Cabinet and
The Fall of Muntasir

The conflict between national and provincial authorities often manifested itself in the form of Palace interference in Cabinet affairs, done in the name of the King without the King's knowledge and resulting in Cabinet crises. This situation disturbed Muntasir, who determined to put an end to it and took up the matter with the King. The King, sympathizing with his Prime Minister, promised to support him; but it was a complex situation intimately connected with the struggle between the advocates of provincial and national authority, and it was exceedingly difficult to control. In the last analysis, it became a duel between Muntasir and the advocates of provincial authority in which Muntasir, because of his strength of character, was able to hold his own; [48] but when he became ill and went abroad for treatment in September, 1953, his opponents took full advantage of the opportunity. On September 18, 1953, the King issued a decree, with the approval of Deputy Prime Minister Fathi al-Kikhya, appointing 'Ali al-'Unayzi as Minister of Finance in place of Abu Bakr Na'ama. Saqizli was transferred to the Royal Diwan and Abu Na'ama replaced him as Minister of Education.

When the news of this important change in the Cabinet reached Muntasir, who was recuperating in Europe, he promptly cabled his resignation to the King. Upon his return it was pointed out to him that the Deputy Premier had approved the change and the King refused to accept the resignation. The Deputy Premier explained to his chief that he had approved the change because 'Unayzi, well-acquainted with the financial problems of the country, was better qualified than Abu Na'ama; but Muntasir, who suspected that the change was made to undermine his position, protested on the ground that such a reshuffling should not have been made without prior consultation with him. Attempts were made to persuade Muntasir to remain head of the

---

[48] Several attempts had been made to force Muntasir to resign, but the King, who hoped that his First Minister's difficulties might be resolved, was not willing to accept the resignation.

national government without Diwan interference; he stayed for a while, but his opponent's influence was too great over the Diwan.

Muntasir had to make a choice between remaining as Prime Minister both in name and in fact and resigning. He chose the latter and relinquished his seal of office on February 15, 1954. The King's admiration for his Prime Minister did not permit the latter to remain in retirement; he was sent to represent the King of Libya at the Court of St. James (July, 1954) and ever since has remained in the diplomatic service. Muntasir's disappearance from the central authority meant the victory of the advocates of provincial authority; but his resignation registered a protest against them. His action reflected the personal courage and the single-mindedness of a man who was determined to govern in name as well as in fact; but it betrayed lack of appreciation for the value of opposition parties—an element necessary for the maintenance of parliamentary government. Had he not suppressed opposition parties, the Congress Party in particular, he might have used them against the advocates of provincial authority; for when the news of his resignation became public, hardly any significant voice was raised in his support.[49]

The Saqizli Cabinet

The King invited Saqizli, Chief of the Royal Diwan, to form a new government on February 18, 1954. In addition to the Premiership, Saqizli assumed the portfolio of Foreign Affairs. At the King's suggestion, Mustafa Bin Halim and Khalil al-Qallal were included in the Cabinet.[50] There was speculation as to why the King had chosen Saqizli to head the new government, since the country, which had just begun its independent life and

[49] Salih Buwaysir, then Vice-President of the House of Representatives, rallied a few members of the House in support of the Cabinet; but his move, since he himself had been a critic of the Government, proved to be of little or no value.

[50] The other members of the Cabinet were: 'Ali al-'Unayzi for Finance, 'Abd al-Rahman al-Qalhud for Justice, Ibrahim Bin Sha'ban for Education, al-Tahir al-'Alim for Health, and Isma'il Bin al-Amin and Khalil al-Qallal as Ministers without portfolios.

was confronted with domestic and foreign problems, needed a more flexible and dynamic head than Saqizli, who possessed a meticulous and legalistic mind. Some contended that the King probably wanted to get rid of his Chief of the Royal Diwan, while others conjectured that he wanted to install one of the pillars of Cyrenaican parochialism as head of the national government.

While all these considerations may have had a bearing on the appointment of a man of Saqizli's character, the King had his own reasons for the appointment. The Cabinet of Muntasir, who was determined to govern the country as the head of a parliamentary government, had raised a number of constitutional issues which needed a strong man, sympathetic with the provincial viewpoint, to handle. Believing that the situation required a man who possessed legal experience and single-mindedness, the King turned to Saqizli. When it was pointed out that Saqizli was not flexible enough, the King remarked that he wanted to try him as head of the national government; at any rate he needed him to solve pending constitutional issues. The tenure of office of the new government, therefore from the start, was not expected to last too long, and Saqizli himself seemed to have understood the purpose of the Royal summons quite well as he then intimated to some of his friends, as well as years later to the author.

One of the constitutional issues that Muntasir had raised, it will be recalled, was the legal status of the wali. Saqizli, it will be recalled, had already advocated the view that the wali, as representative of the King, should be relieved of legal responsibility by shifting it to a chief executive who, instead of the wali, would preside over the executive council of the province. When Saqizli formed the new government he addressed himself to the solution of the issue not by submitting the question to the Supreme Court, but by looking at it from a different angle.[51]

---

[51] Saqizli asked the President of the Supreme Court to postpone action on Muntasir's request for an advisory opinion, and on March 1, 1954, he requested the Court to limit its advisory opinion to the legal status of the wali generally, not to the Royal decrees of May 14 and June 13, 1953, concerning the appointment of the two walis of Cyrenaica and Tripolitania. However, the Supreme Court never actually had given an opinion on the legal status of the wali.

He was of the opinion, as he pointed out in a Cabinet meeting on March 4, 1954, that the Constitution was vague on the legal status of the wali and suggested that the Constitution should be amended so as to relieve the wali of responsibility. Should the wali be made responsible to the national government, Saqizli maintained, he would be subject to political influences and would be likely to be replaced every time a new government was formed. Thus it was on Saqizli's recommendation that the wali was relieved of legal responsibility by shifting it to the executive council, and the Organic Laws were revised so as to provide for the appointment of chiefs of executive councils. This constitutional device, which temporarily resolved the legal issue, resulted in strengthening the provincial governments at the expense of the national government.

The Supreme Court and the Fall of Saqizli

Scarcely had Saqizli gained a short respite when there was suddenly thrust upon him a more serious legal problem bearing on the question of federal and provincial powers. The Tripolitanian Legislative Assembly, which had been functioning satisfactorily for almost a year since its establishment in March, 1953, began to criticize some of the measures adopted by Siddiq al-Muntasir, Wali of Tripolitania. The wali, by direct contact with the Royal Diwan, procured a Royal decree dated January 19, 1954, dissolving the Legislative Assembly; it was unexpectedly delivered to 'Ali al-Dib, President of the Legislative Assembly. The decree stated that in view of the lack of co-operation between the Legislative Assembly and the Executive Council, the King, upon the recommendation of the Executive Council, ordered the dissolution of the Legislative Assembly and new elections to be held within ninety days from the day of dissolution. The Wali of Tripolitania was entrusted with carrying out the Royal decree.

No sooner had 'Ali al-Dib received the order of dissolution than he, as President of the Legislative Assembly, took the matter to the Supreme Court with a request for a judgment as to whether the Royal decree, in the manner in which it was issued, was indeed constitutional. In his letter to the Court (dated January 31, 1954) 'Ali al-Dib raised the following points:

1. Article 36 of the Organic Law of Tripolitania empowers the King, upon the advice of the Executive Council, to dissolve the Legislative Assembly by a decree stating the reasons for the dissolution. The present Legislative Assembly, 'Ali al-Dib said, was dissolved by a Royal order, not by a Royal decree; for, according to Article 36 of the Organic Law of Tripoli and Article 85 of the Constitution, the Royal decree should have been countersigned by the Prime Minister of the national government in order to be valid.

2. The Royal decree stated that the King had ordered the dissolution upon the recommendation—not upon the advice—of the Executive Council, as provided in Article 36 of the Organic Law of Tripolitania.

3. The Royal decree stated that the reason for dissolution was the lack of co-operation between the Legislative Assembly and the Executive Council, while the proceedings of the Legislative Assembly gave no evidence of such lack of co-operation, nor had the Assembly ever failed in any of its duties since its inception.[52]

The Executive Council, assuming the responsibility for the Royal decree, submitted a memorandum [53] to the Court (dated March 7, 1954) in which 'Ali al-Dib's charges were refuted. The memorandum stated that the terms " order " and " decree " have been used interchangeably in the federal Constitution and the Organic Law of Tripolitania, that the word " recommendation " signified " advice " and that the countersignature of the Prime Minister of the national government was not necessary on the ground that the dissolution of the Legislative Assembly was an act belonging to the provincial, not the national, government as provided in the Constitution.

It was announced that the Court would consider the case on April 3, 1954; three sittings of the Administrative and Constitu-

---

[52] The Government of Libya, *Decisions of the Supreme Court*, 1953–1958, Vol. 1: Administrative and Constitutional Decisions (Tripoli, 1959) , pp. 11–13.

[53] Signed by 'Abd al-Halim 'Awad, deputy counsellor of the government of Cyrenaica, on behalf of the Executive Council. For text of the memorandum, see *ibid.*, pp. 13 ff.

tional Division were held and were presided over by ʿAli ʿAli Mansur. Having examined the case thoroughly, Mansur, acting on the principle that the King was not responsible, declared the order of dissolution unconstitutional. The only person to bear responsibility, Mansur held, was the King's Prime Minister and head of the national government.[54]

No sooner had the Court's decision been made public on April 5 than a conflict between the Diwan and Saqizli immediately ensued. Siddiq al-Muntasir, who had advised the King on the dissolution, was enraged to find the Court making a decision in favor of ʿAli al-Dib. Under the guise that the Court's decision was intended to undermine the King's authority, he organized a demonstration by a mob which paraded the streets on April 6 and shattered the Court's windows. The King, who had approved the dissolution of the Legislative Assembly without paying attention to the form in which the decree was signed, found himself in an embarrassing situation. Saqizli's opponents in the Royal Diwan put the matter before the King as a deliberate attempt to oppose his authority by declaring the decree unconstitutional.[55]

It was in this atmosphere that Saqizli faced the crisis on April 10, 1954. He and his Cabinet were attending a parliamentary meeting that day when the news reached him that Siddiq al-Muntasir had been holding elections for a new Legislative Assembly and that demonstrations against the Supreme Court were taking place in Tripoli. Saqizli at once called a meeting of the Cabinet to discuss the situation. Unaware as to what had transpired with the King, he, at the suggestion of one of his Ministers, requested the King in a brief telephone conversation to order Muntasir to stop the elections. The King, dissatisfied with the manner in which Saqizli had approached him, cut short the conversation. On the following day Saqizli held a Cabinet meeting in which it was decided that he should resign. While

---

[54] *Ibid.*, pp. 23–43; and the writer's interview with ʿAli ʿAli Mansur on May 14, 1958.

[55] Under Siddiq al-Muntasir's influence the press did not publish the full text of the Supreme Court's decision in Tripolitania. A summary of the case was published in *Corriere di Tripoli*, March 11, 1954. Articles attacking the Court's decision were inspired by the provincial administration (See *Tarablus al-Gharb*, Tripoli, April 4, 1954).

the Cabinet was still in session, the Acting Chief of the Royal Diwan, 'Ali al-'Abidiya, arrived to communicate the King's lack of confidence in the Cabinet. Saqizli immediately tendered his letter of resignation to the Acting Chief.

By an unhappy coincidence, the first case referred to the Supreme Court touched the ticklish question of Royal powers which had become one of the principal issues between the Diwan and Libya's first Cabinet.[56] The King, who had shown great interest in the work of the National Assembly and in the promulgation of a constitution for the country, was faced with an issue originating from a conflict between the Wali of Tripolitania and the Legislative Assembly. Factional rivalry operating in an atmosphere of confusion inevitably involved the King in a conflict from which he would have preferred to remain aloof, but rival factions fully exploited the issue in order to gain prestige and power over each other. The advocates of provincial authority won another round in the struggle for power, but the battle was unfortunately fought this time on the ground of the judiciary. As a result the Supreme Court suffered a setback which was universally deplored throughout the country.

[56] Saqizli, it will be recalled, tried to spare the Court from facing the issue of Royal powers when he requested the postponement of the case raised by his predecessor; but 'Ali al-Dib, without prior consultation with the national government, took his own case to the Supreme Court and brought matters to a head.

chapteR IX

Trial and Error in Self-Government II:
The Bin Halim Administration

T HE KING INVITED Mustafa Bin Halim, Minister of Communications, to form the new government. When asked to
see the king on the same day on which Saqizli had resigned,
Bin Halim had no idea that he was going to form a government,
since he felt himself too young and inexperienced for such a
responsibility. Thanking the King for his confidence, Bin Halim
requested permission to consider the Royal summons and to
consult some of the prospective members of his Cabinet on the
question of the Supreme Court. One day after Saqizli resigned,
Bin Halim completed the formation of his government.

Bin Halim's Early Career

A little background about the man who so ably steered the ship
of state in troubled waters for more than three years is perhaps
necessary; for Bin Halim, who had suddenly risen from a relatively junior Cabinet position to be the head of government, was
not well-known even in his own country.

He was born in Alexandria, Egypt, on January 23, 1921.
Although his family may have come originally from Zliten, his
father, who was born at Darna, emigrated to Egypt a few days
after the Italian occupation of Libya in 1911, fleeing from a
death sentence. Bin Halim studied in a French school at Alex-

andria before he went to Cairo for a career in engineering. After graduation from the Egyptian (now Cairo) University, he worked in a construction company in Alexandria and became a well-to-do business man. While still in college, young Bin Halim met Amir Idris, who was then in exile in Egypt, and made the acquaintance of Ibrahim al-Shalhi, the Amir's private secretary, upon whom he made a great impression as a brilliant engineer. Bin Halim's personal friendship with Shalhi gave him first the opportunity to be invited to return to his homeland in 1950 and then to reach the highest position in the service of the King and country.

It was the policy of Sayyid Idris after his enthronement as the Amir of Cyrenaica in 1949 to invite Libyans abroad to return and take active part in the rebuilding of their country. Several of them had already assumed responsible positions in the government. Bin Halim was now given his chance. When Saqizli succeeded 'Umar Mansur to form a government in Cyrenaica, Bin Halim, at Shalhi's suggestion, joined it as Minister of Public Works and Communications in July, 1950, replacing 'Ali al-Jirbi, who was named as Cyrenaica's representative on the United Nations Council for Libya.[1] Bin Halim proved to be an active administrator and contributed to the rebuilding of many Cyrenaican towns, particularly the city of Banghazi. He was also often called on for help by other departments, especially in financial matters. He continued to serve in the Cyrenaican administration as a Nazir of Public Works and Communications when Libyan independence was proclaimed in December, 1951, and Cyrenaica became a province within the union.

After his return to Libya, Bin Halim was able to cement his relations with Shalhi and his close associate, Sayyid 'Abd-Allah 'Abid, a member of the Sanusi family; and the three, often referred to as " the triumvirate," collaborated so closely that they attained great success in business and politics. Bin Halim, by far abler and more astute than the other two, fixed his eyes on higher political stakes, while the other two, satisfied only with material reward, inspired the King with the idea that Bin Halim's ability qualified him to be the future Premier of Libya.

[1] See p. 139, above.

When Saqizli formed a government in February, 1954, Bin Halim, who had already served as Nazir under him in the Cyrenaican administration, was offered the portfolio of Communications. Although Bin Halim respected Saqizli's honesty, he disliked his attitude toward Sayyid 'Abd-Allah 'Abid, especially in curbing his financial ventures which was construed to mean favoring his rival, Sayyid Abu al-Qasim; but he agreed to serve again under Saqizli at the King's request and in expectancy of higher political posts. The opportunity came sooner than perhaps was expected; for, as Bin Halim explained to the author, he had no idea that the King's choice of a successor to Saqizli would fall upon him. Bin Halim may have aspired to form a government sometime in the future; but the view held by some critics that the plan for his succession to Saqizli had already been affirmed may have been an afterthought.

Formation of the Bin Halim Government

Within a day following the Royal summons of April 11, 1954, Bin Halim completed the formation of his government. In addition to the Premiership, he assumed the portfolio of Communications. 'Ali al-'Unayzi and Khalil al-Qallal, who had served under Saqizli and Muntasir as Cyrenaican representatives, were given Finance and Defense, and 'Abd al-Salam al-Busiri, Foreign Affairs. Believing that the Supreme Court decision that had wrecked the Saqizli government needed the co-operation of elements enjoying lay popularity, Bin Halim sought the co-operation of 'Abd al-Rahman al-Qalhud and Mustafa al-Sarraj, two influential members of the Congress Party, who agreed to join his government. Qalhud assumed the portfolio of Justice and Sarraj that of National Economy. Ibrahim Bin Sha'ban, a dignitary of the Berber community, was given Education, and Muhammad Bin 'Uthman, a Fazzanese, was assigned Health.

The new Cabinet, headed by a young but energetic chief, was hailed as a strong government, for it received the support not only of the Royal Diwan, but also of opposition elements. Despite several crises, its tenure of office lasted more than three years

(April, 1954, to May, 1957), although it was reshuffled several times.

Bin Halim's Initial Difficulties

The first problem that Bin Halim had to deal with was that of the tension between the Royal Diwan and the Supreme Court resulting from the Court's decision declaring the Royal decree dissolving the Legislative Assembly of Tripolitania to be unconstitutional. The King expressed his desire to respect the Court's decision provided the dissolved Legislative Assembly was not called back into session, since a new Assembly had already been elected. One day before Bin Halim completed the formation of his Cabinet, he discussed the situation with the President of the Supreme Court, Mahmud Sabri al-'Iqari, and it seemed that an agreement had been reached that the Royal decree would be countersigned by the new Prime Minister to meet the Court's objection, while the Tripolitanian Assembly would be regarded as constitutionally dissolved. Bin Halim went so far as to make a statement in Parliament to this effect and the crisis appeared to have passed for the time being.[2]

Upon the advice of 'Uthman Ramzi, Chief of a division in the Supreme Court, that the Court's decision in the 'Ali al-Dib case was void on the ground that when the decision was taken the Attorney-General (Procureur Général) was not present, the Royal Diwan became reluctant to change even the form of the Royal decree. Thus on May 5, 1954, the Court's decision was declared void on the basis that the Court was not sitting properly,[3] and 'Ali 'Ali Mansur, Chief of the Administrative Division, resigned and was given a position on a Court of Appeal in Egypt. A law reorganizing the Court and putting an end to the tension created by its former decision had yet to be enacted later in the year. When the amendment law, stipulating that the President of the Court should be a Libyan citizen and deleting

---

[2] Salih Buwaysir, " al-Wazara al-Jadida wa al-Zuruf al-Hamma al-Rahina," al-Difa', Banghazi, April 15, 1954.
[3] Barqa al-Jadida, Banghazi, May 12, 1954.

the penal clause concerning the enforcement of the Court's decision, was issued (November 3, 1954), it was coupled with a new decree countersigned by the Acting Prime Minister, validating the dissolution of the Tripolitanian Legislative Assembly on January 19, 1954.[4]

The change to a new government carried with it a shift in government favor from one set of businessmen to another. Sayyid 'Abd-Allah 'Abid, who had remained in the background under former administrations, came to the fore; while Sayyid Abu al-Qasim, who heretofore had obtained business transactions, was pushed to the background. Competition for business contracts aroused public criticism and brought Sanusi quarrels more openly into the public eye. Bin Halim himself was not immune from such criticism, which must have made him feel uncomfortable, since it inevitably reflected on the image of his government.

Nor was the impact of this competition confined to a new circle of business speculators. In September, 1954, Conte Marzotto, the Italian millionaire who had acquired vast estates in Cyrenaica under Italian rule, visited Libya while on a cruise through the Mediterranean; he was entertained in Banghazi by Sayyid 'Abd-Allah 'Abid and was taken to the Green Mountain (al-Jabal al-Akhdar) to visit his former estate, now under government control.[5] This visit was insignificant in itself; but it aroused 'Abd-Allah 'Abid's opponents to inform the King that Marzotto's visit, which had already been commented upon unfavorably in the press, was reported to have taken place by Royal permission. Sayyid 'Abd-Allah had, in fact, sought the approval of Husayn Maziq, Wali of Cyrenaica, by hinting to him that he had invited Marzotto with Royal approval. Thus the King's name was unnecessarily involved in an episode arising from personal rivalry. When the news of the affair reached the King he inevitably decided to punish the persons responsible for involving him. On October 2, 1954, the King issued an order, without even consulting his Ministers, depriving 'Abd-Allah 'Abid of his honorific title and confining him to his house pending trial;

---

[4] *The Government Gazette*, Vol. IV, November 3, 1954, pp. 22–23.

[5] Conte Marzotto had paid a similar visit to Tripoli in October, 1951 (see *Sunday Ghibli*, Tripoli, October 21, 1951).

and another suspending Husayn Maziq, the Wali of Cyrenaica, from his functions as Wali for one month.[6] The Royal orders, issued shortly before Shalhi's assassination, were withdrawn three days later; but they had already given Sayyid Abu al-Qasim's group a chance to exploit Sayyid 'Abd-Allah 'Abid's temporary eclipse to their advantage. The inner struggle between the two factions, which had an indirect bearing on the assassination of Shalhi, was the source of considerable public concern before Shalhi's assassination actually took place.

Assassination of Shalhi

The King's confidence which Ibrahim al-Shalhi had enjoyed aroused the curiosity of many foreign observers as well as the suspicion of many a Libyan. Shalhi's loyalty to the King was beyond reproach and his judgment in public affairs was valued. He proved to be equally loyal and helpful to friends and followers; but the power he wielded was resented by his opponents. Above all it was resented by the King's cousins, descendants of Sayyid Ahmad al-Sharif al-Sanusi, who deeply felt that Shalhi had separated them from the King, although the Queen herself was one of their number. The house of Sayyid Ahmad argued that since the King had no issue, succession to the throne should devolve on one of them by legitimate right; for, as the present King himself had admitted, it was agreed that Sayyid Ahmad al-Sharif's eldest son should succeed him as the Chief of the Sanusi order. However, as King Idris has explained in his Memoirs,[7] the agreement dealt with the leadership of the Sanusi order, which was a purely religious organization, and had nothing to do with the monarchical system established in the country following World War II. Moreover, the agreement was based on Sayyid Ahmad's policy of placing Libya under the Sultan of Turkey's authority during World War I in order to secure the independence of the country but the Sultan had not won the war

[6] For text of the Royal orders, see *Barqa al-Jadida*, Banghazi, October 3, 1954.

[7] King Idris, " Memoirs " in *Al-Zaman*, Banghazi, January 27, 1955, p. 4.

nor had the country secured her independence. It was not until Sayyid Idris had associated his country's struggle with the Allied cause both in World War I—which secured for him the title of Amir—and in World War II—resulting in the independence of Libya—that a Royal House was established. Thus it is clear, King Idris argued, that Sayyid Ahmad al-Sharif's house possessed no valid claim to Royal succession. Nonetheless, Sayyid Ahmad's descendants continued to claim the legitimate right of succession and concentrated their attack on Shalhi as the person most responsible for their loss of Royal favor. It was this legend, associated with Shalhi's name, that prompted one of Sayyid Ahmad al-Sharif's descendants to take his life.

Ibrahim al-Shalhi, it is true, was praised for his intelligence, patriotism, and indefatigable industry in looking after the King's personal affairs; but his reserved manners worked against him. His family came originally from Algeria.[8] From early childhood he joined the circle of Sayyid Ahmad al-Sanusi, studying the Qur'an and Sanusi rituals. At Sayyid Ahmad's suggestion, Shalhi entered the service of Sayyid Idris. Ever since his childhood Shalhi proved to be both loyal and devoted in the service of his master.[9] He was courteous in his manner and always polite and respectful to the Amir's (later the King's) public servants and visitors, in whose presence he hardly uttered a word. But due to this very fact, Shalhi was resented by his opponents, because his opinions were privately given to the King. Highly valuing his judgment, the King never concealed his respect for and dependence on Shalhi.

Al-Sharif Bin al-Sayyid Muhi al-Din al-Sanusi, the assassin, was not a fellow-traveler nor an adventurer, for he was no less a dignitary than the grandson of Sayyid Ahmad al-Sharif and a cousin of the King. Sharif received his education in Cairo and Beirut and was imbued with high ideals. But as a young man,

---

[8] Al-Busiri al-Shalhi, son of Ibrahim al-Shalhi, told the present writer that his grandfather, who left Algeria about 1870, was born in a village near Constantine and belonged to a well-known tribe. Ibrahim himself was born about 1899. For a brief account of Shalhi's early life, see Muhammed al-Tayyib al-Ashhab, *Ibrahim Ahmad al-Shalhi* (Cairo, 1956).

[9] King Idris told the author that Shalhi had served him for forty-one years with an honesty and loyalty that could not be surpassed even by a son, if he had one.

he had grown up in an atmosphere of intrigue and rivalry among Sanusi princes. Believing that Shalhi was the greatest obstacle to the realization of the legitimate aspirations of his house, Sharif decided to take the life of the King's favorite confidant, because he had separated the King from his kinsmen.

On October 5, 1954, Shalhi paid a visit to Prime Minister Bin Halim. Having seen Shalhi before he entered the Premier's office, Sharif waited outside the building. When Shalhi came out, Sharif followed him to his car and fired at him. The police immediately arrested him. The Prime Minister and Mahmud Buqwaytin (Abu Quwaytin), Commander of the Cyrenaican Defense Force and son-in-law of Shalhi, went immediately to see the King, to whom they offered their condolences and discussed the situation. The King seemed to have taken the event rather calmly at first. In the afternoon, however, the King, realizing that Sharif had been incited by his kinsmen, became exceedingly angry. A state of siege was proclaimed on October 5, 1954, and the Wali of Cyrenaica, Husayn Maziq, who had been suspended from office for a month, was empowered to enforce the decree imposing the state of siege and the order of his suspension was cancelled.[10] The King also ordered that his Kingdom was to be in a state of mourning for a week, beginning on October 6.

Owing to the assassin's background and the possible complicity of Shalhi's opponents, an extensive investigation was carried out. All the members of the Sanusi house were ordered under house arrest. It was contemplated at the outset that they should be expelled from the country, but it was realized that such an action would be unconstitutional. It was therefore decided to keep the elder members under house arrest and to banish the younger ones to Tripoli. However, due to difficult living conditions, they were kept under house arrest in Cyrenaica.[11] Those who were out of the country, such as Sayyid Ibrahim—who held the post of Libya's Ambassador to Egypt—asked for asylum in that country.

[10] See *Barqa al-Jadida*, Banghazi, October 6, 1954. The order directing Sayyid 'Abd-Allah 'Abid to remain under house arrest was also cancelled.

[11] These were: 'Ali Safi al-Din, Bashir Ibrahim, Kamil Ibrahim, Rida Safi al-Din, Mustafa al-Rida, Ahmad Muhi al-Din, Mustafa Muhi al-Din. The decree of banishment was issued on October 15, 1954. See *Barqa al-Jadida*, October 22, 1954.

Only Sayyid ʿAbd-Allah and his brothers Sayyid Ahmad and Sayyid Siddiq ʿAbid, who publicly repudiated the assassin's criminal act and declared their loyalty to the King, escaped punishment. The case of Sayyid Sharif, who was directly responsible for the assassination, was referred to a criminal court in Banghazi; the trial lasted for a week, beginning on November 29, 1954. Sharif insisted that he had committed the crime on his own, though in the writer's opinion, his mind may have been influenced by factional rivalries. The immediate cause, however, was by no means clear. On December 11, 1954, the Court, finding Sharif guilty, sentenced him to death. An appeal to the Supreme Court was to no avail, and he was executed on February 6, 1955.

The King, disgusted with the city in which the Chief of the Royal Household had been killed, left Banghazi, never again to return to live there. Since Tubruq, to which he moved temporarily for health reasons, proved to be more agreeable to him, he decided to make it the seat of his Royal Diwan. The Manar Palace—formerly Graziani's—was assigned by the King to house the newly established national university in which, three years later, the author had the privilege of serving as Dean. No cause would have been more worthy as a diversion of the King's mind from the loss of a valued friend than the establishment of a higher institution of learning which symbolized the intellectual awakening of the country during his reign.

The Wheelus Base Agreement
and American Aid to Libya

Before Bin Halim formed his government, Libya's relations with other powers had not yet been established on a firm basis. Libya, it is true, had been admitted to membership in the Arab League and her alliance with Great Britain had become the basis of her foreign policy; but Libya's application for membership in the United Nations was still pending and her policy toward other powers had yet to be shaped.

From the time when he took office, Bin Halim showed as much interest in foreign ventures as in Libya's domestic problems.

" Mahmud al-Muntasir," said Bin Halim to the author, " played
the game of foreign policy with one card only—Libya's alliance
with Great Britain." Bin Halim, as he went on to explain his
policy, introduced another card, namely, the establishment of a
firm friendship and co-operation with the United States of
America. The purpose of this policy was not only to obtain
assistance for Libya's economic development, but also to secure
American diplomatic support in solving Libya's pending issues
with France, Italy, and neighboring powers. Bin Halim may
also be credited with having introduced into Libya a policy of
" Arab solidarity "—first applied to Egypt, until it was thwarted
by the Suez crisis in 1956, and then to Tunisia in 1957. He
might have even found it advantageous to flirt with the Soviet
Union, but such a policy was intended to demonstrate Libya's
independent stand in foreign affairs rather than to cultivate
Soviet friendship.

The cornerstone of Bin Halim's foreign policy was Libya's
friendship and co-operation with the United States. In 1952, the
United States had offered Libya financial aid under the Point
Four Program for technical co-operation; [12] but the Wheelus Base
agreement, permitting the United States to maintain a military
base on Libyan territory, proved to be of great help for subsequent economic co-operation.

The right to use a military base near Tripoli was granted by
Great Britain to the United States during the war. The base
rights were intended to be temporary for the duration of the war;
but Soviet desire to obtain the trusteeship over Tripolitania after
the war and the subsequent development of the cold war,
prompted the United States to request the continuation of the
use of the base when British authority was transferred to Libyans,
pending a formal agreement on the matter.

Negotiations over the Wheelus Base, which were carried out
during the same time the British treaty was under discussion,
lasted for some time, mainly because the Libyan government
desired to sign the British Treaty first and because of other
pressing problems facing a newly independent country. The

[12] Point Four Agreement for Technical Co-operation, signed on January 21,
1952.

controversial points centered mainly on the financial arrangements relating to the area of the base; but other matters, such as defining the status of Americans residing in the base also contributed to the prolongation of the negotiations. These matters included the definition of the relationship of American forces to the administration of criminal jurisdiction and the relief of local duties and taxes on American imports.

In July, 1954, Bin Halim visited the United States and the negotiations were finally completed. The formal signing of the agreement, however, was effected in Banghazi on September 9. Bin Halim's visit to Washington was intended mainly to secure American financial assistance for Libya's economic development and for cementing the friendly relations already existing between the two countries. The preamble, stating the broad purposes of the agreement, reads as follows:

> The government of the United States of America and the government of the United Kingdom of Libya, desiring to strengthen the firm friendship and understanding now existing between them; confirming their determination to co-operate amicably and to support each other mutually in the international field, and to contribute to the maintenance of peace and security within the framework of the Charter of the United Nations; and being of the opinion that co-operation within the territory of Libya will assist in achieving these objectives . . .[13]

More specifically, the agreement provided that Libya granted permission to the United States to " occupy and use for military purposes " certain specific areas agreed upon for the duration of the agreement. The United States was to exercise full control over "aircraft, ships and waterborn craft, and vehicles entering, leaving, and while within the agreed areas." The right to construct and maintain communications outside the area was also given. The agreement also provided that the United States may " bring into Libya members of the United States forces in connection with carrying out the purposes of the agreement," and that the laws of Libya " shall not apply to prevent admission or

---

[13] *United States and Other International Agreements*, Vol. V, Part 3 (1954), pp. 2451–95 (text in English and Arabic). See Appendix V.

departure into or from Libya of members of the United States forces."

The significance of the Wheelus Base is as follows:

1. A link in the overseas base system which the United States has erected against the Soviet Union.

2. An important military transit stop in the Mediterranean area.

3. A training base for air personnel in the Mediterranean area.

As a *quid pro quo* for Libya's offer of military facilities, the United States, under a general agreement for technical co-operation, signed in 1954 and revised in 1955, pledged itself to pay during the first year seven million dollars in development assistance and 24,000 tons of grain for relief in drought areas. For subsequent years the United States pledged itself to provide Libya with four million dollars annually for six years, and one million annually for the next eleven years.

The agreement was described in the United States as "an important contribution to the defense of the free world," and an instrument designed to "strengthen the ties of amity which bind together the people of the two countries." [14] For Libya it provided direct association with a Great Power and financial assistance for economic development. The United States also pledged itself to help Libya in the development of its health, education, and agricultural programs.[15]

Since it was an executive agreement, congressional action on the Wheelus Base agreement was not required in the United States. For Libya, however, the agreement was regarded so important that parliamentary action was deemed necessary. A parliamentary bloc of sixteen members raised certain objections to the agreement before it was submitted to Parliament. Early in October, 1954, when Parliament was considering the agreement, Ibrahim al-Shalhi was assassinated. The parliamentary bloc, believing that Bin Halim's position had weakened after Shalhi's assassination, concentrated its attack on the agreement

[14] *State Department Bulletin*, Vol. XXXL (1954), pp. 396–97.
[15] See texts of agreements for co-operative programs in health, education, agriculture, and natural resources, signed on July 28, 1955.

hoping that Bin Halim might resign. Thus some of Bin Halim's supporters suggested the postponement of parliamentary action until conditions had improved. Bin Halim, however, seeking the King's personal support, prompted the King to issue a statement to the effect that the Bin Halim government enjoyed his full confidence.

Before Parliament moved to approve the agreement, Bin Halim had to overcome further difficulties. The four Tripolitanian members in the Cabinet (Qalhud, Sarraj, Abd al-Salam al-Busiri, and Bin Sha'ban) demanded that the government move back to Tripoli in lieu of their support for the Wheelus Base agreement. Bin Halim, who did not want to antagonize the King on the matter, suggested that action be postponed until the agreement was ratified. When Shalhi was assassinated, and the King moved his official residence from Banghazi to Tubruq, it became less difficult for Bin Halim to request the King's approval for moving the government to Tripoli. This action, regarded as a victory for the Tripolitanian members of the government, encouraged them to support Bin Halim in public on the Wheelus Base Agreement.[16] Bin Halim, after Shalhi's assassination, himself wanted to move to Tripoli in order to have a free hand in conducting the business of government.

Nor was this all. 'Umar Mansur al-Kikhya, President of the Senate, was not on good personal terms with Bin Halim. He displayed his personal dissatisfaction by criticizing the American agreement, although his son Fathi had taken active part in the negotiation and tried to explain to his father the advantages of the agreement. When 'Umar Mansur denounced the agreement in public,[17] Bin Halim took up the matter with the King, who was disturbed by 'Umar Mansur's tactlessness. The King, already annoyed at 'Umar Mansur for his failure to attend the funeral of Shalhi, issued an order dismissing him from the presidency of the Senate on October 15, 1954. There had already been criticism levelled at Mansur's conduct as President of the Senate,[18] but his recent utterances against the agreement seem to have

---

[16] The writer's interview with Qalhud and Sarraj.
[17] At a party given at the British Embassy in Banghazi in October, 1954.
[18] See *Barqa al-Jadida*, Banghazi, October 31, 1954.

exhausted the King's patience, though Bin Halim might not have wanted to go as far as to humiliate by dismissal the elder statesman who had spent the whole of his life in the service of the country.

Finally, Bin Halim, trying to impress the parliamentary bloc with the material advantages of the agreement, explained the nature of American economic aid and made an appeal in the interest of the country for support of his policy. On October 1, 1954, four days before Shalhi was assassinated, Bin Halim invited Salih Buwaysir, Vice President of the House of Representatives, to a luncheon at his house, attended by Husayn Maziq and Sayyid 'Abu al-Qasim al-Sanusi. Bin Halim took the opportunity to explain the advantages of the American agreement to his guests and sought Buwaysir's co-operation by hinting to him that Buwaysir might be invited to join the Cabinet. Bin Halim's effort to win Buwaysir was frustrated by Shalhi's assassination; for, after the banishment of Sayyid Abu al-Qasim, Buwaysir's intimate friend, the latter's opposition to the agreement became more vocal.[19]

The agreement was submitted to Parliament for approval on October 30, 1954, having been scrutinized by a parliamentary committee of seven members. It is reported that the majority of the committee recommended the rejection of the agreement, but the recommendation, in a secret meeting of Parliament, was unacceptable to the majority, who voted for its approval. The King ratified the agreement by a Royal decree issued on the same day of its approval by Parliament (October 30, 1954) and put it into force on that day.[20] Its ratification was a great victory for Bin Halim's effort to carry out a policy which proved to be

[19] Buwaysir seems to have indulged in opposition and his close association with Sayyid Abu al-Qasim al-Sanusi, an alleged culprit in Shalhi's assassination, aroused the Royal Diwan. Rumors reached Buwaysir that the government was contemplating his arrest upon his return to Banghazi, where a state of siege had been proclaimed. On August 8, 1955, when the government moved to arrest him, he left Tripoli in disguise and went to Cairo via Tunisia. By a decision of the Executive Council of Tripolitania (August 21, 1955), Buwaysir's estate in Tripolitania was put under government custody (*Tarablus al-Gharb*, Tripoli, August 22, 1955).

[20] The text of the agreement was made public for the first time on November 3, 1954 (*Tarablus al-Gharb*, Tripoli, November 3, 1954).

so successful in achieving the economic development of the country. Shortly before the enforcement of the agreement, the United States announced (September 25, 1954) the elevation of its legation in Libya to the status of an embassy. At the same time it was announced that Col. John L. Tappin, who had served as a liaison officer in North Africa during the last war and later was active in administering the Marshall Plan, was appointed Ambassador, replacing Henry S. Villard who had served as Minister since the proclamation of independence.

The Franco-Libyan Agreement

Before Libya achieved her independence there seems to have been tacit understanding between Britain and France that Cyrenaica and Fazzan, having been given a large measure of independence, were to remain under British and French influence respectively. Britain quickly came to an understanding with Libya after independence—an understanding which gave Britain the right to retain bases in Cyrenaica [21]—and France seemed to have aspired to a similar position in Fazzan. On the same day on which Libya proclaimed her independence (December 24, 1951), two temporary agreements had been signed between Libya and France: a military agreement permitting France to retain her forces in Fazzan for six months, subject to renewal for further periods of six months pending the signing of a treaty of alliance which would replace the temporary agreement, and a financial agreement by virtue of which France promised to contribute financial assistance to Libya, equal to the amount of the deficit in the Fazzan budget.

On November 12, 1956, France proposed to conclude a treaty of alliance with Libya similar to the Anglo-Libyan treaty which was still under negotiation; but Libya, while accepting the principle of retaining French forces in Fazzan, raised objections to the privileges and immunities demanded by France in a note dated November 24, 1952. Negotiations were not resumed until the Anglo-Libyan treaty was signed, but no common ground of

[21] See pp. 226 ff., above.

agreement had been found. The French proposals appeared to Libya to imply the desire to retain a greater influence in Fazzan than the British in Cyrenaica. Thus, neither Muntasir nor Saqizli, who had negotiated with France, was ready to accept the French proposals, although both showed willingness to accept the principle of retaining French forces in Libyan territory (Fazzan).[22]

Changes in government both in Libya and France helped to resolve the deadlock. France, under the liberal government of Mendès-France, was anxious to come to an understanding with French dependencies, and Libya, headed by a Prime Minister who proved to be a skillful negotiator, quickly seized the opportunity and obtained more favorable terms than had been expected. Bin Halim, having successfully completed the Wheelus Base agreement, sought American support in his dealings with France.

Negotiations with France were resumed in May, 1954. By July, after a visit to Paris on his way back from the United States, Bin Halim made it clear to the French government that Libya was not prepared to enter into a military agreement and that the principle of evacutation of French forces should be the basis of the negotiations. At the outset the French refused to accept the principle of evacuation; but Bin Halim sent a note (November 13, 1954) in which he firmly stated that the principle of evacuation should be regarded as the basis of the negotiation and notified France that Libya was not willing to renew the temporary military agreement beyond December 31, 1954. Although France was not prepared to accept Libya's short notice terminating the agreement, Bin Halim remained firm in his stand.

On December 17, 1954, Mendès-France proposed that he negotiate directly with Bin Halim. To this Bin Halim agreed on December 23, 1954, provided that the negotiation would begin before December 31—the date set for the termination of the temporary military agreement. From January 3 to 6, 1955, the Libyan and the French Prime Ministers quickly came to an

---

[22] Saqizli suggested that the uniform of the French forces in Fazzan should be different from the regular French uniform elsewhere.

agreement on the principle of evacuation which became the basis
for subsequent negotiations in Tripoli in July, 1955. The chief
point of difference at this stage was France's insistence on the
return of her forces to Fazzan in the event of an armed attack
by a foreign power. Bin Halim accepted the French request
without commitment, for he deferred the question of defense
for future consultation between France and Libya in the event
of a threat of war.

Having explained the principal terms of the French treaty
both to his government and to Parliament (in a closed meeting),
Bin Halim proceeded to complete his negotiations until the
treaty was formally signed in Tripoli on August 10, 1955.

The treaty made up of 11 clauses in addition to annexes,
financial, cultural, and bon-voisinage agreements, provided that
perpetual peace and friendship should govern the relations
between France and Libya. Libya, however, agreed to consult
with France on matters concerning their mutual interests (Article
1). The treaty also provided for the final rectification of Libya's
frontiers in favor of the French territories in Africa. The principle of future consultation on the defense of Libya is embodied
in Article 5, which reads:

> In the event that one of the two high contracting parties finds itself
> involved in a war resulting from armed aggression, or the threat of
> war by a third power, involving the territories of Africa north of
> the Equator, the two parties shall consult with one another on the
> measures of defense of their respective territories. . . .

France promised to evacuate her forces from Fazzan within
twelve months from the enforcement of the treaty, and to hand
over the airports already in French hands to the Libyan government, provided that Libya would employ French civilian technicians for the operation of the airports. France also promised,
in the financial agreement, to contribute the sum of 130 million
francs in 1955, and 350 million in 1956, for the economic development of Libya. Beyond that, both countries promised to observe
the most-favored nation clause in foreign trade and to promote
close economic and commercial co-operation. Further, both
countries agreed to promote the exchange of cultural facilities

and publications, and Libya promised to introduce instruction in the French language into her institutions of higher learning. Facilities for the movement of tribes, the return of émigrés to Libya, and other matters were all dealt with in separate annexes.[23]

The treaty was ratified on April 10, 1956, having been approved by Parliament in a closed meeting. No serious opposition was raised against it, although a few attacked the treaty on account of Bin Halim's acceptance of the rectification of the frontiers in favor of France.

Diplomatic Relations with the Soviet Union and Libya's Admission to Membership in the United Nations

On the same day when Libya proclaimed her independence (December 24, 1951), she applied for membership in the United Nations. Libya's admission to this organization, which should have been merely a procedural matter (since she was created by an action of the United Nations General Assembly),[24] was rendered the more difficult because her name was added to a list of other pending applications. The Soviet Union had already submitted to the Security Council a draft resolution containing the names of thirteen countries for admission to the United Nations. When Libya formally submitted her application, the name of Libya was quickly added to the list in the Soviet draft resolution. This created a difficult problem for Libya, because the Soviet Union sought to exploit Libya's case in favor of countries which the Security Council was not in the mood to admit.[25] The Pakistani representative tried in the Security Coun-

[23] For text of the Treaty and its annexes, see *Government Gazette*, Vol. VIII (April 30, 1958), No. 7; United Nations, *Treaty Series*, Vol. 300 (1958), pp. 263–95.

[24] In its resolution concerning Libya's independence the General Assembly took the position that " upon its establishment as an independent state, Libya shall be admitted to the United Nations in accordance with Article 4 of the charter."

[25] Vishinsky plainly explained to Muntasir that he opposed Libya's admission because the Western Powers were not prepared to admit Soviet nominees.

cil to save the situation by submitting a separate resolution concerning Libya's admission, but it was vetoed by the Soviet representative (September 6, 1952) on the ground that Libya's application for membership was not a new application, since it had already been in the list of the Soviet resolution with thirteen other countries.[26]

The Soviet veto postponed Libya's admission into the United Nations for another three years until an agreement had been reached on a "package deal" which included some sixteen countries. Attempts had been made to secure Soviet approval on the ground that Libya's case was unique, since the Libyan state had been created by the United Nations, and that there was a moral obligation on the part of the members of this organization to admit Libya. However, this was to no avail.

When Bin Halim came into power, he decided to negotiate directly with the Soviet Union in order to insure its support for Libya's admission to the United Nations. The Soviet Union had already asked to establish diplomatic relations with Libya, and there was sharp criticism in Arab circles that Libya had leaned too heavily on Western support. Having assured the Western Powers of Libya's good will, Bin Halim decided to establish diplomatic relations with the Soviet Union in order to win not only Soviet support for Libya's admission to the United Nations, but also to demonstrate to the Arabs, at a time when Soviet prestige had reached its peak in Arab lands, that Libya could stand on her own feet.

However, diplomatic relations with the Soviet Union, which were established early in 1955, did not mean that Libya's doors had been thrown open to Communist propaganda. Bin Halim made it quite clear to Generalof, the Soviet Ambassador, before the latter presented his letters of credence, that Libya was not prepared to tolerate Communist activities within her frontiers. The Soviet Ambassador is reported to have replied, as Bin Halim told the author, that the Soviet Union did not intend to export Communist ideas to Libya. The opening of diplomatic relations with the Soviet Union may not have enhanced Libya's prestige

[26] The United Nations, *Security Council Official Records*, 7th year, 1952, pp. 11–19.

in Arab circles as much as expected, but it did strengthen Bin Halim's hand in seeking additional Western economic aid against Soviet offers of assistance.

The question of withholding the admission of new members into the United Nations aroused the concern of many a member of the United Nations and prompted the General Assembly on December 9, 1955, to adopt a resolution calling upon the Security Council to "consider, in the light of the general opinion in favor of the widest possible membership of the United Nations, the pending applications for membership of all those eighteen countries about which no problem of unification arises." [27] Upon the request of the General Assembly, the Security Council held meetings on December 10, 13, and 14, 1955, to consider the question of recommending the admission of pending applications. The applications had already been carefully scrutinized by the admissions committee, and a list of eighteen countries, agreeable to all members, was recommended to the Security Council. The Security Council, in its meeting on December 14, 1955, agreed to recommend sixteen members to the General Assembly for admission. This "package deal" broke the deadlock in the Security Council and Libya, having established diplomatic relations with the Soviet Union, secured Soviet support for her admission after her name was placed on the list of sixteen countries as new members of the United Nations. In welcoming their admission, M. José Maza of Chile, President of the Assembly, said:

> We have by this vote fulfilled a deep desire which has existed in the General Assembly for many years—the desire to overcome the obstacles preventing the United Nations from becoming a completely international organization representing all peoples enjoying true universality.[28]

Libya's admission to the United Nations was regarded as "the fulfillment of the moral commitments entered into by the United

[27] United Nations, *Official Records of the General Assembly*, Tenth Session, 1955, Supplement No. 19.
[28] United Nations, *Official Records of the General Assembly*, Tenth Session, p. 436.

Nations," [29] for it had been withheld for a long while by the
deadlock on the admission of new members. When Libya finally
occupied her seat in the General Assembly, her admission was
not only welcomed by all members of the United Nations,[30] but
was particularly valued by the Arab states, who sought to
strengthen their position in the Afro-Asian bloc.

Federal vs. Provincial Powers and the Question of Succession to the Throne

The assassination of Shalhi not only eliminated a great factor
in the controversy over the federal system but also reopened the
question of succession after the exile of the leading pretenders
to the throne; for, in the absence of a direct Royal issue, the
question of succession weighed heavily on the King's mind. The
appointment of the King's brother, Amir Muhammad al-Rida,
as heir apparent in 1953, regulated by a law of succession, temporarily solved the problem; but this was by no means a final
solution, since al-Rida died on July 29, 1955.

After Shalhi's assassination, the King, dissatisfied with the
conduct of the leading members of the Sanusi house, began to
reconsider the question of succession. Bin Halim could not have
chosen a more opportune moment to suggest to the King the
idea of dissolving the federal system and transforming the monarchy into a republic. He suggested that King Idris should become President of the Republic for life, but that after him the
tenure of office would be for ten years only. The President, as
head of state, would be directly responsible for provincial administration, without the need for separate provincial governments.
Next to the President there would be a Vice-President, who
would succeed temporarily in case of the President's death until
a new President was elected; and an elected Parliament representing the nation, whose members, meeting in a national convention, would elect the President and the Vice-President. The

[29] United Nations, *Official Records of the Security Council*, 7th year, 1952,
p. 8.
[30] Only Israel abstained in voting for Libya's admission.

أهدى رسمي
للسكند
خدودي
للذكرى
الحسن الرضا
١٩٧٢/٧/٢

Crown Prince al-Hasan al-Rida

new structure would be that of a presidential—not a parliamentary—form of government.

The King, anxious to solve the question of succession, ordered
Bin Halim to prepare a memorandum on the proposed form of
government. Prompted by a desire to put an end to the conflict
between national and provincial powers, Bin Halim submitted to
the King (December, 1954) a very able memorandum in which he
proposed the dissolution of the federal system and the creation
of a decentralized unitary system. As to the form of government,
he suggested a presidential one, after the American model, rather
than a parliamentary form. Bin Halim's critics remarked that
his eyes were fixed on becoming Vice-President and that, after the
King's death, he hoped to become the future President of the
Republic.[31] Whatever Bin Halim's purpose, the memorandum
was manifestly the work of a man who had observed the regime
with a trained eye and keen interest. Whether the King seriously
considered abolishing the monarchical system is difficult to determine, but he was at the outset impressed by the brilliant scheme
prepared by his Prime Minister.

At several meetings held in Tubruq (January 11-15, 1955) [32]
over which the King presided, the Bin Halim memorandum was
considered. Among those invited were Adrian Pelt, former
United Nations Commissioner in Libya; Husayn Maziq, Wali of
Cyrenaica; 'Abd al-Salam al-Busiri, Chief of the Royal Diwan;
and the younger Shalhi, Nazir of the Royal Household. The
King opened the discussion by raising the question as to whether
the time had not come to transform the federal into a unitary
system. He also raised an objection to the presidential form of
government, which renders the President as head of state responsible, in contrast to the parliamentary form which makes the
Prime Minister responsible, although he was in favor of the
principle of republicanism. The younger Shalhi, who also was

---

[31] Bin Halim made the following comment: " I suggested to the King that
if my proposals were adopted, I would resign. I also suggested that the ages
of the President and Vice-President should be no less than 50 years, so as to
exclude my being a candidate for one of these posts."

[32] The press reported that Bin Halim and Adrian Pelt went to Tubruq on
January 11 and returned to Tripoli on January 15, 1955 (*Tarablus al-Gharb*,
Tripoli, January 13 and 16, 1955) .

in favor of republicanism, suggested the appointment of several vice-presidents, each representing one of the three provinces. If the President passed away, the vice-presidents would elect one of their number as President.

Pelt advised against haste and pointed out that such a change in the form of government required a revision of the constitution, which might meet with opposition. The King made the observation that his desire to change the monarchy into a republic might provide an opportunity for Parliament to revise the constitution and transform the federal into a unitary system. Pelt, who was in favor of a monarchy for Libya, commented that the opponents of the federal system would certainly discover the reason for the constitutional change and might react against the contemplated republican regime. As to the question of succession, Pelt felt that the King might adopt a son and appoint him as an heir apparent. However, the King was not in favor of this expedient. Bin Halim expatiated on the merits of the unitary system and pointed out that the federal system was too expensive for a country with meager resources. He indicated that the unitary form of government would save the country the sum of £750,000 a year (on the basis of the budget of 1955) which might be used for economic development. Husayn Maziq, Wali of Cyrenaica, was doubtful as to the wisdom of dissolving the federal system. No decision was reached at the meeting, but the King gave further thought to the Bin Halim proposals.[33]

As soon as the news of the Tubruq meeting became known, the Cyrenaican tribal chiefs began to visit the Royal Diwan, protesting against the proposed plan for changing the monarchy into a republic and the federal into a unitary system.[34] The tribal protest demonstrated that the time had not yet come to make a change in favor of the unitary system, and they confirmed the King's belief that the federal system, despite the complaints raised against it, was still the best guarantee of Libyan unity. As a result, the King was inspired to give serious thought to the

[33] The writer's interviews with King Idris, Bin Halim, Husayn Maziq, al-Busiri al-Shalhi, and Adrian Pelt.

[34] Bin Halim told the author that the protest of the tribal chiefs to the King was instigated, while Husayn Maziq said that they spontaneously reacted against the news that reached them.

question of the Royal succession and to put an end to Sanusi quarrels over it.

The problem of succession proved to be very delicate and was often the subject of discussion between the King and his principal advisers. Bin Halim, as he told the author, had suggested two alternatives to the rule in force of appointing one of the Sanusis as heir apparent. First, he suggested that the King might marry a second wife, which is permissible in Islamic law, in order to produce a male successor. This subject was discussed several times, but the King, devoted to his first wife, was reluctant to marry a second one. Secondly, he proposed the transformation of the monarchy into a republican form of government.

The King, it will be remembered, tried to tackle the problem by taking up the latter proposal. As the outcome of the Tubruq meetings demonstrated, this proposal proved to be impractical. Then, under the influence of palace advisers, the King decided to take a second wife. The marriage to an Egyptian lady took place on June 30, 1955, but did not result in producing an heir and was subsequently dissolved in January, 1958. The question of succession was further complicated when the King's brother, Amir Muhammad al-Rida, died after a short illness in 1955, having served less than two years as heir apparent.

Prompted by his leading Ministers to appoint an heir apparent, the King settled on Amir al-Hasan al-Rida, a nephew, and announced his decision in the Speech from the Throne in Parliament on November 26, 1956. In 1959, Amir al-Hasan married a Tripolitanian lady, a move intended to elicit Tripolitanian support for the ruling dynasty.

Libyan-Egyptian Relations and the Suez Crisis

As an independent Arab country, Libya had already joined the Arab League and participated in regional Arab conferences; but, as a country in close relationship with Western Powers, she wisely kept aloof from the widely spreading anti-Western feeling in Arab lands following World War II. Such an attitude was often denounced in Arab nationalist circles as submissiveness to

Western influence, but Libya tried earnestly to maintain friendly relations with both the Western and the Arab countries.

When Bin Halim formed a government in 1954, he had, it is true, regarded American-Libyan friendship as the cornerstone of his foreign policy, but he also tried to cultivate friendly relations with Arab countries, Egypt in particular. Although he saw that Libya's future was dependent on Western support, especially for her economic development, he also realized that Libya, as an Arab country, could not possibly detach herself from the Arab World. He maintained that if he did not try to cultivate friendly relations with the Arab World, his government would run the risk of losing the sympathy of the people, because Libyans tend to identify the aspirations of their country with the national aspirations of other Arab countries. Thus in following a policy of Arab co-operation, Bin Halim sought to strengthen the position of his government within Libya no less than to assert Libya's independence in foreign affairs.

Egypt was naturally the principal Arab country with which he sought to cultivate friendly relations. As a young man who grew up in that country, he had known her people and watched the course of her internal political development with a keen eye. He had also known many of her political leaders and established friendly relations with some of them. When he later approached the Egyptian government as the Prime Minister of Libya, he was therefore confident that he would be able to cement friendly relations between his country and Egypt.

In June, 1954, he paid a visit to Cairo. In an intimate conversation with Colonel Jamal 'Abd al-Nasir, who had just succeeded General Muhammad Najib as chief of government, he put an end to the ill feeling created between the two countries following the decision of the Supreme Court of Libya in the 'Ali al-Dib case [35] in which Egyptian judges took part and which was construed as undermining the authority of the King of Libya. Bin Halim also explained to Nasir Libya's policy toward the West—the United States in particular—with which Nasir expressed personal satisfaction.

In November, 1954, Bin Halim was again in Egypt and saw

---

[35] See pp. 240 ff., above.

Colonel Nasir. Nasir intimated to him the contemplated plan of supporting the Algerian revolt and revealed Egypt's readiness to supply the Algerian leaders with arms. He wanted to inquire from Bin Halim whether Libya was prepared to permit the clandestine passage of arms across her frontiers to Algeria. Since a decision on such a matter might compromise Libya's relations with other powers, especially France—with whom Libya was negotiating an evacuation agreement [36]—Bin Halim told Nasir that he had to consult with the King. Upon his return to Libya, Bin Halim gave the King an account of what was agreed upon in Cairo and it was decided to permit the secret passage of arms, provided that no war materials were to be stored in Cyrenaica. A military attaché, Colonel Isma'il Sadiq, was later sent to Tripoli (1955) to take charge of delivering the arms to Algerian leaders.

Relations with Egypt continued to improve and Bin Halim, when approached by 'Iraq to join the Baghdad Pact, refused to do so because he saw no advantage for Libya's adherence to the Pact and felt that it would antagonize Egypt.[37] This friendly attitude toward Egypt gave the impression to some Western observers that he was promoting the neutralist policy of Egypt.[38] When Nasir declared the nationalization of the Suez Canal Company (July 26, 1956), Bin Halim on July 28, 1956, made a statement in support of Egypt's right to do so. He said:

> The decision taken by President Jamal 'Abd al-Nasir to nationalize the Suez Canal Company is a wise and courageous step which we [all] hope will be carried out successfully. This decision has been taken to protect Egypt's [national] interests, and it falls within the domestic jurisdiction of a sovereign independent state. So I do not understand the reason for the objection raised against Egypt by some of the Western Powers, since the decision was dictated by [Egypt's] national interests. However, President Nasir, who appreciates the significance of the Suez Canal as an international maritime

---

[36] See pp. 258-261, above.

[37] The writer's interview with Bin Halim; see also *al-Ahram*, Cairo, July 26, 1956.

[38] See Osgood Caruthers, " Egyptian Wooing of Libya Stirs Concern of Western Diplomats," *The New York Times*, May 24, 1956.

passage, declared his country's readiness to respect [the principle of] the free navigation of the Canal. This should be regarded as a sufficient guarantee for world public opinion. The negative attitude of the Western Powers [toward the nationalization of the Canal] raises doubt as to their [good] intentions in giving free economic aid to small Powers.[39]

The wording of this statement caused some eyebrow-raising in certain political circles, because of Libya's close alliance with Great Britain; but in reality Bin Halim's statement was in line with similar statements made by heads of other Arab governments. Nor did Britain raise an objection to such a declaration of sympathy by one Arab country with the national aspirations of another.

During Bin Halim's absence from Libya in early August when he accompanied the King on his state visit to Turkey, Khalil al-Qallal, the acting Prime Minister, made a statement on August 11 that Libya would not permit any foreign power to launch an attack on Egypt from her territory. Similar statements were made by 'Ali al-Sahili, acting Foreign Minister; and notes were sent to Britain and the United States stating that under no circumstances was Libya to permit the use of her ports and bases for an attack on Egypt.[40]

When, however, Egypt was attacked by Israel and an Anglo-French note, demanding the separation of the two belligerents and a guarantee of freedom of transit through the Suez Canal, was delivered to Egypt and Israel (October 29, 1956), Bin Halim's position became very delicate. He saw at once that the impending attack on Egypt would place him and his country in an embarrassing position and that verbal declarations of sympathy would satisfy neither Libya's close neighbor nor her principal ally. An attack on Egypt by Great Britain was bound to strain both Bin Halim's friendly relations with Egypt and his country's obligations toward Britain.

At the outset Bin Halim tried to support Egypt's position

[39] For text of the original Arabic, see *Tarablus al-Gharb*, Tripoli, July 29, 1956 (writer's translation).

[40] The writer's interview with 'Ali al-Sahili; see also *al-Ahram*, Cairo, August 16, 1956.

without compromising Britain's rights under her treaty with Libya. Thus, when the joint note was delivered to Egypt (October 29), he returned to Tripoli from Tubruq where he was discussing the Egyptian problem with the King and asked to see the British Ambassador, W. G. C. Graham, on the evening of that day. He wanted to know whether, if Britain attacked Egypt, she would use her bases in Libya against Egypt. Graham replied that although nothing specific would prevent Great Britain from using the bases, its preamble clearly indicated that Libya's obligations under the United Nations Charter and the Arab League Pact did not permit Britain to use the bases against Libya's neighbor.[41] He therefore thought that Great Britain was not going to use her rights under the treaty. Bin Halim asked for an " absolute guarantee " that Britain did not intend to use the bases against Egypt, and he indicated that should Britain try to use the bases she would be resisted by Libyan forces. Graham replied that he could not give such a guarantee without authorization from London, and a cable requesting instructions was sent at once to the Foreign Office. When Bin Halim tried on the following day (October 30) again to see the British Ambassador, he found that the Ambassador had already left for London. Graham made a flying visit to London for consultation and was back in Tripoli on the same day that Bin Halim wanted to see him. A reply authorizing Graham to inform the Libyan government that Britain was not contemplating the use of the bases against Egypt had already arrived, and a letter to that effect was handed over to Bin Halim.[42] The British military command may have been contemplating the use of the British bases in Libya against Egypt, but the Foreign Office seems to have been under no illusion that Britain could easily invoke her treaty of alliance with Libya.

Bin Halim and Graham came to a quick understanding as to

[41] Bin Halim had already received a letter from Selwyn Lloyd, delivered to him in August while on a visit to Turkey, in which a general assurance was given to the effect that Britain would respect Libya's treaty obligations as well as her commitment under the Arab League Pact. On August 19 Bin Halim made a statement that Libya received confirmation from Britain that she would not use her Libyan bases for an attack on Egypt (Information supplied by Bin Halim; see also the *New York Times*, August 20, 1956) .

[42] The writer's interviews with Bin Halim and W. G. C. Graham.

the position of the bases and the conduct of the British forces in Libya during the Anglo-French operations in Egypt. Bin Halim asked that the British troops be confined to the bases and not leave them during the period of the military operations. Graham replied that such a condition was unacceptable. Bin Halim then asked that the British troops should at least be as inconspicuous as possible in their movement. Graham agreed to pass Bin Halim's request on to the military authorities and, it seems, the troops remained in camp for a short while, but trucks carrying foodstuffs naturally had to move. The terms of this *modus operandi* seem to have been fairly observed by both parties.[43] Bin Halim acquainted the Egyptian Ambassador with the British assurance and public statements that Libyan bases would never be used against Egypt were reiterated.

The British assurance, which Bin Halim could flatter himself to have secured in favor of Egypt, proved to be inadequate for nationalist demands. For no sooner had the attack on Egypt begun than nationalist elements became very active and demanded full support in favor of Egypt.[44] Some asked for the breaking off of diplomatic relations with Britain and France; others went so far as demand an attack on the British. Bin Halim was willing to restrict the activities of extreme elements but was not prepared to antagonize Egypt at a moment when public opinion had become increasingly hostile to Britain. In the meantime, he was worried lest Libyan territory should become a battlefield between Britain and Egypt; he accordingly began secretly to organize a force against such an eventuality. Because of the inherent weakness of Libya and her government's desire to support Egypt without antagonizing Britain, Bin Halim's position was obviously unenviable.

The British Ambassador, believing that King Idris was either

[43] Bin Halim made the following comment: "Ambassador Graham advised me that it was better not to bother the Foreign Office and the British Command with more conditions. He added that we could work out local ways and means by which British forces would be confined within the bounds of their bases and that General Moore, Commander of the British Forces in Libya, would co-operate with us. This worked out to my satisfaction."

[44] As early as August 16, a demonstration in Tripoli in favor of Egypt's nationalization of the Suez Canal Company was organized by nationalist elements.

incompletely informed about the conduct of his government or that some of its actions had not been accurately reported to him, decided to send Cecil Greatorix, one of the Embassy's officers,[45] to acquaint him with the situation. Greatorix saw the King on October 31 in Tubruq, and the King went to Tripoli on the following day to watch the course of political developments. King Idris, who often expressed himself against involving Libya in international complications, had already advised his Prime Minister to keep Libya out of trouble. In the past he had found his country entangled in conflicts among foreign powers which resulted in intervention in his country's affairs. He therefore urged Bin Halim to avoid exposing Libya to similar risks.

Meanwhile, signs of internal unrest due to the influence of nationalist elements and foreign broadcasts had become apparent, and the Wali of Tripolitania, Muhammad Jamal al-Din Bash Agha, warned the government of impending disturbances. The government moved to take measures necessary for internal security. It had already, on October 31, issued a decree declaring the country in a state of siege and the provincial administrations imposed restrictions on the movements of the people. But the activities of the Egyptian Military Attaché, Isma'il Sadiq, which received the support of those favorable to Egypt, rendered Bin Halim's position exceedingly difficult. Sadiq distributed arms to Libyans and encouraged attacks on British installations.[46] Such attacks, despite government precautions, caused some damage to several British and American installations. The activities of the Egyptian Military Attaché proved to be embarrassing to the government at a time when it had just been able to secure the immobilization of the British bases in favor of Egypt, provided that no attacks were to be permitted on British installations. The British Embassy sent notes of protests to the Libyan government, and the Wali of Tripolitania, who found the internal situation exceedingly difficult to control, asked the government to expel the Military Attaché.

[45] Greatorix, who spoke Arabic fluently, had been in Libya since the war and had known the King previously in Egypt.

[46] It was later revealed that the Military Attaché had distributed some 300 machine guns among Libyans, taken from the arms sent by Egypt to Algerian leaders across Libyan territory.

Bin Halim, trying to avoid antagonizing Egypt, took up the matter first with the Egyptian Ambassador and asked him either to inform his home government to recall the Attaché or to give him a long-term leave. The Ambassador was reluctant to accept either solution and promised only to ask the Attaché to remain in his house. However, the Attaché failed to do so and had already moved arms into the Egyptian Embassy and employed Libyans to defend its quarters. When the news of the Attaché's action reached Bin Halim, he asked the Egyptian Ambassador to send the Attaché back to Egypt. Pleading that the Attaché was responsible directly to the Ministry of Defense in Cairo, not to him, he asked for a formal note on the matter. A note demanding the recall of the Attaché was sent to the Egyptian government and the Attaché, within three days, on November 12, was escorted by the Libyan police to the Egyptian frontier. The Egyptian government disavowed the action of its Military Attaché and President Nasir sent a letter of apology to King Idris. Perhaps to counteract the action taken against the Egyptian Military Attaché, Bin Halim asked the British government to recall Greatorix, presumably on the ground that he went to see the King over the Premier's head.[47]

Bin Halim's handling of the affair was decisive, but it cost him his popularity in Egypt. He was denounced by the Egyptian press as the tool of Western imperialism and, after the fall of his government, the press made unfavorable comments on the record of his government.[48] Unaffected by his critics, Bin Halim paid lip service to Egypt at the Beirut Conference (November 13–14, 1956) held by Arab states to discuss their attitude toward England and France, but refused to sever Libya's diplomatic relations with those Powers since they had agreed to comply with the United Nations resolutions demanding withdrawal from Egypt. Relations between the Libyan and Egyptian peoples, however, had not been affected, because outside of official circles the feeling of the two sister countries remained undisturbed.

[47] Bin Halim made the following comment: " I asked the British government to recall Cecil Greatorix solely because he went without my knowledge to complain to King Idris against my government and presented to the King a very gloomy picture of the situation. I understood that Greatorix said that I was looking after Egyptian, not Libyan interests."

[48] See *al-Ahram*, Cairo, June 1, and 3, 1957.

The Italian-Libyan Treaty

The exodus of the Italian settlers from Cyrenaica and the subsequent occupation of the entire Libyan territory by the British forces created the problem of control of property belonging to absentee owners. The British military administration appointed a Custodian of Enemy Property whose functions and powers were based principally on the Hague Convention. Since all the Italian settlers of Cyrenaica had left, the control of the property they abandoned raised no problem for the Custodian and the eventual settlement of the question became part of the larger question of the disposal of Italian territory. In Tripoli, the Italians remained largely in physical possession of their property and when Italy herself capitulated to the Allied Powers, resulting in the Italian settlers' co-operation with the British military administration, the Custodian's work became more in the nature of that of a trustee than of an administrator.[49]

After the war, the question of Italian property was dealt with for the first time in a United Nations resolution (December 15, 1950) giving the Libyan government the right to " receive, without payment, the movable and immovable property located in Libya owned by the Italian State." [50] As to private property of Italian nationals in Libya, including Italian juridical persons, their rights were naturally respected. A tribunal was set up to decide disputes arising from the application of the United Nations resolution. Great Britain, as an administering power, carried out the resolution and handed over to the Libyan authorities all public property. However, disputes arose in connection with returning to Italian nationals property which the Libyan authorities regarded as being in the public domain. These disputes were referred to the tribunal, but the whole question of Italian property was not finally settled until Libya signed a treaty with Italy in 1956.

[49] See Lord Rennell of Rodd, *British Military Administration of Occupied Territories in Africa*, 1941–1947 (London, 1948), pp. 418–19, 438–39, 467–68.

[50] For text of resolution, see *Yearbook of the United Nations, 1950* (New York, 1951), pp. 357–59.

Early in 1953, Italy took the initiative by sending a delegation
to Tripoli and a Libyan delegation, headed by Saqizli—then
Minister of Education under Muntasir—opened the negotiation.
There was no common ground for agreement, since Saqizli asked
for a substantial amount of compensation for war damages and
for the reopening of the subject of public and private property.
The Italian Foreign Office maintained that the subject of war
damages was outside the scope of negotiation on the ground that
Libya was part of Italy during the war—thus she had no legal
claim for compensation—and that the question of the distinction
between private and public property had already been settled
between Italy and Britain.

Negotiations were interrupted for almost two years. Italy again
took the initiative and discussion of the subject was resumed early
in 1955. Libya held that legal considerations could not be regarded as the sole basis of discussion and asked that the negotiations should include political factors also. To this the Italian
government agreed, and an Italian delegation proceeded to
Tripoli to negotiate in June, 1955. The negotiations on general
principles were conducted satisfactorily, but they broke down
on the question of war damages, because the Italian delegation
held that Libya had no right to ask for compensation.

In October, 1955, a Libyan delegation, headed by Sahili, was
invited to Rome, and Italy offered Libya the sum of half a
million pounds, later raised to £2,750,000, and so the question
of war damages was settled. In the meantime, the tribunal set
up under the United Nations Resolution (December 15, 1950)
to settle pending issues concerning public property made a decision in favor of Libya. Thus the final obstacle in the way of
reaching an agreement had been removed.

Matters of detail were worked out by committees of experts
and the final draft treaty, agreed upon in Rome, was signed on
October 2, 1956. The treaty not only settled pending issues
between the two countries, but also provided a basis for agreement on financial and cultural matters. Sahili, who proved to be
a skillful negotiator, resolved one of Libya's most complicated
problems with one of her former rulers.

The treaty provided that Libya should succeed the Italian

government in the ownership of public property, but that private property belonging to individuals would be respected by the Libyan government.[51] The technical matters of ownership were dealt with in separate annexes. Other matters, such as the sale of Italian private property and the settlement of business transactions that had been made under the Italian regime, were also dealt with. The Italian government, on its part, pledged to pay pensions and compensations to Libyans who had served under its former civil or military administrations.

In lieu of compensation for war damages, the Italian government pledged to contribute one million Libyan pounds for economic reconstruction, to be paid in cash within three months from the enforcement of the treaty, and £1,750,000 as credit for buying Italian goods, to be used by Libya within three years. The treaty also stated that both governments would soon begin to negotiate a commercial and navigation treaty and a cultural agreement within the framework of a broader treaty between the two countries.

In a closed session the Libyan Parliament approved the treaty and the King ratified it on March 30, 1957.[52]

The Libyan-Tunisian Treaty of Friendship

Ever since the Cairo conference of North African leaders held (February 15–22, 1947) to co-ordinate their activities for achieving independence, the idea of forming some kind of a North African union had appealed to the people of North Africa.[53] Libya proved to be the first North African country to achieve independence, and the idea of a North African Union attracted Libyan nationalists. When, however, independence was achieved

[51] A number of establishments owned by companies or semigovernmental agencies, such as the building of the Banco di Roma, were also taken over by the Libyan government.

[52] For text of the Treaty, see *Official Gazette*, Vol. VIII (March 25, 1958), No. 5.

[53] For a background of this movement, see 'Allal al-Fasi, *The Independence Movements in Arab North Africa* (Cairo, 1948), pp. 375–80; English translation by H. Z. Nuseibeh, American Council of Learned Societies, Washington, D. C., 1954.

by Morocco and Tunisia in 1956, Algeria, because of her special relation to France, failed to reach the position of statehood achieved by her North African neighbors. In the circumstances, the possibility of achieving an ultimate North African Union seemed remote, and many North African leaders deemed it necessary to co-operate for the liberation of Algeria before they could work for unity. Thus, when the Algerian nationalists led the revolt against France, they received the support of all Arab countries, but the future relations of the Algerian nation with other North African counties would necessarily depend on the nature of the new regime to be created following a settlement with France.

Libya, occupying a central position between the Western and the Eastern Arab countries, was bound to respond to the call of nationalist leaders on both sides of her. When her Western neighbors were still struggling to obtain their freedom, Libya, preoccupied with her own internal problems, had to wait for participation in nationalist activities until those countries had achieved independence. For a short while Libya herself was not able to conduct her foreign relations independently; but, after she had firmly established her position in international councils, she moved to cement her relations with neighboring countries.

It was Bin Halim, after he formed a government in 1954, who saw that the time had come for Libya to enter into treaty relationship with other North African countries and began, it will be recalled, to cultivate friendly relations with Egypt. It was indeed not an easy task to maintain equally friendly relations with Nasir's Egypt when Nasir decided that Egypt's interests were not in accord with those of the Western Powers. Tunisia, finding her future development dependent on the West, shaped her policy of co-operation with Western Powers, and Libya, for financial and strategic considerations, found herself even more dependent on those powers than was Tunisia. Thus a policy of co-operation between Libya and Tunisia, based not merely on geographical propinquity, was bound to develop.[54]

[54] Libyan leaders had already been in touch with Tunisian leaders who supported them in their struggle with France.

The initiative for the conclusion of a Libyan-Tunisian agreement came from Libya. 'Ali al-Sahili, Minister for Foreign Affairs, proceeded to negotiate with Bourguiba (Abu Ruqayba), then Prime Minister of Tunisia. Bourguiba responded promptly and favorably, having himself been trying to lead a Northwest African bloc—counteracting Nasir's East Arab bloc—hoping to secure support for his policies by collaboration with Western Powers. A draft treaty, agreed upon by Bourguiba and Sahili, was later formally signed in Tunis by Bin Halim, who went on a visit to Tunisia, and Bourguiba on January 6, 1957.[55]

The treaty provided for " a permanent friendship " and " fraternity " betwen Libya and Tunisia, and declared that its object was " to strengthen the ties between the two neighboring states, to co-ordinate their policies, and to ensure their co-operation in the interest of safeguarding their independence and sovereignty." Libya and Tunisia pledged to " consult [one another] with a view to harmonizing their policies toward neighboring sister countries and toward the Western and Eastern states, with a view to safeguarding security and peace." Each one of them pledged to " refrain from taking part in any alliance likely to be harmful to the interests of the other party, and from engaging in any action likely to harm the other." If an attack were directed against one of them, it would be considered as directed against the other—in such a case the other party " will come to the aid of the party threatened or injured by all means which may be appropriate to its particular circumstances and possibilities."

The treaty also provided possibilities of co-operation in economic, commercial, cultural, health, social, and other matters. Finally, the two parties promised to respect each other's established regime, recognizing its legitimacy, and " agree not to make an effort to modify such regime."

The treaty, ratified on May 11, 1957, was hailed as a model of collaboration between two North African countries, because it was regarded as a basis for a broader scheme of co-operation

---

[55] During his visit to Tunis, Bin Halim impressed upon Bourguiba the need for Arab solidarity and Tunisia's entry into the Arab League. He also suggested that either Tunis or Tripoli should be the headquarters for the provisional Algerian government; but Bourguiba, who did not want then to antagonize France, failed to agree (information supplied by Bin Halim).

which was to include other North African countries, although formally it was signed as a bilateral, not a multilateral, treaty. Its critics denounced it as an instrument for co-ordinating the policies of the two signatories and harmonizing them with those of the West, although no specific clause dealt with such an objective. The treaty may also be regarded as an important milestone in the development of North African solidarity and may well be the first step for attracting others, either in adhering to it or revising it to make room for the adherence of other countries.[56] The implementation of this treaty was carried out by the signature of several agreements in 1961.

The Eisenhower Doctrine and the Richards Mission

From the time when Egypt entered into an arms deal with the Soviet Union in 1955, Communist activities in the Middle East became more prominent. While some of the Middle Eastern countries sought the backing of the Soviet Union for the sole purpose of asserting their newly won independence, Communist elements exploited this drift to their advantage at the expense of the pro-Western elements. The United States, which has often declared that she did not seek either political or economic domination over any people, was pictured by the Communist bloc as seeking to encroach on the independence of Middle East countries in the guise of defending their independence. To American policy makers, the Communist danger appeared to be alarming by the end of 1956, a situation which prompted President Eisenhower to ask the Congress of the United States on January 5, 1957, to authorize the launching of an American economic program to oppose Communist aggression against the Middle East.[57] Eisenhower urged Congress to authorize him to

[56] For a favorable assessment of the Libyan-Tunisian Treaty, see *La Dépêche Tunisienne*, Tunis, January 9, 1957; *Tarablus al-Gharb*, Tripoli, May 12 and 17, 1957. For an attack on Bourguiba's policy see *al-Ahram*, Cairo, October 10, 1957.

[57] For text of President Eisenhower's speech at the joint meeting of Congress, see the *Department of State Bulletin*, Vol. 36 (1957), p. 85.

assist economically and militarily the nations of the Middle East that needed American support against Communist domination. More specifically he proposed to Congress that the United States should:

1. Co-operate with and assist any nation or group of nations in the general area of the Middle East in the development of economic strength for the maintenance of national independence.

2. Undertake programs of military assistance and co-operation with any nation or group of nations which desire such aid.

3. Employ armed forces to secure and protect the territorial integrity and political independence of Middle East nations requesting such aid against overt armed aggression from any nation controlled by international Communism. These measures were to be undertaken in accordance with treaty obligations of the United States, including her obligations under the United Nations Charter.[58]

On March 9, 1957, Congress passed a joint resolution authorizing the President of the United States to carry out the proposals he had submitted on January 5. The resolution, *inter alia*, reads:

> The President is authorized to undertake, in the general area of the Middle East, military assistance programs with any nation or group of nations of that area desiring such assistance. Furthermore, the United States regards as vital to the national interest and world peace the preservation of the independence and integrity of the nations of the Middle East. To this end, if the President determines the necessity thereof, the United States is prepared to use armed forces to assist any such nation or group of such nations requesting assistance against armed aggression from any country controlled by international Communism, provided that such employment shall be consonant with the treaty obligations of the United States and with the Constitution of the United States.[59]

Despite the protest of the Soviet Union against the American offer of aid to the nations of the Middle East,[60] Congress passed

---

[58] *Ibid.*, p. 86 and J. F. Dulles' statements before the House Foreign Relations Committee and the Foreign Relations and Armed Services Committees on January 14, 1957, *ibid.*, pp. 126–29.

[59] *Ibid.*, p. 481.

[60] *Ibid.*, pp. 524–25; for text of the American reply see *ibid.*, pp. 523–24.

a resolution authorizing the President to spend $200,000,000 for the economic development of Middle Eastern countries and their support againt Communist domination. The joint resolution was signed and formally declared by the President on March 9. Henceforth the declaration came to be known as the Eisenhower Doctrine.

On January 7, 1957, Eisenhower appointed James P. Richards [61] as his special assistant to advise him on the implementation of the joint resolution of Congress. Richards left the United States on March 11 and visited North Africa and the Middle East in an effort to explain the Eisenhower Doctrine to the governments of these regions, to remove misunderstanding that had arisen in connection with the purposes of the doctrine, and to offer American aid. During his visit, Richards tried to determine the extent to which each country showed willingness to participate in the program offered. Upon leaving each country, a joint communiqué was issued setting forth a statement of common purpose and indicating the points of agreement.

Before Richards had arrived in Libya, Richard M. Nixon, the Vice-President of the United States, paid a visit to Tripoli on March 15, 1957, and exchanged views with Bin Halim on American aid and the security of the Middle East. At a state dinner given in honor of Nixon, Bin Halim said:

> The American people know, from their own history, how difficult the first years of independence can be . . . [America] understands by her own experience the difficulties facing us and as a result is determined to help us.
>
> That is the main reason why Libya welcomes the Eisenhower Doctrine in principle, the details of which are to be discussed with Ambassador Richards.
>
> We are convinced . . . that this doctrine is aimed at assisting us to maintain our independence in [the] face of any . . . attempt to sabotage that independence. . . .
>
> We, like the American people, abhor international Communism— it is contrary to the principles of our faith. . . .
>
> It is fortunate indeed that the United States takes the long view in her assistance to the under-developed countries; that America

---

[61] A former democratic Congressman from South Carolina.

really believes that in helping such countries and people America is also helping herself. We, too, believe in that far-sighted policy, and we people of Libya will be eternally grateful to America for her generous assistance in helping us to regain our national pride . . . [until] we can stand . . . as equal partners in the community of free nations of the world. . . .

In reply Nixon said:

We deeply appreciate the very generous comments that you have made with regard to the policy of the United States internationally, and in particular the comments that you have made with regard to the Eisenhower Doctrine, one which has a direct relationship to the problems of this country. . . .

I was impressed by the fact that you, Mr. Prime Minister, recognized a very fundamental fact, and that is that the Eisenhower Doctrine, and this, may I say, applies to all of the aid programs of the United States, is designed to assist nations to maintain their independence, and in no way is designed to compromise that independence.

. . . I can assure you that as far as the devotion to the principle of independence and freedom for peoples and peace for humanity is concerned, that our hearts and the hearts of the people of Libya and people like us throughout the world are as one. . . .

We know that when the independence of other nations is threatened that our own is threatened. It is for that reason that we welcome the opportunity to work with you and to work with other nations to build up the strength which will enable you to maintain your independence against any form of aggression.[62]

Two days later Richards arrived in Tripoli and exchanged views with leading Libyan statesmen. Although the initial economic aid offered to Libya was relatively small, Bin Halim declared that he had accepted the Eisenhower Doctrine as a matter of principle, not as a *quid pro quo* for material reward.

[62] For text of the Bin Halim and Nixon speeches, see *The Sunday Ghibli*, Tripoli, March 17, 1957. On March 9, 1957, shortly before Nixon's visit *al-Ra'id*, in a leading article entitled " An Open Letter to Mr. Nixon," written by Ibn al-'As, reputed to be the pen name of Bin Halim, more specific demands were made, including the increase of economic aid to Libya, solving the Palestine and Algerian problems, and bringing pressure to bear on America's allies to abandon imperialistic aims in the Middle East (see *Al-Ra'id*, Tripoli, March 9 and 14, 1957) .

However, he indicated that economic assistance to Libya should be substantially increased. Richards left Libya on March 20, and a communiqué, embodying the points discussed with the Libyan government was issued. It reads:

> On his visit to Libya from March 17 to 20, the Special Assistant to President Eisenhower, Ambassador James P. Richards, has conferred with the Prime Minister of the government of Libya. They have reached agreement on the meaning and purpose of President Eisenhower's proposals for the Middle East. This exchange of views revealed an identity of interests of the two nations and agreement to work together for the successful applications of the Middle East plan, which provides: (1) if requested, defense against any armed aggression by forces of international communism which may be directed at any nation of the Middle East; (2) assistance in developing the security forces of countries of the Middle East which request help for the purpose of protecting their freedom and independence; (3) aid in strengthening the economic systems of Middle East countries as the best defense against the threat of subversion. The government of Libya and the special Mission of Ambassador Richards agreed that the aggressive intentions of international communism offer the greatest present threat to national independence and the peace and security of the world community. They also confirmed that it is the general cry of both countries to oppose any aggression from any source. The government of Libya received with approval Ambassador Richards' assurance that the United States Middle East policy does not seek to establish spheres of influence or special positions of power in the Middle East but is devoted to strengthening the nations of the area so that they may be masters of their own destinies. In support of the principles enunciated above, it was agreed that additional economic aid to Libya is needed and will be forthcoming from the United States.[63]

Criticism was made that Libya should not have taken sides in the East-West conflict, due to the failure of the West to solve the Algerian as well as other Arab issues.[64] In answer to his critics, Bin Halim pointed out that the joint communiqué

[63] Only a summary of the communiqué was published in the Libyan press (see al-Ra'id, Tripoli, March 23, 1957; and Barqa al-Jadida, Banghazi, March 22, 1957). For full text see State Department Bulletin, Vol. 36 (1957), p. 726.
[64] Tarablus al-Gharb, Tripoli, March 26, 1927.

stressed Libya's readiness to resist aggression from any source, not only from the Soviet bloc, and that Libya's main purpose in supporting the Eisenhower Doctrine was to maintain her independence.[65] Since Libya had already entered into projects with Western Powers more formidable in nature than those specified under the Eisenhower Doctrine, Bin Halim was essentially right in accepting an offer promising additional economic aid to his country without further commitments.

Bin Halim demanded an increase in American aid in his negotiations with Richards, and his position was stronger when he called attention to the criticism levelled against the Eisenhower Doctrine in the Arab press. Richards returned to Tripoli on his way back to the United States on May 4 and was able to pledge additional aid to Libya after further conversations with Bin Halim. A sequel to the joint communiqué was issued which reads as follows:

> In accordance with the statement made on March 20 that the United States would provide additional economic assistance to Libya, the government of Libya and Ambassador Richards have now completed studies of economic activities which would contribute to Libya's needs. The Ambassador has agreed in principle that the United States government will immediately undertake the necessary procedural and legal steps to initiate projects in the following fields, among others:
>
> 1. A general survey of Libyan development needs.
> 2. The development of broadcasting.
> 3. Assistance in education, including scholarships and instructional material.
> 4. Further aid toward electrical power development.
> 5. Improvement of telecommunications.
> 6. Development of domestic water supplies.[66]

By her acceptance of the Eisenhower Doctrine, Libya received seven million dollars which raised the amount of American contribution by the end of the fiscal year of 1957, to $23 million.[67]

[65] See a leading article by Ibn al-'As in *Al-Ra'id*, Tripoli, March 23, 1957.
[66] *The Sunday Ghibli*, Tripoli, May 5, 1957; *al-Ra'id*, Tripoli, May 11, 1957; *Department of State Bulletin*, Vol. 36 (1957), p. 845.
[67] See a statement to this effect issued by the Prime Minister in *Tarablus al-Gharb*, Tripoli, May 9, 1957.

The Fall of Bin Halim's Government

From the time when he formed his government to the assassination of Shalhi (April 11–October 5, 1954), Bin Halim was the most effective Prime Minister Libya had had since independence. After Shalhi's assassination, however, he suffered a temporary setback, since Shalhi's support was deemed essential for his government's strength. Encouraged by the King's public expression of confidence in his capacity to carry out his constructive plans of reform, Bin Halim showed remarkable ability in carrying on successfully the business of government after Shalhi's assassination. He gained further strength when the second Parliamentary elections, held in the autumn of 1955, returned an overwhelming majority in support of the government. It is true that Bin Halim had taken careful steps to control the elections, but no disturbances, such as those which the country had witnessed in the elections of 1952, had taken place. Opposition elements, to which Bin Halim prudently listened while negotiating with foreign powers, were allowed to enter Parliament, although the number of seats given them hardly exceeded ten in the lower House.[68] Nor was there any serious opposition outside Parliament to reckon with, for political parties had been suppressed since Muntasir's time, and the politically conscious public had been carefully brought under control, except during the Suez crisis.

Opposition to Bin Halim, therefore, came neither from the public nor from Parliament, although the latter, next to the King's expression of displeasure with his Premier, was the only organ that could withdraw confidence from the government. Bin Halim's initial difficulties arose from within his own Cabinet. Some members, who joined the government at the King's instance, felt perhaps just as strong as Bin Halim and wanted to be on their own; others, who came from an opposition party—the Congress—were not expected to support all of Bin Halim's pro-

[68] The leaders of the opposition were: Mahmud Subhi, al-Ziq'ar, al-Sarraj, al-Qalhud, al-Zaqalla'i, Miftah 'Urayqib, 'Abd al-Qadir al-Badri, and others. Bin Halim made the following comment: " Except for 'Ali al-Dib, no opposition leader or member of any organization was prevented from taking part in the elections."

posals. Lack of harmony proved to be the perennial weakness of Bin Halim's government, but so long as his position was strong, the reshuffling of the Cabinet was carried out with relative ease; but when Bin Halim's position became weak, his inability to reconcile opposition elements gave an opportunity to his opponents to exploit dissension and cause the eventual fall of his government.

The first Cabinet reshuffling, in which Bin Halim dropped Khalil al-Qallal, took place on December 19, 1954. The portfolio of 'Abd al-Salam al-Busiri, Minister of Foreign Affairs, who had already been appointed as Wali of Tripolitania (December 3, 1954), was assumed by Bin Halim himself. The two departing Ministers were replaced by 'Ali al-Sahili and Salim al-Qadi, the first as Minister of Communications, the other as Minister of National Economy. Sarraj was transferred from National Economy to Education, and Ibrahim Bin Sha'ban from Education to Defense. While these changes brought a temporary spell of harmony, dissension was by no means ended. A split within the Cabinet again manifested itself, which compelled Bin Halim to drop Sarraj on April 26, 1955, who was replaced by 'Abd al-Salam al-Bisaykiri. 'Unayzi, Minister of Finance, who was appointed Governor of the newly created National Bank, was replaced by Sahili. The portfolio of Communication, vacated by Sahili, was given to 'Abd al-Majid Ku'bar, who also acted as Deputy Premier. Three more changes in the Cabinet took place before Bin Halim finally resigned. The first was on March 26, 1956, when he dropped Qalhud and 'Ali Ju'uda, replacing them with Muhi al-Din al-Fakini, and 'Abd al-Qadir al-'Allam. Bin Halim reinstated Qallal, and Ku'bar went back to take his position as Speaker of the House. The other took place on October 30, 1956, when Qallal, who often opposed the Premier's proposals, was dropped. The new members of the Cabinet were Muhammad Abu Dajaja for National Economy, Allam for Defense, and Tahir Bakir for Education. The third change took place when Sahili was transferred from Foreign Affairs to Justice on March 14, 1957, and Ku'bar entered the Cabinet as Foreign Minister. Salim al-Qadi left the Cabinet when he was elected Speaker of the House in Ku'bar's place.

Dissension within the government was not the immediate cause of Bin Halim's fall; for, as the several reshufflings have demonstrated, he was able to reconstitute the Cabinet without much difficulty, although continued dissension must have contributed to the weakening of the Cabinet.

While Bin Halim's domestic policy proved to be successful on the whole, especially the provision of funds for many constructive projects, his foreign ventures were often subjected to sharp criticism. The opening of diplomatic relations with the Soviet Union in 1955, which may have pleased the public at a time when Soviet Russia enjoyed high prestige, was received with much misgiving in pro-Western circles, although Bin Halim's leaning toward the United States was quite clear. His acceptance of the Eisenhower Doctrine brought him criticism from anti-Western elements who paid little attention to the additional millions of dollars he brought to the Treasury in return for virtually no new commitment by his country. As a result, his policy appeared to be mercantilistic, aiming at enriching the country's treasury. Bin Halim, however, was essentially right in following a policy which aimed at obtaining the maximum support for economic reconstruction without which Libya would, perhaps, never have been able to stand on her feet.

Most damaging of all was his policy during the Suez crisis which satisfied neither Britain nor Egypt, although he earnestly tried to help Egypt without compromising his country's position toward Britain.

Bin Halim's policy appeared too complicated and involved to the King, who preferred a straightforward fulfillment of Libya's treaty obligations. British representations must have added conviction to the King's evaluation of his Prime Minister's policy, especially when he proposed to revise the British Treaty with a view to specifying that in no way was the treaty directed against any neighboring Arab country. He went on to announce in Parliament, at its opening session in November, 1956, that his government was contemplating opening treaty negotiations with Britain in the following year. For this the King showed no great enthusiasm, and the question of treaty revision was postponed. Subsequent events also indicated that the King was reluctant to accept his Prime Minister's advice.

What made the situation more difficult was Bin Halim's conflict with al-Busiri al-Shalhi, Nazir of the Royal Household. The younger Shalhi, who stepped into his father's position, at the outset kept aloof from interference in politics and was on good terms with Bin Halim. But very soon the younger Shalhi, who became conscious of the power he could wield at the Royal Diwan, began to take an interest in public affairs. The struggle that ensued between the two men was in the last analysis a struggle for power. The dissension in Bin Halim's Cabinet was cleverly exploited by Shalhi, which rendered Bin Halim's position untenable. Attempts to drop the opposition elements, Sahili in particular, from the Cabinet were not successful, although the King approved Sahili's transfer from Foreign Affairs to Communications.

Matters came to a head on the question of transferring Siddiq al-Muntasir, Libya's Ambassador in Cairo, to a similar post in the United States. Bin Halim did not want to reward Muntasir, who had supported dissatisfied Libyan students studying in Egypt in their demand for an increase in their stipends, by transferring him to Washington. Thus, Bin Halim proposed to the King that Muntasir should be recalled to Tripoli, pending an appointment to one of the embassies other than that in Washington. To this the King, who himself was dissatisfied with Muntasir's support of Libyan students, agreed. When, however, Bin Halim was on a visit to Italy in May, 1957, a Royal decree was issued transferring Muntasir from Cairo to Washington. Finding that the order of transfer was issued during his absence, Bin Halim threatened to resign. On May 22 he sent a confidential cable to the King intimating that he did not want to continue in office in the face of continued obstruction by elements opposed to him in the Royal Diwan.

In a formal letter of resignation, dated May 24, 1957, Bin Halim requested the King to relieve him of the responsibility of his office. The letter was carried from Tripoli to Tubruq by two of his friends, 'Abd al-Majid Ku'bar, Speaker of the House, and 'Abd al-Raziq Shaqluf, Director-General of Finance. The two carriers having delivered the resignation, the King invited Ku'bar to form a government. Thus ended the life of a government headed by a man who proved to be one of Libya's most potent public leaders. Nevertheless this may not yet be the end of the political career of this young statesman; for, having served two years as Ambassador in Paris, he resigned to become the head of a business firm in Tripoli and to watch the course of internal politics of his country with keen interest.

chapter X

Trial and Error in Self-Government III:
From Ku'bar to Bin 'Uthman

THE KING's fourth Prime Minister was a Tripolitanian, the second and third having been from Cyrenaica. 'Abd al-Majid Ku'bar, a member of a family that had distinguished itself in nationalist activities, was born on May 9, 1909, and worked his way up in local Tripolitanian politics until he was appointed a member of the National Constituent Assembly in 1950, having been nominated as a representative of the Istiqlal (Independence) Party. In the first general elections (1952), he entered Parliament and subsequently was Speaker of the House almost uninterruptedly until he formed a government in 1957. He relinquished that position twice only (April 26, 1955, and March 14, 1957), to serve short terms in the Bin Halim government as Deputy Premier and Minister of Communications in 1955 and Deputy Premier and Foreign Minister in 1957.

Ku'bar quickly selected his colleagues on the same day on which he was invited to form a government (May 26, 1957). Only three new members were added to the former Cabinet, namely, Wahbi al-Buri for Foreign Affairs, Siddiq al-Muntasir for Defense, and 'Abd al-Hamid al-Dibani for Justice, replacing Bin Halim, Sahili, and Fakini.[1] Saqizli was invited to be Minister of Justice, but declined. Thus six members of the government were Tripolitanians, five Cyrenaicans, and one Fazzanese.[2]

---

[1] See p. 287, above.

[2] For text of the decrees inviting Ku'bar to form a government and appointing the members of that government, see *Tarablus al-Gharb*, Tripoli, May 27, 1957.

Not only had Ku'bar retained the same membership of the Bin Halim government, but also declared in Parliament three days following the formation of his government that his policy " would follow closely the lines laid down by the previous government." He had, it is true, included in his government Siddiq al-Muntasir, who precipitated the crisis in the Bin Halim Cabinet; but he had also dropped Sahili and Fakini, who had opposed Bin Halim. Bin Halim, who was a member of the Lower House, sought to support the new government in Parliament; perhaps he aspired to succeed Ku'bar as the Speaker of the House, as it was then suggested, for after his resignation, he declared in Parliament: " I shall look forward to sitting with you in this honored House." [3]

The King, however, sought to keep Parliament beyond Bin Halim's influence and decided to give him a post at the Royal Diwan. This idea attracted Bin Halim who, perhaps, thought he might be able to reduce Shalhi's influence over the King by taking an appointment at the Royal Diwan. Ku'bar also toyed with the idea of counteracting Shalhi's influence and nominated Mahmud al-Muntasir for a similar position. Thus a " triumvirate," composed of two former Premiers and one in power, was formed to counteract Palace interference; but Shalhi's insistence that Muntasir and Bin Halim were appointed merely as personal advisers and should not take up their offices at the Royal Diwan rendered the power of the two former Premiers devoid of political influence. They accordingly requested the King that they be relieved of their offices and sought to serve their country in diplomatic posts. Royal decrees appointing Muntasir Ambassador to Italy and Bin Halim Ambassador to France, were issued on March 1, 1958.

Trying to avoid involvement with competing elements vying for power, Ku'bar decided to follow an independent policy. He came to terms with the Diwan entourage, dissociated himself from the influence of former Premiers, and avoided a conflict with provincial governors, who had proved to be the pillars of

[3] Bin Halim made the following comment: " I had no aspiration for the post of Speaker of the House, because the Speaker is, by tradition, Tripolitanian. However, I aspired to lead a large group in the House which would support or oppose in a constructive manner the government's conduct."

opposition to his predecessors. Asked about his domestic policy by the present writer,[4] Ku'bar tried to explain that he was on his own, and stressed the friendly personal relations he had established with the three Walis. The "personal" approach to the position of the Wali vis-à-vis the federal government meant in practice his submission to their demands, although after his resignation he complained about their relations with the federal government.[5] Ku'bar had to choose between a struggle with the palace entourage and one with provincial authority, if he wished to exercise his full powers with the possible fall of his government at any moment, or to accept the position of head of a government with limited powers. Nor was Ku'bar's temper suited for a struggle for the assertion of federal powers. He was quite satisfied to be the head of a benign administration and his policy proved to be successful in ensuring him a long tenure of office, although it could hardly have given him the same degree of power and prestige enjoyed by his predecessors.

Ku'bar's Problems and Achievements

As in the case of predecessors, one of Ku'bar's chief preoccupations was to ensure the continuation of foreign aid in order to balance the budget. Under the Anglo-Libyan treaty, concluded in 1953, the British financial contribution was to be reconsidered every five years. The first consideration was due in 1958 and Ku'bar began to make preparations for the forthcoming negotiations.

The idea of reviewing British financial assistance had been in Bin Halim's mind since 1956, when the Soviet Union offered economic aid and Egypt offered military equipment. Bin Halim seized the opportunity and informed Selwyn Lloyd, the British Foreign Secretary, when he paid a visit to Tripoli in that year, that Libya was in need of further financial assistance for her economic development. As a result, Bin Halim went to London for negotiations and a slight increase in assistance was obtained.

[4] The writer's interview with Ku'bar on August 4, 1959.
[5] The writer's interview with Ku'bar on July 14, 1961.

But Bin Halim, who aspired to obtain a substantial increase, resigned before a treaty revision was accomplished.

It devolved therefore upon Ku'bar to try his hand. But after the Suez crisis, the British government was not willing to give Libya the same amount of financial assistance, since it had already begun to withdraw the major portion of its forces from Libya. Negotiations began in Libya on January 21, 1958, and Britain proposed to reduce the financial assistance from four to one million pounds a year. It was suggested that the United States might be invited to take part in the negotiations and might be persuaded to meet Libya's financial needs. The British proposals were unacceptable to the Libyan government and Ku'bar decided to negotiate directly with the British Foreign Office. He left for London on April 27, 1958, and an agreement was reached with Selwyn Lloyd on May 3 by virtue of which British financial assistance was slightly reduced, fixing it at £3,250,000 a year for five years.[6] Britain also pledged to provide military equipment and free military training for Libyan officers.

After Britain, Ku'bar approached the United States. Following negotiations with Washington, the American Ambassador to Libya, J. Wesley Jones, was authorized to send a letter to Ku'bar, dated May 21, 1959, in which American economic assistance was increased for 1959. In addition to the fund provided under the American-Libyan agreement of September 9, 1954,[7] the American government agreed:

> to place at the unrestricted disposal of the Libyan government for this year only and subject to transfer arrangements to be agreed between representatives of our two governments, the sum of $4,000,000 from funds available to the United States government for commitment during its fiscal year 1959, as a special indication of support for the government of the United Kingdom of Libya, without

---

[6] Under the original financial agreement, it will be recalled (see p. 228 above), Britain pledged to pay during the first five years (1953–58) one million a year to Libyan development organizations and £2,750,000 a year to the Libyan budget. Under the present agreement Britain pledged to provide £3,250,000 a year in the form of budgetary aid for further five years, but with no additional contribution to development.

[7] See page 255, above.

prejudice or commitment in regard to aid programs or procedures in future years.[8]

In 1960 further negotiations resulted in raising American assistance to ten million dollars, given directly to the federal government without reference to specific programs. When it was announced, the agreement was rightly regarded by Ku'bar as a great success in balancing the Federal budget.[9]

Having secured adequate financial support from Britain and the United States, Ku'bar was not in the mood to flirt with rival powers. It was stated in the press as early as April 1958, that the Soviet Ambassador presented Ku'bar a letter from Khrushchev in which he offered financial assistance to Libya, but Ku'bar himself seemed to have been vague in his public statements concerning Soviet economic assistance.[10] In an interview with the author, Ku'bar said that the Soviet Ambassador offered his government's readiness to establish a hospital and supply it with Soviet physicians and assistants, but while he was ready to accept the offer of Soviet physicians, he rejected the assistants whom he thought might indulge in subversive activities. Asked by Zaqalla'i in Parliament (May 20, 1958), as to why the Soviet offer was rejected, Ku'bar replied that the offer was still under consideration, but that it consisted of establishing only one hospital in al-Bayda. No further Soviet offers seem to have been made to Libya.

The first important issue that confronted Ku'bar, and one in which he tried to play the role of the honest broker, was the complaint of Lebanon to the Council of the Arab League on May 21, 1958, against the United Arab Republic's intervention in

---

[8] See *United States Treaties and Other International Agreements* (Washington, D. C., 1959), Vol. X (1959), Part 2, pp. 2017–18.

[9] *Tarablus al-Gharb*, Tripoli, August 3, 1960. In 1958 it was agreed that the American government would supply Libya with arms, equipment, and ammunition under arrangements made in June 1956. This assistance was designed to help equip about one thousand men for the Libyan army (See *Department of State Bulletin*, Vol. 39 [1958], p. 84).

[10] See *Tarablus al-Gharb*, Tripoli, April 17 and October 31, 1958. In an interview with the correspondent of *al-Ahram*, Ku'bar is reported to have said that the Soviet offer consisted of substantial financial aid (*al-Ahram*, Cairo, October 20, 1958).

inspiring and directing the civil strife that had been going on in that country. Libya's policy, as manifested in the past, was to maintain strict neutrality in inter-Arab conflicts; but in this instance the matter touched directly Libya's neighbor, to which Libyan public opinion was well-disposed, and the meeting of the League's Council in Banghazi (June 1-5, 1958) in an atmosphere of intense rivalry between 'Iraq and Egypt rendered Ku'bar's position very delicate. Both Libya and the Sudan, concerned lest a drastic decision be rejected by one or another of the parties and wreck the organization, sponsored a resolution requesting Lebanon to withdraw the complaint and addressed an appeal to the contending parties in Lebanon to put an end to civil strife and settle their dispute by peaceful and constitutional means. This compromise resolution, though it failed to solve the problem, saved the Arab League from falling apart. Libya's prestige was enhanced when the United Nations' resolution proved to be essentially similar in nature to that sponsored by her at the Arab League Council.

A more serious problem that confronted Ku'bar was the revolution in Baghdad on July 14, 1958. The manner in which the Royal Family had been liquidated grieved King Idris, not only on the ground of kin relationship—since the Sanusi and the Hashimi houses were lineally descendants from the Prophet Muhammad—but also on purely humanitarian grounds, since the King of 'Iraq was an innocent young man who had nothing to do with the events leading up to the revolution. King Idris ordered the Chief of his Royal Diwan to declare the country in a state of mourning for two weeks, beginning from July 21, 1958, and refused to recognize the new regime in 'Iraq for three weeks.

Libyans, however, especially those who espoused the ideals of Arab unity, displayed undisguised delight in the liquidation of the 'Iraqi Royal House and regarded the event as a victory for the movement of Arab unity led by President Nasir of Egypt. They accordingly expected the Libyan government to recognize the new 'Iraqi regime in line with other Arab governments. When Libya failed to extend recognition quickly, the Egyptian radio spread the news throughout the Arab World that only Libya and Israel had not yet recognized the new national government of 'Iraq.

Ku‘bar, who was in sympathy with the humanitarian ideals of the King, was undoubtedly in a difficult position, especially since he had been denounced as the tool of the imperialists. Nor was his government strong enought to oppose an already excited public opinion in favor of Arab unity and, perhaps, one that expected that Libya herself might soon join such union. To improve his position, Ku‘bar impressed upon the King the necessity of recognizing the new government in Baghdad, and the King, in giving his assent, made it clear that he was not prepared to receive an ‘Iraqi Ambassador other than the one who already had represented the former regime. Thus, the new ‘Iraqi government agreed to keep ‘Abd al-Mun‘im al-Gaylani as Ambassador in Tripoli, and the Libyan government formally declared its recognition on August 4, 1958.[11]

One of Ku‘bar's far-reaching achievements, which proved to be the immediate cause of the fall of his own government, was the revision of the federal electoral law and the holding of relatively free elections. The second Parliamentary session was due to expire in 1960, and Ku‘bar, before the elections, decided to revise the electoral law. The chief criticism against the law was the distinction made in the elections between rural and urban districts. By a decree issued on September 24, 1959, abolishing this distinction and empowering rural communities to exercise secret voting as in urban communities, Ku‘bar put an end to the criticism levelled against the law and hoped that the forthcoming elections would be carried out in a peaceful atmosphere.[12]

The government moved back to Tripoli City on November 25, 1959, and preparations for the elections began in January, 1960. A change in the distribution of certain electoral colleges, which aroused criticism, was announced on January 8, and the Minister of Justice issued an order on January 9 prohibiting the carrying of arms during the elections.[13] The elections, held in accordance with the procedure provided for in the electoral law, were completed on January 17, 1960. There was general satisfaction that the new elections were carried out with a minimum government

[11] *Tarablus al-Gharb*, Tripoli, August 8, 1958.
[12] For a text of the amendment law, see *Official Gazette* (October 5, 1959).
[13] *Tarablus al-Gharb*, Tripoli, January 8 and 9, 1960.

control, so much so that two members of the government, who were candidates, failed to be elected, while several opposition leaders won the elections.

Parliament met on February 15, 1960, and elected Miftah 'Urayqib as Speaker of the House. Mahmud Abu Hidma was appointed President of the Senate by the King. Several new members took their seats in Parliament, and there were signs from the very beginning that these members were determined to be active Parliamentarians and oppose government measures ordinarily carried out without difficulty in previous sessions. The role of this opposition bloc, especially in causing the fall of Ku'bar himself, will be discussed later.

Deterioration in Administration

Conciliatory and easy-going by nature, Ku'bar managed to keep on good terms with almost all leading personalities; but this policy, though it helped him to enjoy a longer tenure of office than his predecessors, detracted from the efficiency of his government. In an administration where there was an increasing responsibility devolving on heads of departments owing to the rapid development of the country, there was a noticeable decline in efficiency and a tardiness in conducting the business of government. Moreover, transfer of government officials and new appointments of personnel were not always on a purely merit basis or in accordance with the laws and regulations of the country, and personal and political factors were often involved.

To overcome bureaucratic delay Libyans often resorted to influencing government personnel with material blandishments in order to get work done quickly. Such inducements were new neither in Libya nor in any other Middle Eastern country. But in a country whose people languished a long time under foreign domination and were deprived of the benefit of her resources, these practices are likely to continue for a long time to come. Coincidentally it was during the Ku'bar administration that foreign business firms and corporations that had already been given contracts to exploit the economic resources of the country, especially oil companies, began to pour into the country sums of money such as Libya had never seen in the past. Not infrequently it was these foreign firms who placed themselves in situations where they had to resort to local practices. These practices, beginning on a small scale in the lower echelons of administration, continued into upper echelons (and Ku'bar himself could not escape criticism from such practices), although it became known that such accusations were in most cases either untrue or grossly exaggerated. Nevertheless, damage was done by the mere fact that the public kept talking about corruption, bribery, and exploitation which the Ku'bar government obviously could not do much to stop.

The talks of deterioration in administration, resulting from corruption and exploitation, did not fail to reach the King, who showed great concern both morally, as the official head of a religious order, and politically, as the head of State. With great courage, and without even consulting his Prime Minister, he took the unprecedented step of issuing a letter dated July 13, 1960, to all heads of government, federal and provincial, calling their attention to the corruption and exploitation that had swept the country and admonishing them concerning its evil consequences. The text of the letter is of particular interest and, therefore, deserves to be quoted in full:

> In the name of God, the Compassionate, the Merciful:
> This is an announcement to the people by virtue of which they would be admonished.
> To the Head of the federal government, the Ministers, the Deputy Ministers, and all those responsible [in the federal government]; to the Wali of Tripolitania, the Wali of Cyrenaica, and the Wali of Fazzan; to their Nazirs, Directors, Mutasarrifs and all those who are responsible [in the provinces].
> Matters have come to a climax, as have deafening reports of the misconduct of responsible state personnel in taking bribes—in secret and in public—and in practicing nepotism—the two [evils] which will destroy the very existence of the state and its good reputation both at home and abroad, as well as the squandering of the [country's] wealth in secret and in public. [God], the Blessed and Most High, said:
> " Do not consume your wealth amongst yourselves in vain and

do not dangle it before the judges that you may sinfully and know-
ingly consume a part of the wealth of the people " (Qur'an, II, 184).

And the Prophet, God's blessing and peace be upon him, said
in a Tradition of his:

"You shall command good and forbid evil, otherwise [God] will
let those of you who are evil-doers dominate you, so that those of
you who are good shall pray for you, but they will not be answered."

The Prophet also said in a Tradition of his:

"He of you who will see a wrong, he should correct it with his
hand; if he cannot do so, then with his tongue; if he cannot do
so thus, then by his heart—the latter is the weakest in degree of
faith."

I, by God's blessing and His might, shall [try to] correct [evil]
with my hand, God willing. I shall not be deterred from carrying
out God's command to re-establish the good reputation of my
country. Salutation.

(signed) Muhammad
Idris al-Mahdi al-Sanusi.[14]

This letter circulated at the outset among department heads,
became the subject of discussion in Libya's political circles and
no longer remained a secret document. The press published first
its contents and then the full text.[15] There was an apparent
satisfaction throughout the country that the King was not unaware of the deterioration in administration, but no immediate
action was taken against those responsible for it. The significance
of the letter lies therefore not so much in its immediate effect
on the conduct of public personnel, but in its encouragement of
opponents of the government, both in Parliament and in public,
to denounce all those in authority who had failed in their public
responsibility. The position of Ku'bar was greatly weakened, but
he made no move either to resign or to conduct an investigation
of the conduct of those who were directly responsible for the
public concern. The damage to his government was done, and
his main effort seems to have been merely to focus public attention on the achievements of his government. He made a speech,
broadcast to the people on August 2, 1960, in which the satis-

---

[14] *Al-Masa'*, Banghazi, July 29, 1960; *al-Zaman*, Banghazi, August 4, 1960.
[15] See *Tarablus al-Gharb*, Tripoli, July 26, 1960.

factory negotiation with the United States government had been completed, resulting in the increase of American aid to ten million dollars.[16] Thus Ku'bar, unmindful of public dissatisfaction, remained in office for another two months before the opposition in Parliament moved to withdraw confidence from his government.

The Crisis over the Fazzan Road

In accordance with his conciliatory policy, which proved to be successful with the Palace entourage and the provincial authorities, Ku'bar tried also to accommodate himself to pressure groups and influential leaders, although such a policy was not always in the best interest of the country. Most dangerous of all, perhaps, was his acquiescence to the demands of certain influential persons for favors even when such demands proved to be excessive. The manner in which Sayyid 'Abd-Allah 'Abid obtained the Fazzan Road was a case in point.

The need for a road connecting the interior of the Fazzan province with the Mediterranean coast was universally acknowledged throughout the country and the plan was especially impressed upon the government by Fazzanese leaders.[17] It was contemplated that oil and other mineral resources, the existence of which in immense quantities had been indicated by experts, might attract foreign companies to the Fazzan fields if a road were opened to connect this province with a suitable Mediterranean port.[18] Sayyid 'Abd-Allah 'Abid, who had demonstrated his skill in obtaining government contracts, quickly applied to construct the road and signed the contract on December 20, 1958. Ku'bar's initial mistake was not so much in giving the contract

[16] See page 295, above.

[17] The road connects the coastal road at a point about 120 kilometers south of Misrata to Sabha in Fazzan. It was estimated that the road would be about 600 kilometers of black-top road.

[18] The government's decision may be said to have been based in the main on political and administrative grounds rather than on economic consideration (See Report of the International Bank on *The Economic Development of Libya*, pp. 233, 491–92) .

to Sayyid 'Abd-Allah on easy terms as in the hasty way it was
given, without a thorough scrutiny of the terms offered by other
firms. News of the award of the road contract to Sayyid 'Abd-
Allah for one million and nine hundred thousand pounds,[19] to be
completed in three years, rather than to another firm on the
ground that the 'Abid firm offered the least estimate of the cost of
construction, was not favorably received. It was suspected that
the cost would inevitably be much higher and that Sayyid 'Abd-
Allah had exerted personal influence on Ku'bar to obtain the
contract.

In 1960 Sayyid 'Abd-Allah, as it was expected, submitted a
statement to the Ministry of National Economy requesting further funds for the completion of the road on the ground that,
in accordance with the terms of the contract, he had completed
one unit, for which he had received the one million and nine
hundred thousand pounds and asked for funds for the other
units. Unaware of the precise terms of the contract, the government transferred the Fazzan Road project from the Ministry of
National Economy to the newly-established Development Council
for a decision. After careful examination of the matter, it was
decided to revise the contract in such a way as to allow Sayyid
'Abd-Allah to receive a further four million Libyan pounds for
the completion of the remaining portion of the road rather than
permit him to ask for more funds after the completion of each
unit. This arrangement was satisfactory to Sayyid 'Abd-Allah,
who received an advance of one million Libyan pounds on the
basis of the revised contract. The difficulty seemed to have been
settled in June 1960, although the whole affair was dealt with
behind closed doors.

A month later the King, it will be recalled, disturbed by the
news that had reached him concerning corruption and exploitation, issued his famous letter of July 13, 1960. In mid-August,
a few members of Parliament learned that Sayyid 'Abd-Allah
had been given four million pounds on the basis of a revised
contract of the Fazzan Road, and the story of the road appeared
for the first time in the press.[20] On August 18, 1960, Bashir

---

[19] The exact figure specified in the contract was 1,896,000 Libyan pounds.

[20] *Al-Masa'*, Banghazi, August 20, 1960. *Al-Masa'* was the first paper to dis-
close the news to the public.

al-Mughayribi, an opposition leader in the Lower House, sent
a cable to the Prime Minister protesting against the government's
action in giving four million Libyan pounds to Sayyid 'Abd-Allah
and stating that the action was contrary to statements made
earlier in Parliament that the full cost of the road was only one
million nine hundred thousand pounds.[21]

During September, the press published further sidelights on the
Fazzan Road and al-Masa', whose editor had a personal conflict
with Sayyid 'Abd-Allah over the ownership of a house, indulged
in derogation of Sayyid 'Abd-Allah's personal conduct.[22] Sayyid
'Abd-Allah, it is true, had often in the past used his personal
influence to obtain government contracts, but the Fazzan Road
became a target for public unrest and general dissatisfaction with
government administration with which Sayyid 'Abd-Allah had
nothing to do. Since Ku'bar was neither capable of stopping
corruption nor willing to resign following the King's dissatisfaction with the conduct of his government, the opposition moved
to overthrow him by Parliamentary action.

The Fall of Ku'bar

The Prime Minister was out of the country when the crisis
occurred. During his absence, the opposition, led by Bashir al-
Mughayribi and 'Abd al-Mawla Lanqi, two young Cyrenaican
members of Parliament, skillfully managed to circulate letters to
members of Parliament urging them to sign a petition to the King
for an extraordinary session of Parliament to discuss the government's action on the Fazzan Road. A petition, signed by more
than two-thirds of the members of both Houses of Parliament, was
submitted to the King in August, 1960. In accordance with
Article 66 of the Constitution, the King issued a decree, dated
September 17, 1960, calling Parliament to an extraordinary
session to be held on October 3, 1960. This decree, rightly
acclaimed as a great success by the opposition, sealed the fate
of the Ku'bar government, since the Parliamentary opposition

[21] Al-Masa', Banghazi, August 26, 1960; al-Zaman, Banghazi, August 25, 1960.
[22] Al-Masa', Banghazi, September 2, 9, 16, 23 and October 4, 1960.

had already held several secret meetings in which the majority of the members of Parliament committed themselves in writing to cast a vote of no confidence in the government.[23] What followed after Parliament convened was a drama that had already been skillfully rehearsed several weeks earlier.

Ku'bar's fall might have been less tragic, and even postponed, if he had not handled himself so poorly shortly before Parliament met. He returned to Tripoli on September 20 without the faintest idea as to what was going on behind the scenes. He decided at the outset to break the opposition by reshuffling his government and elevating one of the leaders of the opposition, 'Abd al-Mawla Lanqi, to a Cabinet position, without even obtaining his prior approval. Thus he not only revealed the weakness of his government, but he also faced a showdown when Lanqi, declaring his solidarity with fellow opposition leaders, declined the offer of a Cabinet position. The decree reshuffling the Cabinet was issued on September 29, five days after Ku'bar had gone to see the King, and he stayed there longer than he had expected in an effort to obtain Palace support against Parliamentary action. He seems to have suggested to the King that Parliament be dissolved to resolve the issue that had arisen between him and the opposition. The King, without committing himself to dissolution, told Ku'bar to see what would result from the parliamentary session.

Parliament met on October 3 before Ku'bar had returned from Tubruq. When the Speaker of the House, Miftah 'Urayqib, opened the session only Muhammad Bin 'Uthman, the Minister of Finance, represented the government. Thirty-five cables had already been received from Fazzan Province requesting Parliament not to stop the completion of the Fazzan Road. 'Ali Mustafa al-Misrati, one of the opposition, moved that a public statement be made to the effect that the purpose of the parliamentary meeting was not to stop work on the Fazzan Road, but to discuss the reason for the increase of the cost of the road from one million nine hundred thousand Libyan pounds to six million pounds. Misrati's motion, intended to calm Fazzanese concern about the future of the road, was carried out by the majority of the House.

[23] Information supplied by 'Abd al-Mawla Lanqi and Bashir al-Mughayribi.

Muhammad Bin 'Uthman, Minister of Finance, suggested the postponement of the meeting until Ku'bar had returned. He pointed out that the reshuffling of the Cabinet caused Ku'bar to delay his return from Tubruq. To this suggestion there was a violent reaction from the opposition, who pointed out that Ku'bar had not cared to appear on time and tried to escape the censure of Parliament. Mughayribi hinted that Ku'bar went so far as to "conspire" against the opposition by taking one of its leaders, 'Abd al-Mawla Lanqi, into the Cabinet. Misrati endorsed Mughayribi's position and indulged in a scathing personal attack against Ku'bar which prompted the Speaker to call his attention to irrelevant statements made in his speech.[24]

The Minister of Finance asked again that the House postpone the meeting to October 15 and, if this date were not agreeable, to October 10. The opposition insisted that the meeting should not be postponed beyond October 7 and a vote to that effect was carried by the majority of the House.

When Parliament met on October 7, the Ku'bar Cabinet had not yet returned from Tubruq and the Minister of Justice, 'Abd al-Hamid al-Dibani, made a statement giving the reason for Ku'bar's inability to return, which was mainly because the new Ministers had to take the constitutional oath before the King. Dibani then asked Parliament to postpone the meeting till October 10.

Ku'bar's absence from the parliamentary meeting on October 7 aroused the suspicion of the opposition and one of them, Mahmud Subhi, doubted Ku'bar's willingness to appear before Parliament. He therefore suggested a censure of the government in absentia. Misrati, though he pointed out that Ku'bar deliberately tried to disregard the date set by Parliament, moved to postpone the meeting to October 10. He asked the Minister of Finance, Muhammad Bin 'Uthman, whether the Cabinet would really appear before Parliament if the meeting were postponed till October 10.

Bin 'Uthman replied that when he previously asked Parliament to postpone its meeting till October 10, he wanted to give

---

[24] *Proceedings of the House of Representatives*, Extraordinary Session, 1960, p. 7 (mimeographed).

the government sufficient time to return and prevent Parliament from fixing a date which might be impossible to meet. Now, he said, he would like to thank Parliament for the motion to postpone the meeting till October 10, and wanted to assure the members that "if the government does not appear before Parliament on Monday [October 10] they [the opposition] should regard [its failure to do so] as an insult to me personally and I will then desert the government and join you." [25] Having been given this assurance, Parliament readily agreed to postponement.

On October 10, the full Cabinet appeared before Parliament. An avalanche of cables was received, some supporting the opposition, but most of them requesting Parliament not to take any action that might hinder the completion of the Fazzan Road.

The first member who asked to speak was 'Abd al-Salam al-Tuhami. He made a brief speech in which he criticized the action of the government concerning the Fazzan Road and its subsequent contradictory statements in Parliament concerning its dealings with the firm that had been given the contract. He also pointed out that the Minister of Communications had made a statement in Parliament assuring the members that the cost of the Fazzan Road was not to exceed the two million pounds already fixed by experts; during the Parliamentary recess, however, the government modified the contract and more than doubled the original estimated cost without the approval of Parliament. This action, concluded Tuhami, was a violation of Article 169 of the Constitution.[26]

The Minister of Defense, Ahmad al-Hasa'iri, read a short but careful statement explaining the position of the government. The statement may be summed up as follows: The original cost fixed by the experts was greatly underestimated and, according to the contract, the estimate was made on the basis of dividing the road into three units, the first of which alone proved to cost the original estimated total amount. This was entirely unexpected by the Government, and the whole question was referred

[25] *Proceedings of the House of Representatives*, Extraordinary Session, 1960, Second Meeting, p. 4 (mimeographed).

[26] Article 169 states: " No public loan or undertaking that is likely to be a charge on the Treasury for one or more of the following years may be contracted without the consent of Parliament."

to a committee of experts headed by the Minister of Communications. The Committee found that the request of Sayyid 'Abd-Allah 'Abid was legitimate, and it sought to revise the contract in such a way as to prevent another request by Sayyid 'Abd-Allah for further money for the other units. The cost of the remaining two-thirds of the road was fixed at four million Libyan pounds and the project was transferred from the jurisidiction of the Ministry of Communications to that of the Development Council. This revision of the contract was to take effect on March 31, 1961. This revision was completed after the Minister of Communications had made his statement in Parliament that the cost of the road was not to exceed the two million Libyan pounds.[27]

The statement indicated that there was a mistake in the expert's estimate of the cost of the road of which the government was unaware when it made its statements in Parliament. More significantly, it was pointed out that the government's effort to revise the contract in such a way as to put an end to a possible repetition of Sayyid 'Abd-Allah's request for funds by fixing the cost of the remaining units at four million Libyan pounds. For, as the action of Parliament in rejecting this arrangement demonstrated, the subsequent decision of the Supreme Court in favor of Sayyid 'Abd-Allah might still give him the opportunity to present future requests to the government on the basis of the original contract. The fundamental weaknesss of the government, however, lies in its agreeing to pay an advance on this new estimate before securing parliamentary approval of the new undertaking.

Ignoring the government's candid admission of error in the estimate of the cost, the opposition reverted again to the theme as to why the estimate was raised from two to four million pounds when it had asserted earlier that the estimate of two million was to cover the whole cost of the road. Almost all opposition members denounced the government's action in assigning the Fazzan Road project to Sayyid 'Abd-Allah 'Abid as an act of favoritism. Mahmud Subhi, 'Ali al-Misrati, and Bashir al-Mughayribi engaged in a scathing attack on the Ku'bar government

[27] For text of the statement, see *Proceedings of the House of Representatives,* Extraordinary Session, 1960, pp. 4–5 (mimeographed) .

and attributed all the corruption and exploitation in the country to the manner in which its personnel had been handling public affairs. The Fazzan Road was obviously not the only reason for the opposition's attack on the government; for, as Mahmud Subhi pointed out,[28] the road was but one of several cases which prompted the public to believe that the government's financial policy had resulted in the squandering of public funds. One of the members, Miftah al-Shari'a, went so far as to say that it had become a tradition that the government always took advantage of parliamentary recess to issue decrees for temporary budgets to be spent without prior parliamentary approval and then to submit them to Parliament when it reconvened. Miftah's criticism prompted the Speaker to remark that his criticism was irrelevant to the subject under discussion.[29]

This was followed by an interrogation between Misrati and the Minister of Communications concerning other projects; some of them had actually been acted upon by previous Cabinets. These were nonetheless answered, although Misrati declared himself dissatisfied with the Minister's answers.

'Abd al-Mawla Lanqi, one of the leaders of the opposition, made a long statement in which he tried to assert parliamentary right of supervision and control but, he said, Ku'bar had ignored Parliament and disregarded the public interest. He went on to reiterate in detail the various violations committed when the Fazzan Road contract was awarded.[30]

Finally, one of the opposition, Yunus 'Abd al-Nabi Bilkhayr, having found that all fellow opposition leaders had completed their speeches, made the following statement:

> I move that Parliament pass a resolution concerning the Fazzan Road demanding that the government should carry out the following five points:
>
> 1. To cancel the government's undertaking relative to the payment of four million pounds to SASCO [Sayyid 'Abd-Allah 'Abid's Company] and to stop any financial arrangements made for the payment of funds.
>
> 2. To prevent SASCO from completing the work and cancel its contract.

---

[28] *Ibid.*, p. 6.   [29] *Ibid.*, p. 23.   [30] *Ibid.*, pp. 28–31.

3. To make every possible effort to prepare a sound plan for the completion of the road and to assign it to another company, after announcing it publicly to all business firms, provided that it shall never be given again to SASCO.

4. To appoint a committee of experts, subject to the approval of Parliament, to investigate the work done so far and the money spent on the Fazzan Road and the firm's compliance with the terms of the contract. The Committee shall submit its report to Parliament at the earliest possible time.

5. To appoint a financial committee composed of one member of the Financial Committee of the House of Representatives, one member of the Communications Committee of the House of Representatives, one member of the Financial Committee of the Senate, one member of the Communications Committee of the Senate, the Supervisor-General of the federal government, a representative of the Ministry of Finance, and a representative of the Ministry of Communications for the purpose of investigating the payments made by the government to SASCO and the latter's compliance [with the regulations], whether in receiving the money or in the payment of its customs duties or any other matter connected with the [Fazzan Road] contract. The Committee shall report to Parliament at the earliest possible time.[31]

The motion was presented to the House in a written statement signed by thirty-one members. Another declared himself orally in favor of the motion, raising the number of supporters to thirty-two. Another opposition member, Misrati, read a written statement, signed by thirty-two members, embodying a motion to withdraw confidence in the government.[32]

The Speaker pointed out that the motion concerning the withdrawal of confidence in the government would have to be treated in accordance with Article 87 of the Constitution,[33] but that the

[31] Ibid., p. 33.
[32] Ibid., p. 34.
[33] Article 87: "If the House of Representatives by a majority of all its members passes a vote of no confidence in the Council of Ministers, the Council of Ministers must resign. If the decision concerns one of the Ministers, he must resign. The House of Representatives shall not consider the request for a vote of confidence, whether such request be direct or implied, unless it has been presented by fifteen or more of the deputies. Such request may not be discussed except after eight days from the date of its presentation and shall not be voted upon except after two days from the completion of the discussion thereon."

other motion might be discussed and voted upon immediately. The Prime Minister, who had hardly uttered a word, at last asked to speak. He showed his surprise at the speed in which the opposition presented its motion, because he expected that the discussion of such an important subject would last two or three days, at the end of which the government would consider its reply to its critics. He had noted, he said, that most of the speeches contained repetition of the same points of criticism, mostly directed against him personally. He said that he was not opposed to criticism, since he was a responsible person, but regretted that the government was not given an opportunity to reply.[34]

The Speaker remarked that no Cabinet member had expressed a desire to speak, for if anyone had asked he would have been given the opportunity to do so. "Now," he added, "that the Government has asked to defend itself it can do so even if the meeting lasts till morning." The Prime Minister replied that the government would have been willing to reply before the motions were presented to the House, but since these motions had already been made he would like to see the outcome of the voting.

Before the Speaker moved to put the first motion—presented by Bilkhayr—to the vote, he asked the Prime Minister whether he wanted to give his opinion about it. Ku'bar said that if the House adopted the motion he would be willing to carry it out.

At this point Miftah al-Shari'a, one of the opposition, said that if the government were willing to carry out the opposition's proposals concerning the Fazzan Road, there would be no longer any need for the motion to withdraw confidence in the government. This statement caused a sensation in the House and it might have been exploited by Ku'bar and his supporters had they known how to defend themselves. A verbal duel ensued between Miftah and a few members of the opposition in which he was told that he could speak only for himself. The Speaker reminded the House that the motion concerning the withdrawal of confidence would have to be postponed in accordance with Article 87 of the Constitution.

[34] *Ibid.*, p. 35.

Since neither Ku'bar nor any of his Cabinet colleagues expressed a desire to speak, the Bilkhayr motion was carried by 53
votes for to one against. Because the motion concerning lack
of confidence required a period of eight days before it could be
discussed, the Speaker declared that the next meeting of Parliament would be on October 19, 1960.[35]
No sooner had Ku'bar left Parliament than he addressed a
letter to the King in which he depicted the opposition to his
government as having been organized by a few ring leaders,
instigated by such irresponsible persons as Mughayribi, Lanqi,
Misrati, and Mahmud Subhi, supported by Mustafa Bin 'Amir,
Misbah Ruqruq, 'Abd al-Hamid Bin Halim, and others of the
former 'Umar al-Mukhtar Club. When Parliament met on
October 10 these elements, Ku'bar explained, indulged in unwar-
ranted criticism of the Fazzan Road and the government, making
such threatening remarks as to imply that they feared no one
in the country and presented a motion, signed by thirty-two,
for withdrawal of confidence in the government. For this reason
Ku'bar in his letter requested the King to issue a decree dissolving
Parliament and ordering new elections in order to enable him
to appeal to the electorate for a decision on the matter.[36]
Ku'bar's appeal to the King to dissolve Parliament before he
exhausted the possibilities of defeating his parliamentary opponents prematurely brought the King to act as the arbiter in an
issue that had arisen between Ku'bar and the opposition. Neither
Ku'bar nor any member of his Cabinet had actually made a
serious effort to answer his critics. It is true that some of the
criticism was justified, but not all the points were unanswerable.
As a former Speaker of the House, Ku'bar should have known
how to handle the opposition and he might have been able to
refute it if he made a real effort to do so. Nor had some of his
colleagues, such as Qalhud, who had distinguished himself as an
able speaker, uttered a word in defense of the government.

[35] The Senate held one meeting on October 3, on the same day when the
Lower House held its first extraordinary meeting, and appointed a committee
of investigation under the chairmanship of Senator 'Umar Abu Ghandura,
but saw no need to hold another meeting, since the right of withdrawing
confidence from the government belonged to the Lower House only.
[36] A copy of the letter supplied by Ku'bar.

Instead Ku'bar made up his mind to dissolve Parliament and sought to silence the opposition by an appeal to the electorate. However, by requesting the King to dissolve Parliament, he brought matters to a head. The King, it is true, under Article 65 of the Constitution, can dissolve Parliament for any reason; [37] but he ordinarily does so only if a conflict takes place between Parliament and the government on a specific issue. Since Ku'bar had already agreed to carry out the decision of Parliament concerning the Fazzan Road, the specific issue that had arisen between Ku'bar and Parliament was changed from that of the Fazzan Road to the withdrawal of confidence from his government. This question naturally would involve the King personally vis-à-vis the opposition if he ordered dissolution, and perhaps later the public also when the elections were carried out. In either case the King would be in an embarrassing situation. Due to circumstances, the King was reluctant to order dissolution and since Ku'bar insisted on either his own resignation or dissolution in a letter sent to the King on October 12, 1961, the King decided to accept the resignation of Ku'bar.[38] The King might have also felt that the time had come for the Ku'bar Cabinet to resign in favor of another that could inspire confidence following the controversy that had been stirred up over the question of corruption and exploitation. Ku'bar had, after all, served a longer term in office than any other Premier before him. The King, in a letter dated October 16, sincerely thanked him for the services he had rendered to the country.[39]

Formation of the Bin 'Uthman Government

Ku'bar's letter of resignation was carried to Tubruq by Muhammad Bin 'Uthman, who shrank at first from fulfilling the task, but agreed only as a final duty to his chief, having failed to

[37] See also Article 106 of the Constitution.
[38] In an interview with the author, King Idris pointed out that Ku'bar's reasons for dissolving Parliament were not quite convincing, for he was not sure that the elections, unless controlled by the government, would return a House that would support Ku'bar.
[39] For text of the letter, see *Tarablus al-Gharb*, Tripoli, October 17, 1960.

persuade the opposition to effect a reconciliation with the government. Bin 'Uthman arrived at Tubruq on Wednesday (October 12) and delivered the letter to the King's secretary. The King sent word to Bin 'Uthman asking him to wait until Saturday (October 15) for a reply.

On Saturday morning Bin 'Uthman had an audience with the King. He gave an account of the crisis at the King's request and explained the issue that had arisen between the government and Parliament. He pointed out that the immediate cause of the conflict was the government's statement in Parliament concerning the Fazzan Road, which gave Parliament a version that differed from what actually had taken place. Had there been no difference, Bin 'Uthman said, between the government's statement and the news that had reached the opposition as to what actually had happened, probably no crisis would have developed. The King asked Bin 'Uthman to wait until he could give him a decision in the afternoon.

At 5:00 p. m., Bin 'Uthman was told by 'Ali al-Sahili, the Chief of the Royal Diwan, that the King had accepted Ku'bar's resignation and that he would like to invite Bin 'Uthman to dinner in the evening. An hour later Bin 'Uthman went to the Royal Diwan and Sahili told him that the King had decided to invite him to form a new government. Bin 'Uthman told Sahili that he had not come to replace Ku'bar, but to help him. Sahili, however, intimated that the King's mind had already been made up and that Bin 'Uthman should begin to think about whom he should nominate for the new Cabinet.

At dinner the King impressed upon Bin 'Uthman the need to improve governmental administration and restore popular confidence in it. He went on to explain that the country was disturbed as a result of the conflict between Parliament and the government and that he had chosen him (Bin 'Uthman) because he was confident that the new Premier would make an effort to advance the welfare of the people. In an interview with the author, the King stated that the time had come to ask a Fazzanese to form a government so that the people of Fazzan would feel that they could aspire to this high position. Moreover, Bin 'Uthman's previous support for the Sanusi Amirate and his personal loyalty to the King should be mentioned; for, it will be recalled, he was one of those Fazzanese nationalists who advocated the Sanusi Amirate over Fazzan, and who supported the federal system in the National Assembly. After dinner Bin 'Uthman immediately informed Ku'bar by telephone as to what had transpired between him and the King. It did not take long to form the new Cabinet, for the names suggested by Bin 'Uthman, derived in the main from his predecessor's Cabinet, were at once approved by the King. The whole Cabinet was ready at Tubruq to take the oath before the King on Sunday, October 16.

Bin 'Uthman's government was composed of fourteen Ministers: seven Tripolitanians, five Cyrenaicans, and two Fazzanese.[40] Seven months later Bin 'Uthman reshuffled his Cabinet and enlarged its composition so as to include two new ministries— Petroleum Affairs and Industry. Dropping five of the ministers, he introduced new elements, including 'Abd al-Mawla Lanqi, one of the leaders of the opposition who caused the fall of the Ku'bar Cabinet. This change, which strengthened Bin 'Uthman's Cabinet, took place on May 3, 1961.[41]

Bin 'Uthman's Policy

As a self-made man who had distinguished himself in Fazzan's local politics, Bin 'Uthman entered the national scene seeking the support of the entire Libyan public. He had gained exper-

[40] The composition of the Cabinet was as follows: Bin 'Uthman for the Premiership; 'Abd al-Rahman al-Qalhud for Justice; Salim al-Qadi for Finance; 'Abd al-Qadir al-'Allam for Foreign Affairs; Muhammad Abu Dajaja for Agriculture; Ahmad al-Hasa'iri for Defense; Mahmud al-Bishti for Education; Ahmad 'Awn Sawf for Communications; Abd al-Qadir al-Badriya for National Economy; Salim Sadiq for Health; Ta'i' al-Biju for Labor and Social Affairs; Hasan Zafir Burkan for Propaganda and Publication; and Wahbi al-Buri and Fu'ad al-Ku'bazi, Ministers without portfolios.

[41] The Cabinet was composed as follows: Bin 'Uthman for the Premiership; Ahmad 'Awn Sawf for Communications; Wahbi al-Buri for Justice; Ahmad al-Hasa'iri for Finance; Mahmud al-Bishti for Education; Salim al-Sadiq for National Economy; 'Abd al-Qadir al-Badriya for Health; Hasan Zafir Burkan for Information and Guidance; Sulayman al-Jirbi for Foreign Affairs; Hamid al-'Ubaydi for Agriculture; 'Abd al-Mawla Lanqi for Labor and Social Affairs; Yunus 'Abd al-Nabi for Defense; Abu al-Qasim al-Alaqi for Industry; and Muhamad Buhayh, Minister without portfolio.

ience in working with the rank and file in Fazzan and learned
how to appeal to them. He also had learned to build up his
party from among personal supporters in order to strengthen his
own position. After forming a government, he realized that there
were groups, made up of former Ministers and Prime Ministers,
who would oppose him and were determined to achieve power
themselves. He, accordingly, made a few changes in high government posts, placing some of his confidants in key positions, and
made an effort to inspire efficiency in the administration. The
Ministry of Guidance and Information, which controls the press
and radio, proved to be an effective instrument in the hands of
Bin 'Uthman for publicizing government news and activities.
Propaganda literature as well as books and magazines were distributed among the politically conscious public and placed in
public libraries sponsored by the government; they were designed
to demonstrate the government's keen interest in educating the
public and enlightening them concerning public affairs.

Nor was this all. Bin 'Uthman began to pay visits to the various
parts of the country, mixing with the people and giving public
addresses. He appealed directly to the people and tried to
explain the policy of his government. In one of his major
addresses, delivered on the occasion of the opening of an agricultural bank in Misrata (June 1961), he denounced his political
opponents as a small set of aristocratic politicians who avoided
contact with the public. He hinted that he himself had risen
from the common people and that his government, under the
King's guidance and support, sought to pay attention to the
people's welfare and aspirations.[42]

Bin 'Uthman tried his utmost to satisfy both Parliament and
the provincial administration in his dealings with them. He tried
to carry out the Parliament's decision to cancel the Fazzan Road
contract, but Sayyid 'Abd-Allah 'Abid took his case to the Supreme
Court. Tht Supreme Court made a decision in favor of Sayyid
'Abd-Allah, which forced the Bin 'Uthman government to pay
the amount due him, on the ground that the original contract
was valid, while the arrangement made to pay him four million
pounds for the remaining part of the road was not made on the

---

[42] For text of the speech see al-Ra'id, Tripoli, June 17, 1961.

basis of funds that had been approved by Parliament. This decision caused Parliament to approve payment for the road in its budget for 1961.

Bin 'Uthman took the drastic step of appointing Fadil Bin Zikri, who had been appointed the first Wali of Tripolitania,[43] to serve as the seventh Wali. Bin Zikri, well-known for his strong position as a Tripolitanian politician, recommended to the King the appointment of 'Ali al-Dib, whose case had caused the fall of Saqizli,[44] and who had been a trenchant critic of former administrations. Thus Bin 'Uthman's relations with Tripolitania were made satisfactory to the Tripolitanians by investing Provincial authority in the hands of these influential politicians. He had also satisfied the Tripolitanians by making a decision in favor of placing the municipal electric project undertaken by the federal government under Tripolitanian authority. Most satisfactory, perhaps, was the settlement of a frontier dispute between Tripolitania and Fazzan in which Bin 'Uthman, as a Fazzanese, supported Tripolitanian claims against Fazzan—a dispute which his predecessors had been unable to settle.[45] Owing to his Fazzanese origin and his being on good terms with the house of Sayf al-Nasr, who supplied leadership for that province, he had the support of Fazzanese. His relations with Cyrenaicans have proved to be on the whole satisfactory, since he has obtained the support of former opposition elements, although a few extremists denounced the government with criticism as sharp as that directed against its predecessors. Leaflets, originating from a clandestine Ba'thist society under the influence of Arab national socialist ideas, were circulated; but the government arrested ring leaders and brought them to trial. Libyan young men, sensitive to neighboring Arab nationalist influences, will perhaps always try to press for a more rapid and spectacular progress for their country than is being achieved under the

[43] See p. 214, above.

[44] See pp. 240 ff., above.

[45] During the author's visit to Libya in the summer of 1961, he witnessed the conference of the three Walis held in al-Bayda in late July during which the Premier used his good offices to settle the frontier dispute between Tripolitania and Fazzan. The Conference was regarded as a great success for Bin 'Uthman's government.

present administration. The problem, as the discussion in the following chapter will indicate, is more complex than these young men realize.

Owing to a widespread belief among Libyans that foreign business firms have come to their country to exploit her resources solely to their advantage, Bin 'Uthman tried to impress upon the people that his government's policy was to protect the country's rights and that under no circumstances were foreigners to acquire rights beyond their specified ones in contractual arrangements. The decree revising the Petroleum Law of 1955, issued on June 3, 1961, was partly intended to clarify certain ambiguities in the original law, but mainly, perhaps, to impress upon the people that their rights would be adequately protected. As Bin 'Uthman told the author (August 27, 1961), his policy was to specify clearly the rights acquired by foreign firms in Libya without compromising Libyan rights. His principal concern, it seems, was to bridge the gulf created between government and people, a problem to which Libyan leaders should pay proper attention, for failure to solve it might render public order and stability exceedingly difficult to maintain.

chapter **XI**

Prospects of Reform

D URING THE DECADE that followed the proclamation of
independence, the need for sweeping reforms and constructive economic development was often reiterated in Parliament
and in the press, and all were agreed that constructive reforms,
both in the structure of government and in the ways and means
of carrying out plans for development, were urgently needed
if Libya were to take her proper place in the community of
nations. But no agreement seems to have been reached as to
what particular branch or branches of government should be
changed or overhauled. As a result criticism was sharply levelled
against particular politicians or public leaders, who were singled
out as scapegoats for general dissatisfaction with existing conditions, and against the federal regime itself. It is intended in
this chapter to assess some of the factors operating to promote
internal unity and cohesion as well as the efforts made for the
development of the country.

The King, the Federal System, and National Unity

The role which King Idris played in the establishment of the
Libyan state is of prime importance, for he had taken not only
the bold step in the original movement for the recovery of
Cyrenaica from Italy during World War II, but also used his
personal influence and statesmanship to persuade influential

Tripolitanian leaders to rally in favor of federalism, without which the unity of Libya would probably never have been achieved. As the grandson and successor of Muhammad Bin 'Ali al-Sanusi, the founder of the Sanusi order, his influence over Sanusi followers was unquestionable; but he was also able to win the confidence of Cyrenaican tribal chiefs and gathered around him a number of able men who were ready to support him with devotion. Some of these men had followed him to exile, and others who remained to oppose Italian rule acted under his direction. When after the war he returned to Cyrenaica, there was no question as to who would be the future head of Cyrenaica.

Nor were the Tripolitanian leaders unaware of the unifying influence of King Idris, for they realized that he was the only person who could command respect in the country; but they disagreed on the form of government they wanted to establish and the constitutional limitations on his powers. It was also realized that he was not very anxious to rule over Tripolitania and that he would have been satisfied with the Amirate of Cyrenaica, but accepted the throne of Libya as a patriotic duty in order to supply leadership for a divided country.

King Idris' greatest asset is perhaps his ability to hold a balance among disruptive centrifugal forces and competing personalities. In a country torn by tribal feuds and rival houses vying for leadership, the need for a man whose prestige and integrity are universally acknowledged is essential for the maintenance of internal order and stability. He placed himself above factional rivalries and allowed competing leaders to air their differences and grievances in his presence, but he refused to take sides. Thus he became the ultimate arbiter among rival personalities and preferred to delay decisions, allowing emotions and personal feuds to cool off. His withdrawal to Tubruq, prompted at the outset by health reasons, proved to be of great political significance, for it removed him from the center of rivalries and intrigues which might have inevitably involved him if he had resided in one of the two capitals. When important disputes were brought to his attention, emotions often had subsided and his wise judgment was gratefully accepted. Due to poor health, the King is not always available to visitors, and his detached living in isolated Tubruq does not encourage many to make the trip from Tripoli—or even from Banghazi. Thus his name has already become a legend, which serves for the maintenance of the country's unity and stability.

Occupying such a unique position in public life, King Idris inevitably has emerged as the most powerful and unrivalled statesman in his country. It is true that as a constitutional monarch his powers are limited and he is not responsible under the terms of the constitution; but in identifying himself with Libya's needs and aspirations, he has played the role of the benevolent monarch and the powerful leader who could call and dismiss Cabinets at his own pleasure. He has been reproached for concentrating as much power as possible in his own hands; but this concentration of power, in a country where local divisions and factional rivalries are still very strong, is probably necessary in order to ensure the unity and the progress of the country.

King Idris, however, is not working for the glory of his house nor perhaps for the consolidation of a monarchical system of government; for, as his desire to change the monarchy to a republic indicated in 1956, he was quite willing to adopt a republican system of government that would ensure the unity and stability of Libya. He has struggled so long to achieve the liberation of his country that his main concern now may be said to be chiefly to ensure the preservation of the unity and independence of the country. Faced with grave domestic problems threatening the unity of the country, he often has admonished his countrymen that the preservation of the unity and independence of the country is more difficult than achieving them.

Next to the King, the federal system has provided the constitutional framework under which the three provinces have agreed to unite and and co-ordinate their activities. It was a compromise between the advocates of unitarianism in Tripolitania and the advocates of separatism in Cyrenaica and Fazzan. They all admitted that the federal system, which virtually led to the establishment of four governments, four parliaments, and four administrative bodies, is expensive for a country small in population and resources; but they hoped that the time would come when the system might be transformed into a unitary system. However, the constitution, which was drawn up somewhat in a hurry, left much to be desired in the way of providing adequate means of co-ordination and some of its articles are vague and ambiguous. As a result, the operation of the constitution gave rise to many problems concerning the relations between federal and provincial authorities.

No sooner had Libya proclaimed her independence than the advocates of the unitary system began to criticize the federal system and demand the immediate dissolution of the federal in favor of the unitary system. They argued that since Libyan unity and independence had been achieved, there was no justification for its continuation. The advocates of federalism admit that the present constitutional structure is more elaborate and more costly than the unitary system, but they point out that its critics overlook the continuing value of the system, without which Libyan unity might be in danger of falling apart. If the federal system were destroyed before local particularism was superseded by national feeling, the disappearance of the federal structure might lead to separatism. Gradual transfer of powers from provincial to federal authorities should be encouraged, but the process, in order to be salutary, should be evolutionary and coupled with a conscious effort to create conditions favorable for unity. What the advocates of the unitary school demand with justice is the simplification of the elaborate provincial system reducing the provincial legislative assemblies to local elective councils, and combining the functions of the wali and the chief of the Executive Council in those of one responsible head. The wali should eventually be made responsible to the federal government. The King, who is aware of the dangers of haste, has been, it will be recalled, exceedingly reluctant to allow his Prime Ministers to move too fast to meet the desires of the unitary school. The federal system might even become more necessary if King Idris passes away, since the King has been himself a uniting factor and his demise might encourage local particularism to assert itself if the advocates of the unity school move hastily. If the present equilibrium between national and local forces can be maintained within a working constitutional structure long enough to develop sufficient cohesion to hold the three provinces together, Libya's problem is likely to be solved. If such an equilibrium should prove impossible to maintain, especially after the King's death, internal stability and the progress of the country might be difficult to achieve.

Foreign Aid and the Development Council

Long preoccupied with the problem of opposing Italian domination of their country, the Libyans had little time to spare for social and economic development. Nor did the Italian administration enjoy a period of peace after the pacification of the country to enable it to carry out its plans for the demographic and economic reconstruction of the country. Before some of the Italian-developed lands began to produce, the war wrought havoc with many of them, and some of the service industries as well as foreign trade came to a standstill. As a result, the British and French administering authorities bore to a large extent the burden of extending economic assistance until Libya achieved independence.

Even after independence it was realized that Libya would have to be economically dependent for a long while on foreign aid, both for balancing the budget and for economic reconstruction. In February, 1952, the General Assembly of the United Nations requested the Economic and Social Council to study ways and means by which the United Nations could furnish assistance to Libya for the purpose of " financing its fundamental and urgent programs of economic and social development." But in fact it was Great Britain and the United States, two interested powers with whom Libya entered into political and military ventures, who were to supply the greater portion of foreign aid. To a lesser extent other powers, such as France, Italy, Egypt, Pakistan, and Turkey, extended a variety of financial and technical assistance.

The United Nations and its specialized agencies have provided several programs of technical assistance, some based on reports framed by experts,[1] and others in the form of technical advice.

[1] Such as the report on Libyan economy by Lindbergh, see John Lindbergh,

The United Nations technical assstance, as described in a memorandum on the subject, may be summed up in the following quotation:

> The technical assistance provided by the United Nations to Libya covers a very wide field and experts from the several UN agencies are giving invaluable aid in almost every aspect of the country's development. For the most part these experts serve in an advisory capacity, but in several cases they have also been required to assume executive responsibilities within the Libyan government where this is made necessary by the nonavailability of appropriately qualified Libyan personnel. A number of UN experts have also been assigned to Libya to carry out specialist investigations in some of the fields where basic information is most urgently required. Financial assistance for the country's development needs is not, of course, provided by the United Nations, although in a few instances the UN agencies do provide limited amounts of equipment and supplies; many UN technical assistance projects in Libya are therefore supported by funds provided by the government and received under bilateral agreements for economic aid.[2]

The economic assistance extended by Great Britain and the United States was, it will be recalled, given partly as a *quid pro quo* for rights granted by Libya to these powers for military purposes and partly for economic development.[3] For the purpose of handling the funds given by foreign powers, the Libyan government at first created two special agencies. The first was the Libyan Public Development and Stabilization Agency, established in 1952 to supervise programs financed by funds received from Great Britain. The second was the Libyan-American Reconstruction Commission, established in 1955 to assist in the implementation of programs financed under American aid.

A General Economic Appraisal of Libya (New York, 1952) ; the UN Economic Mission led by Higgins, see Benjamin Higgins, *The Economic and Social Development of Libya* (New York, 1953) ; the report on the balance of payments, see Stanislaw Kirkar, *Balance of Payment of Libya* (New York, 1953) , and the report on education, see UNESCO, *Report of the Mission to Libya* (Paris, 1952) .

[2] Cited in International Bank for Reconstruction and Development, *The Economic Development of Libya* (Baltimore, 1960) , pp. 53–54.

[3] See pp. 228, 255, above.

The Libyan Public Development and Stabilization Agency began to operate in April, 1952. The first Chairman of its board was Salim Shirmit, later replaced by 'Abd al-Raziq Shaqluf, the permanent Under-Secretary of Finance. The general manager was British and his deputy Libyan. The three provinces were represented on the board, as was a representative from the contributing countries. Britain was the principal contributor from the time of the agency's establishment to April, 1958, when she ceased to contribute directly to development funds and was replaced by the United States. Egypt and 'Iraq contributed nominal grants annually. A five-year program was established in 1954 and was completed in 1961, when the functions of this board were transferred to the Development Council.

The Libyan-American Reconstruction Commission was established in 1955 under the chairmanship of 'Ali al-Sahili, who was succeeded by 'Abd al-Raziq Shaqluf, permanent Under-Secretary of Finance. Its board was composed of representatives of the three provinces and of the contributing power (USA); thus Libya had the majority of votes. There was an American advisor to the board, Marcus Gordon, but the Commission's work, like that of its counterpart, the Development and Stabilization Agency, was transferred to the Development Council. The Commission operated mainly as a programming agency and worked in co-operation with American personnel connected with the American Embassy. The principal projects were in the fields of agriculture, natural resources, health, and education.

As an adjunct to the Libyan-American Commission a separate agency, called the Libyan-American Joint Services, was created in 1955 to assist in the implementation of programs financed by the United States. Moreover, the United States, like the United Nations, provided technical assistance to Libya, and the United States Operations Mission in Libya, whose personnel were either American officials or private American consultants.[4]

Foreign aid has undoubtedly been received by Libyans with gratitude, for it not only assisted their government in the

[4] Information supplied by 'Abd al-Raziq Shaqluf. See also International Bank for Reconstruction and Development, *The Economic Development of Libya*, pp. 46–53.

balancing of the budget, but also helped to launch several important projects. During the decade following independence, Libya
has made significant strides in social and economic development,
thanks to foreign aid. However, Libyans have not confined themselves to expressing thanks to the contributing powers, for they
often have voiced sharp criticism both as to the amount of funds
and the manner in which they have been spent. First, Libyans
have always demanded larger contributions from Britain and the
United States than these powers have been willing to give,
although both have generously aided Libya before and after
independence. Secondly, Libya has not obtained the utmost
benefits from foreign funds due partly to organizational defects
of the various agencies and commissions established, and partly
from the lack of co-ordination of the programs laid down. As
a result, several of the programs have either partially been completed or not carried out at all. There has also been criticism
levelled against foreign experts and personnel, either from choice
of wrong persons or because the experts did not stay long enough
to carry their contribution to fruition and ensure continuity in
the execution of their projects. Moreover, lack of co-ordination
resulted in duplication of effort. As the Economic Mission of
the International Bank noted:

> There has been much overlapping of technical investigations and
> research, a quite unnecessary profusion of experts' reports dealing
> with almost every conceivable aspect of social and economic develop-
> ment and conspicuous lack of central libraries or record offices where
> the results of the research work done in various fields before and
> since the war are available for reference. As a result, development
> has proceeded in a rather piecemeal and haphazard fashion.[5]

To co-ordinate the programs and work of the various agencies
it was deemed necessary to establish a Development Council in
1956 whose main function at first was co-ordination.[6] By 1960
it was realized that Libya needed not only the co-ordination
of her program under the Council, but supervision and the

---

[5] *Ibid.*, p. 57.
[6] See text of the Prime Minister's speech on the occasion of the opening of
the Council on June 7, 1956, in *Tarablus al-Gharb*, Tripoli, July 8, 1956.

financing of her projects by an agency with a special budget for economic development. For this purpose the Development Council was reorganized as a Development Board, after the 'Iraqi pattern, regulated by a law passed by Parliament in 1961. The Board is an independent agency governed by a Council composed of the permanent Under-Secretary of Finance, 'Abd al-Raziq Shaqluf,[7] as chairman, one member representing the federal government, appointed by the Council of Ministers, and three members representing the provinces, each appointed by the Executive Council of the province. The Council undertakes to establish both long and short-term projects of economic development and provides funds for their execution. The Council is solely responsible for its work and is kept free from political influences.

The chief source of revenue for the Council's budget is oil royalties. The government has already made a decision to allocate seventy per cent of the royalties accruing to Libya for economic development and has put this sum at the disposal of the Development Council. A five-year plan has been tentatively formulated for the period 1961-65, which includes, among other long-term projects, the improvement of the Banghazi harbor and the municipal electric power supply of Tripoli.[8] Once Libya has begun to receive large amounts of oil royalties, the Council should be in a position to play an increasingly important role in the economic reconstruction of the country.

The Petroleum Law

From the time of the achievement of independence, Libyan leaders realized that their country would remain dependent on foreign aid and subsidies unless serious efforts were made to exploit her subsoil resources. Some mineral deposits were already known, but no petroleum exploration had yet been conducted.

---

[7] On June 5, 1962, Shaqluf has been replaced by Khalifa Musa as an acting chairman.

[8] Funds for the establishment of an electric power center in Tripoli were secured from the American Development Loan Fund under an agreement signed on June 29, 1959, in the amount of $5,000,000.

The Libyan government could not afford to spend large sums of money to carry out geological exploration in such a vast area as the Libyan desert. It was deemed necessary, therefore, to throw open Libya's gates to foreign enterprise. Thus a provisional mining law was rushed through Parliament in 1953, authorizing the grant of exploration permits to foreign firms. The companies that obtained the permits did not actually acquire concessionary rights, but were allowed to carry out work that helped them determine the area of their interest when the time came to apply for rights under the contemplated petroleum law.

While the oil companies were busy conducting exploration, the Bin Halim government began to make preliminary preparation for the enactment of a permanent petroleum law. A draft law, prepared by a committee of experts, was circulated for comments to foreign companies engaged in exploration. The comments having been received, Bin Halim appointed Anis al-Qasim, a Palestinian lawyer in the employment of the Libyan government, as chairman of a committee composed of experts who met with representatives of oil companies to discuss the draft law. As a result of meetings held in the autumn of 1954 an elaborate draft petroleum law was ready for Parliament; it was passed in 1955 and came into force on July 18 of that year.

One of the chief purposes of the law was not only to attract foreign oil companies but also to offer them concessionary rights on a competitive basis. In this the drafting committee tried to take full advantage of the experience of older oil countries, both Middle Eastern and Western. Moreover, there was an internal constitutional problem, for under Article 38 of the Constitution the subsoil wealth of the country was to be dealt with under the so-called joint powers which enabled each province individually to carry out legislation passed by Parliament. Since a vital problem such as a unified negotiation of oil contracts with foreign companies required a unified policy, the question of the participation of both federal and provincial authorities in the discharge of the joint powers was resolved by the creation of a Petroleum Commission, composed of members representing federal and provincial authorities. It was entrusted not only with all oil affairs but also with the granting, in the name of the government, of concessionary rights. To meet the constitutional requirements concerning the supervision, execution, and management of foreign affairs, one member of the Cabinet, the Minister of National Economy, was empowered to supervise and approve (or reject) any permit or concessionary right given by the Petroleum Commission.

As stated in the Petroleum Law, oil is a national, not a private property, and " no person shall explore or prospect for, mine or produce petroleum in any part of Libya, unless authorized by a permit or concession issued under this law." As a result the owner of land does not own the oil that may be found under it nor is he entitled to participate, or even to have priority in acquiring petroleum rights. But he continues to be the owner of the surface and of such deposits other than minerals that may be found on the land and is entitled to receive compensation for any damages resulting from the exploitation of the subsoil. The owner is under legal obligation to allow access to his land for exploration and operation in return for reasonable compensation. The law divides operations into two stages: the preliminary stage of exploration, for which a renewable permit is granted for one year and a concession stage for which concessionary rights are granted for a maximum period of fifty years with a possible extension for ten years. The procedure for granting concessionary rights, the qualifications of applicants, and the detailed regulations governing relations between the companies and the Libyan government are set forth in the Petroleum Law and its amendments to which the reader may refer.[9]

Petroleum affairs are dealt with by the Petroleum Commission. It is an autonomous body having a separate budget annexed to the federal budget. The Commission is composed of a chairman appointed by the Cabinet and three members representing the provinces. No person who holds a responsible government position may be allowed to serve on this Commission. The Commission appoints a Director of Petroleum Affairs who carries out the duties specified under the Petroleum Law and is assisted by

[9] See the *Official Gazette*, Vol. V (1955), No. 4; and *Tarablus al-Gharb*, Tripoli, November 14, 1961.

a sufficient number of personnel appointed by the Commission. On May 21, 1955, the first membership of the Commission was set up, composed of Anis al-Qasim, Abu Bakr Ahmad, Muhammad Asifat, and al-Tahir al-Bishti.

Following a considerable discussion among responsible government personnel and in Parliament, Libya finally arrived at a formula satisfactory to both national and provincial authorities which fixed the ratios of the royalties to be received from oil production. It was agreed that seventy per cent of the royalties would be exclusively devoted to economic development and would be assigned to the autonomous Development Council with no direct interference by national or provincial authorities. The remaining portion would normally be added to the regular budgets of the federal and provincial Governments: fifteen per cent for the Federal and fifteen per cent for the budget of the province from which the oil was obtained.

More than a dozen American, British, French, German, and Italian companies have begun exploratory work and operation and the first (Esso) struck oil in commercial quantities in 1959. The same company has completed a 100-mile thirty-inch pipeline connecting the Zeltern oil fields with an oil terminal built at Marsa al-Burayqa. On October 25, 1961, the pipeline was completed and began to operate, after having been opened by King Idris in an official ceremony. The completion of other pipelines is underway and Libya is expected to be among the important oil producing countries in the near future.

It is too early to speculate as to the future impact of oil on this relatively vast country that possesses but meager resources. The oil companies have already spent millions of dollars for exploration and have attracted thousands of unskilled laborers from the countryside. With an expanding oil operation, perhaps the bulk of Libya's younger men will seek the more lucrative positions in the oil industry rather than employment in government. If the government tries to attract them by higher salaries, the normal budget will have to absorb a higher proportion of oil royalties at the expense of economic development.

Nor will oil have an impact only on the economy of the country. A larger national income will enable Libya to be less dependent on foreign aid and may afford her greater freedom in her relations with powers with which she has had treaty relationships. The freer the Libyan government becomes from foreign powers, the more dependent it will be on popular support. However, Libya needs a strong government to maintain public order and stability so as to make possible the continued operation of the oil industry, without which no progress can be achieved. There are, however, several other factors which influence the public and the government in their relations with foreign powers and business firms—the upsurge of nationalism and the influx of radical ideas.

The Impact of Ideologies

The rise of Libya to statehood in 1952 coincided with the rising tide of nationalism in the Middle East and agitation in neighboring North African countries for their liberation from French control. Thus Libyans were caught in an atmosphere of confusion and agitation, which was unfavorable to the West when their country had just achieved independence and their dream of freedom from foreign domination had become a reality. As a result, the politically conscious public was inevitably influenced by the grievances and aspirations of fellow compatriots, both in Northwest Africa and in the Eastern Arab world.

The extreme nationalists in Libya advocated Pan-Arab ideas and wished to join an Arab union. At the outset, those who advocated Pan-Arabism were limited to the articulate intelligentsia who had received their education in neighboring Arab countries; but when President Nasir adopted the policy of Arab unity, calling for the establishment of an empire extending from the Atlantic to the Persian Gulf, the imagination of many Libyans was fired and an increasing number of them aspired to join such a union. Like many young Arab nationalists in the Eastern Arab World, Libyan nationalists regarded the regime established under the federal union as an artificial structure imposed upon them by foreign powers; the only truly national regime would be that in which Libya would be part of a larger

Arab empire including North Africa and the Eastern Arab world. The ideology of this school of thought was derived from the Arab nationalism advocated by the new generations in Syria and Egypt, who demanded the full unity of the Arab World, reorganized on a socialist basis and playing the role of a non-aligned force—in fact, a policy of positive neutralism—in foreign affairs. The most outspoken advocates of this school are the Ba'thist (Resurrectionist) group who combine Pan-Arab ideas with socialist reforms and are opposed to any alignment with the West.

Until 1959, when President Nasir, who supplied leadership for the advocates of the new Pan-Arab ideas, repudiated the association of Communism with Arab nationalism, the Communists joined with the Arab nationalists in demanding the emancipation of Arab lands from Western influence. Before 1959, Libyan nationalists, in line with their compatriots in Eastern Arab lands, displayed a sympathetic attitude toward those who advocated co-operation with the Soviet bloc. When the Communists in Iraq, having made headway in domestic politics following the revolution of 1958, sought to establish a *bona fide* Communist regime, in distinction to one of nationalist character, the nationalists in other Arab countries reacted against the Communists and their sympathizers and the Communist movement suffered a setback from which it has never recovered. The advocates of nationalism in Libya, who have become receptive to leftist ideas only under the influence of nationalist-communist collaboration in Eastern Arab lands, began to argue that Communism was a danger to their national existence and inconsistent with Islamic traditions. Thus Communist ideas, which appeared at one time to constitute a danger in Libyan society, have been greatly discredited partly because of the prevailing religious sentiment among the majority of the people and partly because of the rapidly increasing wealth in the country since the discovery of oil and the percolation of this wealth down to the masses.

No less articulate in their views are religious groups, whether they represent the old-fashioned al-Azhar graduates and Sanusi followers or younger men who are influenced by the Muslim Brotherhood. The old-fashioned groups are motivated by traditional Islamic ideas rather than by secular nationalism and tend to agree with the nationalists only in their opposition to foreign influence and radical ideologies. The new generation, mainly under the influence of the Muslim Brotherhood, has accepted nationalism mixed with religion. They also advocate social and economic reforms, but are not prepared to accept Ba'thist socialist views. Because of the overlapping of religion with nationalism in the whole nationalist movement in North Africa, religious groups tend to exercise more influence in this region than in some other parts of the Arab World. In Libya, where the Sanusi order played an important role in the liberation movement, religion may continue as a significant element in nationalism for a very long time, especially in Cyrenaica. There is now a noticeable tendency to revive the role of the Sanusi order in religious preaching and in the education of the young tribesmen.

More realistic in their views than extremists of both the right and the left are the advocates of a North African Union, comprising Libya, Tunisia, Algeria, and Morocco. Libyans who advocate such a union hope that Libya may play the role of a pivot between the North African and the Eastern Arab unions. The immediate objective of this group would be the liberation of Algeria from French rule and the establishment of a federal union among the four North African countries. But no clear program of action has yet been framed by them, despite the wide prevalence of such ideas and their appeal among North African peoples. Some have accepted the broad ideas of President Bourguiba of Tunisia, often referred to as Bourguibism, which advocate a loose confederal system; [10] others, who agree with Bourguiba on a North African union, do not accept his close collaboration with the West; and still others aspire to a more perfect union among the North African countries and assert that these countries should play an independent role in international affairs. The conservative advocates of this school of thought may be found in both official and nonofficial circles of Libya, but no organized group

[10] Bin Halim, who negotiated with Bourguiba the Libyan-Tunisian treaty, made the following comment: " I was pressing for the Maghrib (North African) Union as the left wind of Pan-Arabism. Bourguiba never accepted the last part of my formula. He told me that he did not believe in Pan-Arabism."

advocating such a union exists as yet. There are, however, small organized groups that have been actively supporting the Algerian national liberation movement.

More moderate views of nationalism are held by an increasing number of Libyans and represent the more mature ideas of leaders who have held responsible positions in the government. This school of thought, which may be called the Libyan school, sees grave danger in exposing Libya to foreign ideological influences and tends to concentrate on that which serves Libya's own national interest. Its advocates are sensitive to foreign influence and, in spite of the independence enjoyed by their country, aspire to achieve complete freedom from dependence on any kind of foreign aid or influence. Libya's future will, perhaps, depend on the advocates of this school, since they are more concerned with the internal unity of the country and the creation of a Libyan nation that could play its proper role in regional and international politics than with its identification with competing ideologies. When Libya was completely dependent on foreign aid and the support of Western Powers, the Pan-Arab school could argue that unless Libya joined an Arab union she would remain indefinitely dependent on Western support. Now that oil is leading Libya to depend on her own resources, the the moderate school of thought is gaining ground and its assertion of Libyan independence appears to command respect in wider circles. "We appreciate the value of certain ideologies advocated by our neighbors," said one Pan-Arab leader to the author (1961), "but these ideologies should not be accepted by us without regard to our special circumstances." This mature reflection of a relatively young leader is in contrast to his earlier declarations in favor of the acceptance of ideological views. The more independent Libya becomes economically, the more self-concerned with her politically conscious public she tends to be in her political orientation. The spread of education, one of the main concerns of both national and provincial authorities, is likely to enforce the growing tendency toward cohesion and solidarity among the population of the three provinces and the eventual strengthening of a Libyan nation-state that existed only in the form of a constitutional structure when independence was proclaimed a decade ago.

Foreign Policy

The achievement of unity and independence fulfilled the fundamental aspiration of Libyan nationalists, especially after Libya's admission to the Arab League in 1953 and to the United Nations in 1956. But this achievement, thanks to favorable international circumstances, was marred by certain limitations dictated by Libya's dependence on foreign aid and treaty obligations. As a result, Libyan nationalists have regarded independence and unity as a step toward the realization of their ultimate objective—full independence and membership in a union with the Arab World.

After Libya's rise to statehood, the politically conscious public may be said to have been divided into two schools of thought on the country's foreign policy. These schools, however, should not be regarded as representing well-defined objectives in foreign policy, but rather as tendencies—in certain respects as aspirations —which often overlap and on certain matters are quite vague and nebulous, as reflected in the minds of the less articulate public.

The first, which may be called the idealistic school, includes the advocates of Pan-Arab and North African groups who insist on an aggressive foreign policy in order to help Libya's neighbors in their struggle for liberation or the achievement of Arab unity. They see no hope in the independent struggle of each Arab country against colonialism and urge the Libyan government to give active support to the Pan-Arab cause. On purely emotional grounds this school of thought has a wide appeal in the country, and at times when there is an outburst of nationalism or when one of the Arab countries is exposed to danger—as in the Suez crisis—the Libyan government finds itself in a difficult position with regard to its pressures.

The other school, which may be called the Libyan or realistic school, advocates an independent foreign policy for Libya and hesitates to follow the hazardous foreign policy advocated by the Pan-Arab and North African groups which might expose her to danger. This school, which includes the country's more mature statesmen, has been influential in formulating Libya's foreign policy and is guided in many respects by the King, who keeps a watchful eye on the conduct of his country's foreign relations.

King Idris, though he has directed Libya's foreign policy since independence, has witnessed her shifting fortunes since the Ottoman period. Except for a short period of rapprochement with Italy following World War I, he indirectly guided those who opposed Italian control of his country. With basic wisdom and a calculating sense of the play of political forces, he could, while in exile, wait patiently for the circumstances in which he could seek the support of Italy's enemies to liberate his country. His greatest venture, which to a large extent resulted in the expulsion of Italy from Libya, was his support of Britain against the Axis Powers in 1940, at a time when almost all other Arab leaders thought that she had lost the war. His subsequent alliance and co-operation with the British earned him their support for the establishment of Cyrenaican self-government and eventually Libyan unity and independence. He thought it more prudent to accept what Britain was prepared first to give, while he waited for further concessions under more favorable circumstances. Thus, when King Idris ascended the throne of Libya he already possessed rich experience gained during the decades in which he had handled Libya's domestic and foreign problems.

As an Arab who had spent a considerable period in exile watching the struggle of Arab countries for independence, King Idris naturally sympathized with all Arab countries and hoped that they might achieve their unity and independence. But as the architect of the Libyan state that achieved its independence by earning the good will of Western Powers, he hesitates to follow a foreign policy which would expose Libya to dangers. The King's foreign policy, accordingly, appears to have been based on four fundamental principles which in turn have become the foundation of Libya's foreign policy.

First, Libya has earned the good will of Western Powers which helped her to achieve independence and provided the substantial economic aid necessary for her economic reconstruction. The King and his leading Ministers are agreed that this continued good will is absolutely essential for the maintenance of Libya's independence and her social and economic development. With the discovery of oil and other mineral resources, this co-operation with the West will, perhaps, become even more essential in order to encourage foreign business firms to expoit Libya's hidden resources for the benefit of her people.

Secondly, the King advocates a " good neighbor " policy with all Arab countries; but since responsible Arab leaders have often followed conflicting policies, he has advised his Ministers to follow a neutral course with regard to inter-Arab differences.

Thirdly, the King has also advised his government, while taking no sides in Arab conflicts, to offer its services to help to repair Arab differences and reconcile their conflicting viewpoints. Libya's policy vis-à-vis inter-Arab relations has been well reflected in the wise conduct of her delegations at the Arab League and in her treaty relations with her neighbors.

Fourthly, as the head of a religious order, the King is opposed to radical ideologies inherently incompatible with Islam, and as the head of a state over which the Soviet Union has in the past desired tutelage and whose admission to the United Nations it had opposed, he is against both the Soviet creed and Soviet ambitions which might result in the destruction of his country's independence.

The King's ideas and aspirations, especially his " good neighbor policy," have been shared by all his Ministers, although ways and means of carrying them out have varied slightly from one Cabinet to another. The King's ideas have become the basis of what might be called Libya's traditional foreign policy, although these ideas were by no means shared by radical ideological groupings. But even among these groups, the King's views on foreign affairs are respected and often highly valued.

Conclusion

Viewing in retrospect the past development of Libya, the progress achieved in building a modern state is remarkable; for, following the departure of her Italian rulers, Libya did not possess even the basic elements necessary for the making of a state. Poor and internally divided, her Arab supporters at the

United Nations tried to arrange for her a short-term tutelage under the aegis of a friendly Great Power. But Libyan leaders, defying the realities of existing conditions, insisted on unity and complete independence. Thus Libyan leaders, almost by an act of will, realized their cherished national aspirations beyond the expectation of their well-wishers, thanks to the rivalry of the Great Powers and to favorable international circumstances.

The task ahead of Libyan leaders in developing a stable and progressive " nation-state," as the problems dealt with in this work have demonstrated, are even greater than the establishment of unity and independence; for unless the Libyan people develop cohesion and maintain internal stablity, Libyan unity and independence might be reduced to a mere legal fiction which can be easily destroyed by a change in the present balance of forces. The Libyan national (federal) government should, therefore, be considerably strengthened in order to be able to maintain the equilibrium necessary for the development of a modern Libyan " nation-state." To achieve this task, the Libyan government needs both sufficient resources and know-how.

The natural wealth at the disposal of the Libyan regime, if spent on cultural development and social and economic reconstruction, would make it possible for it to muster sufficient power to maintain public order and harmony to the satisfaction of the people. This power can also be used to silence opposition elements and groups. If, during the reconstruction period, the government can inspire confidence and maintain harmony among the provinces, Libya may well emerge as the model of a stable North African nation and might even eventually become the most powerful one. If, on the other hand, the wealth of the country is spent unwisely without regard to the real needs of the people, dissatisfaction is likely to increase and the resulting gap between the people and governing authorities would be difficult to bridge. Such a situation might generate continuous unrest and social upheavals, thus exposing the very existence of the state to danger.

Appendix I

The Sanusi Family

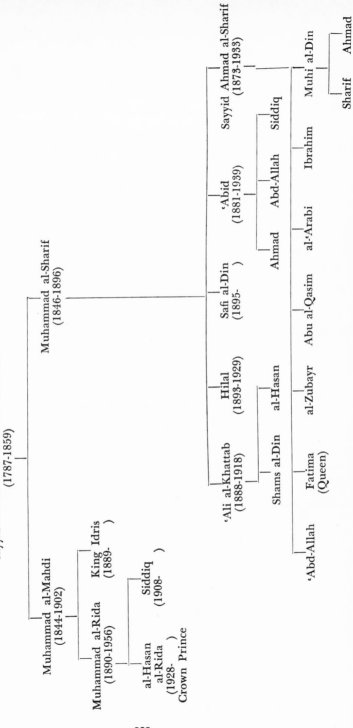

Appendix II
Libyan Cabinets

Premiers	Period
1. Mahmud al-Muntasir	December 24, 1951-February 18, 1954 (Reshuffled on September 18, 1953)
2. Muhammad al-Saqizli	February 18, 1954-April 11, 1954
3. Mustafa Bin Halim	April 12, 1954-May 23, 1957 (Reshuffled on December 19, 1954; April 26, 1955; March 26, 1956; October 30, 1956; and March 14, 1957).
4. ʿAbd al-Majid Kuʿbar	May 26, 1957-October 16, 1960 (Reshuffled on April 24, 1958; October 11, 1958; November 15, 1958; February 6, 1960; and September 29, 1960).
5. Muhammad Bin ʿUthman	October 16, 1960- (Reshuffled on May 3, 1961; January 27, 1962; October 11, 1962).

Appendix III

In the name of God the benificent, the merciful.

We, the representatives of the people of Libya from Cyrenaica, Tripolitania and the Fezzan, meeting by the will of God in the cities of Tripoli and Benghazi in a National Constituent Assembly.

Having agreed and determined to form a union between us under the Crown of King Mohammed Idriss el Mahdi el Senussi to whom the nation has offered the Crown and who was declared constitutional King of Libya by this the National Constituent Assembly.

And having decided and determined to establish a democratic independent sovereign State which will guarantee the national unity, safeguard domestic tranquillity, provide the means for common defence, secure the establishment of justice, guarantee the principles of liberty, equality, and fraternity and promote economic and social progress and the general welfare.

And trusting in God, Master of the Universe, do hereby prepare and resolve this Constitution for the United Kingdom of Libya.

CONSTITUTION OF LIBYA

CHAPTER I.

The Form of the State and the System of Government.

1. Libya is a free independent sovereign State. Neither its sovereignty nor any part of its territories may be relinquished.

2. Libya is a State having a hereditary monarchy, its form is federal and its system of government is representative. Its name is " the United Kingdom of Libya."

3. The United Kingdom of Libya consists of the Provinces of Cyrenaica, Tripolitania and the Fezzan.

4. The boundaries of the United Kingdom of Libya are:
   On the north, the Mediterranean Sea;

---

[1] Spellings of original reproduced.

On the east, the boundaries of the Kingdom of Egypt and of the Anglo-Egyptian Sudan;

On the south, the Anglo-Egyptian Sudan, French Equatorial Africa, French West Africa and the Algerian Desert;

On the west, the boundaries of Tunisia and Algeria.

5. Islam is the religion of the State.

6. The emblem of the State and its national anthem shall be prescribed by a federal law.

7. The national flag shall have the following dimensions: Its length shall be twice its breadth, it shall be divided into three parallel coloured stripes, the uppermost being red, the centre black and the lowest green, the black stripe shall be equal in area to the two other stripes together and shall bear in its centre a white crescent, between the two extremities of which there shall be a five-pointed white star.

CHAPTER II.

Rights of the People.

8. Every person who resides in Libya and has no other nationality, or is not the subject of any other State, shall be deemed to be a Libyan if he fulfils one of the following conditions:

(1) that he was born in Libya;

(2) that either of his parents was born in Libya;

(3) that he has had his normal residence in Libya for a period of not less than ten years.

9. Subject to the provisions of article 8 of this Constitution, the conditions necessary for acquiring Libyan nationality shall be determined by a federal law. Such law shall grant facilities to persons of Libyan origin residing abroad and to their children and to citizens of Arab countries and to foreigners who are residing in Libya and who at the coming into force of this Constitution have had their normal residence in Libya for a period of not less than ten years. Persons of the latter category may opt for Libyan nationality in accordance with the conditions prescribed by the law, provided they apply for it within three years as from the 1st of January 1952.

10. No one may have Libyan nationality and any other nationality at the same time.

11. Libyans shall be equal before the law. They shall enjoy equal civil and political rights, shall have the same opportunities and be subject to the same public duties and obligations, without distinction of religion, belief, race, language, wealth, kinship or political or social opinion.

12. Personal liberty shall be guaranteed and everyone shall be entitled to equal protection of the law.

13. No forced labour shall be imposed upon anyone save in accordance

with law in cases of emergency, catastrophe or circumstances which may endanger the safety of the whole or part of the population.

14. Everyone shall have the right of recourse to the Courts, in accordance with the provisions of the law.

15. Everyone charged with an offence shall be presumed to be innocent until proved guilty according to law in a trial at which he has the guarantees necessary for his defence. The trial shall be public save in exceptional cases prescribed by law.

16. No one may be arrested, detained, imprisoned or searched except in the cases prescribed by law. No one shall under any circumstances be tortured by anyone or subjected to punishment degrading to him.

17. No offence may be established or penalty inflicted except by law. Only offences committed after the promulgation of a law shall be subject to the penalties specified therein for those offences; the penalty inflicted shall not be heavier than the penalty that was applicable at the time the offence was committed.

18. No Libyan may be deported from Libya under any circumstances nor may he be forbidden to reside in any locality or compelled to reside in any specific place or prohibited from moving in Libya except as prescribed by law.

19. Dwelling houses are inviolable; they shall not be entered or searched except in cases and according to the manner prescribed by law.

20. The secrecy of letters, telegrams, telephonic communications and all correspondence in whatever form and by whatever means shall be guaranteed; they shall not be censored or delayed except in cases prescribed by law.

21. Freedom of conscience shall be absolute. The State shall respect all religions and faiths and shall ensure to Libyans and foreigners residing in its territory freedom of conscience and the right freely to practice religion so long as it is not a breach of public order and is not contrary to morality.

22. Freedom of thought shall be guaranteed. Everyone shall have the right to express his opinion and to publish it by all means and methods. But this freedom may not be abused in any way which is contrary to public order or morality.

23. Freedom of the Press and of printing shall be guaranteed within the limits of the law.

24. Everyone shall be free to use any language in his private transactions or religious or cultural matters or in the Press or any other publications or in public meetings.

25. The right of peaceful meetings is guaranteed within the limits of the law.

26. The right of peaceful association shall be guaranteed. The exercise of that right shall be regulated by law but the establishment of secret associations and those which have as their purpose the realization of political objectives by means of organizations of a military nature shall be prohibited.

27. Individuals shall have the right to address public authorities by means of letters signed by them in connection with matters which concern them but only organized bodies or juristic persons may address the authorities on behalf of a number of persons.

28. Every Libyan shall have the right to education. The State shall ensure the diffusion of education by means of the establishment of public schools, and of private schools which it may permit to be established under its supervision, for Libyans and foreigners.

29. Teaching shall be unrestricted so long as it does not constitute a breach of public order and is not contrary to morality. Public education shall be regulated by law.

30. Elementary education shall be compulsory for Libyan children of both sexes; elementary and primary education in the public schools shall be free.

31. Property shall be inviolable. No owner may be prevented from disposing of his property except within the limits of the law. No property of any person shall be expropriated except in the public interest and in the cases and in the manner determined by law and provided such person is awarded fair compensation.

32. The penalty of general confiscation of property shall be prohibited.

33. The family is the basis of society and shall be entitled to protection by the State. The State shall also protect and encourage marriage.

34. Work is one of the basic elements of economic life. It shall be protected by the State and shall be the right of all Libyans. Every individual who works shall be entitled to fair remuneration.

35. The State shall endeavour to provide as far as possible for every Libyan and his family an appropriate standard of living.

CHAPTER III.

PART I.

Powers of the Federal Government.

36. The Federal Government shall exercise legislative and executive powers in connection with the matters shown in the following list:—

  (1) Diplomatic, consular and commercial representation
  (2) Affairs of the United Nations and its specialized agencies
  (3) Participation in international conferences and bodies and the implementation of the decisions adopted by them
  (4) Matters relating to war and peace
  (5) The conclusion and implementation of treaties and agreements with other States
  (6) The regulation of trade with foreign States
  (7) Foreign loans
  (8) Extradition
  (9) The issue of Libyan passports and visas

(10) Immigration into Libya and emigration from Libya

(11) Admission into residence of foreigners in Libya and their expulsion

(12) Matters relating to nationality

(13) All other matters relating to foreign affairs

(14) Provision for the land, sea and air forces, their training and maintenance and the employment thereof

(15) Defence industries

(16) Libyan military, naval and air force arsenals

(17) The limitation of powers in cantonment areas, the appointment of personnel for these areas and determining their powers and the regulation of residence therein. The boundaries thereof shall be delimited after consultation with the Provinces

(18) Arms of all kinds for national defence, including firearms, ammunition and explosives

(19) Martial law

(20) Atomic energy and materials essential to its production

(21) All other matters relating to national defence

(22) Air lines and agreements relating thereto

(23) Meteorology

(24) Posts and telegraphs, telephones, wireless, federal broadcasting and other forms of federal communication

(25) Federal roads and other roads which the Federal Government, after consultation with the Provinces, decides do not belong to a particular Province

(26) The construction and control of federal railways, after agreement with the Provinces which they cross

(27) Customs

(28) Taxation necessary to meet the expenditure of the Federal Government, after consultation with the Provinces

(29) Federal Bank

(30) Currency, the minting of coins and the issue of notes

(31) Federal finances and public debt

(32) Exchange and stock exchanges

(33) Inquiries and statistics relating to the Federal Government

(34) Matters relating to the officers of the Federal Government

(35) In consultation with the Provinces, the promotion of agricultural and industrial production and commercial activities and the ensuring to the country of essential foodstuffs

(36) Properties of the Federal Government, the acquisition, management and disposal thereof

(37) Co-operation between the Federal Government and the Provinces in the work of the criminal police and the establishment of a central bureau for the criminal police and the pursuit of international criminals

(38) Education in universities and other institutions of higher education and the determination of educational degrees

(39) All matters assigned by this Constitution to the Federal Government.

37. The Federal Government may, with the agreement of any Province, delegate to it or to its officers the executive power concerning any matter which is within its competence under this Constitution, provided the Federal Government will bear the expense of the execution.

PART II.

Joint Powers.

38. In order to ensure a co-ordinated and unified policy between the Provinces, the legislative power relating to the following matters shall be within the competence of the Federal Government, while the executive power in connection with the implementation of that legislation shall be within the competence of the Provinces acting under the supervision of the Federal Government:

(1) Companies
(2) Banks
(3) Organization of imports and exports
(4) Income tax
(5) Monopolies and concessions
(6) Sub-soil wealth and prospecting and mining
(7) Weights and measures
(8) All forms of insurance
(9) Census
(10) Shipping and navigation
(11) Major ports which the Federal Government considers to be of importance with regard to international navigation
(12) Aircraft and air navigation, the construction of airports, the regulation of air traffic and the administration of airports
(13) Lighthouse, including lightships, beacons and other provisions for the safety of sea and air navigation
(14) The establishment of the general judicial organization subject to the provisions of Chapter 8 of this Constitution
(15) Civil, commercial and criminal law, civil and criminal procedure, the legal profession
(16) Literary, artistic and industrial copyright, inventions, patents, trademarks and merchandise marks
(17) Newspapers, books, printing presses and broadcasting
(18) Public meetings and associations
(19) Expropriation
(20) All matters relating to the national flag and the national anthem and official holidays
(21) Conditions for practicing scientific and technical professions
(22) Labour and social security

(23) The general system of education
(24) Antiquities and archaeological sites and museums, libraries, and other institutions declared by a federal law to be of national importance
(25) Public health and the co-ordination of matters relating thereto
(26) Quarantine and quarantine stations
(27) Conditions for licences to practice the medical profession and other professions connected with health.

39. The Provinces shall exercise all powers connected with the matters which have not been assigned by this Constitution to the Federal Government.

CHAPTER IV.

General Federal Powers.

40. Sovereignty is vested in the nation and the nation is the source of powers.

41. Legislative power shall be exercised by the King in conjunction with Parliament. The King promulgates the laws when they have been approved by Parliament in accordance with the procedure prescribed by this Constitution.

42. Executive power shall be exercised by the King within the limits of this Constitution.

43. Judicial power shall be exercised by the Supreme Court and other courts, which shall give judgments within the limits of this Constitution, in accordance with the law and in the name of the King.

CHAPTER V.

The King.

44. The sovereignty of the United Kingdom of Libya is vested in the nation. By the will of God the people entrust it to King Mohammed Idris el Mahdi el Senussi and after him to his male heirs, the oldest after the oldest, degree after degree.

45. The Throne of the Kingdom is hereditary. The order of succession to the Throne shall be determined by Royal Decree promulgated by King Idris I within a year of the date of the promulgation of this Constitution. No one may accede to the Throne unless he is of sound mind, a Libyan and a Moslem born of Moslem parents legally wedded. The Royal Decree which shall regulate the succession to the Throne shall have the same force as an article of this Constitution.

46. In the event of the King's death and the Throne remaining vacant owing to the lack of a successor to the King or to no successor having been appointed, the Senate and the House of Representatives shall at once hold a joint meeting without convocation to appoint a successor within ten days; three quarters at least of the number of members of the two Chambers

shall be present and the voting shall take place openly by a majority of two-thirds of the members present. If the choice cannot take place within the time specified, the two Chambers shall jointly proceed to make the choice on the eleventh day, in the presence of an absolute majority of the members of each of the two Chambers and by a proportionate majority. If the House of Representatives has been dissolved the Old House shall immediately meet until the King has been chosen.

47. Before assuming his constitutional powers, the King shall take the following oath before a joint session of the Senate and the House of Representatives: " I swear by Almighty God to observe the Constitution and the laws of the country and to devote all my efforts to the maintenance of the independence of Libya and to defending the safety of its territory ".

48. Whenever the King wishes to travel outside Libya or when circumstances prevent or delay him temporarily from exercising his constitutional powers, he may appoint one or more Deputies to perform such duties and to exercise such right and powers as the King may delegate to such Deputy or Deputies.

49. The King shall attain his majority upon the completion of his eighteenth lunar year.

50. If the King is a minor, or if any circumstances prevent or delay him from exercising his constitutional powers and he himself is unable to appoint a Deputy or Deputies, the Council of Ministers shall with the consent of Parliament appoint a Regent or a Council of Regency to perform the duties of the King and to exercise his rights and powers until such time as he become of age or is capable of exercising his powers. If Parliament is not in session it shall be convened. If the House of Representatives has been dissolved the old House shall immediately meet until such time as the Regent or Council of Regency has been appointed.

51. No person may be appointed a Deputy to the Throne or a Regent or a member of the Council of Regency unless he is a Libyan and a Moslem and has completed his fortieth year (Gregorian); however, a male of the Royal family who has completed his twenty-first year (Gregorian) may be appointed.

52. During the period between the death of the King and the taking of the constitutional oath by his successor to the Throne, by the Regent or by the members of the Council of Regency, the Council of Ministers shall, on its own responsibility, exercise the constitutional powers of the King in the name of the Libyan nation.

53. The Regent or any member of the Council of Regency shall not assume office unless he has taken the following oath before a joint meeting of the Senate and the House of Representatives: " I swear by Almighty God to observe the Constitution and the laws of the country, to devote all my efforts to the maintenance of its territory and to be loyal to the King ".

A Deputy to the Throne shall take this oath before the King or some person designated by the King.

54. A Minister or any members of a legislative body may not be Regent or a member of a Council of Regency. If a Deputy to the Throne is a member of any legislative body he shall not take part in the activities of that body during the time he is acting as Deputy to the Throne.

55. If a Regent or a member of the Council of Rgenecy, appointed in accordance with article 50, dies or is prevented by any circumstances from performing his duties as Regent or as a member of the Council of Regency, the Council of Ministers may with the consent of Parliament appoint another person to replace him, in accordance with the provisions of articles 51, 53 and 54.

If Parliament is not in session it shall be convened. If the House of Representatives has been dissolved, the old House shall immediately meet until such time as a Regent or a member of the Council of Regency has been appointed.

56. The Civil List of the King and of the Royal Family shall be fixed by federal law; it may not be reduced during his reign but it may be increased by resolution of Parliament. The law shall limit the salaries of Deputies to the Throne and of Regents which shall be paid from the Civil List of the King.

57. The judicial procedure to be followed in cases brought by the Royal Estate or against it shall be regulated by a federal law.

58. The King is the supreme head of the State.

59. The King shall be involable. He shall be exempt from all responsibility.

60. The King exercises his power through his Ministers and responsibility rests with them.

61. The King shall not assume a throne outside Libya except after the consent of Parliament.

62. The King sanctions and promulgates the laws.

63. The King shall make the necessary regulations for carrying out the laws without modifying or suspending the laws or dispensing with their execution.

64. If, when Parliament is not in session, exceptional circumstances arise which necessitate urgent measures, the King may issue decrees in respect thereof which shall have the force of law provided that they are not contrary to the provisions of this Constitution. Such decrees must be submitted to Parliament at its first meeting; if they are not submitted to Parliament or if they are not approved by either of the Chambers they shall cease to have the force of law.

65. The King shall open the sessions of Parliament and close them, and shall dissolve the House of Representatives in accordance with the provisions of this Constitution, and he may, when necessary, convene a joint meeting of the two Chambers to discuss any important question.

66. The King may, if he deems necessary, convene Parliament to meet

in an extraordinary session; he shall also convene it upon the presentation of a petition signed by an absolute majority of the members of the two Chambers. The King shall pronounce the closure of an extraordinary session.

67. The King may adjourn the session of Parliament but the adjournment may not exceed a period of thirty days nor may it be repeated during the same session without the consent of both Chambers.

68. The King is the supreme commander of all the Libyan armed forces.

69. The King shall declare war and conclude peace and enter into treaties which he ratifies after the approval of Parliament.

70. The King shall proclaim martial law and a state of emergency provided that he shall present the proclamation of martial law to Parliament in order to decide whether it shall continue or be repealed. If that proclamation is made when Parliament is not in session, Parliament must be urgently convened.

71. The King shall create and confer titles, ranks, decorations and all other signs of honour.

72. The King shall appoint the Prime Minister, he may remove him from office or accept his resignation; he shall appoint the Ministers, remove them from office, or accept their resignation at the proposal of the Prime Minister.

73. The King shall appoint diplomatic representatives and remove them from office at the proposal of the Minister of Foreign Affairs. He shall accept the credentials of the heads of foreign diplomatic missions accredited to him.

74. The King shall establish the public services and appoint senior officials and remove them in accordance with the provisions of the law.

75. Currency shall be issued in the name of the King, according to law.

76. No death sentence imposed by any Libyan court shall be executed except under the consent of the King.

77. The King shall have the right to grant pardon or to commute a sentence.

Chapter VI.

The Ministers.

78. The Council of Ministers shall consist of the Prime Minister and of the Ministers whom the King deems fit to appoint at the proposal of the Prime Minister.

79. Before assuming office the Prime Minister and Ministers shall take an oath before the King.

80. The King may appoint Ministers without portofolio in case of necessity.

81. No non-Libyan may be a Minister.

82. No member of the Royal Family may be a Minister.

83. A Minister may at the same time be a member of Parliament.

84. The Council of Ministers shall be responsible for the direction of all the internal and external affairs of the State, in accordance with the powers given to the Federal Government by this Constitution and in accordance with the provisions of this Constitution.

85. For the signatures of the King concerning the affairs of State to be effective, they must have the countersignature of the Prime Minister and of the competent Ministers, provided that decrees appointing the Prime Minister or relieving him of office shall be signed by the King alone and decrees appointing Ministers or relieving them of office shall be signed by the King and countersigned by the Prime Minister.

86. The Ministers are collectively responsible to the House of Representatives for the general policy of the State and each of them individually is responsible for the activities of his Ministry.

87. If the House of Representatives by a majority of all its members passes a vote of no confidence in the Council of Ministers, the Council of Ministers must resign. If the decision concerns one of the Ministers, he must resign.

The House of Representatives shall not consider the request for a vote of no confidence, whether such request be direct or implied, unless it has been presented by fifteen or more of the deputies. Such request may not be discussed except after eight days from the date of its presentation and shall not be voted upon except after two days from the completion of the discussion thereon.

88. Ministers shall have the right to attend the meetings of both Chambers and must be heard whenever they so request; they may not take part in the voting unless they are members. They may have the assistance of any officer they choose of their Ministry or may appoint any such officer as a deputy to represent them. Each Chamber may when necessary request any Minister to attend its meeting.

89. In the event of the dismissal or resignation of the Prime Minister all the Ministers are considered thereby to have been dismissed or to have resigned.

90. The Ministers may not while holding office assume any other public office, exercise any other profession or purchase or rent any property belonging to the State, and they may not directly or indirectly take part in the undertakings concluded and tenders invited by the public administration or the institutions falling under the administration or control of the State. They may not be members of the Board of Directors of any company nor may they take an active part in any commercial or financial enterprise.

91. The salaries of the Prime Minister and the other Ministers shall be determined by federal law.

92. A federal law shall prescribe the civil and criminal responsibilities of the Ministers and the manner in which they may be charged and tried in respect of offences committed by them in the exercise of their duties.

CHAPTER VII.

Parliament.

93. Parliament shall consist of two Chambers, the Senate and the House of Representatives.

PART I.

The Senate.

94. The Senate shall consist of twenty-four members. Each of the three Provinces of the Kingdom of Libya shall have eight members.

95. The King appoints one half of the members. The other members shall be elected by the Legislative Councils of the Provinces.

96. A Senator must be a Libyan and have completed the fortieth year of his age (Gregorian) and possess such qualifications as are provided in the federal electoral law.

Members of the Royal Family may be appointed to the Senate but may not be elected.

97. The President of the Senate shall be appointed by the King. The Senate shall elect two Vice-Presidents. The result of the election shall be submitted to the King for approval. The appointment of the President and the election of the two Vice-Presidents shall be for a period of two years and the President may be reappointed and the two Vice-Presidents may be re-elected.

98. Membership of the Senate shall be for eight years. Half the appointed Senators and half the elected Senators shall be replaced every four years. Retiring Senators may be re-appointed or re-elected.

99. The Senate shall meet at the same time as the House of Representatives; its sessions shall close at the same time as the House of Representatives.

PART II.

The House of Representatives.

100. The House of Representatives shall consist of members elected in the three Provinces in accordance with the provisions of a federal electoral law.

101. The number of Deputies shall be determined on the basis of one Deputy for every twenty thousand inhabitants or fraction of that number exceeding half, provided that the number of Deputies in any of the three Provinces shall not be less than five.

102. A voter must be:

    (1) a Libyan and

(2) shall have completed his twenty-first year (Gregorian), in addition to the conditions prescribed by provisions of a federal electoral law.

103. A Deputy must:—

(1) have completed his thirtieth year (Gregorian)

(2) be inscribed on one of the electoral rolls of the Province in which he resides, and

(3) not be a member of the Royal family, in addition to the conditions prescribed by the federal electoral law.

104. The term of office of the House of Representatives shall be four years unless it is dissolved earlier.

105. At the opening of every session, the House of Representatives shall elect a President and two Vice-Presidents, who shall be eligible for re-election.

106. If the House of Representatives is dissolved on account of any matter, the succeeding House of Representatives may not be dissolved on account of the same matter.

107. The order whereby the House of Representatives is dissolved shall call upon the electors to carry out new elections in the three Provinces within a period not exceeding three months. It must also provide for the new Chamber to be convened within twenty days of the completion of the elections.

PART III.

Provisions Common to the Two Chambers.

108. Each member of Parliament represents the whole people; his electors or the authority that appoints him may not make his mandate subject to any conditions or restrictions.

109. No one may be both a Senator and Deputy at the same time. No member of Parliament may at the same time be a member of a provincial Legislative Council or the holder of any public office. Other cases of incompatibility shall be determined by the federal electoral law.

110. Before assuming his duties each Senator and each Deputy shall take publicly in the place of meeting of his Chamber the following oath:—" I swear by Almighty God to be loyal to the country and to the King, to observe the Constitution and the laws of the country and to carry out my duties honestly and truthfully ".

111. Each Chamber decides upon the validity of the election of its members in accordance with its rules of procedure provided that, in order to decide that the election of a member is invalid, a majority of two-thirds of the members of the Chamber shall be required. This power may be delegated to another authority by virtue of a federal law.

112. The King shall call Parliament annually to hold its regular meeting in the first week of November. Failing such convocation Parliament shall

meet on the tenth day of the same month. Unless the Chamber of Deputies is dissolved, the regular session shall last for at least five months and the King shall pronounce the closure of the session.

113. The period of sessions shall be common to both Chambers. If both Chambers meet, or either of them meets, at a time other than the legal time the meeting shall be unlawful and any resolutions taken shall be void.

114. The meeting of the two Chambers shall be public but each Chamber shall, at the request of the Government or of ten of its members, go into secret session in order to decide whether the discussion on the question before it is to be held in public or in secret.

115. During extraordinary sessions Parliament shall not discuss, except with the consent of the Government, questions other than those for which it has been convened.

116. The meetings of either of the two Chambers shall not be valid unless the majority of the members are present at the opening of the meeting. Neither of the two Chambers may take a decision unless the majority of its members are present at the time of the decision.

117. Except in cases where a special majority is required, decisions in each of the Chambers shall be adopted by a majority of the members present. If the vote is equally divided, the proposal in question shall be considered to have been rejected.

118. Voting on questions under discussion in each Chamber shall take place in the manner prescribed in its rules of procedure.

119. Neither Chamber may discuss a bill before it has been considered by the appropriate committees in conformity with its rules of procedure.

120. Every bill adopted by one of the two Chambers shall be transmitted by the President of that Chamber to the President of the other Chamber.

121. A bill which has been rejected by either Chamber may not be re-introduced at the same session.

122. Every member of Parliament has the right, in conditions which shall be determined in the rules of procedure of each Chamber, to address questions and interpellations to Ministers. Discussion on an interpellation shall not take place until at least eight days after it has been presented, except in cases of emergency and with the consent of the person to whom the interpellation is addressed.

123. Each Chamber shall have the right to investigate, in accordance with its rules of procedure, specific questions within its competence.

124. Members of Parliament shall have immunity with regard to opinions they have expressed in either Chamber or in the committees thereof, subject to the provisions of the respective rules of procedure.

125. Except in cases of *flagrante delicto*, no member of either Chamber may be prosecuted or arrested for criminal offences while Parliament is in session, without the authorization of the Chamber of which he is a member.

126. Members of Parliament other than those who exercise governmental offices compatible with parliamentary membership may not be granted any title or decoration, with the exception of military ranks and decorations, during their term of office.

127. The conditions under which a member of Parliament forfeits his membership shall be determined by the federal electoral law and the decision of such forfeiture shall be taken by a majority of all the members of the Chamber to which such member belongs.

128. If a seat becomes vacant in either of the Chambers, it shall be filled within three months by election or appointment in conformity with the provisions of this Constitution; the period of three months shall commence on the date on which the Chamber informs the Government of the vacancy. The term of office of a new Senator shall be limited to the term of office of his predecessor. The term of office of a new member of the House of Representatives shall expire upon the termination of the period of office of the Chamber.

129. Elections for a new House of Representatives shall take place within the three months preceding the expiration of the period of office of the old House of Representatives. If it is not possible to carry out elections within the said period the term of office of the old House of Representatives shall extend until elections are held, notwithstanding the provisions of article 104.

130. The replacement of half the members of the Senate shall take place by means of election or appointment within the three months preceding the expiration of the terms of office of the retiring Senators. If it is impossible to effect the replacement within that period, the term of office of the Senators whose period of office has expired shall be prolonged until the election or appointment of the new Senators, notwithstanding the provisions of article 98.

131. The remuneration of members of Parliament shall be fixed by federal law, provided that no increase in such remuneration shall take effect until after the expiration of the term of office of the House of Representatives which decided it.

132. Each Chamber shall lay down its own rules of procedure and it shall specify therein the manner in which it will exercise its functions.

133. The President of each Chamber shall be responsible for maintaining order in his Chamber; no armed force may enter either Chamber or be stationed near its doors except by request of the President.

134. No one may present a request to Parliament except in writing. Each Chamber may transmit the petitions addressed to it to the Ministers. The Ministers shall be bound to give the Chamber necessary explanations regarding such petitions whenever the Chamber so requires.

135. The King shall sanction the laws passed by Parliament and shall promulgate them within thirty days of the date of their communications to him.

136. Within the period prescribed for the promulgation of a law, the King may refer the law back to Parliament for reconsideration, in which case Parliament must reconsider the law. If the law is passed again by a two-thirds majority of the members composing each of the two Chambers, the King shall sanction and promulgate it within the thirty days following the communication to him of the last decision. If the majority is less than two-thirds the bill shall not be reconsidered during that session. If Parliament in another session passes such bill again by a majority of all the members composing each of the two Chambers the King shall sanction and promulgate it within the thirty days following the communication of the decision to him.

137. Laws which are promulgated by the King shall become effective in the United Kingdom of Libya after thirty days from the date of their publication in the official gazette. This period may be increased or decreased by a special provision in the law concerned. The laws must be published in the official gazette within fifteen days of their promulgation.

138. The right to initiate laws shall be vested in the King, the Senate and the House of Representatives, except when they concern the budget or the imposing of new taxes or the modification of taxes or exemption or part exemption from taxes or their abolition, when the right to initiate such laws shall be vested in the King and the House of Representatives.

139. The President of the Senate shall preside whenever the two Chambers meet together in Congress. In his absence the President of the House of Representatives shall preside.

140. The meetings of the Congress shall be valid only when the absolute majority of the members of each of the two Chambers composing the Congress are present.

CHAPTER VIII.

The Judiciary.

141. The general judicial organization of the State shall be determined by federal law in accordance with the provisions of this Constitution.

142. The judges shall be independent; in the administration of justice, they shall be answerable only to the law.

Federal Supreme Court.

143. The Supreme Court shall consist of a President and of judges appointed by the King.

144. Before taking office the President and members of the Supreme Court shall take oath before the King.

145. Should the office of a judge fall vacant, the King, after consulting the President of the Court, shall appoint another judge.

146. The President and judges of the Court shall retire when they have completed the sixty-fifth year of their age (Gregorian).

147. The President and judges of the Court may not be removed from office; nevertheless, if it appears that for reasons of health, or because he has lost the confidence or respect which his office requires, one of them can no longer exercise his functions, the King, with the approval of the majority of the members of the Court, excluding the member concerned, shall relieve him of his office.

148. The basic salaries, allowances and provisions concerning leave of absence and pensions or provident fund of judges of the Supreme Court shall be determined by a federal law; no modification which would be prejudicial to a judge shall apply to a judge after he has been appointed.

149. When the President of the Court is absent or otherwise unable to perform his duties the King may appoint a member of the Court to perform the duties of the President.

150. When a judge is absent or otherwise unable to perform his duties the King may, after consultation with the President, appoint some person to replace him during his absence; the member thus appointed shall enjoy all privileges of the other judges of the Court while he is so acting.

151. The Supreme Court exclusively shall be competent to hear disputes which may arise between the Federal Government and one or more Provinces or between two or more Provinces.

152. The King may refer important constitutional and legislative questions to the Supreme Court for an opinion; the Court shall examine such questions and inform the King of its opinion, taking into account the provisions of this Constitution.

153. An appeal may be lodged with the Supreme Court, in accordance with the provisions of the federal law against any judgment by a provincial court in civil or criminal proceedings if such judgment included a decision in a dispute concerning this Constitution or the interpretation thereof.

154. Subject to the provisions of article 153, the cases in which an appeal against the judgment of a provincial court or an appeal for cessation may be lodged with the Supreme Court shall be determined by a federal law.

155. The legal principles embodied in the decisions of the Supreme Court shall be binding on all courts within the United Kingdom of Libya.

156. All civil and judicial authorities in the United Kingdom of Libya shall give the Supreme Court any assistance it may require.

157. Other functions may be conferred on the Supreme Court by federal law, so long as they are not contrary to the provisions of this Constitution.

158. The Supreme Court, with the approval of the King, shall determine the rules regulating the practice and procedure in the Court and fixing the fees to be charged.

CHAPTER IX.

Federal Finance.

159. The general budget shall be submitted to Parliament for study and approval at least two months before the beginning of the financial year. The budget shall be approved head by head. The beginning of the financial year shall be determined by a federal law.

160. The budget shall be discussed and approved in the first instance by the House of Representatives.

161. The parliamentary session may not be terminated before the budget has been approved.

162. In all cases where the budget has not been approved before the beginning of the financial year, provisional monthly credits shall be opened by Royal Decree on the basis of one twelfth of the credits for the preceding year, and revenue shall be collected and sums expended in accordance with the laws in force at the end of the preceding financial year.

163. Any expenditure for which provision has not been made in the budget or which exceeds the budget must be authorized by Parliament and any transfer of funds from one head of the budget to another must also be so authorized.

163. Any expenditure for which provision has not been made in the budget or which exceeds the budget estimates must be authorized by Parliament and any transfer of funds from one head of the budget to another must also be so authorized.

164. Between sessions or during the period when the House of Representatives is dissolved, and in cases of urgent necessity, new expenditure for which provision has not been made in the budget may be approved or sums may be transferred from one head of the budget to another on condition that such action is taken by Royal Decree and submitted to Parliament within a period of not more than one month after the next meeting.

165. A draft exceptional budget may in cases of necessity be drawn up for more than one year to provide for revenue and expenditure of an exceptional nature; such a budget shall not be put into force until it has been approved by Parliament.

166. The Audit Office shall audit the Federal Government accounts and shall report to Parliament on the result of the audit. The powers of the Audit Office and its constitution and the rules for exercising its auditing powers shall be determined by federal law.

167. No tax may be imposed, modified or abolished except by law. No one may be exempt from the payment of taxes except in cases provided by law. No one may be asked to pay any amounts of fees except within the limits of the law.

168. No pension, compensation, gratuity or payment from provident fund may be approved for payment out of the Government Treasury except within the limits of the law.

169. No public loan or undertaking that is likely to be a charge on the Treasury for one or more of the following years may be contracted without the consent of Parliament.

170. The currency system shall be determined by federal law.

171. Any dispute between the Senate and the House of Representatives concerning the approval of a head of the budget shall be settled by a decision taken by an absolute majority of the two Chambers meeting in Congress.

172. The receipts from all taxes and fees relating to matters which are within the legislative and executive competence of the Federal Government under article 36 of this Constitution shall be paid to the Federal Government.

173. Each Province shall have the revenue from taxes and fees accruing from matters within its competence in accordance with article 39 of this Constitution, and also from matters within its executive competence in accordance with article 38 of this Constitution.

174. The Federal Government must allocate annually to the Provinces from its receipts sufficient funds to enable them to discharge their obligations subject to the condition that their financial capacity is not less than it was before independence. The method and amount of such allocation shall be determined by federal law in a manner that will guarantee to the Provinces an increase in the amounts to be allocated to them by the Federal Government, such increases to be proportionate to the growth of the federal revenue and such as will guarantee to them a constant economic progress.

175. In cases of the imposition of federal taxes for which provision is made in article 36, paragraph 28, the Provinces shall be consulted before the bill relating to such taxes is submitted to Parliament.

CHAPTER X.

The Provinces.

176. The Provinces shall exercise all powers which have not been assigned to the Federal Government under the provisions of its Constitution.

177. Each Province shall formulate its own Organic law provided that its provisions are not contrary to the provisions of this Constitution. The formulation of such laws and their promulgation shall take place within a period not exceeding one year from the promulgation of this Constitution.

178. The Province shall be bound to observe the provisions of this Constitution and to enforce the federal law in the manner prescribed in this Constitution.

179. Each Province shall have a governor who shall be called the " Wali."

180. The King shall appoint the Wali and may relieve him of office.

181. The Wali shall represent the King within the Province and shall supervise the implementation of this Constitution and of the federal laws therein.

182. Each Province shall have an Executive Council.

183. Each Province shall have a legislative Council, three-quarters of the members of which at least shall be elected.

184. The functions of the Wali shall be determined by the Organic Law in each Province, subject to the provisions of article 181, and the functions of the Executive and Legislative Councils shall also be so determined.

185. Judicial power shall be exercised by the local tribunals in the Provinces in accordance with the provisions of this Constitution.

CHAPTER XI.

General Provisions.

186. Arabic shall be the official language of the State.

187. Cases in which a foreign language may be used in official transactions shall be determined by a federal law.

188. The United Kingdom of Libya has two capitals, Tripoli and Benghazi.

189. The extradition of political refugees shall be prohibited. International treaties and the federal laws shall prescribe the grounds for the extradition of ordinary criminals.

190. Foreigners shall be deported only in accordance with the provisions of the federal law.

191. The legal status of foreigners shall be prescribed by federal law in accordance with the principles of international law.

192. The State shall guarantee respect for the systems of personal status of non-Moslems.

193. General amnesty shall not be granted except by federal law.

194. A federal law shall determine the manner in which the land, sea and air forces are established and regulated.

195. No provision of this Constitution may be suspended under any circumstances except where such suspension is temporary in time of war or during the operation of martial law and is in accordance with law. In any event a parliamentary session may not be suspended when the conditions prescribed by this Constitution for the holding of such a session exist.

196. The King or either of the two Chambers may propose the revision of this Constitution either by the amendment or deletion of one or more of its provision or by the insertion of additional provisions.

197. No proposal may be made to review the provisions relating to the monarchal form of government, the order of succession to the Throne, the representative form of government or the principles of liberty and equality guaranteed by this Constitution.

198. For the purpose of reviewing this Constitution, each of the two Chambers shall, by an absolute majority of all its members, adopt a resolusion stating the necessity for the review and prescribing the subject thereof. The two Chambers shall, after discussing the matters subject to review, adopt their decisions in respect thereof. Discussion and voting in each of the two Chambers shall not take place unless two-thirds of its members are present. The resolution to be valid must be adopted by a majority of two-thirds of the members present in each of the two Chambers and must be sanctioned by the King.

199. In the event of a review of the provisions concerning the federal form of government, such review must be approved, in addition to the provisions laid down in the preceding article, by all the Legislative Councils of the Provinces. Such approval shall be expressed by a resolution taken in this respect by the Legislative Council of each Province before the review is presented to the King for his sanction.

200. Immigration into Libya shall be regulated by a federal law. No immigration shall be permitted into a Province without the approval of the Province having been secured.

CHAPTER XII.

Transitory and Provisional Provisions.

201. This Constitution shall come into force upon the declaration of independence, which must take place by 1st January 1952 in accordance with the resolution of the United Nations General Assembly dated 21st November 1949. Nevertheless the provisions of Article 8 of this Constitution and of this chapter shall come into force on the promulgation of this Constitution.

202. Until the establishment of a government constituted in accordance with the provisions of article 203 of this Constitution, the Provisional Federal Government shall exercise all the powers concerning the matters transferred to it by the two Administering Powers and by the existing Provincial Governments, provided that the provisions laid down by it shall not be contrary to the fundamental principles established by this Constitution.

203. Upon the declaration of independence the King shall appoint the duly constituted Government.

204. The Provisional Federal Government shall draw up the first electoral law for Parliament, provided it is not contrary to the provisions laid down in this Constitution. The law shall be summitted to the National Assembly for approval and promulgation. The said law must be promulgated within a period not exceeding thirty days from the date of the promulgation of this Constitution.

205. The first elections to the House of Representatives must take place within a period not exceeding three and a half months from the date upon which the electoral law is promulgated.

206. In the first elections to the House of Representatives and until a census of the Libyan people has been made, the Province of Cyrenaica shall have fifteen Deputies, the Province of Tripolitania thirty-five Deputies and the Province of the Fezzan five Deputies.

207. Notwithstanding the provisions of articles 95 and 98 of this Constitution, the King shall appoint all members of the first Senate. Its term of office shall be four years as from the date of the first session of Parliament.

208. Articles 95 and 98 shall become operative as from the date of the expiration of the term of office of the first Senate. The members of the Senate who will retire at the end of the first four years in accordance with the provisions of articles 95 and 98 shall be selected by lot.

209. Notwithstanding the provisions contained in article 47 of this Constitution, the first King of the United Kingdom of Libya shall exercise his constitutional powers upon the declaration of independence, provided that he shall take the prescribed oath before Parliament at its first session in a joint meeting.

210. Unless they are inconsistent with the principles of liberty and equality guaranteed by this Constitution, all laws subsidiary legislation, orders and notices which may be in operation in any part of Libya upon the coming into force of this Constitution shall continue to be effective and in operation until repealed or amended or replaced by other legislation enacted in accordance with the provision of this Constitution.

211. The first Parliament shall be convened within a period of not more than twenty days from the date on which the final results of the elections are announced.

212. Article 36 (27) and article 174 of this Constitution shall not come into operation before 1st April 1952.

213. The National Assembly shall continue in existence until the declaration of independence.

The Libyan National Assembly prepared and resolved this Constitution in its meeting held in the city of Benghazi on Sunday, 6th Muharram, Hagera 1371, corresponding to 7th October 1951, and delegated its President and the two Vice-Presidents to promulgate it and submit it to His Majesty, the Exalted King, and publish it in the Official Gazettes in Libya.

In pursuance of the Resolution of the National Assembly we here promulgated this Constitution in the city of Benghazi on Sunday, the 6th day of Muharram, Hegera 1371, corresponding to the 7th day of October, 1951.

MOHAMED ABUL ASSAAD,
President of the National Assembly.

OMAR FAYEK SHENNIB,
BUBAKER AHMED BUBAKER,
Vice-President of the National Assembly.

Appendix IV

TREATY OF FRIENDSHIP AND ALLIANCE BETWEEN HER
MAJESTY IN RESPECT OF THE UNITED KINGDOM OF
GREAT BRITAIN AND NORTHERN IRELAND AND HIS
MAJESTY THE KING OF THE UNITED KINGDOM OF LIBYA

Benghazi, July 29, 1953

ARTICLE 1

There shall be peace and friendship and a close alliance between the High
Contracting Parties in consecration of their cordial understanding and their
good relations.

Each of the High Contracting Parties undertakes not to adopt in regard
to foreign countries an attitude which is inconsistent with the alliance or
which might create difficulties for the other party thereto.

ARTICLE 2

Should either High Contracting Party become engaged in war or armed
conflict, the other High Contracting Party will, subject always to the provisions of Article 4, immediately come to his aid as a measure of collective
defence. In the event of an imminent menace of hostilities involving either
of the High Contracting Parties they will immediately concert together the
necessary measures of defence.

ARTICLE 3

The High Contracting Parties recognise that it is in their common interest
to provide for their mutual defence and to ensure that their countries are in
a position to play their part in the maintenance of international peace and
security. To this end each will furnish to the other all the facilities and
assistance in his power on terms to be agreed upon. In return for facilities
provided by His Majesty The King of Libya for British armed forces in
Libya on conditions to be agreed upon, Her Britannic Majesty will provide
financial assistance to His Majesty The King of Libya, on terms to be agreed
upon as aforesaid.

ARTICLE 4

Nothing in the present Treaty is intended to, or shall in any way, prejudice
the rights and obligations which devolve, or may devolve, upon either of

the High Contracting Parties under the Charter of the United Nations or under any other existing international agreements, conventions or treaties, including, in the case of Libya, the Covenant of the League of Arab States.

ARTICLE 5

This Treaty shall be ratified and shall come into force upon the exchange of instruments of ratification which shall take place as soon as possible.

ARTICLE 6

This Treaty shall remain in force for a period of twenty years except in so far as it may be revised or replaced by a new Treaty during that period by agreement of both the High Contracting Parties, and it shall in any case be reviewed at the end of ten years. Each of the High Contracting Parties agrees in this connexion to have in mind the extent to which international peace and security can be ensured through the United Nations. Before the expiry of a period of nineteen years either High Contracting Party may give to the other through the diplomatic channel notice of termination at the end of the said period of twenty years. If the Treaty has not been so terminated, and subject to any revision or replacement thereof, it shall continue in force after the period of twenty years until the expiry of one year after notice of termination has been given by either High Contracting Party to the other through the diplomatic channel.

ARTICLE 7

Should any difference arise relative to the application or interpretation of the present Treaty and should the High Contracting Parties fail to settle such difference by direct negotiations, it shall be referred to the International Court of Justice unless the parties agree to another mode of settlement.

In witness whereof the above-named Plenipotentiaries have signed the present Treaty and affixed thereto their Seals.

Done in duplicate at Benghazi this 29th day of July, 1953, in the English and Arabic languages, both texts being equally authentic.

(L.S.)   A. KIRKBRIDE.   (L.S.)   MAHMUD MUNTASSER.

AGREEMENT BETWEEN THE GOVERNMENT OF THE UNITED KINGDOM OF GREAT BRITAIN AND NORTHERN IRELAND AND THE GOVERNMENT OF THE UNITED KINGDOM OF LIBYA REGARDING MILITARY FACILITIES

Benghazi, July 29, 1953

The Government of the United Kingdom of Great Britain and Northern Ireland (hereafter referred to as the United Kingdom Government) and the Government of the United Kingdom of Libya (hereafter referred to as the

Government of Libya), desiring to give effect to Article 3 of the Treaty of Friendship and Alliance signed at Benghazi on the 29th day of July, 1953, between Her Majesty The Queen of the United Kingdom of Great Britain and Northern Ireland and of Her other Realms and Territories and His Majesty The King of the United Kingdom of Libya, have agreed as follows:—

ARTICLE 1

Co-operation regarding Training Methods and Equipment

The two Governments agree to concert together from time to time with a view to taking appropriate steps to secure that their armed forces attain the necessary efficiency in co-operation with each other and that uniformity of training methods and equipment of their armed forces is established and maintained as far as possible. The United Kingdom Government will use their good offices to facilitate the supply from the United Kingdom of arms, ammunition and equipment for the Libyan armed forces in a manner consonant with the natural continuous development of these forces. Nothing in this Agreement shall, however, oblige Libyan armed forces to serve outside Libyan territory.

ARTICLE 2

Military Facilities in Libya

(1) As a contribution to the maintenance of international peace and security in accordance with the provisions and principles of the Charter of the United Nations[1], the Government of Libya grant permission to the United Kingdom Government to enjoy for the duration of this Agreement and subject to its terms and conditions the facilities within the territory of Libya for military purposes which are hereinafter set forth.

(2) The United Kingdom Government for their part recognize that all members of the British forces in Libya must honour the independence and sovereignty of Libya and respect its laws and abstain from any activities inconsistent with this obligation or with the spirit of the aforesaid Treaty, and in particular abstain from any political activity in Libya. The United Kingdom Government will take appropriate measures to these ends.

ARTICLE 3

Use of Lands for Military Purposes

(1) The Government of Libya will permit the United Kingdom Government to have the exclusive and uninterrupted use for military purposes of the lands and buildings, and anything therein or thereon, set out in Annex I to this Agreement. The United Kingdom Government will vacate the lands and buildings set out in Annex II to this Agreement within the periods indicated therein, but may use them as aforesaid meanwhile. All lands and

---

[1] " Treaty Series No. 67 (1946) ," Cmd. 7015.

buildings used in pursuance of this Agreement by the United Kingdom Government (except the lands referred to in paragraph (3) of this Article) are hereinafter referred to as agreed lands.

(2) The United Kingdom Government may adapt the agreed lands for military purposes, but will not demolish any buildings existing on the land at the time of first entry into occupation of the British forces, or remove trees in any substantial number, without the consent of the Libyan authorities.

(3) The Government of Libya will from time to time make available to the United Kingdom Government areas of land to be agreed between the two Governments to be used for short periods for training and exercise. Such areas shall not be in the neighbourhood of centres of population and shall not be cultivated areas.

(4) The Government of Libya will also take steps to make available for the use of the United Kingdom Government further areas of land of a reasonable size, agreed to be suitable for the reasonable extension of incomplete installations included in Annex I to this Agreement, and for the replacement as necessary of lands or buildings surrendered in accordance with paragraph (1) of this Article.

(5) In general, items may be added to or deleted from the list of agreed lands by agreement between the two Governments.

(6) This Article shall apply to State properties and, subject to the terms of Article 18 of this Agreement, to properties in private ownership.

ARTICLE 4

Control of Aircraft, Vessels and Vehicles

(1) Save as may be otherwise agreed between the two Governments, the United Kingdom Government may exercise full control over aircraft, vessels and vehicles entering, leaving and within the agreed lands.

(2) The Libyan Government shall arrange for such controls over aircraft, vessels and vehicles entering, leaving and within areas near the agreed lands as are agreed by the two Governments to be necessary to carry out the purposes of this Agreement and ensure the security of British forces and property in Libya.

ARTICLE 5

Rights of Way

At the request of the United Kingdom Government and by agreement between the two Governments, the United Kingdom Government shall be accorded rights, for military purposes, to lay pipes, to construct drainage and irrigation channels and railways and to lay cables and wires, on or over or below the surface of any lands or waters, and to maintain the same. This Article shall apply to State lands and, subject to the provisions of Article 18 of this Agreement, to lands in private ownership.

ARTICLE 6

Communications

Provided that the Government of Libya agree, the United Kingdom Government may construct and maintain necessary roads and bridges, and improve and deepen harbours, channels, entrances and anchorages, affording access to the agreed lands.

ARTICLE 7

Power to Construct and Use Telegraphic, Telephonic and Broadcasting Systems

(1) The Government of Libya will permit the United Kingdom Government to construct and use telecommunications systems (including wireless and electromagnetic systems) within the agreed lands and connecting any such lands. These systems may also be connected with the systems of the Government of Libya and with systems outside Libya on terms and conditions to be agreed by the two Governments.

(2) The Government of Libya will also permit the United Kingdom Government to construct and use service broadcasting stations within the agreed lands.

ARTICLE 8

Generation of Light and Power and Winning of Building and Construction Materials

Within the agreed lands, and elsewhere in Libya by agreement between the two Governments, the United Kingdom Government may, for military purposes—

(a) generate light and power;

(b) search for and win by any means water and indigenous building and construction material such as stone, sand, gravel, earth, gypsum and clay:

Provided that any archæological remains and mineral resources, including petroleum but excluding building and construction material, which the United Kingdom Government discover during their operations under this Agreement, shall remain the property of Libya.

ARTICLE 9

Transmission of Commodities and Goods

The United Kingdom Government may, directly or through their contractors and authorised service organizations, transmit to, from, between and within the agreed lands for military purposes light, power, commodities and goods.

ARTICLE 10

Security of the Agreed Lands

(1) The Government of Libya empower the United Kingdom Government to maintain the security of lives and property within the agreed lands.

(2) In particular no person will be allowed to be in or enter any such lands without permission of a member of the British forces authorised by the competent military authority to give permission. The competent military authority will, however, cause all facilities consistent with security to be given to officials of the Government of Libya to enter any such lands for the purpose of carrying out official duties.

ARTICLE 11

Postal Services

The Government of Libya permit the United Kingdom Government to operate without restriction, by means of post offices established within the agreed lands, postal services in Libya and to and from Libya, exclusively for the use of the authorities of the United Kingdom Government and of members of the British forces.

ARTICLE 12

Hygiene

The United Kingdom Government will do all things in their power that are necessary for the maintenance of hygiene within the agreed lands.

ARTICLE 13

Surveys

The Government of Libya permit the United Kingdom Government to make surveys of any kind in any part of Libya and the adjacent waters (including carrying out aerial photography on which such surveys may be based) for the purpose of operations under this Agreement. The United Kingdom Government will inform the Government of Libya before any survey is made outside the agreed lands and, if the Government of Libya so desire, a representative of the Government of Libya may be present when any survey is made outside the agreed lands; and the results of such surveys and all data in connexion therewith, such as maps, air photographs, triangulation or other control data, will be supplied by the United Kingdom Government to the Government of Libya. The rights conferred by this Article shall not extend to areas access to which is prohibited by the Government of Libya.

ARTICLE 14

Special Institutions

The United Kingdom Government may establish within the agreed lands, directly or through authorised service organizations, the institutions necessary to provide canteens, messes and facilities for the social, recreational and cultural activities of, and the sale of goods and commodities to, members of the British forces. These institutions and any authorised service organisations through which they may be established, their equipment, the services they provide and the goods and commodities they sell, will not be subject to any taxes, duties or imposts or to legislative requirements as to the constitution or activities of the institutions or organisations. The United Kingdom Government will take administrative action designed to prevent the resale to unauthorised persons of goods and commodities sold by such institutions and generally to prevent abuse of the privileges granted under this Article and there shall be co-operation between the two Governments to this end.

ARTICLE 15

Public Services and Facilities

Upon the request of the United Kingdom Government and provided the Government of Libya agree that public and private interests in Libya receive no hurt thereby, the public services and facilities in Libya shall, as far as practicable, be made available for the use of the United Kingdom Government and authorised service organisations and members of the British Forces. The charges therefor shall be the same as those paid by other users, unless otherwise agreed.

ARTICLE 16

United Kingdom Government Property

(1) When the United Kingdom Government vacate any part of the agreed lands which is State land, or any lands which they have purchased from a private owner and used for military purposes under this Agreement, permanent constructions erected on the lands at the expense of the United Kingdom Government under or prior to this Agreement shall not be disposed of except with the consent of the Government of Libya.

(2) Permanent constructions erected at the expense of the United Kingdom Government under or prior to this Agreement on private lands rented by them, and used for military purposes under this Agreement, shall become the property of the owner of the land unless otherwise agreed between the United Kingdom Government and the owner.

(3) Except as provided in paragraphs (1) and (2) of this Article, all property constructed, installed, brought into or procured in Libya under or prior to this Agreement by the United Kingdom Government, shall remain the property of the United Kingdom Government and may be removed from Libya free of restrictions, or disposed of in Libya by the United Kingdom Government in agreement with the Government of Libya, at any time before the termination of this Agreement or within a reasonable time thereafter. Any such property not so removed or disposed of before the termination of this Agreement or within a reasonable time thereafter will cease to be the

property of the United Kingdom Government and the United Kingdom Government will not be entitled to compensation for such property.

ARTICLE 17

Vacating of Land

When the United Kingdom Government vacate any State land which has been made available by the Government of Libya under Article 3, they are not obliged to leave such land in the condition in which it was when the use of the land by the United Kingdom Government began, and no compensation shall be payable to or by the United Kingdom Government in respect of any increase or decrease in the value of the land.

ARTICLE 18

Arrangements with Private Owners of Land

(1) The two Governments may agree that the use of any land in private ownership by the United Kingdom Government for military purposes shall be the subject of direct arrangements between the United Kingdom Government and the private owners, and in such case the United Kingdom Government may purchase or rent the lands direct from the private owners or acquire direct from them any interests in or relating to the lands.

(2) If satisfied that there is unreasonable refusal by a private owner, after he has received an offer of equitable compensation, to make available land necessary for the purposes of this Agreement, the Government of Libya will take the necessary steps to ensure that such land is made available. In this event equitable recompense to the owner shall be paid by the United Kingdom Government, by agreement with the Government of Libya.

(3) During or within a reasonable time after the expiry of this Agreement, the United Kingdom Government shall dispose, with the consent of the Government of Libya, of any lands purchased by them, and used for military purposes, under the provisions of this Agreement.

(4) Subject to the terms of any agreement with the Government of Libya and of any arrangements with the private owners, the lands referred to in this Article will be regarded as agreed lands for the purposes of this Agreement.

ARTICLE 19

Maintenance and Development of Certain Facilities

If the Government of Libya, at the request of the United Kingdom Government, agree to maintain at or develop to a level which would not have been reached but for such request any facilities such as harbours, ports, anchorages, aerodromes, roads or railways in Libya, the United Kingdom Government will make to the Government of Libya a payment of which the basis will be agreed by the two Governments before the proposed work is begun.

ARTICLE 20

Movement of British Forces, Vessels, Aircraft and Vehicles

(1) The Government of Libya grant to the British forces and United Kingdom public vessels, aircraft and vehicles, including armoured vehicles, freedom of entry to and egress from and movement between the agreed lands by land, sea or air. This right shall include freedom from compulsory pilotage and all toll charges. Her Britannic Majesty's Ships may visit Libyan ports on reasonable notification.

(2) The Government of Libya permit United Kingdom public aircraft to fly over and, in an emergency, land on and take off from any of the territory of Libya, including territorial waters. United Kingdom public aircraft shall not, however, fly over towns, except in case of emergency or under conditions to be agreed between the two Governments, nor over areas prohibited by the Government of Libya to foreign aircraft in general. United Kingdom public aircraft shall be permitted to use Libyan airports under the conditions applicable to foreign military aircraft generally, save that they shall enjoy transit facilities at Benina civil airport on notification, and that the status of the Royal Air Force at Tripoli civil airport shall be governed by Article 21 of this Agreement.

(3) By agreement between the two Governments, the British forces and United Kingdom public vessels, aircraft and vehicles shall have freedom of movement in other districts of Libya for the purposes of this Agreement.

(4) In the exercise of the privileges described in this Article all reasonable precautions will be taken by the United Kingdom Government to avoid damage to Libyan public facilities.

(5) Members of the British forces will, in their individual capacity, enjoy the same freedom of movement in Libya as is enjoyed by foreigners in general. The United Kingdom Government accept the principle that military members of the British forces should not wear uniform in Tripoli and Benghazi when off duty. Normally, therefore, military members of the British forces when in Tripoli and Benghazi will wear civilian clothes when not on duty. In exceptional circumstances, however, the military authorities may, after consultation with the Libyan authorities, issue orders or grant permission to such members to wear uniform. This arrangement will be reconsidered after five years.

ARTICLE 21

Tripoli Civil Airport

(1) Full responsibility for the operation and maintenance of Tripoli civil airport shall be assumed as rapidly as possible by the Libyan authorities.

(2) In the meanwhile, the Royal Air Force will continue to afford at their cost such technical and other assistance as may be agreed for the efficient operation of the airport.

(3) The Government of Libya will make available to the Royal Air Force the necessary lands adjacent to the East side of Tripoli civil airport to enable them to reprovide facilities to the extent of those which they enjoy at present in the airport. The latter shall be handed over gradually by the Royal Air Force to the Government of Libya in a period not exceeding five years. The Royal Air Force will continue thereafter to afford to the Libyan authorities when so requested such technical and other assistance as may be agreed between the two Governments.

(4) The Royal Air Force may continue to station in the agreed lands at Tripoli civil airport two Squadrons or such other number as may be agreed with the Government of Libya.

ARTICLE 22

Entry into, and Departure from, Libya of the British Forces

(1) The Government of Libya permit the United Kingdom Government to bring into Libya members of the British forces, and to remove any such members from Libya. The United Kingdom Government will keep the Government of Libya informed as to the number of the British forces present in Libya, which shall not exceed such number as shall have been agreed between the two Governments.

(2) Passport and visa requirements will not apply to military members of the British forces, but they will be furnished with appropriate identification cards by the United Kingdom Government and specimens of such cards will be supplied to the Government of Libya. The laws of the Government of Libya will not apply to prevent their admission or departure. Passport and visa requirements will, however, be applicable to other members of the British forces.

(3) No toll charges will be payable in respect of the entry into, or departure from, or movement in Libya of members of the British forces.

ARTICLE 23

Laws as to Registration and Control of Aliens not Applicable

The Government of Libya exempt members of the British forces from any laws providing for the registration and control of aliens. The United Kingdom Government will take every step open to them to ensure the correct behaviour of all members of the British forces and will provide such information as the Government of Libya may require about the civilian members, bearing in mind their status as members of the British forces.

ARTICLE 24

Repatriation of ex-Members of the British Forces

The United Kingdom Government shall make provision for the repatriation at their own expense of any member of the British forces who ceases to be such while serving in Libya. This repatriation shall be effected as soon as possible after the change of status takes place. Meanwhile, the United Kingdom Government shall prevent the person in question from being a public charge in Libya. These provisions shall not apply if the Government of Libya permit the person in question to remain in Libya.

ARTICLE 25

Possession and Carriage of Arms

Military members of the British forces in Libya may possess and carry arms as required in the performance of official duties.

ARTICLE 26

Local Purchases

(1) Members of the British forces may purchase locally goods and commodities necessary for their own use or consumption, and such services as they need, under the conditions generally applicable in Libya.

(2) The United Kingdom Government and their contractors and authorised service organisations may purchase locally goods and commodities which they require in connexion with operations under this Agreement and, subject to any wishes expressed by the Government of Libya, it will be the policy of the United Kingdom Government for such goods and commodities to be purchased locally if they are available and of the standard required.

ARTICLE 27

Employment of Local Labour

(1) Subject to any wish expressed by the Government of Libya, the United Kingdom Government and their contractors and authorised service organisations shall save in special circumstances employ Libyan civilians provided that they are available and qualified to do the work. The conditions of employment of the Libyan nationals and persons normally resident in Libya shall conform to the conditions generally applicable under Libyan law, with particular reference to wages and extra pay and insurance and conditions for the protection of workers.

(2) At the request of the appropriate Libyan authorities the United Kingdom Government and their contractors and authorised service organisations will deduct and pay to the Libyan authorities, in accordance with the requirements of Libyan law, income tax or any other impost upon the wages which they pay to employees not exempt from taxation under the provisions of this Agreement.

(3) The United Kingdom Government will avail themselves when possible, in agreement with the Government of Libya, of the services of the Departments of Public Works in Libya.

ARTICLE 28

Vehicles and Driving Permits

(1) In the case of members of the British forces who hold driving licences valid in the United Kingdom of Great Britain and Northern Ireland, or driving permits issued to them by the competent military authority after they have passed a driving test valid for the issue of driving licences in the United Kingdom of Great Britain and Northern Ireland, the Government of Libya agree either to honour such licences and permits without driving test or fee, or to issue their own driving permits without driving test or fee.

(2) The Government of Libya will not require United Kingdom public vehicles to be licensed under the laws of Libya or to bear the identification marks ordinarily required by the laws of Libya, but all such vehicles will bear identification marks issued by the appropriate authorities of the United Kingdom Government.

(3) The Government of Libya will not require United Kingdom public vehicles to comply with the laws of Libya as regards construction and equipment, but all reasonable precautions will be taken by the United Kingdom Government and authorised service organisations to avoid damage to Libyan public facilities.

ARTICLE 29

Customs Laws and Regulations

(1) The United Kingdom Government and their contractors, whether Libyan or otherwise, and authorised service organisations may import into Libya free of customs duty goods and commodities required for the purpose of operations under this Agreement or exclusively for use or consumption by members of the British forces.

(2) Members of the British forces may at the time of their first arrival in Libya or at the time of the first arrival of any of their dependants to join them, import into Libya free of customs duty their personal effects and household goods and their private motor vehicles for personal use.

(3) The laws and regulations administered by the customs authorities of Libya, including any right to inspect and seize, will not apply to any property imported under this Article nor to any official documents brought into Libya by the United Kingdom Government.

(4) Property imported into Libya under this Article may be exported from Libya without regard to the customs laws and regulations of Libya, but it shall not be disposed of in Libya except for the purpose of operations under this Agreement, or to members of the British forces, or in any other cases authorised by the appropriate authorities of the Government of Libya and subject to such conditions as they may impose.

(5) The United Kingdom Government will take administrative action designed to prevent abuse of the privileges granted by this Article and there shall be co-operation between the two Governments to this end.

(6) Property acquired in Libya which is referred to in paragraph (3) of Article 16 may be exported without regard to the customs laws and regulations of Libya.

ARTICLE 30

Miscellaneous Fiscal Provisions

(1) The temporary presence in Libya of a member of the British forces will constitute neither residence nor domicile therein and will not of itself subject him to any tax, duty or charge in Libya, either on his income or on his movable property the presence of which in Libya is due to his temporary presence there, nor, in the event of his death, will it subject his estate to death duties. This paragraph shall not apply to income derived from any immovable property or from any commercial interests in Libya.

(2) British subjects or corporations organised under the laws of the United Kingdom of Great Britain and Northern Ireland, resident in the United Kingdom of Great Britain and Northern Ireland, shall be exempt from all taxes in respect of income derived under a contract with the United Kingdom Government in connexion with operations under this Agreement, provided that this exemption shall not apply to such persons or corporations who are engaged in business in Libya otherwise than under such contracts with the United Kingdom Government.

(3) No tax, duty or charge will be payable in respect of any such importation or exportation as is referred to in Article 29.

(4) Save as otherwise provided in this Agreement no tax, duty or impost shall be payable by the United Kingdom Government in respect of anything done in Libya (including the acquisition, ownership, possession, occupation, use or disposal of any property) by the United Kingdom Government in connexion with operations under this agreement; but this exemption shall not extend to any payment due in respect of any services rendered.

(5) Nothing in this Article shall exempt any member of the British forces from—

    (a) any fee under the laws of Libya in respect of any privately owned radio or television set;

    (b) any tax or registration fee under the laws of Libya in respect of the possession or use of any privately owned vehicle.

(6) Nothing in this Article shall require the refund or remission by the Government of Libya or any tax, duty or charge payable in Libya or any goods or commodities prior to their acquisition in Libya by the United Kingdom Government or its contractors or by authorised service organisations, except that the Government of Libya will make arrangements to remit all duties and taxes on any fuel, oil and lubricants so acquired which are certified by an authorised officer of the United Kingdom Government to be for the exclusive use of the British forces in connexion with operations under this Agreement. Fuel, oil and lubricants acquired by members of the British forces for their private use shall not be exempt from duties and taxes.

ARTICLE 31

Jurisdiction—Civil Matters

(1) The United Kingdom Government will pay equitable compensation in respect of claims which arise out of the performance of their official duties by members of the British forces who are directly employed by the United Kingdom Government, not being claims arising from military operations in war-time; and the courts will not entertain any such claims.

(2) The Government of Libya will pay equitable compensation in respect of claims by the United Kingdom Government or by members of the British forces which arise out of the performance of their official duties by persons who are directly employed by the Government of Libya, not being claims arising from military operations in war-time.

(3) Save as provided in paragraph (1) of this Article, the Libyan Courts shall be entitled to entertain civil cases against members of the British forces. In such cases the competent military authorities shall, on request by the appropriate Libyan authorities, take all measures open to them to secure compliance with the judgments and orders of the Libyan Courts, and, so far as security considerations allow, to assist the Libyan authorities in the execution of any such judgment or order. A military member of the British forces shall not, however, be liable to be taken out of the service by any judgment or order of a court, and execution of such a judgment or order shall not issue against his person, pay, arms, ammunition, equipment, regimental necessaries and clothing.

ARTICLE 32

Jurisdiction—Criminal Matters

(1) The service tribunals and authorities of the United Kingdom Government may exercise such jurisdiction and authority in relation to members of the British forces as is conferred by the Law of England in the following cases, namely—

(a) Offences solely against the property of the Government of the United Kingdom, or against the person or property of another member of the British forces;

(b) Offences committed solely on the agreed lands;

(c) Offences solely against the security of the United Kingdom, including treason, sabotage, espionage or violation of any law relating to official secrets, or secrets relating to the national defence of the United Kingdom;

(d) Offences arising out of any act or omission done in the performance of official duty;

and in every such case where such jurisdiction and authority exist the members of the British forces shall be immune from the jurisdiction of the Libyan Courts.

(2) In other cases the Libyan Courts shall exercise jurisdiction unless the Government of Libya waive their right to exercise jurisdiction. The Government of Libya will give sympathetic consideration to any request from the authorities of the United Kingdom for a waiver of their right in cases where those authorities consider such waiver to be of particular importance, or where suitable punishment can be applied by disciplinary action without recourse to a court.

(3) The Libyan and United Kingdom authorities will assist each other in the arrest and handing over to the appropriate authority of members of the British forces for trial in accordance with the above provisions, and the Libyan authorities will immediately notify the United Kingdom authorities if they arrest any member of the British forces. The Libyan authorities will, if the United Kingdom authorities request the release on remand of an arrested member of the British forces, release him from their custody on the United Kingdom authorities' undertaking to present him to the Libyan Courts for investigatory proceedings and trial when required.

(4) The Libyan and United Kingdom authorities will assist each other in the carrying out of all necessary investigations into offences, and in the collection and production of evidence, including the attendance of witnesses at the trial and the seizure and, in proper cases, the handing over of objects connected with an offence. The handing over of such objects may, however, be made subject to their return within the time specified by the authority delivering them.

(5) Whenever a member of the British forces is prosecuted in a Libyan court he shall be entitled—

(a) to a prompt and speedy trial;

(b) to be informed, in advance of trial, of the specific charge or charges made against him;

(c) to be confronted with the witnesses against him;

(d) to have compulsory process for obtaining witnesses in his favour, if they are within the jurisdiction of the Libyan Courts;

(e) to have legal representation under the conditions prevailing for the time being in Libya;

(f) if he considers it necessary, to have the services of a competent interpreter; and

(g) to communicate with the United Kingdom authorities and to have a representative of those authorities present at his trial.

(6) The Libyan authorities will notify the United Kingdom authorities of the result of any trial in a Libyan court of a member of the British forces.

(7) Witnesses who are alleged to have committed perjury or contempt of court in proceedings before the service tribunals or authorities of the United Kingdom Government and who are not subject to the law administered by those tribunals and authorities will be turned over to the authorities

of the Government of Libya. Provision will be made by the Laws of Libya for the trial and punishment of such offenders.

(8) The United Kingdom Government will have the right to police the agreed lands and to maintain order therein and may arrest therein any alleged offenders and, when they are triable by the Libyan Courts, will forthwith turn them over to the Libyan authorities for trial.

(9) Outside the agreed lands, members of the British forces may be employed on police duties by arrangement with the appropriate authorities of the Government of Libya. The Libyan authorities shall be primarily responsible for the protection of cables carrying light, power or communications to any of the agreed lands, whether such cables are the property of the United Kingdom Government or otherwise, but they may make arrangements with the United Kingdom authorities for the employment of members of the British forces for this purpose. In such cases, the Libyan police with whom members of the British forces may be serving shall have paramount authority with respect to the persons and property of inhabitants of Libya.

ARTICLE 33
Definitions

(1) In this Agreement—

(a) " the Government of Libya " means the Federal Government of the United Kingdom of Libya;

(b) " the United Kingdom Government " means the Government of the United Kingdom of Great Britain and Northern Ireland;

(c) "the two Governments" means the two Governments above-mentioned;

(d) " British forces " means the personnel of the British land, sea and air armed services (referred to in this Agreement as " the military members ") and accompanying civilian personnel who are employed by or serving with such services directly, or through authorised service organisations. This definition includes also the dependants of such military and civilian personnel but excludes all persons who are nationals of or ordinarily resident in Libya, or whose presence in Libya does not arise from operations under this Agreement;

(e) " dependant " in relation to a person means any of the following, that is to say—

(a) the wife or husband of that person; and

(b) any other person wholly maintained by, or in the custody, charge or care of, the first person;

(f) " authorised service organisations " means organisations customarily accompanying the British armed forces and specified in Annex III to this Agreement, and any further organisation of a like kind which the United Kingdom and Libyan Governments shall agree to regard as an authorised service organisation;

(g) "military purposes" means, within the agreed lands and elsewhere as provided in this Agreement, the installation, construction, maintenance, use and operation of military equipment and facilities, including facilities for the training, accommodation, hospitalisation, recreation, education and welfare of members of the British forces; and the operations of the United Kingdom Government and their contractors and of authorised service organisations under this Agreement; and the storage of the property of the United Kingdom Government and their contractors and authorised service organisations which is in Libya in connexion with operations under this Agreement;

(h) "competent military authority" means the officers commanding the branches of the British armed services in Libya;

(i) "vessel" includes water-borne craft of all kinds;

(j) "goods" includes military equipment and services and construction material;

(k) the terms "United Kingdom public vessel" and "United Kingdom public aircraft" means vessels and aircraft operating under charter or otherwise for the purposes of the armed services of the United Kingdom;

(l) "United Kingdom public vehicle" means a vehicle exclusively in the service of the United Kingdom Government or authorised service organisations.

(2) If any doubt arises as to whether any person is a member of the British forces, a certificate that he is such a member signed by an authorised officer will be accepted by the courts of Libya as proof of that fact. The names of the officers authorised to issue such certificates and specimens of their signatures will be notified by the United Kingdom Government to the Government of Libya through diplomatic channels.

(3) A certificate by Her Britannic Majesty's Minister in Libya to the effect that any claim has arisen out of the performance of official duties by a member of the British forces employed by the United Kingdom Government will be accepted by the courts of Libya as proof of that fact.

ARTICLE 34

Disputes

Any disputes between the Government of Libya and the United Kingdom Government arising out of this Agreement shall, unless otherwise settled or unless other provision is made in this Agreement for such determination, be determined by arbitration by a special tribunal composed of one member appointed by the Government of Libya, one member appointed by the United Kingdom Government, and one member appointed jointly by the two Governments. In the event of the two Governments being unable within two months to agree on the person to be appointed as the third member, the President of the International Court of Justice shall be requested to appoint the third member. If the President is a citizen of the United Kingdom and Colonies or of Libya, the Vice-President shall be requested to act; and, if he also is such a citizen, the next senior Judge of the Court.

ARTICLE 35

Ratification and Duration of Agreement

This Agreement shall be subject to ratification and the instruments of ratification shall be exchanged as soon as possible. It shall enter into force on the date of the exchange of instruments of ratification and shall remain in force for a period of 20 years, except in so far as it may be revised or replaced by agreement between the two Governments. It shall in any case be reviewed at the end of 10 years. Before the expiry of a period of 19 years either Government may give to the other through the diplomatic channel notice of termination at the end of the said period of 20 years. If the Agreement has not been so terminated, and subject to any revision or replacement thereof, it shall continue in force after the expiry of the period of 20 years until the expiry of one year after notice of termination has been given by either Government to the other through the diplomatic channel.

In witness whereof the undersigned, being duly authorised by their respective Governments, have signed the present Agreement and have affixed thereto their seals.

Done in duplicate at Benghazi this 29th day of July, 1953, in the English and Arabic languages, both texts being equally authentic.

Signed on behalf of the United Kingdom Government:

(L.S.)   A. KIRKBRIDE.

Signed on behalf of the Government of Libya:

(L.S.)   MAHMUD MUNTASSER.

FINANCIAL AGREEMENT BETWEEN THE GOVERNMENT OF
THE UNITED KINGDOM OF GREAT BRITAIN AND
NORTHERN IRELAND AND THE GOVERNMENT OF THE
UNITED KINGDOM OF LIBYA

Benghazi, July 29, 1953

The Government of the United Kingdom of Great Britain and Northern
Ireland (hereinafter referred to as the United Kingdom Government) and
the Government of the United Kingdom of Libya (hereinafter referred to
as the Government of Libya), desiring to give effect to Article 3 of the Treaty
of Friendship and Alliance signed at Benghazi on the 29th day of July, 1953,
between Her Majesty The Queen of the United Kingdom of Great Britain
and Northern Ireland and of Her other Realms and Territories and His
Majesty The King of the United Kingdom of Libya, have agreed as follows:—

ARTICLE 1

The purpose of this Agreement is to assist Libya to enjoy conditions of
financial stability and orderly economic development appropriate for securing,
in relation to Libya, the objectives referred to in Article 3 of the aforesaid
Treaty of Friendship and Alliance.

ARTICLE 2

In order to carry out the purpose of this Agreement the United Kingdom
Government, taking account of the needs of Libya in consultation with the
Government of Libya, will give financial assistance annually to the Government of Libya for the duration of the Agreement. For the five financial years
from the 1st of April, 1953 to the 31st of March, 1958 £1,000,000 (one million
pounds sterling) will be paid annually to Libyan development organisations
existing on the 1st of April, 1953 or, as may be agreed between the two
Governments from time to time, to other development organisations set up
thereafter and £2,750,000 (two million seven hundred and fifty thousand
pounds sterling) will be paid as financial assistance towards the Libyan
budget. The sums already paid by the United Kingdom Government under
interim arrangements during the current financial year, prior to the entry
into force of this Agreement, shall be regarded as payments on account for
that year. Before the end of each succeeding period of five years during the
currency of this Agreement, the United Kingdom Government will, taking
into account the needs of Libya in consultation with the Government of
Libya, undertake to give such suitable assistance annually during the following
period of five years as may be agreed between the two Governments.

ARTICLE 3

The Government of Libya will apply the United Kingdom Government's
payments in accordance with the purpose of this Agreement and, with the
object of aiding the United Kingdom Government to assess the financial
assistance to be given during an ensuing period of five years, will provide

that Government with copies of the annual consolidated Estimates as approved
by the Libyan Parliament and with copies of the annual reports of the
Libyan auditors as adopted by the appropriate legislatures.

ARTICLE 4

This Agreement is made subject to the continuance, except as agreed
between the two Governments, of the existing Libyan currency arrangements.

ARTICLE 5

This Agreement shall be subject to ratification and the instruments of
ratification shall be exchanged as soon as possible. It shall enter into force
on the date of the exchange of instruments of ratification and shall remain
in force for a period of 20 years, except in so far as it may be revised
or replaced by agreement between the two Governments. It shall in any
case be reviewed at the end of 10 years. Before the expiry of a period
of 19 years either Government may give to the other through the diplomatic
channel notice of termination at the end of the said period of 20 years.
If the Agreement has not been so terminated, and subject to any revision
or replacement thereof, it shall continue in force after the expiry of the
20 years until the expiry of one year after notice of termination has been
given by either Government to the other through the diplomatic channel.

In witness whereof the undersigned, being duly authorised by their
respective Governments, have signed the present Agreement and have affixed
thereto their seals.

Done in duplicate at Benghazi this 29th day of July, 1953, in the English
and Arabic languages, both texts being equally authentic.

Signed on behalf of the United Kingdom Government:

(L.S.)   A. KIRKBRIDE.

Signed on behalf of the Government of Libya:

(L.S.)   MAHMUD MUNTASSER.

Appendix V

AGREEMENT

BETWEEN

THE GOVERNMENT OF THE UNITED STATES OF AMERICA

AND

THE GOVERNMENT OF THE UNITED KINGDOM OF LIBYA

PREAMBLE

The Government of the United States of America and the Government of the United Kingdom of Libya, desiring to strengthen the firm friendship and understanding now existing between them; confirming their determination to cooperate amicably and to support each other mutually in the international field, and to contribute to the maintenance of peace and security within the framework of the Charter of the United Nations; and being of the opinion that cooperation within the territory of Libya will assist in achieving these objectives; have entered into the present Agreement.

ARTICLE I

AGREED AREAS

(1) The Government of the United Kingdom of Libya grants permission to the Government of the United States of America to occupy and use for military purposes, for the duration of the present Agreement and in accordance with its terms and conditions, those areas which are presently used and occupied by the Government of the United States of America as well as such additional areas as may be agreed upon in writing from time to time by the two Governments. All areas used and occupied by the Government of the United States of America pursuant to this paragraph shall hereinafter be referred to as " agreed areas."

(2) A particular agreed area shall cease to be considered as such whenever the Government of the United States of America shall notify the Government of the United Kingdom of Libya that it no longer requires such area.

ARTICLE II

DEVELOPMENT AND SECURITY OF AGREED AREAS

The Government of the United States of America may make arrangements for and carry out directly or through its contractors the installation, construction and removal of facilities within the agreed areas to improve and adapt such areas for military purposes and to provide for the internal security of such areas. The authorities of the Government of the United States of America will not, however, demolish any buildings existing on public lands at the time of first entry of the United States forces on such lands or cut or remove trees in any substantial number growing on such lands without the consent of the appropriate authorities of the Government of the United Kingdom of Libya.

ARTICLE III

CONTROL OF AIRCRAFT, VESSELS AND VEHICLES

(1) The Government of the United States of America may exercise full control over aircraft, ships and water-borne craft, and vehicles entering, leaving and while within the agreed areas.

(2) The Government of the United Kingdom of Libya shall arrange for such controls over aircraft, vessels and vehicles entering, leaving and while within areas near the agreed areas as are agreed by the two Governments, to be necessary to carry out the purposes of the present Agreement and ensure the security of United States forces and property in Libya.

ARTICLE IV

COMMUNICATION AND PIPELINE FACILITIES

The Government of the United States of America may construct and maintain such wire communication and pipeline facilities outside of the agreed areas as the two Governments agree are necessary to carry out the purpose of the present Agreement.

ARTICLE V

PUBLIC SERVICES AND FACILITIES

Upon the request of the Government of the United States of America and provided that the Government of the United Kingdom of Libya is assured that the public and private interests in Libya will be duly safeguarded, the public services and facilities in Libya shall be made available as far as practicable for the use of the Government of the United States of America and members of the United States forces. The charges therefor shall be the same as those paid by other users, unless otherwise agreed.

ARTICLE VI

USE OF AGREED AREAS

(1) The agreed areas shall be used and occupied exclusively by the Government of the United States of America except as otherwise provided in this Article. Agreed areas used exclusively by the Government of the United States of America will be maintained at its expense.

(2) The two Governments, as an element in collective military measures to maintain or restore international security, may agree to a joint use and occupancy of an agreed area by the two Governments, or by the United States of America and any nation with which the United Kingdom of Libya has a Treaty of Friendship and Alliance. The cost of maintenance of an agreed area which is used jointly by the two Governments, or by the United States of America and any other nation, shall be apportioned on the basis of usage, at rates and charges which are mutually satisfactory to the users.

(3) The Government of the United States of America may request the Government of the United Kingdom of Libya to permit the use of the agreed areas for training purposes by small groups of military personnel of countries other than the United States of America, such personnel to be at all times while in Libya under the United States auspices and control. The Government of the United Kingdom of Libya is prepared to examine all such requests expeditiously on a case by case basis and inform the Government of the United States of America of its decision.

ARTICLE VII

ACQUISITION OF LAND

(1) Except as otherwise agreed by the two Governments in accordance with paragraph (2) of this Article, the Government of the United Kingdom of Libya will make all acquisitions of land and other arrangements required to permit occupation and use of lands and interests in lands for the purpose of the present Agreement. The Government of the United States of America shall not be obliged to compensate any Libyan national or other person for the occupation or use of lands in which he has an interest and which are made available to the Government of the United States of America under the provisions of this paragraph, but it agrees to pay to the Government of the United Kingdom of Libya on behalf of such national or person annually an equitable rental for such occupation or use. The two Governments agree that once the equitable annual rental for such lands has been determined, the amount of that rental shall not be changed for the duration of the present Agreement without the consent of both Governments.

(2) Subject to agreement between the two Governments, the Government of the United States of America may rent lands or any interest in or relating to lands directly from private owners or make other arrangements with private owners as required to permit occupation and use of agreed areas in

accordance with the provisions of the present Agreement. If satisfied that there is unreasonable refusal by a private owner, after he has received an offer of equitable compensation, to make available land or an interest in land necessary for the purpose of the present Agreement, the Government of the United Kingdom of Libya will take the necessary steps to ensure that such land or interest in land is made available.

(3) The rentals paid by the Government of the United States of America on the date of the entry into force of this Agreement for the occupation and use of lands and interests in lands within the agreed areas shall be deemed to be the equitable rentals payable for such occupation or use.

(4) Lands or interests in lands occupied or used by the Government of the United States of America under the provisions of this Article shall be regarded as agreed areas for the purposes of the present Agreement.

(5) Compensation to private owners for damage arising out of the occupation and use of property, if not otherwise paid, shall be paid by the Government of the United States of America under the provisions of Article XIX.

Article VIII
MOVEMENT OF FORCES, AIRCRAFT, VESSELS AND VEHICLES

(1) The Government of the United Kingdom of Libya grants to the United States forces and United States public vessels, aircraft, and vehicles, including armor, the right of free access and egress to and from the agreed areas and movement within and between the agreed areas, by land, air and sea, for the purpose of the present Agreement. The right shall include freedom from compulsory pilotage and all toll charges anywhere within Libya, including territorial waters. With a view to facilitating control of harbor traffic within Libyan port areas open to commerce, reasonable notice will be given to the appropriate port authorities of the arrival of a United States public vessel in any such port area. The provisions of this paragraph shall not apply to courtesy visits of United States Government vessels unrelated to the present Agreement. Such visits shall be governed by customary international practice.

(2) By agreement between the two Governments, United States forces and United States public vessels, aircraft and vehicles, including armor, shall have freedom of movement in other districts of Libya, including the territorial waters, in order to carry out the purposes of the present Agreement.

(3) Subject to such conditions (including conditions governing flight over towns) as may be agreed upon by the appropriate authorities of the two Governments, United States public aircraft may fly over any of the territory of Libya, including territorial waters. United States public aircraft shall not fly over areas prohibited by the Government of the United Kingdom of Libya to foreign aircraft in general, except as may be agreed. In an emergency United States public aircraft may land on and take off from any of the territory of Libya, including territorial waters, and, under such

conditions as may be agreed upon by the appropriate authorities of tne two Governments, United States public aircraft may use airports and other aviation facilities outside the agreed areas.

(4) In the exercise of the privileges described in this Article all reasonable precautions will be taken by the Government of the United States of America to avoid damage to public facilities.

(5) The Government of the United States of America accepts the principle that military members of the United States forces should wear civilian clothes when in Benghazi and Tripoli in an off-duty status.

ARTICLE IX
ACCESS FACILITIES

The Government of the United States of America may, at its own expense, and in agreement with the Government of the United Kingdom of Libya, and without the right to claim compensation from that Government at any time, construct and maintain necessary roads and bridges, and improve and deepen harbors, channels, entrances and anchorages, affording access to the agreed areas.

ARTICLE X
VACATING AGREED AREAS

When the Government of the United States of America permanently vacates an agreed area, permanent constructions thereon shall not be removed and the Government of the United States of America shall not be entitled to any compensation for such constructions. Except as provided in the preceding sentence, all property constructed, installed, brought into or procured in Libya under or prior to the present Agreement by the Government of the United States of America shall remain its property and may be removed from Libya, free of any restrictions, or disposed of in Libya by the Government of the United States of America as agreed with the Government of the United Kingdom of Libya, at any time before the termination of the present Agreement or within a reasonable time thereafter. Any such property not so removed or so disposed of before the termination of the present Agreement or within a reasonable time thereafter will cease to be the property of the Government of the United States of America and the Government of the United Kingdom of Libya shall not be obligated to compensate the Government of the United States of America for such property.

ARTICLE XI
CONDITION OF AGREED AREAS UPON RELEASE

The Government of the United States of America is not obligated to turn over the agreed areas to the Government of the United Kingdom of Libya at the expiration of the present Agreement in the condition in which they were at the time of their occupation by the Government of the United States of America.

ARTICLE XII
OTHER OBLIGATIONS

The present Agreement is made in accordance with the principles laid down in the Charter of the United Nations and nothing in the Agreement shall be construed to conflict with the obligations assumed by the United States of America under that Charter, which obligations the United Kingdom of Libya also accepts pending its admission to the United Nations. Further, the two Governments declare that nothing in the present Agreement conflicts with or prejudices or is intended to conflict with or prejudice international obligations assumed by either Government under any other existing international agreements, conventions or treaties, including, in the case of the United Kingdom of Libya, the Covenant of the League of Arab States.

ARTICLE XIII
MILITARY AND CIVILIAN PERSONNEL

The Government of the United Kingdom of Libya authorizes the Government of the United States of America to employ and supervise military and civilian personnel as required in connection with operations under the present Agreement.

ARTICLE XIV
SURVEYS

The Government of the United States of America may make engineering, topographic, hydrographic, coast and geodetic, and other technical surveys (including aerial photographs) in any part of Libya and the waters adjacent thereto. The Government of the United States of America shall notify the Government of the United Kingdom when any survey is to be made outside the agreed areas, and the Government of the United Kingdom of Libya may, if so desired, designate an official representative to be present when any survey is made outside the agreed areas. A sufficient number of copies with title and triangulation and other control data of any such survey shall be furnished to the Government of the United Kingdom of Libya.

ARTICLE XV
POST OFFICES

The Government of the United States of America may establish, maintain and operate United States post offices in the agreed areas for domestic use between United States post offices in the agreed areas and between such post offices and other United States post offices. Such post offices shall be for the exclusive use of the authorities, agencies and offices of the Government of the United States of America under the provisions of this Article shall be the United States of America, the members of the United States forces and nationals of the United States of America holding an official position in Libya with the Government of the United States of America.

Article XVI

ENTRY AND DEPARTURE OF UNITED STATES FORCES

(1) The Government of the United States of America may bring into Libya members of the United States forces in connection with carrying out the purpose of the present Agreement.

(2) The laws of the Government of the United Kingdom of Libya shall not apply to prevent admission or departure into or from Libya of members of the United States forces. Passport and visa requirements shall not be applicable to military members of United States forces, but they shall be furnished with appropriate identification cards or tags and samples of such identification cards or tags shall be filed with the Government of the United Kingdom of Libya. Passport and visa requirements shall be applicable to non-military members of the United States forces.

(3) The Government of the United Kingdom of Libya shall exempt members of the United States forces from any laws providing for the registration and control of aliens. The Government of the United States of America shall take every step open to it to ensure the correct behavior of all members of the United States forces and will provide such information as the Government of the United Kingdom of Libya may require about the civilian members, as may appropriately be furnished, bearing in mind their status as members of the United States forces.

(4) If the status of any member of the United States forces brought into Libya by the Government of the United States of America is altered so that he would no longer be entitled to such admission, the Government of the United States of America shall notify the Government of the Kingdom of Libya and shall, unless the Government of the United Kingdom of Libya permits him to remain, remove him from Libya as soon as possible, and shall in the meantime prevent him from becoming a public responsibility of the United Kingdom of Libya.

(5) If the Government of the United Kingdom of Libya requests the removal of any member of the United States forces whose misconduct renders his presence in Libya undesirable, the Government of the United States of America shall remove him from Libya as soon as possible.

Article XVII

AGENCIES OF UNITED STATES FORCES

The Government of the United States of America may establish agencies in the agreed areas, including concessions such as sales commissaries, military service exchanges, messes and social clubs for the exclusive use of members of the United States forces and nationals of the United States having comparable privileges; and such agencies shall be free of all licenses, fees, excise, sales or other taxes or imposts. The merchandise or services sold or dispensed by such Government agencies shall be free of all taxes, duties, imposts and inspection by the Government of the United Kingdom of Libya. Administrative measures will be taken by United States military authorities to prevent the resale of goods which are sold under the provisions of this Article to persons not entitled to buy goods at such agencies, and generally to prevent abuse of the privileges granted under this Article. There shall be cooperation between such authorities and the appropriate authorities of the government of the United Kingdom of Libya to this end.

Article XVIII

HEALTH AND SANITATION

The appropriate authorities of the two Governments will cooperate in making arrangements in the interest of sanitation and health. Any measures in the interests of sanitation or health which are required to be taken in the agreed areas to meet acceptable international standards will be the responsibility of the Government of the United States of America.

Article XIX

CLAIMS AND JURISDICTION IN CIVIL MATTERS

(1) The Government of the United States of America agrees to pay just and reasonable compensation for valid claims of the Government of the United Kingdom of Libya for damage, loss or destruction of its property caused by military members of the United States forces who are in Libya under the terms of the present Agreement, or by civilian employees of the United States armed services, including those who are nationals of or ordinarily resident in Libya, in connection with operations under the present Agreement.

(2) The Government of the United States of America agrees to pay just and reasonable compensation for valid claims of persons who are nationals of Libya or inhabitants of that country, for damage, loss or destruction of property, or for injury or death, caused by military members of United States forces who are in Libya under the terms of the present Agreement or by civilian employees of the United States armed services, including those who are nationals of or ordinarily resident in Libya, in connection with operations under the present Agreement.

(3) All such claims will be processed and paid in accordance with the applicable provisions of United States law, and the courts of Libya will not entertain any such claims against members of the United States forces.

(4) In all other civil cases involving members of the United States forces the Libyan courts will have jurisdiction.

Article XX

JURISDICTION—CRIMINAL MATTERS

(1) The United States military authorities shall have the right to exercise within the United Kingdom of Libya all criminal and disciplinary juris-

diction conferred on them by the laws of the United States of America over members of the United States forces in the following cases, namely:

   (a) Offenses solely against the property of the Government of the United States of America, or against the person or property of another member of the United States forces.

   (b) Offenses committed solely within the agreed areas.

   (c) Offenses solely against the security of the United States of America, including treason, sabotage, espionage or violation of any law relating to official secrets, or secrets relating to the national defense of the the United States of America.

   (d) Offenses arising out of any act or omission done in the performance of official duty.

and in every such case where such criminal and disciplinary jurisdiction exists, the members of the United States forces shall be immune from the jurisdiction of the Libyan courts.

(2) In other cases the Libyan courts shall exercise jurisdiction unless the Government of the United Kingdom of Libya waives its right to exercise jurisdiction. The Government of the United Kingdom of Libya will give sympathetic consideration to any request from the United States authorities for a waiver of its right in cases where the United States authorities consider such waiver to be of particular importance, or where suitable punishment can be applied by disciplinary action without recourse to a court.

(3) The United States and Libyan authorities will assist each other in the arrest and handing over to the appropriate authority of members of the United States forces for trial in accordance with the above provisions, and the Libyan authorities will immediately notify the United States authorities if they arrest any member of the United States forces. The Libyan authorities will, if the United States authorities request the release on remand of an arrested member of the United States forces, release him from their custody on the United States authorities' undertaking to present him to the Libyan courts for investigatory proceedings and trial when required.

(4) The United States and Libyan authorities will assist each other in the carrying out of all necessary investigations into offenses, and in the collection and production of evidence, including the attendance of witnesses at the trial and the seizure and, in proper cases, the handing over of objects connected with an offense. The handing over of such objects may, however, be made subject to their return within the time specified by the authority delivering them.

(5) Whenever a member of the United States forces is prosecuted in a Libyan court he shall be entitled:

   (a) to be presumed innocent until proved guilty according to law in a trial in which he has had the guarantees necessary for his defense,

   (b) to a prompt and speedy public trial,

(c) to be informed, in advance of trial, of the specific charge or charges made against him,

(d) to refuse to testify against himself,

(e) to be confronted with the witnesses against him,

(f) to be permitted full opportunity to examine all witnesses,

(g) to have compulsory process for obtaining witnesses in his favor, if they are within the jurisdiction of the Libyan courts,

(h) to have legal representation of his own choice for his defense or to have free or assisted legal representation under the conditions prevailing for the time being in Libya,

(i) to have his legal representatives present during all stages of proceedings against him,

(j) to have, if he considers it necessary, the services of a competent interpreter,

(k) to communicate with the United States authorities and to have a representative of those authorities present at his trial, and

(l) to such other rights as are guaranteed under the constitution and laws of the United Kingdom of Libya to persons on trial in those courts.

(6) The Libyan authorities will notify the United States authorities of the result of any trial in a Libyan court of a member of the United States forces.

(7) Witnesses who are alleged to have committed perjury or contempt of court in proceedings before the United States service tribunals or authorities and who are not subject to the law administered by those tribunals and authorities will be turned over to the Libyan authorities. Provision will be made by the laws of Libya for the trial and punishment of such offenders.

(8) The Government of the United States of America will have the right to police the agreed areas and to maintain order therein and may arrest therein any alleged offenders and, when they are triable by the Libyan courts, will forthwith turn them over to the Libyan authorities for trial.

(9) Outside the agreed areas, members of the United States forces may be employed on police duties by arrangement with the appropriate Libyan authorities. The Libyan authorities shall be primarily responsible for the protection of cables carrying light, power or communications to any of the agreed areas, whether such cables are the property of the Government of the United States of America or otherwise, but they make arrangements with the United States authorities for the employment of members of the United States forces for this purpose. In such cases, the Libyan police with whom members of the United States forces may be serving shall have paramount authority with respect to the persons and property of persons who are nationals of or ordinarily resident in Libya.

Article XXI

DRIVING PERMITS

The Government of the United Kingdom of Libya either shall honor, without driving test or fee, driving permits issued by the Government of the United States of America or a subdivision thereof to members of the United States forces; or issue its own driving permits without test or fee to such persons who hold such United States permits. Members of the United States forces who do not hold driving permits issued by the Government of the United States of America or a subdivision thereof shall be required to comply with whatever regulations Libya may establish with regard to driving permits.

Article XXII

POSSESSION AND CARRIAGE OF ARMS

Military members of the United States forces in Libya may possess and carry arms as required in the performance of official duties.

Article XXIII

LOCAL PURCHASES AND EMPLOYMENT OF LOCAL LABOR

(1) Members of the United States forces may purchase locally goods necessary for their own consumption and such services as they need under the same conditions as Libyan nationals.

(2) The Government of the United States of America may purchase locally goods required for the subsistence of the United States forces and it shall be the policy of the Government of the United States of America to purchase such goods locally if they are available and of the standard required by United States authorities. In order to avoid any such purchases having an adverse effect on the Libyan economy, the appropriate authorities of the Government of the United Kingdom of Libya will indicate, when necessary, any articles the purchase of which should be restricted or forbidden.

(3) The Government of the United Kingdom of Libya consents to the employment of Libyan civilians by the Government of the United States of America, or its contractors, and it shall be the policy of the Government of the United States of America and its contractors to prefer the employment of Libyan civilians when they are available and qualified to do the work involved. The conditions of employment for Libyan nationals and persons normally resident in Libya, particularly in respect to wages, supplementary payments, insurance, and conditions for the protection of workers, shall be generally those laid down by Libyan law.

(4) Upon the request of the appropriate authorities of the Government of the United Kingdom of Libya, the United States military authorities will withhold and pay over to the Government of the United Kingdom of Libya all income tax or other deductions from the wages of persons other than members of the United States forces employed by the Government of the

United States of America, who may by Libyan law be subject to such tax or deductions in the same manner and to the same extent as any other employer.

Article XXIV
TAXES, DUTIES, ETC.

(1) The temporary presence in Libya of a member of the United States forces shall constitute neither residence nor domicile therein and shall not of itself subject him to taxation in Libya, either on his income or on his property the presence of which in Libya is due to his temporary presence there, nor, in the event of his death, shall it subject his estate to a levy of death duties. Land and permanent structures thereon located in Libya which are purchased by a member of the United States forces shall be subject to the laws of the United Kingdom of Libya as to taxation.

(2) No national of the United States of America or corporation organized under the laws of the United States of America, resident in the United States of America, shall be liable to pay the Government of the United Kingdom of Libya any tax in respect of any income derived under a contract with the Government of the United States of America in connection with operations under the present Agreement. The provisions of this paragraph shall not, however, apply to any such national or corporation engaged in business in Libya otherwise than under such a contract with the Government of the United States of America.

(3) No tax, duty or other charge of any nature shall be levied or assessed on material, equipment, supplies or goods brought into Libya or procured in Libya by United States authorities for the use of the Government of the United States of America or its agents or for the use of persons present in Libya only in connection with operations under the present Agreement.

(4) Members of the United States forces may at the time of their first arrival in Libya or at the time of the first arrival of any of their dependents to join them, import into Libya free of customs duty their personal effects and household goods and their private motor vehicles for personal use.

(5) The provisions of this Article shall not exempt members of the United States forces from the payment of any license fees imposed under the laws of the United Kingdom of Libya on private radios outside the agreed areas and any registration or license fee imposed under the laws of the United Kingdom of Libya in respect of private motor cars.

Article XXV
CUSTOMS LAWS AND REGULATIONS

(1) The laws and regulations administered by the customs authorities of the Government of the United Kingdom of Libya, including the right to inspect and seize, shall have no application to:

(a) Service and construction material, equipment, supplies, provisions and other goods, brought into Libya by the Government of the United States of America or its contractors in connection with operations under the present Agreement for the exclusive use of the United States forces.

(b) Personal effects, household goods, including privately owned automobiles and furniture, and other goods brought into Libya by the authorities of the Government of the United States of America directly or through the customary civil channels of Libya for the personal use of members of the United States forces at the time of their first arrival in Libya or at the time of the first arrival of any of their dependents to join them.

(c) Official documents under seal.

(d) Mail sent to and from the United States post offices established pursuant to Article XV.

(2) Property falling within the provisions of Paragraph (1) of this Article may be exported from Libya, without regard to the customs laws and regulations of the United Kingdom of Libya.

(3) Property brought into Libya under the provisions of Paragraph (1) of this Article may not be disposed of in Libya except for the purposes of operations under the present Agreement, or, to any person or corporation having the right to bring property into Libya in accordance with Paragraph (1) of this Article, or, under conditions imposed by the appropriate authorities of the Government of the United Kingdom of Libya. The Government of the United States of America may, however, dispose of such property to the government of any nation entitled to make use of agreed areas in accordance with the provisions of the present Agreement or to the personnel of such government engaged in activities connected with such use of an agreed area. The United States military authorities will prescribe and enforce regulations designed to prevent the sale or supply to individual members of the United States forces of quantities of goods imported into Libya free of charge which would be in excess of personal requirements of such personnel and which in consultation with the appropriate authorities of the Government of the United Kingdom of Libya, are determined to be most likely to become items of gift, barter or sale in the free market in Libya.

ARTICLE XXVI
USE OF CURRENCY

(1) The United States authorities will take the necessary measure in cooperation with the appropriate Libyan authorities to safeguard Libyan foreign exchange legislation or regulations.

(2) With respect to the acquisition of Libyan currency, the United States forces will have the authority to purchase local currency with United States dollars at the most favorable rate from authorized banking facilities and institutions, provided that Libyan currency now available or which may

become available to the Government of the United States of America may be used by the Government of the United States of America for such purposes as it desires.

(3) The United States authorities may import, export, possess and use United States currency, the currency of any third state, and instruments or scrip expressed in United States currency.

(4) The United States authorities may pay the United States forces in instruments expressed in United States currency, or scrip denominated in units of United States currency, or in Libyan currency, or in United States currency, provided that payment in United States currency shall take place after consultation between the appropriate authorities of the two Governments. The United States authorities will take appropriate measures to assure that the use of scrip denominated in units of United States currency is restricted to internal transactions within installations and areas in use by the United States forces.

ARTICLE XXVII

COMPLIANCE

The Government of the United States of America shall take the necessary measures to prevent abuse of the privileges granted by the Government of the United Kingdom of Libya under the present Agreement.

ARTICLE XXVIII

DEFINITIONS

In the present Agreement the following expressions have the meanings hereby respectively assigned to them:

" The two Governments " means the Government of the United Kingdom of Libya and the Government of the United States of America.

" The Government of the United Kingdom of Libya " means the federal Government of the United Kingdom of Libya.

" United States forces " included personnel belonging to the armed services of the United States of America and accompanying civilian personnel who are employed by or serving with such services (including the dependents of such military and civilian personnel), who are not nationals of, nor ordinarily resident in Libya; and who are in the territory of Libya in connection with operations under the present Agreement.

" Agreed areas " means those areas and their component parts (including land, buildings, structures, water, stone and other construction materials, and things other than minerals, including petroleum, and archeological remains which are on, in, or over land and land covered by water) which the two Governments shall agree may be occupied and used by the Government of the United States of America under the terms and conditions of the present Agreement.

" Military purposes " means, within the agreed areas and elsewhere as provided in the present Agreement, the installation, construction, maintenance, use and operation of military equipment and facilities, including facilities for the training, accommodation, hospitalization, recreation, education, and welfare of members of the United States forces; and the operations of the Government of the United States of America and its contractors and of authorized service organizations under the present Agreement; and the storage of the property of the Government of the United States of America and its contractors and of authorized service organizations which are in Libya in connection with the operations under the present Agreement.

"United States public vessel" and "United States public aircraft" mean vessels (including waterborne craft of all kinds) and aircraft belonging to the Government of the United States of America or operating under charter, contract or otherwise for the purposes of the United States armed services.

ARTICLE XXIX

DISPUTES

Matters relating to the interpretation of the present Agreement and to the settlement of disputes arising therefrom shall be examined in common by the appropriate authorities of the two Governments. In the event it is not possible for such authorities to reach agreement, the two Governments will consider the practicability of submitting the dispute to an independent third person or body.

ARTICLE XXX

RATIFICATION AND DURATION

The present Agreement shall come into force upon the date of receipt by the Government of the United States of America of a notification from the Government of the United Kingdom of Libya of its ratification of the present Agreement and without having any retroactive effect shall replace the existing arrangements between the two Governments on the matters covered in the present Agreement. The present Agreement shall continue in force until December 24, 1970, and after that date shall continue in force until either of the two Governments gives to the other notice of termination, in which event, the Agreement shall cease to be effective one year after the date of receipt of such notice.

IN WITNESS WHEREOF, the undersigned duly authorized representatives of the Government of the United States of America and the Government of the United Kingdom of Libya have signed the present Agreement.

Done in duplicate at Benghazi in the English and Arabic languages, both texts being equally authentic, the ninth day of September 1954.

FOR THE GOVERNMENT OF THE UNITED STATES OF AMERICA:
                    LIONEL M. SUMMERS   [seal]

FOR THE GOVERNMENT OF THE UNITED KINGDOM OF LIBYA:
                    BEN HALIM   [seal]

Index

Certain names, especially place names, of very common occurrence, such as al-Sanusi, Tripoli, Banghazi and Libya, are either omitted or designated as passim.